1963

The Methods of English Prose

W. ARTHUR TURNER

OBERLIN COLLEGE

The Odyssey Press • New York

Teaching Objectives of This Book

PART ONE

The Paragraph

Unity and the topic sentence
Methods of development
Organization and coherence

The Whole Composition

Purpose
Explicit meaning
Unity and theme statement
Main divisions
Methods of development
Organization and outlining

The Sentence

Conciseness
Parallel structure
Some attention to balance and antithesis

Diction

Increase of vocabulary
Exactness of meaning
Distinction between concrete and abstract words and between
specific and general words

v

Preference for concrete and specific words
Connotation (introduced)

Ornament

Usefulness of simple metaphors and similes
Allusion and quotation (introduced)

PART TWO

The Whole Composition

Purpose and its relation to method
Meaning: explicit, implicit, and inferential
The logical basis of proof and of discussion
Main divisions
Emphasis

The Sentence

Balance, antithesis, regression, and gradation
Euphony (all elements)
Emphasis

Diction

Increase of vocabulary
Exactness of meaning
Connotation

Ornament

Various figures of speech

Tone

Throughout the book, the exercises are designed to teach the careful observation of writing techniques and to promote close reading.

The materials and exercises in Part I progress from simple

problems of organization, theme type, and the accurate use of words to the more complicated problems involved in longer pieces developed by more than one method and in styles more effective than straightforward prose.

The materials and exercises in Part II continue the study of style as indicated in the outline above. As to form and content, the selections are more flexible than those in Part I and may be used in two main ways in the study of composition. They may simply serve to stimulate more advanced thinking and writing, for the later part of the course, of the same kinds practised during the first part. Or they may be used as three units in the study of logic, the long factual article or research paper, and the essay. Sections A and B provide a good study of logic and its practical application, both in diction and in the whole composition; most of the pieces in sections B and C demonstrate the use of information gained by research on a specific topic; sections D and E demonstrate the interpretation of knowledge already in the author's mind and can stimulate similar essays by the student. This progression from logic to research to the essay coincides with the pattern now given to the second half of many college composition courses.

In addition, these materials can be used for the study of intensive reading methods in those courses which combine the teaching of reading and composition.

W. A. T.

What Is Composition?

(A Talk with the Student)

Let me introduce to you some good writers from several periods. They have written with different purposes and used a variety of methods, but each in his own way has so pleased and educated his readers that he has been honored and sometimes even well paid. Primitive people have always, quite properly I think, regarded words as having mysterious power and good speakers as darlings of the gods. Writing, which embodies this mysterious power in permanent symbols, has always been honored as an art. Yet, like drawing or singing, it is an art which most intelligent people can practise. Though the finished composition has a total effect which can be felt but not fully explained, the methods of writing are clear enough. The best writers have always understood these methods.

This is not an "idea" book with a "new approach." In the decade and a half in which I have been teaching English, I have developed an aversion to such books. Books of essays organized only around such themes as modern problems or designs for living may be interesting to read, but they take the student by a long and roundabout path in his search for the principles of good writing. Similarly, books which "approach" composition through only one of its elements, such as logic, organization, or purpose, distort the problem and mislead the student. The expression of human experience in language is an almost universal human activity, like love, complicated and perhaps even mysterious, but eternal and subject to slight change if any. One who thinks that the essential nature of love has changed during the last 2500 years, in any of its aspects, should read, for example, *The Song of Songs,* the Gospels, Plato, or Ovid. Writing, like love, has superficially responded to the fluctuations of taste, as you will see; but the essential process is unchanged. The speech of Odysseus as he roused the Greeks to battle or the funeral oration of Marcus Antonius in *Julius Caesar* could not be improved by anything we have learned since the time of Homer or of Shakespeare; indeed, Shakespeare learned from Homer. If this book offers anything new, it is a return to the basic methods of writing which have been employed since the time of the ancients. The student who has learned only such special skills as how to analyze a character or how to analyze a "social pattern" stands dumb before a machine or an emotion which he needs to explain. But the student who has gone to the bottom of the matter and learned the fundamentals of all prose composition can explain a character, a group, a machine, or anything else within his comprehension.

The Process of Expression

The writer, a human being who wants to tell something to other human beings, puts his experiences, feelings, and thoughts into language and puts the language on paper. His experiences with life come from participation in and observation of the world about him and from reading. He responds to many experiences with emotions, such as love, fear, or hate. To others he makes intellectual reactions, such as approval, respect, disbelief, or merely understanding. If he is given to reflection, he relates one experience to another and arrives at new meanings; he "has an idea." If he thinks that one of his experiences is so vivid and unusual or one of his ideas so worthwhile that other people might like to share it, he makes a series of statements which he hopes will convey his experience or explain his idea. These statements he puts on paper according to certain conventions. Several parts of this whole process are beyond explanation, even by psychologists; but the main steps—*experience to language to paper*—must be clear to anyone who thinks about them. The reader then reverses the process. From the printed page he takes the language into his own mind and tries to re-create there the experience or idea exactly as it was in the mind of the writer. Obvious as they seem, it is well to keep these processes in mind when we read or write.

The Subject

Nearly everyone is potentially the writer of at least a few good pieces; for the subject matter of writing is infinite, and each human being is unique. In composition classes we speak of *primary* sources and *secondary* sources of subject matter. Primary sources are personal experiences and observations; secondary sources are books, magazines, newspapers, documents, and oral reports—all information which we receive at second hand. Ordinarily college composition classes depend upon primary sources during the first part of the course and reserve the treatment of secondary material for the second part of the course, when the fundamental skills of writing have been mastered. The course usually leads up to the research paper, which allows the student to demonstrate all his skills by finding suitable material on a given subject and then composing a paper by whatever methods are appropriate to the subject.

The Four Forms

Most pieces of writing can be classified as description, narration, exposition, or argument—the four forms of discourse. Description conveys the appearance of a place, object, or person; narration relates an action or a series of actions; exposition explains; and argument attempts to gain the reader's assent to an idea or a plan of action. Because most college students need skill in exposition more than in any other form, the major emphasis of this book is on exposition. But the other three forms are often useful in exposition or are mingled with it, and they are therefore studied as adjuncts.

Unity, Purpose, and Worth

Every composition, like every paragraph, must have unity of subject and a clear central purpose. That is, its statements must not only be restricted to a single subject but they must also say something definite about that subject. And both subject and purpose must be worth the reader's time. An article on the general subject "automobile accidents" might be very dull and pointless. What *about* the accidents? An article which presented a sure way of preventing even one kind of accident would have millions of grateful readers.

Methods of Development

When a writer has carefully stated his purpose to himself, what then? If he wants to describe a scene, relate an adventure, or explain an idea, how does he begin? Where does he find statements to put together, one after another, to make his meaning clear? *Development,* the process of unfolding or revealing the central idea, is one of the major concerns of composition. The basic methods of development are (1) by analysis, or giving details, (2) by giving examples, (3) by comparison, and (4) by definition. The selections in Part I of this book demonstrate these methods separately. When you have studied each group of models until you can, in your own writing, use the methods employed in them, you will have mastered the principles of development. You will be able to develop an idea either in a single paragraph or in a whole composition. The longer selections in Part II use combinations of methods and therefore show how a writer turns naturally from one method to another, according to the requirements of his subject and of his purpose. They also illustrate the larger principles of organization and expression.

Organization

And how does one arrange his material into a clear, coherent pattern? Again, a few simple and fairly obvious orders of arrangement serve nearly all needs; and, again, the writer follows the order which best suits his subject and his purpose.

Some kinds of material easily fall into patterns inherent within their very nature. A description of a candy shop might begin with the outside appearance, move on to the inside walls and decoration, then to the display cases, and finally to the sales counter; this would be a space arrangement. An account of a day in the life of a doctor would surely follow a time arrangement. It would not necessarily proceed directly from morning to evening; it might begin with the doctor's afternoon office hours, then relate his account of his morning's work to his assistant as they pause for coffee, then follow him on his final round of house calls. Directions for changing a tire would unavoidably follow a functional order; functional order is only incidentally chronological, for its time sequence is decided by the necessary order of the steps in a process and rearrangement is seldom possible. These three natural or *inherent orders,* based on (1) space, (2) time, and (3) function, provide the basic organization of a large portion of all writing. But the writer can never disregard organization, even when he can follow an inherent order; for the order is inherent in the subject, not in his pen. He needs to arrange his statements so that the subject will seem to have the same order in his theme which it has in actuality.

Material which a writer collects to illustrate a discussion or to support an assertion must usually have some order imposed upon it. Such an order is therefore *attributed,* or *rational.* Most attributed orders are based upon one of four sets of relationships: (1) the general and the specific, (2) the familiar and the unfamiliar, (3) climax (small to large, least important to most important, etc.), or, (4) cause and effect.

Style

Finally, each composition has a certain style in its language, as unavoidably as its writer has a certain style in his dress. It may be as unconscious, incorrect, and sloppy as the rags of a tramp; or as studied, correct, and pleasing as the attire of a Brooks Brothers customer. The writer cannot choose whether he will have style or not; he can only choose between good and bad style.

Style in writing is a complex quality which has never been very well defined because it is intangible in nature and infinite in variety. We can say here that a good style has four main sets of qualities: (1) clear, economical, and rhythmical sentences; (2) accurate, concrete, and appropriate diction; (3) appropriate ornament used to promote clarity and vividness; and (4) tone appropriate to the subject and the purpose. But only through careful study can you actually come to know what style is. Consequently most sets of exercises in this book will call your attention to some aspect of style.

Learning the basic principles of composition so well that they become an active part of your consciousness, guiding all your writing, may appear difficult. Yet you must learn them, and you may take some comfort from other apprentices. The unfledged pilot's first glimpse of the instrument panel almost makes him long for a horse and buggy. Such an array of dials and pointers! Before he wins his wings he must learn them all—air temperature, oil temperature (in each engine), air speed, motor speed (in each engine), altitude, drift, bank, and so on—and keep them all in mind at once. He does learn, though. He studies intensively every aspect of airplane design, construction, and operation, and the main principles of flight. Of equal importance, he watches and admires expert pilots. Under their guidance he learns to imitate every motion they make, every trick of maneuvering. Finally, one good day, his teacher claps him on the back and says, "Today you're on your own. Take 'er up!"

You are going to be a writer. Perhaps you did not have that intention uppermost in your mind when you enrolled in college. But all college students and college graduates are writers. It is true that they are not all good writers; they are not all equally successful, either. Since I believe so strongly in good writing, I should try to persuade you to learn your lesson well while you have the best chance in the world; and I could find many arguments. Do you want money? The Human Engineering Laboratory has shown that skill in the use of language is essential to business success. Do you want fame and power? Julius Caesar, Queen Elizabeth I, Benjamin Franklin, and Winston Churchill all owed much to their mastery of language. Do you want what is better than either fame or money— an effective and loved character? One of the gentlest of human documents went from the pen of Abraham Lincoln, the most beloved President, to a mother whose son had been killed in battle. But these good examples will not necessarily move you. You will decide for yourself whether any private motive impels you to learn composition. It is a matter which you must decide for yourself because, quite simply, it is your own business and no one can push you.

You will find the models of writing in this book as useful for your purposes as demonstrations by Heifetz or other great violinists would be to a young student of the violin. Study them carefully. The exercises will direct your attention to the significant principles to be observed. Your teacher will check your observations and understanding, teach you the fundamentals of writing, and assign themes—and grade them patiently far into the night.

Contents

PART ONE: Methods of Development

Development by Analysis

Development by Example

PART TWO: Essays, Articles, and Addresses

Section B: The Logic of Freedom

Section C: Man and His Resources

Section D: The Nature and Uses of Knowledge

Section E: Human Values

PART ONE

Methods of Development

Development by Analysis

To analyze means to take apart, to reduce a whole to its parts or details. Development by analysis gives such parts for the purpose of revealing the nature of a scene, an action, an object, a person, an idea, or some other whole. As a matter of fact, it is not always accurate to say that a theme or a paragraph so developed is developed by analysis; what often happens is that the writer analyzes a subject in his mind, then develops the composition by giving the resulting details, or particulars. This method is often called "development by giving details" or "development by particularization." But a whole composition developed in this way is ordinarily called an analysis; in general this familiar term is satisfactory so long as we understand its meaning, and the method it designates is clear enough. A theme analyzing a fountain pen would deal with such parts as the cap, clip, barrel, ink tube, filling lever, and point. Such a treatment is clearly different from giving examples of pens, from comparing different pens, and from defining a pen; example, comparison, and definition are the other main methods of development.

Analysis is the simplest method of exposition. We can explain a hammer to a child by showing him that it has two main parts, a handle and a head, and that the head is so formed as to have a striking face for driving nails and a claw for pulling nails which we have not driven well. We can explain a committee to an adult by giving its general purpose, its specific duties, its subdivisions if any, the extent of its power, and any other attributes it may

3

possess. One of these subjects is concrete and the other mainly abstract; yet the explanatory process is the same.

Partition and Classification

Partition, or simple analysis, presents each item and perhaps explains its particular nature and function. It does not arrange parts into related groups, usually because no groups are possible. The hammer has only one handle and one head; classification is neither necessary nor possible. Classified analysis deals with parts by groups. Rifle handbooks, for instance, explain the structure of rifles under the headings *stock assembly, receiver assembly,* and *barrel assembly.* A rifle is more complicated than a hammer and consequently has, instead of a one-piece handle, a group of parts which can be classified as a stock assembly.

The basis on which parts are classified must always be consistent and clear. The reader of a rifle handbook needs to learn the functional relationship among the parts; therefore the parts are classified by function. But the purchasing department of a rifle factory would need to have rifles analyzed on the basis of the materials required for their manufacture: walnut, steel, brass, and leather. The plant manager in charge of producing the steel parts would need a classification on the basis of production methods: stamping, casting, forging, and machining. And so on. The writer need only choose the basis of classification which serves his purpose and follow it consistently and clearly.

The Two Kinds

It would be profitless to try to list all the kinds of subjects which may be developed by analysis, such as "character analysis," "analysis of a mechanism," "analysis of a process." But we can make one useful distinction. One kind of analysis explains objects, places, ideas, personalities, and other subjects which need to be explained simply as structures or entities. Another kind relates actions or explains processes, or machines in operation. These categories actually include plain description and narration, of course, as well as simple exposition. The beginning writer need not be detained by terminology; what matters for him is the method used in all these prose forms. Whether he describes a place, tells a simple story, or explains a process, he must first see each detail of the subject himself and then set down enough of these details to make a fully developed composition.

Katrina's Home

WASHINGTON IRVING

[1] As Ichabod jogged slowly on his way, his eye, ever open to every symptom of culinary abundance, ranged with delight over the treasures of jolly autumn. On all sides he beheld vast store of apples; some hanging in oppressive opulence on the trees; some gathered into baskets and barrels for the market; others heaped up in rich piles for the cider-press. Farther on he beheld great fields of Indian corn, with its golden ears peeping from their leafy coverts, and holding out the promise of cakes and hasty pudding; and the yellow pumpkins lying beneath them, turning up their fair round bellies to the sun, and giving ample prospects of the most luxurious of pies; and anon he passed the fragrant buck-wheat fields, breathing the odor of the bee-hive, and as he beheld them, soft anticipations stole over his mind of dainty slapjacks, well buttered, and garnished with honey or treacle, by the delicate little dimpled hand of Katrina Van Tassel.

[2] Ichabod Crane had a soft and foolish heart toward the sex; and it is not to be wondered at, that so tempting a morsel soon found favor in his eyes; more especially after he had visited her in her paternal mansion. Old Baltus Van Tassel was a perfect picture of a thriving, contented, liberal-hearted farmer. He seldom, it is true, sent either his eyes or his thoughts beyond the boundaries of his own farm; but within those every thing was snug, happy, and well-conditioned. He was satisfied with his wealth, but not proud of it; and piqued himself upon the hearty abundance, rather than the style in which he lived. His stronghold was situated on the banks of the Hudson, in one of those green, sheltered, fertile nooks, in which the Dutch farmers are so fond of nestling. A great elm-tree spread its broad branches over it; at the foot of which bubbled up a spring of the softest and sweetest water, in a little well, formed of a barrel; and then stole sparkling away through the grass, to a neighboring brook, that bubbled along

From *The Legend of Sleepy Hollow,* by Washington Irving.

among alders and dwarf willows. Hard by the farmhouse was a vast barn, that might have served for a church; every window and crevice of which seemed bursting forth with the treasures of the farm; the flail was busily resounding within it from morning to night; swallows and martins skimmed twittering about the eaves; and rows of pigeons, some with one eye turned up, as if watching the weather, some with their heads under their wings, or buried in their bosoms, and others swelling, and cooing, and bowing about their dames, were enjoying the sunshine on the roof. Sleek unwieldy porkers were grunting in the repose and abundance of their pens; whence sallied forth, now and then, troops of sucking pigs, as if to snuff the air. A stately squadron of snowy geese were riding in an adjoining pond, convoying whole fleets of ducks; regiments of turkeys were gobbling through the farmyard, and guinea fowls fretting about it, like ill-tempered housewives, with their peevish discontented cry. Before the barn door strutted the gallant cock, that pattern of a husband, a warrior, and a fine gentleman, clapping his burnished wings, and crowing in the pride and gladness of his heart—sometimes turning up the earth with his feet, and then generously calling his ever-hungry family of wives and children to enjoy the rich morsel which he had discovered.

[3] When he entered the house the conquest of his heart was complete. It was one of those spacious farmhouses, with high-ridged, but lowly-sloping roofs, built in the style handed down from the first Dutch settlers; the low projecting eaves forming a piazza along the front, capable of being closed up in bad weather. Under this were hung flails, harness, various utensils of husbandry, and nets for fishing in the neighboring river. Benches were built along the sides for summer use; and a great spinning-wheel at one end, and a churn at the other, showed the various uses to which this important porch might be devoted. From this piazza the wandering Ichabod entered the hall, which formed the centre of the mansion and the place of usual residence. Here, rows of resplendent pewter, ranged on a long dresser, dazzled his eyes. In one corner stood a huge bag of wool ready to be spun; in another a quantity of linsey-woolsey just from the loom; ears of Indian corn, and strings of dried apples and peaches, hung

in gay festoons along the walls, mingled with the gaud of red peppers; and a door left ajar gave him a peep into the best parlor, where the claw-footed chairs, and dark mahogany tables, shone like mirrors; and irons, with their accompanying shovel and tongs, glistened from their covert of asparagus tops; mock oranges and conch-shells decorated the mantelpiece; strings of various colored birds' eggs were suspended above it; a great ostrich egg was hung from the centre of the room, and a corner cupboard, knowingly left open, displayed immense treasures of old silver and well-mended china.

EXERCISES

Each paragraph in this section is a simple analysis of a scene; that is, it gives the details of the scene, or the elements that constitute it. The whole passage is description of course, though it is used to explain something about Ichabod and about the Sleepy Hollow farm. But we need not decide whether it is mainly descriptive or mainly expository. Our concern is with the method of development: the explanation of a general term by a presentation of its parts or details.

1. What is the topic sentence of paragraph 1?
2. What phrase or phrases in the topic sentence summarize the impressions and sights mentioned in the rest of the paragraph?
3. Each item such as "store of apples" is a specific *detail* of one or both of the general terms in the topic sentence. List other details.
4. The organization of the first paragraph follows two of the inherent orders mentioned on page xii. What are they?
5. Would you call the description in the paragraph vivid? Why?
6. What is the topic sentence of paragraph 2?
7. Find several details which develop a general term in the topic sentence.
8. What is the main impression established by the paragraph?
9. Notice that the scene in this paragraph has a marked pattern; first our attention is directed to a cove on the Hudson, then focused on the single farm, then fixed on the tree—house—barn group, then turned to the activities of the farmyard. This pattern also follows one of the natural or inherent orders of arrangement. Would the author have organized his material in this way automatically or "unconsciously," or do you suppose he knew what he was doing?

10. Irving evidently intends to present the Van Tassel farm as a complete little kingdom or barony. How is this extended metaphor developed? Find details or words which represent the domestic, the social, and the military spheres of the realm.
11. Point out the three main sections of the third paragraph. Is there an orderly arrangement of details within each section? Why?
12. How are these details related to "the conquest of his heart"?
13. Surely Irving's own love for the autumn harvest is partly responsible for the selection of details in this passage from "The Legend of Sleepy Hollow," but he is also selecting for Ichabod. What does the passage tell us about Ichabod?
14. For each paragraph write a sentence which states the subject and the purpose of the entire paragraph.
15. Point out the statements which aid transition between paragraphs.
16. List several details which might be used to develop each of the following statements.
    a. My desk is littered with miscellaneous articles.
    b. Huck Finn's costume was not elaborate.
    c. Every object on the mantel meant something to me.
    d. The barnyard at sundown was a scene of peace and quiet.
    e. The instrument panel on the modern car tells the driver many things.
    f. A woman's powder compact is actually composed of several parts.

The Theatre at Athens

ENCYCLOPEDIA AMERICANA

[1] From the remains of various Greek theatres which have been excavated it is possible to reconstruct, at least in its main features, one of these edifices. In the centre the orchestra formed an exact circle in the middle of which stood the altar of Dionysus. Later the circle was cut on the side next the stage. Round the orchestra,

From *The Encyclopedia Americana* (1947 Edition), XXVI, 492.

in size rather more than a semi-circle, the seats for the audience
rose tier upon tier like a modern baseball field-stand. These seats
were at first of wood, but owing to a collapse of the benches in
499 B. C., it was resolved at Athens to erect a permanent stone
theatre. This was the theatre of Dionysus, which exists today, although it has been partly reconstructed. It consists of three parts
—the orchestra, the stage building and the auditorium. The
orchestra was occupied solely by the chorus. Behind it rose the
stage building, usually a long, narrow rectangle, facing the audience; the most ancient one at Athens was 55 yards long and only
11 yards deep. But then little scenery was used. In front the
buildings represented a palace or a temple. There were usually
three doors opening on to the stage, which was a wooden platform,
standing 8 or 10 feet above the orchestra. On it the actors appeared. The auditorium was of great extent as the theatre was
intended to accommodate practically the whole population of the
city in which it stood. The rows of seats were, in consequence,
of enormous size, the theatre of Dionysus at Athens holding
27,500 persons, and that at Megalopolis being computed to seat
44,000. In order to obtain the necessary slope for the tiers of
seats as well as a natural substructure for the same the Greeks
always chose some natural hollow, where the shape of the ground
aided the design of the architect. Tiers of seats rose one above
another, divided vertically by passages for access and in many
cases horizontally also. The lowest or first row of seats at Athens
is of marble, and was reserved for persons of distinction; the rest
are of ordinary stone. Between the auditorium and the stage were
the passages of entrance (*parodoi*) which in some instances were
of great breadth. The back-wall was called the *scena,* the side-
walls, or wings, in each of which was an entrance door being
called *paraskēnia*. The stage was called the *proscenium*. A flight
of steps, later two, connected the stage with the orchestra and
these steps, continued out of sight beneath the orchestra floor,
were the means by which apparitions from the lower world
ascended. The front of the stage nearest the orchestra was called
the . . . *logeum*. The back-wall represented a suitable background or setting for the play, and, before the performance, was
covered by a curtain (*aulaia*) which was let down, not drawn up as

is usual to-day. When the action of the play required a different scene, the back of the stage was covered with a painted curtain or boards. At either end of the stage were large revolving triangular prisms, each side of which bore a different scene, thus providing three sets of wings. In dealing with the early Greek theatre it must always be remembered that the stage was only of secondary importance, the orchestra being deemed the chief point of interest. There was a certain amount of machinery, of which the most famous was a species of crane by which a god could be let down from on high or drawn up again as occasion required. The Greek theatre was open to the sky and attendance at it was a species of religious observance; performances took place only on festal days, when the whole population turned out to witness them. The acoustic properties appear to have received little attention. Actors used a species of megaphone device, concealed in their masks, in order to make their voices carry to a distance.

EXERCISES

This selection is part of the article on the theatre in the *Encyclopedia Americana*. As such, it is only a small portion of a long composition and is, perhaps logically, in one paragraph. Yet it has its own subdivisions and could be broken into more than one paragraph.

1. How many main divisions can you discern? Put a mark in the margin at each point where you would begin a new paragraph.
2. Why is this selection not really description? Do we *see* the theatre?
3. Why is the selection expository? What is explained?
4. Look up the following words in your college dictionary. Give the etymology (see Glossary) of each. Explain the use of each in the article and also in general modern usage: *orchestra, auditorium, scene (scena), proscenium, prism*.
5. The author says that the orchestra was the chief point of interest to the Greeks; yet he gives a great deal more attention to the stage than to the orchestra. Explain this emphasis in terms of the author's purpose in a general article on "the theatre."
6. Why can this selection be called an analysis? List several details of one of the main divisions which you marked off in doing Exercise 1.
7. Are the details arranged in an inherent pattern or a rational one?
8. Give the etymology of each of the words in the following pairs, and distinguish between them in meaning.

edifice — building
circle — round
audience — listeners
require — need

Sometimes exactness requires us to use one word rather than another; at other times substitution is possible and desirable. Why does the author say "one of these edifices" instead of "one of these buildings"? Why, probably, does he say "chief point of interest" instead of "primary point of interest"?

9. Write an analysis of one of the following topics.

a. The modern stage
b. The organization of a restaurant
c. A drive-in theatre
d. The floor plan (or arrangement) of a church building, a supermarket, or any building with which you are familiar
e. An electric motor
f. A desk lamp
g. The structure of a flower

Types of College Students

HENRY SEIDEL CANBY

[1] At first one's class was a sea of faces, pimply, vacuous, keen, sulky, and amiable, all dissolving into a blur of washed and rosy youth. But soon (and Buddhist priests and doctors of the Sorbonne must have the same experience), the room disintegrated into familiar types. The pleasantest, I think, was the well-mannered, neatly dressed boy from orthodox preparatory schools. He was deferential to teacher, polite to the scrawny high school boy beside him. Yet he was still all boy and at each moment of relaxation would tickle his schoolmate on the other side, and be slyly

punched in return, the two of them like puppies trying hard not
to roll over and cuff and bite. Yet put those well-trained boys
on the football field where serious life for them began, and they
would tackle low, and slug and viciously kick when the umpire
was not looking. A faint aroma of cereal and cream exuded from
these preparatory school boys. They had nice mothers and generous
fathers. Their world was already made for them, and, like blooded
colts, they were expected to play, because their future work was to
be a fierce competition to make the family richer. They had the
arrogance and the gentleness of the aristocrat, without his detach-
ment from life. They were being groomed for the capture or
retention of privilege, and its enjoyment. Every one of them
expected to start in business or professional life at the bottom and
to come to the top as easily as he rushed a ball past untrained
opponents. The type was Spartan rather than Athenian; and, like
the Spartans, they were quite inaccessible to new ideas, having
closed their minds at sixteen or seventeen upon a code of success
which left no room for speculation.

[2] These fine boys with their good voices, their courtesy and self-
assurance, would sit out the hour in deferential boredom, then, at
the word of dismissal, crowd the doorway in a sudden release of
energy, leaving the young teacher in an agony of frustration. For
they had everything—health, good looks, will, character, reserves
of energy—everything but open minds, everything but cracks
in their stiff brains into which ideas could flow! With consummate
skill gained in long experience with clever teachers and the right
textbooks, they gave to Caesar exactly what Caesar was supposed
to get from them, the modicum of facts, the statements of the
last lecture reduced to a formula, enough to get a B in Freshman
year when the footing was still unsteady, just enough for a C in
Senior year when the danger of flunking was past. You liked them
as you liked blooded show dogs. Like show dogs they defeated
every attempt to teach their well-bred intellect new tricks.

[3] Scattered here and there in every class were the "grinds,"
called by the preparatory school dilettantes either "greasy grinds"
or just "grinds." Actually the differences between the two varieties
were subtle. The typical grind was a survival of the old college
that trained chiefly for teaching and the ministry. He was usually

the quiet and bloodless member of a family, afraid of rough sports, averse to competition, seeking refuge in books. His face was blank, his mind was a sponge which squeezed dry and filled again without cellular change. The young teacher found him trying, since he did everything he was told, believed all he heard, studied everything assigned to him, and at the end wrote papers that were correct with a deathly perfection of the commonplace which showed how ineffective education could be unless it touched the emotions, of which he had none.

[4] The "greasy grind" was a racial or social variant of the plain grind. The greasy grind seldom changed his collar. He had a sneaking cleverness which taught him to snap up the hard questions in easy courses, thus collecting high marks as a protection against a world that, quite properly, wished to keep him down. He would argue with teacher for ten minutes trying to get a B changed into an A; but he had no intellectual curiosity. Education for him was a coin, useless unless you could buy something with it. The dilettante could sometimes be shocked into a realization that there were other worlds than his, and so other values in living; but the greasy grind was both unchangeable and inescapable, a fly buzzing about your weary head.

[5] Another and very different type of industrious student in those classes is well recognized now, but was then regarded by the pink and well-soaped elect as just another undesirable. The second generation from the East of Europe was beginning to come to college:—Polish Jews with anemic faces on which were set dirty spectacles, soft-eyed Italians too alien to mix with an Anglo-Saxon community, seam-faced Armenian boys, and now and then a Chinese. These, except the last, were all in college to learn how to live in America. Their mien was apologetic; you could see them watching with envious curiosity the courteous indifference of the superior race; they took little part in discussions, and asked for no credit. Yet often their more flexible minds could be felt playing round and round the confident Anglo-Saxons, admiring, skeptical, puzzled, and sometimes contemptuous. Occasionally there would be a revelation of intellect or a hint of the future, when some Chinese boy, caught off his guard, and forgetting the convention of the classroom which was to answer a question and sit down,

would give a précis of the entire lesson, and perhaps the previous one and the next, which only a French intellectual could have equaled. Or some Russian Jewish exile, asked to comment on an Ibsen play, and losing control of his guarded intellect, would expound a social philosophy that made the class squirm as if a blast of fire had scorched the seats of their comfortable pants.

[6] Every class had also its freaks, which in those college days was a familiar term with a definite meaning. And nothing could have better revealed the nature of our college community than the diversity of types which were all called, for convenience, and to indicate their difference from the true-blue college men, freaks. A freak was a nonconformist. He might be a preparatory school boy of good family who had failed somehow to take the right impress from the preparatory school mold. He might be, and often was, a son of the very rich, or of artistic bohemians, who had been educated in Europe, and was ill at ease in our Philistine Zion. He might be a potential homosexual distracted by his own unrecognized perversity. He might be, but rarely was, a little crazy. Sometimes he was merely an adult intellect in the society of adolescents, who refused to waste his time in organized athletics, although obviously competent, who declined fraternity elections, and was obsessed by a morbid interest in chemistry or philology. All such were freaks.

[7] The Spartan parallel again holds good, since the arts in this question of freakishness were especially suspect. To be musical and indulge in music privately was a sure sign of freakishness, as bad as private drinking or the reading of poetry in seclusion. The banjo, the mandolin, and the guitar were respectable, since skillful players could "make" the instrumental clubs and so gain social recognition; but proficiency on the violin was a sure sign of something wrong, as was skill on the piano not confined to "beating the box," and also the singing of "classic" music. Radical ideas, a taste for the society of professors, silk pajamas, an interest in art, careful English, long hair (except on football heroes), uncollegiate clothes, and a lack of interest in sports, all designated the freak, who was a person dangerous to make friends with. Only religion, thanks to our evangelical heritage, was allowed eccentricities of self-expression, for it was a part of the code.

[8] Hence the young teacher, himself a mild nonconformist since otherwise he would never have gone into teaching, was often embarrassed by the sudden drop in classroom temperature when, misled or ignorant, he gave a freak the floor and his approval. The boy who looked at him with dumb, devoted eyes, the boy who compared Milton to Bach, the youth who knew the Italian primitives in the Art School, the freak who asked whether Christ was not a good socialist, and the exquisite who actually articulated his English, and quoted French in a foreign accent—call upon any one of these and all motion forward was stopped for that day. An Alexandrian Greek could have met with no more disapproval if asked to address the Conscript Fathers of the Roman republic.

[9] I soon grew accustomed to this so variegated class, learning to play one faction against another, soap, so to speak, against dirty finger nails, agile intellect against the solidity of a confident code. Yet what saved those of us who tried to be philosophers in our role of teaching, was another, and fortunately unfailing, contribution from America to our college classes. I remember well those first days of each teaching year: the confident moment when one looked down upon fresh faces in the old seats, and hoped that this time at last faith would be justified. And then the quick disillusion as the herd rounded up into the same old assortment of mavericks, mixed breeds, and stolid beef cattle. Yet as with ranging question and hopeful reading of test papers we sifted and searched, always in some unexpected corners would be found those quiet minds, tenacious, reserved, cautious, practical, and yet ready to sight an idea and pursue it, and apply it, and keep faith with it—not speculative, not logical, but unshakable in the confidence that most problems can be solved—which are the best products of the great American experiment.

EXERCISES

This selection is an analysis by classification. Professor Canby has analyzed the personalities of many students and has finally grouped all students in five classes on the basis of certain attributes. Perhaps in the beginning he did not know what bases of analysis and classification would prove significant. He could have classified them according to hair color, political affiliation, and major subject interests. But in the end the bases which seemed most significant were these: economic and national background, attitude toward study, attitude toward fellow students, attitude toward life, and reasons for being in college. He does not need to take his readers through his preliminary thinking. He simply designates each class, then gives the traits manifested by members of that class. Sometimes, as in his paragraph on the "grind," he lets a typical individual represent the group.

1. What phrase in the second sentence is the general term which the author begins to explain?
2. Mark off portions of the selection which might serve as *introduction* and *conclusion*.
3. The remaining portion, the *body*, falls into five *main divisions*. Mark them off.
4. Is there any reason for the arrangement of the main divisions in relation to one another? Would another arrangement have been possible?
5. Do all of the bases of classification given above apply to all of the classes?
6. On a sheet of paper write the term used to designate one of the classes, as a kind of heading, and under it list all the traits of that class.

Such an analytical list for all five groups would constitute a fairly good *outline* of the selection. A careful writer prepares at least a rough outline to guide his writing. He jots down details or illustrations as they occur to him until he has enough to develop his main ideas fully; then he arranges them in the order which best suits his purpose. Thus he assures himself of full development and strong coherence.

7. This selection obviously has unity of subject; it concerns only students. It also has unity of purpose; state the author's main purpose in a single sentence.
8. Locate the topic sentence of each paragraph.
9. Paragraphs may be made coherent by orderly arrangement or by verbal links, or by both. The orders of arrangement discussed under *Organization* in the Introduction (page xi) serve for paragraphs as well as for whole compositions. The most commonly used verbal links are transition words and phrases, such as *consequently, thereupon, on the other hand,* and *yet* (all conjunctions and conjunctive adverbs), and pronouns with clear antecedents in a preceding sentence. Which method does the author use in paragraph 1? Which in paragraph 9?

10. Notice the emphatic endings of several of the paragraphs. Are these sentences striking because of what the author says or because of his language?

11. The author uses several metaphors and some plain comparisons to help the reader visualize certain qualities in his interesting students. ". . . the two of them like puppies trying hard not to roll over and cuff and bite" and ". . . made the class squirm as if a blast of fire had scorched the seats of their comfortable pants" are examples with obvious meaning. "A faint aroma of cereal and cream exuded from these preparatory school boys" is not so obvious, but it is a very concrete way of representing a quality of character. What is that quality? Find several other striking metaphors.

12. Could the adjectives (in line 1) "pimply, vacuous, keen, sulky, and amiable" all apply to all the faces in the classroom? Could they all apply to any one face? Why does the author use them all in this way?

13. What is the meaning of *vacuous* as it is used in line 1? Compare this meaning with that of the word *blank* in the middle of paragraph 3. Do the etymologies of the words help you to understand these modern usages?

14. Distinguish between *vacuous* and *vacant;* between *vacate* and *evacuate.*

In addition to strong *unity,* effective *organization,* and complete *development,* every composition must have *interest* or it is nearly worthless. Interest can be achieved by one or more of four elements: (1) style, (2) originality, (3) novelty, and (4) immediacy. All these terms are defined in the Glossary (pages 447–461). Both style and immediacy give interest to this selection. Perhaps the most attractive feature of Mr. Canby's style is his facility in using fresh and vivid metaphors, some of which you have studied. Immediacy, briefly defined, is the quality of being directly related to our intimate and strong desires and interests or to our condition in life. Mr. Canby holds your attention because he is writing about college students—about *you.* Into which group would he put *you?* Are his classifications just? Is there any group of which he approves? Would his classifications fit *your* English class? Such questions as these keep your interest keenly awake.

You may now wish to reflect upon whether the preceding two selections held your interest, and if so, why.

15. Write a theme (or prepare an outline for a theme) in which you analyze and classify several separate items on subjects of some one kind: motion pictures, salesmen, college students, ways of

dressing or eating, vacations, etc. Your classification of students
would be on a different basis from Mr. Canby's. You might classify
them by style of dress, by their reasons for coming to college, by
their study methods, or on any of a score of other bases. Or perhaps
you would like to retaliate by classifying your teachers!

Elizabeth

JOHN RICHARD GREEN

[1] England's one hope lay in the character of her Queen. Elizabeth
was now in her twenty-fifth year. Personally she had more than
her mother's beauty; her figure was commanding, her face long
but queenly and intelligent, her eyes quick and fine. She had
grown up amidst the liberal culture of Henry's court, a bold horse-
woman, a good shot, a graceful dancer, a skilled musician, and an
accomplished scholar. She studied every morning the Greek
Testament, and followed this by the tragedies of Sophocles or
orations of Demosthenes, and could "rub up her rusty Greek"
at need to bandy pedantry with a Vice-Chancellor. But she was
far from being a mere pedant. The new literature which was
springing up around her found constant welcome in her court.
She spoke Italian and French as fluently as her mother-tongue.
She was familiar with Ariosto and Tasso. Even amidst the affectation and love of anagrams and puerilities which sullied her later
years, she listened with delight to the *Faerie Queen,* and found a
smile for "Master Spenser" when he appeared in her presence. Her
moral temper recalled in its strange contrasts the mixed blood
within her veins. She was at once the daughter of Henry and
of Anne Boleyn. From her father she inherited her frank and
hearty address, her love of popularity and of free intercourse with
the people, her dauntless courage and her amazing self-confidence.
Her harsh, manlike voice, her impetuous will, her pride, her
furious outbursts of anger came to her with her Tudor blood. She

From *A Short History of the English People,* by John Richard Green.

rated great nobles as if they were schoolboys; she met the insolence
of Essex with a box on the ear; she would break now and then
into the gravest deliberations to swear at her ministers like a fish-
wife. But strangely in contrast with the violent outlines of her
Tudor temper stood the sensuous, self-indulgent nature she
derived from Anne Boleyn. Splendor and pleasure were with
Elizabeth the very air she breathed. Her delight was to move in
perpetual progresses from castle to castle through a series of
gorgeous pageants, fanciful and extravagant as a caliph's dream.
She loved gaiety and laughter and wit. A happy retort or a finished
compliment never failed to win her favor. She hoarded jewels. Her
dresses were innumerable. Her vanity remained, even to old age,
the vanity of a coquette in her teens. No adulation was too fulsome
for her, no flattery of her beauty too gross. "To see her was
heaven," Hatton told her, "the lack of her was hell." She would
play with her rings that her courtiers might note the delicacy of
her hands, or dance a coranto that the French ambassador, hidden
dexterously behind a curtain, might report her sprightliness to his
master. Her levity, her frivolous laughter, her unwomanly jests
gave color to a thousand scandals. Her character in fact, like her
portraits, was utterly without shade. Of womanly reserve or self-
restraint she knew nothing. No instinct of delicacy veiled the
voluptuous temper which had broken out in the romps of her
girlhood and showed itself almost ostentatiously throughout her
later life. Personal beauty in a man was a sure passport to her
liking. She patted handsome young squires on the neck when they
knelt to kiss her hand, and fondled her "sweet Robin," Lord
Leicester, in the face of the court.

[2] It was no wonder that the statesmen whom she outwitted held
Elizabeth almost to the last to be little more than a frivolous
woman, or that Philip of Spain wondered how "a wanton" could
hold in check the policy of the Escurial. But the Elizabeth whom
they saw was far from being all of Elizabeth. The wilfulness of
Henry, the triviality of Anne Boleyn played over the surface of
a nature hard as steel, a temper purely intellectual, the very type
of reason untouched by imagination or passion. Luxurious and
pleasure-loving as she seemed, Elizabeth lived simply and frugally,
and she worked hard. Her vanity and caprice had no weight what-

ever with her in state affairs. The coquette of the presence-chamber became the coolest and hardest of politicians at the council-board. Fresh from the flattery of her courtiers, she would tolerate no flattery in the closet; she was herself plain and downright of speech with her counsellors, and she looked for a corresponding plainness of speech in return. If any trace of her sex lingered in her actual statesmanship, it was seen in the simplicity and tenacity of purpose that often underlies a woman's fluctuations of feeling. It was this in part which gave her her marked superiority over the statesmen of her time. No nobler group of ministers ever gathered round a council-board than those who gathered round the council-board of Elizabeth. But she was the instrument of none. She listened, she weighed, she used or put by the counsels of each in turn, but her policy as a whole was her own. It was a policy, not of genius, but of good sense. Her aims were simple and obvious: to preserve her throne, to keep England out of war, to restore civil and religious order. Something of womanly caution and timidity perhaps backed the passionless indifference with which she set aside the larger schemes of ambition which were ever opening before her eyes. She was resolute in her refusal of the Low Countries. She rejected with a laugh the offers of the Protestants to make her "head of the religion" and "mistress of the seas." But her amazing success in the end sprang mainly from this wise limitation of her aims. She had a finer sense than any of her counsellors of her real resources; she knew instinctively how far she could go, and what she could do. Her cold, critical intellect was never swayed by enthusiasm or by panic either to exaggerate or to underestimate her risks or her power.

EXERCISES

This sketch of Queen Elizabeth, like most brief character sketches, is developed by analysis. From the vast number of known facts about Elizabeth's appearance, habits, and disposition, Green selected those which would best serve his purpose. His sketch is so well organized that we can see he must have made an outline in which he arranged the details under main headings and subheadings; that is, his analysis is classified according to different aspects of Elizabeth's character.

1. Make an outline such as Green must have used by adding headings and details to the framework suggested here:

    I. Elizabeth as a person
        A. Her personal appearance
            1. . . . . . .
            2. . . . . . .
        B. Her liberal culture
            1. . . . . . .
            2. . . . . . . (etc.)
        C. Her moral temper
            1. Qualities inherited from her father
                a. . . . . . .
                b. . . . . . . (etc.)
            2. Qualities inherited from her mother
                a. . . . . . .
                b. . . . . . . (etc.)
    II. Elizabeth as . . . . (Finish this heading and complete the outline.)

2. What words or phrases (not complete statements) in the second half of the first paragraph reiterate or echo the ideas of vanity and love of pleasure?

3. What is the topic sentence of the second paragraph? Which words in the sentence state the general quality to be explained in the paragraph? Point out, as you did for paragraph 1, several words or phrases which designate specific qualities or actions which make up this general quality.

4. Explain the meaning of the following words as they are used in this selection: *personally, pedant, rated, sensuous.*

5. The *Oxford English Dictionary,* which you will find in the reference room of your library, gives all the meanings of a word throughout its existence in English. The meanings of some words change with the passing of time. For instance, in Chaucer's day the word *anon* meant *immediately;* in Shakespeare's day it meant *after a while.* Thus a word quoted from a former period may have no meaning for us or, worse, a wrong meaning. Green puts quotation marks about "a wanton" near the beginning of paragraph 2 to show that the term was taken from some contemporary document. Consult the *O. E. D.* for the meaning of *wanton* in Elizabeth's day and in ours. Would a failure to ascertain the historical meaning of the word have led you to a wrong understanding of what Philip thought of Elizabeth?

6. Green uses fewer metaphors than Canby, but he achieves vividness through the use of examples which illustrate Elizabeth's qualities of

character. Although we are not yet ready to study example as a major method of developing ideas, we may notice here that examples can make writing concrete and vivid. Green speaks of Elizabeth's "furious outbursts of anger" and then says, "She rated great nobles as if they were schoolboys; she met the insolence of Essex with a box on the ear . . . ," and so on. Find a few other examples.

7. This portrait holds our attention for other reasons than those which made Canby's essay interesting. We are not all queens or nobles. But we are always interested in unusual people, as regular features in such different types of magazines as the *New Yorker* and the *Reader's Digest* show.

Write a character sketch of someone you know. Be sure you take a really unusual person: one with striking contrasts of qualities, one whose personal qualities or dramatic achievements set him apart from most of us. Probably you should not write of someone very dear to you but of one you can analyze—"take apart"—without pangs of conscience and without bias. On the other hand, you must know the subject well enough that you will not lack information.

The details which you jot down as they first occur to you, you will later classify under appropriate headings, such as

I. At home
II. At the office
III. On the golf course
IV. In church

Be certain you have enough details, properly organized, then go ahead.

The Grand Jury

BROOKS ATKINSON

[1] February session of the county grand jury begins. Before eleven o'clock more than a hundred men and women silently collect in a large courtroom downtown in Centre Street, take off their overcoats, and wait rather morosely. We have been caught by the

From *Once Around the Sun,* copyright, 1951, by Brooks Atkinson. Reprinted by permission of Harcourt, Brace and Company, Inc.

summons that comes about every thirteen or fourteen months. No matter when it comes, it finds us unprepared, unwilling, and affronted. But the style in which it is written is explicit and ominous. The summons mentions penalties that sound alarming. The mood of the courtroom is portentous. Uniformed guards patrol the courtroom. The clerk is grave and vigilant. At eleven o'clock he starts reading our names in a slow, precise and imposing voice that rumbles with authority and warning. Only a reckless man would dare intrude matters of personal convenience into this solemn assembly. When the clerk has registered the names of all the people present, he puts their slips in the ballot wheel, turns it over a few times and calls the names he draws in a voice that sounds like an awful prison sentence. Aware of all the sins we have ever committed, and silent about all the laws we have broken (I occasionally smoke on subway platforms), we meekly take our respective places in the jury seats when our miserable little names are boomed across the room. Being selected for a jury is a chastening experience. After taking the oath on the battered Bibles kept in stock, and listening to the judge's charge, we retire to our respective jury rooms to begin a month's service in the administration of democratic justice.

[2] The grand jury is one of the most venerable institutions in the judicial system. Justice cannot be administered democratically without it. The grand jury does not try cases. It authorizes legal accusations: before a defendant can be tried on a criminal charge the legal evidence on which the county will base its case must be presented to a grand jury. The prospective defendant can appear before the grand jury if he wants to and can bring witnesses to support his case if the grand jury consents. After all the evidence has been heard the witnesses, the attorneys, the stenographer, and the court attendants leave the room. Behind closed doors the members of the jury discuss the evidence informally. If the grand jury thinks that the uncontested evidence argues a presumption of guilt on the part of the accused, it votes an indictment (known as a "true bill"), and thereby gives consent to a formal trial in a regular court. If the grand jury is not persuaded by the evidence, it finds "no bill" and the accused is dismissed.

[3] Since the evidence in most cases is simple, real and clear, the

grand jury is usually convinced that the accused should be brought to trial. But occasionally the evidence is neither complete nor convincing, even when the accused does not appear; and in defense of a private citizen, the grand jury of private citizens does not permit a trial. In this way the grand juries introduce a decisive democratic influence into the administration of justice at the beginning and at the top; and erect a formidable hurdle over which careless or unscrupulous attorneys have some difficulty in crossing.

[4] Although composed of citizens, grand juries have quasi-judicial functions. Apart from their function in the court they can and are supposed to investigate the administration of the prisons, the conduct of the police, the alertness and integrity of the justice department, the honesty of elections, the conduct of public officials, and any crime, whether or not it is formally presented by the department of justice. Grand juries have the right and also the duty to inquire into anything bearing on the honest conduct of public business. And since the grand jury represents the people's interest in the administration of justice it has a number of autonomous rights: individual grand jurors cannot be held to account for their votes or opinions in the jury room; nor can they be coerced or instructed by the courts, attorneys, or police. The jurors have complete immunity under law for their official actions.

[5] Being a "body of citizens" they outrank the people's servants. Grand juries can call any public official to appear for questioning and for inquiry into official business, and can use the county apparatus for the purpose.

[6] Since the grand jury interposes the judgment of ordinary, disinterested citizens between the accused and the district attorney's office, some political organizations have tried to eliminate the grand jury system or devise ways of circumventing it, for it keeps the district attorney and public officials under observation. Without the grand jury system the citizens would have no control over flagrant or organized abuses of justice, coercion of citizens by corrupt or dictatorial departments of justice, or political domination of the courts. In this huge city with its formidable bureaucracy and unscrupulous political organizations, a "body of citizens,"

representing all businesses, professions, races, and religions, has the responsibility and the authority to guard the public's interest in the conduct of public affairs.

[7] Now we settle down to the month-long grind of appearing in the jury room every morning at eleven, and for two hours listening to, inquiring into, and judging the human frailties of the law, on the one hand, and the human frailties of fellow-citizens, on the other. Neither one is above suspicion.

EXERCISES

This selection is perhaps the most thorough analysis we have studied. Authors of the preceding selections have presented only limited aspects of their subjects; but Mr. Atkinson presents all aspects of the grand jury in as much detail as is likely to interest the general reader. The jury on which he served was in New York.

1. Mark off the selection into divisions which might be given these main headings: *introduction* (one sentence), *manner of selecting jury members, judicial duty of jury, quasi-judicial duties, the importance of the grand jury in the democratic administration of justice, conclusion.*
2. Does paragraph 1 have a topic sentence?
3. Upon what inherent order is the paragraph organized?
4. How does the author establish a portentous mood?
5. How does he make the courtroom and judicial duty seem great and awful and the individual small?
6. What is the topic sentence of paragraph 2?
7. Does the organization of the paragraph follow an almost necessary functional order or a merely chronological order? (Both are inherent orders.)
8. Is the subject of paragraph 3 really different from that of paragraph 2, so that the principle of paragraph unity makes the division a desirable one?
9. Are paragraphs 4 and 5 on different subjects? Might they be combined without violating the principle of unity?
10. Explain the meaning of the following words and phrases as they are used in the selection:

morosely (paragraph 1)   quasi-judicial (paragraph 4)
portentous (paragraph 1)   autonomous (paragraph 4)
prospective defendant (paragraph 2)   apparatus (paragraph 5)
presumption of guilt (paragraph 2)   interposes (paragraph 6)

11. In paragraph 6, would it be possible to substitute *uninterested* for *disinterested? power* for *authority?*

12. Write a theme in which you analyze a group of people who function as a unit. Unlike Mr. Atkinson, you will not be able to go into great detail on all aspects of your subject; but you can explain the group very well in a general way. You will probably write best of a group of which you have been a member. Some suggestions: the High-Y, the student council, a Red Cross fund drive committee, a dormitory council, an intramural council.

The Great Ravelled Knot

GEORGE W. GRAY

[1] Thousands of millions of nerve cells are woven into the texture of the human brain, and each can communicate with near or distant neighbors. Judson Herrick, the University of Chicago neurologist, has calculated that if only a million of these nerve cells were joined two by two in every possible way, the number of combinations would total $10^{2,783,000}$. This is a figure so tremendous that if it were written out and set up in the type you are reading, more than 350 pages of *Scientific American* would be required to print it. And we may be sure that the brain has many times a million nerve cells, each capable of groupings of far more than two cells per hookup.

[2] Life has created innumerable patterns in its long climb from the Archeozoic ooze, but none can compare in intricacy of design and virtuosity of function with "The great ravelled knot," as the famous English physiologist Sir Charles Sherrington described it, by which we feel, see, hear, think and decide. This "master tissue of the human body" is perhaps the most challenging of all biological researches.

[3] One can trace the evolution of the master tissue from fish to man, and observe brain part after brain part originate as each

From "The Great Ravelled Knot," *Scientific American,* October, 1948.

succeeding species becomes better adapted to the complex conditions of life on land, more versatile in its capacity for survival—
and more intelligent. Similarly, in the developing human embryo
the brain forms by the dual process of multiplying the number
of cells and increasing their specialization. In the beginning,
a few days after conception, certain skin cells are selected as tissue
for nerve function. From this microscopic neural tube the spinal
cord forms, and simultaneously the hindbrain, midbrain and forebrain develop from the same germinal structure.

[4] It is the forebrain that attains the crowning organization and
integration of the nervous system—the cerebral cortex. Beginning
as an insignificant segment of the embryonic brain, this gray mantle
eventually grows so large that it must fold in on itself in wrinkles
to accommodate its expanding surface to the walls of the skull.
When fully grown, the cerebral cortex completely covers the brain
structures from which it developed. It overshadows and dominates
them, taking control of many of their functions. From every
nerve cell, or neurone, fibers pass to other neurones, both of the
cortex and of the other brain parts. Millions of lines of communication connect one region of gray matter with another, and these in
turn with distant organs. By such means the brain is in communication with the lungs, the heart and other organs; with the
specialized cells which serve as the receptors of touch, taste,
smell, vision, hearing and other sensations; and with the muscles
which produce action.

[5] The cortex may be compared to a holding corporation formed
to integrate and extend the services of a number of older companies which are housed in the stem of the brain. Under the
consolidation the older companies are not abolished. They are
continued as useful adjuncts of the more modern organization: to
take care of routine activities such as breathing and digestion, to
serve as channels of communication, perhaps to be held in reserve
as stand-by agencies capable of resuming their former higher functions in emergencies. But the offices of inquiry and foresight, of
planning, initiative, the creating of new ideas, the venturing into
new projects, are executed by the holding corporation upstairs, and
control of the consolidated system is administered there.

[6] This roof brain is the supremely distinctive organ of the

human species. What goes on within its network of cells makes the fundamental difference between man and brute. The functioning of the cerebral cortex not only distinguishes man from the animals, but more than any other faculty it distinguishes man from man. It marks the fateful difference between the meek follower and the dynamic leader, between the scholar and the artist, between the genius and the moron.

[7] If the proper study of mankind is man, surely the supreme biological interest of man is his brain, particularly the gray cortex of two billion cells without the orchestration of which "there can be no thought, no sweet sonnets of Shakespeare, no joy and no sorrow."

EXERCISES

This selection is not an analysis of an action or process, for it does not really show the brain at work. But it does explain the principle upon which the brain operates, because an understanding of the principle is essential to an understanding of the structure.

1. State the topic of each paragraph in a phrase.
2. Mark off the introduction and the conclusion.
3. Why should paragraph 3 precede paragraph 4?
4. Which *attributed* or *rational* order (p. xii) do these paragraphs follow?
5. Why must paragraphs 3 and 4 precede paragraph 5?
6. Explain the meanings of the following words as they are used in this selection.

   intricacy (paragraph 2)   holding corporation (paragraph 5)
   virtuosity (paragraph 2)   consolidation (paragraph 5)
   organization (paragraph 4)   distinctive (paragraph 6)
   integration (paragraph 4)   orchestration (paragraph 7)

7. Why is the subject of this selection of interest to most readers?

The principle of economy underlies much good writing. The whole composition must be developed by the most efficient means possible, the paragraph must not be overdeveloped, and the sentence must not contain unnecessary words. Anything which promotes economy is good, and anything which interferes with it is bad unless it promotes some other good end, such as vividness.

Sentence economy is usually called *conciseness*. It is achieved, negatively, by the avoidance of *deadwood* and *wordy constructions,* and positively by the use of such rhetorical devices as *parallelism*. Dead-wood and wordy constructions are faults and so do not often appear in books of readings such as this one; they are dealt with adequately by your English handbook and, if they appear in your papers, by your instructor. But parallelism is a regularly used device and can readily be studied in these model compositions and subsequently imitated. The last sentence of paragraph 6 is a good example. The sentence might be diagrammed thus, to make the construction clear:

It marks the fateful difference ‖ between the meek follower and
                                                        the dynamic leader,
                                     ‖ between the scholar and the artist,
                                     ‖ between the genius and the moron.

The three parallel phrases all depend upon the same main predication for their full meaning. What is the alternative? "It marks the fateful difference between the meek follower and the dynamic leader. It also makes the difference between the scholar and the artist. The genius and the moron likewise differ mainly in the functioning of their cerebral cortexes." The advantage of parallel construction is obvious.

8. Find another sentence in this selection which uses parallel con-struction and diagram it to indicate the parallel elements. Then try to express the same ideas without using parallelism.

9. Express the following ideas in one sentence, using parallel construc-tion: "In a broader and more meaningful way, we cannot really dedicate this ground. Neither can we set it apart any more than it has already been set apart. We cannot make it any more holy, either."

Break-Through

ERNIE PYLE

[1] The general's lined face was a study in emotion. Sincerity and deep sentiment were in every contour and they shone from his eyes. General Barton was a man of deep affections. The tragedy of war, both personal and impersonal, hurt him. At the end his

From *Brave Men,* by Ernie Pyle. Copyright, 1943, 1944 by Scripps-Howard Newspaper Alliance. Copyright, 1944, by Henry Holt and Company, Inc. Reprinted by permission of the publishers.

voice almost broke, and I for one had a lump in my throat. He ended: "That's all. God bless you and good luck."

[2] Then we broke up and I went with one of the battalion commanders. By field telephone, radio, and liaison men, word was passed down to the very smallest unit of troops that the attack was on. There was still an hour before the bombers, and three hours before the infantry were to move. There was nothing for the infantry to do but dig a little deeper and wait. A cessation of motion seemed to come over the countryside and all its brown-clad inhabitants, a sense of last-minute sitting in silence before the holocaust.

[3] The first planes of the mass onslaught came over a little before 10 A. M. They were the fighters and dive bombers. The main road, running crosswise in front of us, was their bomb line. Our kickoff infantry had been pulled back a few hundred yards from the near side of the road. Everyone in the area had been given the strictest orders to be in foxholes, for high-level bombers can, and do quite excusably, make mistakes.

[4] We were still in country so level and with hedgerows so tall there simply was no high spot—neither hill nor building—from which we could get a grandstand view of the bombing as we used to do in Sicily and Italy. So one place was as good as another unless we went right up and sat on the bomb line. Having been caught too close to these things before, I compromised and picked a farmyard about 800 yards back of the kickoff line. And before the next two hours had passed I would have given every penny, every desire, every hope I ever had, to have been just another 800 yards farther back.

[5] Our front lines were marked by long strips of colored cloth laid on the ground, and with colored smoke to guide our airmen during the mass bombing. Dive bombers hit it just right. We stood and watched them barrel nearly straight down out of the sky. They were bombing about half a mile ahead of where we stood. They came in groups, diving from every direction, perfectly timed, one right after another. Everywhere we looked separate groups of planes were on their way down, or on the way back up, or slanting over for a dive, or circling, circling, circling over our heads, waiting for their turn.

[6] The air was full of sharp and distinct sounds of cracking

bombs and the heavy rips of the planes' machine guns and the splitting screams of diving wings. It was all fast and furious, yet distinct. And then a new sound gradually droned into our ears, a sound deep and all-encompassing with no notes in it—just a gigantic faraway surge of doomlike sound. It was the heavies. They came from directly behind us. At first they were the merest dots in the sky. We could see clots of them against the far heavens, too tiny to count individually. They came on with a terrible slowness. They came in flights of twelve, three flights to a group and in groups stretched out across the sky. They came in "families" of about seventy planes each. Maybe those gigantic waves were two miles apart, maybe they were ten; I don't know. But I do know they came in a constant procession and I thought it would never end. What the Germans must have thought is beyond comprehension.

[7] The flight across the sky was slow and studied. I've never known a storm, or a machine, or any resolve of man that had about it the aura of such a ghastly relentlessness. I had the feeling that even had God appeared beseechingly before them in the sky, with palms outstretched to persuade them, they would not have had within them the power to turn from their irresistible course.

[8] I stood with a little group of men, ranging from colonels to privates, back of the stone farmhouse. Slit trenches were all around the edges of the farmyard and a dugout with a tin roof was nearby. But we were so fascinated by the spectacle overhead that it never occurred to us that we might need the foxholes.

[9] The first huge flight passed directly overhead and others followed. We spread our feet and leaned far back trying to look straight up, until our steel helmets fell off. We'd cup our fingers around our eyes, like field glasses, for a clearer view. And then the bombs came. They began like the crackle of popcorn and almost instantly swelled into a monstrous fury of noise that seemed surely to destroy all the world ahead of us. From then on for an hour and a half that had in it the agonies of centuries, the bombs came down. A wall of smoke and dust erected by them grew high in the sky. It filtered along the ground back through our orchards. It sifted around us and into our noses. The bright day grew slowly dark from it. By now everything was an indescribable caldron

of sounds. Individual noises did not exist. The thundering of the motors in the sky and the roar of bombs ahead filled all the space for noise on earth. Our own heavy artillery was crashing all around us, yet we could hardly hear it.

[10] The Germans began to shoot heavy, high ack-ack. Great black puffs of it by the score speckled the sky until it was hard to distinguish smoke puffs from planes. And then someone shouted that one of the planes was smoking. Yes, we could all see it. A long faint line of black smoke stretched straight for a mile behind one of them. And as we watched there was a gigantic sweep of flame over the plane. From nose to tail it disappeared in flames, and it slanted slowly down and banked around the sky in great wide curves, this way and that way, as rhythmically and gracefully as in a slow-motion waltz. Then suddenly it seemed to change its mind and it swept upward, steeper and steeper and ever slower until finally it seemed poised motionless on its own black pillar of smoke. And then just as slowly it turned over and dived for the earth—a golden spearhead on the straight black shaft of its own creation—and disappeared behind the treetops. But before it was down there were cries of, "There's another one smoking— and there's a third one now." Chutes came out of some of the planes. Out of some came no chutes at all. One of white silk caught on the tail of a plane. Men with binoculars could see him fighting to get loose until flames swept over him, then a tiny black dot fell through space, all alone.

[11] And all that time the great flat ceiling of the sky was roofed by all the other planes that didn't go down, plowing their way forward as if there were no turmoil in the world. Nothing deviated them by the slightest. They stalked on, slowly and with a dreadful pall of sound, as though they were seeing only something at a great distance and nothing existed between. God, how we admired those men up there and sickened for the ones who fell.

EXERCISES

This is our first specimen of a true action analysis. The subject of such analysis may be a process or a mechanism, and the whole composition may be an expository narrative, or just a plain narrative; what-

ever the subject or the purpose, the method is the same. The method is
to present details of an action or a process, just as ordinary analysis gives
the details or parts of a scene, an object, a personality, or an idea. For
example, the action in paragraph 2 is presented in definite little steps:

"Then we broke up"
"and I went"
"word was passed down"
the infantry dug deeper
and waited
"A cessation of motion seemed to come over the countryside"

1. What is the main action presented in this selection? Give the general
   course of the action. Analyze the action in some paragraph, step by
   step, as the author gives it; paragraph 10 is especially easy to do.
2. Give the general plan of the scene of operation. Is it all presented at
   once? Point out the sentences in which the author sketches the
   scene.

It is now necessary to say something more about organization. In
the selections preceding "Break-Through" there was little action. In the
analyses of places, "Katrina's Home" and "The Theatre at Athens,"
both paragraphs and whole compositions were organized largely by the
natural space arrangements inherent in the subjects. In the analyses of
more abstract subjects, the body of the whole composition has usually
not followed a necessary pattern. Canby's student classifications, for
example, could have been differently arranged. Likewise, many individual paragraphs have lacked a necessary order, and coherence has
depended upon verbal links. But we have seen some paragraphs organized chronologically, for example the first paragraph of "Grand Jury"
and the last paragraph of "Types of College Students." And at least
one paragraph, the second of "Grand Jury," followed a functional order.
For "touchstone" paragraphs, then, upon which you can model your
own organization of similar material, you can remember these examples:

No order (coherence achieved by verbal links): paragraph 1 of
"Types of College Students"
Inherent orders
  Space: paragraph 2 of "Katrina's Home"
  Time: paragraph 1 of "Grand Jury"
  Function: paragraph 2 of "Grand Jury"

In "Break-Through" and the other pieces which follow, we shall observe two main kinds of order, both in paragraphs and in whole compositions: chronological and functional. Sometimes they are difficult to
distinguish; but we can best apply the principles in our own writing if

we understand the difference. Functional order *is* usually, but incidentally, chronological also. But, more important, it is inflexible or nearly so. It is necessary. There is only one possible order of steps in making coffee in a vacuum coffee maker: (1) put the water into the bottom part, (2) fit the top part into the bottom part, (3) put the ground coffee into the top part, (4) put the whole apparatus over heat, (5) let the steam pressure in the bottom part drive the water into the upper part, (6) remove the apparatus from the heat, (7) let the vacuum in the bottom part draw the water through the ground coffee and back into the lower part, (8) remove the upper part. Only then is the coffee ready. In explaining such a process, *you cannot rearrange these steps significantly;* you must put them down in 1, 2, 3 order. This arrangement according to a necessary succession is functional order.

On the other hand, some actions are not so restricting. An incident in the life of a small boy might be related in this fashion:

> Rick was maneuvering his imaginary power shovel over the front lawn, intending to excavate for one of his building projects, when he ran out of imaginary Diesel oil and did a terrible thing: he used a swear word—a *bad* one. Earlier in the day he had used one, and Aunt Tabitha had promised him a sound thrashing if he did it again. Now he had transgressed. As Aunt came down the steps he abandoned his machine and fled through the spirea.

The arrangement is a chronological one, although it does not follow the actual sequence of events. The details are presented in the order of 3–9–4–5–1–2–5–6–7–8. For reasons of economy and suspense, this is better than relating the details in their actual sequence.

3. Are the steps in the action in paragraph 10 related in the order in which they occurred?

4. Are the events mentioned in paragraph 3 presented in actual chronological order? (You can use 1–2–3, 2–1–3, 3–2–1, etc., to indicate the order in which they are related.) Is the actual order clear?

5. Observe that paragraph 4 begins with what was to Ernie Pyle the present, goes back to the past, then to the present, then to the past, then to the present, then to the future. Is the actual time sequence clear? What is the advantage, if any, of this handling of time? Could the events mentioned have been put into the order of their actual occurrence? Try to rewrite the paragraph according to the actual order.

6. The language of this selection is very vivid. Study paragraph 9 and make a list of the particularly vivid images and metaphors.

7. How does the author make the action of paragraph 10 vivid?

8. Find a sentence in paragraph 5 which has some parallel constructions.
9. Write a theme on one of the following topics or on something similar.
   Be sure to give adequate attention to the scene of action, but emphasize the action itself.

   a. Airplane races   e. A parade
   b. A motor speedway race   f. A symphony performance
   c. A boat race   g. A football rally
   d. A ship coming into port   h. A fire company fighting a large fire

---

Making Sugar

THOMAS BARBOUR

[1] Cuba produces more sugar than any other area on the globe.
For economy, the whole system is predicated on the fact that the
mill must run continually throughout the grinding season, which,
generally speaking, is the duration of the dry weather, four or five
months. When the fields become muddy with the spring rains the
bulls cannot pull the heavy, high-wheeled carts out to get the
cane to the scales. These weighing points are situated at varying
distances along the complicated lines of plantation railroad. Empty
cars must be distributed to each scale and loaded cars picked up
and hauled to the mill to supply cane to the crushers during all of
the twenty-four hours of every day.

[2] Reduced to the human equation, this means that the men who
cut the cane rise early, long before daylight, drink a cup of black
coffee, usually about two o'clock in the morning, take their horses,
and ride to the field. Cane cutting is not by any means the simple
process that it would appear to be. The cutter grasps a stalk of
cane in his left hand about five or six feet above the ground. Then
with a slash or two of his machete he strips loose the dried leaves

From *A Naturalist in Cuba,* by Thomas Barbour, copyright 1945. Reprinted by permission of Little, Brown & Company and the Atlantic Monthly
Press.

—*paja* they are called. Then he swings his machete and cuts off the cane stalk just above the ground. He next swings the stalk to the left and brings it back sharply to the right against the blade of his knife. The weight of the stalk and the swing against the sharp blade cut it in half. He lops off the green top which is tossed into a separate pile, away from where he throws the cane. These tops or *cogollo* are later bundled up and used for cattle and horse feed. The cut stems of cane, the *trozas,* are picked up by women and boys, helped by the cutters when the task which they set out to accomplish that day is finished. They are gathered and piled into the cane cart, on top of chains laid across the bottom of the wagon.

[3] After this work is finished, the bulls which have been feeding on the green cane tops are gathered together, yoked up, and the great load, weighing a number of thousand pounds, is hauled to the scales. Here the load is weighed and the amount cut is credited to the account of the individual cutters and the bull driver as well. The chains are gathered together so that the whole load is hoisted up in the air by a winch, usually activated by a mule walking round and round in a circle hitched to a hoisting apparatus. Drawn up in the air, it is swung over and dropped into a special type of railroad car.

[4] In due time these cars are gathered into trains by locomotives and hauled to the mill yard. Here they are shunted about, hauled hither and yon among a maze of switches by a pair of oxen until they finally are brought in a steady stream to the foot of the conveyor. The car next is made fast to a turning platform, the railing on one side of each car is loosened and the car tipped up sideways. The cane falls directly on an endless belt which carries it up to the several sets of rollers whence the juice goes to the boilers. Here it is concentrated until finally the heavy thick mass is poured into the centrifuges, the molasses thrown off, and the sugar dropped into jute sacks of 240 pounds each. Formerly it was supposed that the centrifuges had to be managed by a Chinese, the idea being that the strictest possible attention was necessary. The maximum amount of molasses was to be extracted but not too much, for on this depended the color of the sugar and the color indicated the purity, and the purity indicated the duty which it would or would not pay upon entry into the United States.

EXERCISES

1. What are the three main divisions of the whole process explained here?
2. Are the scenes of operation clear enough to enable us to understand the processes?
3. Could the main divisions be arranged in another order? What order of arrangement do they follow?
4. Paragraph 1 has a confusing lack of unity in purpose. Exactly what is the difficulty?
5. Does paragraph 2 have a topic sentence? If so, which is it?
6. List the steps, in order, in the process explained in paragraph 2.
7. What order of arrangement do they follow? Could they be given in any other order?
8. Does paragraph 3 have a topic sentence? Does it need one?
9. What order does paragraph 3 follow? Could it be rearranged? Why?
10. Point out the verbal links in paragraph 2.
11. Paragraph 4 gives a brief, general summary of the final process; actually, it involves several distinct processes, each of which could have been given fuller treatment. The sentence "The cane . . . goes to the boilers" summarizes a whole process. Supply some details which are lacking. Point out another sentence which similarly summarizes another process.
12. Explain the meaning of the following words as they are used in this selection: predicated (paragraph 1), apparatus (paragraph 2. Compare with same word as it is used in "Grand Jury."), shunted (paragraph 4), centrifuge (paragraph 4).
13. Is the term "turning platform" in paragraph 4 entirely clear?
14. Comment on the advisability of the following changes in wording in paragraph 4: "The car next is" to "Here the car is"; "sacks of 240 pounds each" to "sacks holding 240 pounds each."
15. Rewrite the last sentence so that "The maximum amount of molasses . . . but not too much" is clearer.
16. In spite of some faults, this selection is generally clear and vivid. Point out several concrete details which make it vivid. Tell why it is clear.
17. Write a theme or prepare an outline for a theme on one of the following topics:
    a. Making sorghum molasses
    b. Making maple syrup

   c. Making ice cream
   d. Harvesting corn (wheat, cotton, potatoes, etc.)
   e. Preparing a field for seeding
   f. Preparing spaghetti and meatballs
   g. Lubricating a car

Deserts on the March

PAUL B. SEARS

[1] The Sand Hills of Nebraska contain about eleven million acres—an area larger than the agricultural portion of Egypt. It consists of billowing, grass-covered hills lying in a vast rock bowl which holds the meager rainfall and slowly passes it up through the loose sand. In summer, when the pastures east of it are parched and dry, the grass here is green and fresh. But here and there [in the "dustbowl" area], as fateful warnings which spoke plainly to the practised eye, were great blowouts. These were funnel-shaped craters dug by the wind into the sand wherever the grass had been removed and the weak turf destroyed. Within these craters is a summertime inferno with temperatures often as high as one hundred and forty degrees, while even a moderate wind converts them into a withering, etching sand-blast. With all her resources, nature has a painful task to reclaim these blowouts. Given time, she can do it by means of the wiry creeping rootstocks of Redfield's grass, followed slowly by other venturesome plants, and ultimately by the original turf-forming grasses.

[2] So long as this land remained in public domain, it was leased in large blocks and used as cattle range. Between the hills were numerous lakes where the underground water came to the surface, and about their shores were meadows of grass which could be cut and cured for winter feed. By the use of large areas for each indi-

From *Deserts on the March,* by Paul B. Sears. Copyright, 1937 and 1947, by University of Oklahoma Press. Used by permission.

vidual operator, overloading of the pasture on the hilltops could have been prevented, as doubtless it frequently was, and the turf thus allowed to remain and hold the sand in place. But a kingdom like this, the size of Egypt, was too tempting to be allowed such use. It became a political issue. The Sand Hills should be carved up into homesteads, each one mile square, and given to the people. Finally a man was elected to Congress on the issue—Moses Kincaid. He secured the passage of the necesssary homestead law, and the settlers who thronged in on these claims were known after him as "Kincaiders."

[3] The Kincaiders often lacked sufficient capital, as well as previous experience with the difficulties which lay ahead of them. Most unfortunately, the area assigned to each homestead, one square mile, was too small to support a family under the conditions which prevailed there. Some confined their activities to cattle but were faced with the fact that enough cattle to support them made too heavy a load on the range. The close-cropped turf broke through, and the sand began to blow, spreading ruin. Others boldly attempted to plow the ground and plant crops. On the lowland there was some return for this trouble, but at the expense of the hay meadows. On the upland, the wind swept down and across the planted rows, swirling the sand into the leaves of the planted crop and shredding them to pieces, finally either burying the crop or uncovering its roots.

[4] Easter week of 1920 a family of these homesteaders extended their hospitality to two foot-travelers, with a grace that would have adorned a more stately mansion than the tiny sod house. In the house was a little flour, a little coffee, a few potatoes, and happily, water with which to prepare all three. No milk, no butter, no eggs, no meat. Not one sign was there that the guests might be making inroads on a scant provision—only regret that the repast was not more varied. These brave people were the lords of six hundred and forty acres—a space which in Egypt keeps alive one thousand —yet they were slowly starving. When the travelers took their leave, they were cheerfully urged to return in August to help eat watermelons because "that's sure one thing we kin grow in these valleys, melons."

[5] As the discouraged and defeated Kincaiders retreated from the picture their homesteads were gradually acquired once more by the larger cattle operators, this time as owners instead of lessors. Gradually the pitted and scarred landscape is resuming its proper function as a range region, but in the meantime, the loss, both in potential wealth and in human effort and happiness, has been appalling. Here again, as in the monotonous story of exploitation we have rehearsed, it is not possible to fix individual blame. Certainly not on the homesteaders, nor the cattlemen. Not on the well-meaning, humane politician whose name is associated with the experiment. Rather it rests upon a system which tolerates private privilege in utter disregard of public policy, and which as yet does not understand how science may be made to help in the determining of policy. At the time these measures were planned there were men who knew the Sand Hills from the scientific side, and who could have predicted exactly the outcome, but their views were not consulted in any effective way. Like the expert witnesses in our courts, scientists are only supposed to talk when they have arguments for, not against, a popular or influential project.

EXERCISES

1. What is the general scene of action?
2. What is the time relation between the first paragraph and the rest of the selection?
3. Why is this a natural way to introduce this particular selection?
4. Is the time return in paragraph 2 (popularly called "flashback") clearly indicated?
5. What are the two main parts of the conclusion? Would it have been permissible to present these in two separate paragraphs?
6. What does each paragraph of the body contribute to the development of the theme?
7. The organization of paragraph 3 follows a cause-to-effect order. The author has not given all the details of the ruining of the grassland by any means. Out of his knowledge of the land, he picked out only those items which could be used to explain the dustbowl; the result is, in a sense, his interpretation. This is not the only pos-

sible arrangement of all the possibly significant details; the order is therefore attributed rather than simply inherent. List in separate columns the narrative details of each of the other paragraphs. Notice the order in which the details are arranged.

8. One suspects that Professor Sears was one of the two foot-travelers so graciously entertained, but he has chosen not to say so. Can you suggest a reason?

Tone is that element of style which reflects an author's attitude toward his subject or toward life in general. It corresponds roughly to tone of voice in speech. It can reflect bitterness, love, sadness, disgust—any emotion or intellectual attitude; it can even reflect an author's desire *not* to betray his personal point of view. An objective or impersonal tone is usually adopted by an author who is trying to deal reasonably with his subject and his readers. A subjective or personal tone of some kind (the possibilities are infinite) is used when it is appropriate.

9. The tone of this selection is objective enough for accurate reporting, but personal enough to reveal some of Professor Sears's opinions. How does he feel toward the land and its plant life? Toward the people? Toward government agencies?

10. Point out sentences which contain his comment.

11. How does the author try to make his style vivid?

12. What practical purpose did the author evidently have in mind?

13. Find sentences in paragraphs 1 and 3 which use parallel construction.

14. Write a paragraph which develops one of the following sentences; organize it according to a time pattern.
    a. Spring seems to arrive slowly; yet a new change comes every few days.
    b. My summer vacation was gone before I knew it.
    c. The weeks leading up to high school commencement are filled with activities.

15. Write a paragraph which develops one of the following sentences; organize it by functional order.
    a. Registration for my freshman year in college was a slow process.
    b. Making fudge is the great event in our Sunday afternoons at home.
    c. I changed the tire without much difficulty.

16. Write a paragraph which develops one of the following sentences; organize it by cause-and-effect order.
    a. Ultimately, my habit of sleeping late is the cause of my poor grades.

b. The training and care John received in early childhood have made him a very self-confident young adult.

c. Success in school work may lead to success in other things and to a happy life in general.

Learning to Write

BENJAMIN FRANKLIN

[1] So I escaped being a poet, most probably a very bad one; but as prose writing has been of great use to me in the course of my life, and was a principal means of my advancement, I shall tell you how, in such a situation, I acquired what little ability I have in that way.

[2] About this time I met with an odd volume of the *Spectator*. It was the third. I had never before seen any of them. I bought it, read it over and over, and was much delighted with it. I thought the writing excellent, and wished, if possible, to imitate it. With that view I took some of the papers, and, making short hints of the sentiment in each sentence, laid them by a few days, and then, without looking at the book, tried to complete the papers again by expressing each hinted sentiment at length, and as fully as it had been expressed before, in any suitable words that should come to hand. Then I compared my *Spectator* with the original, discovered some of my faults, and corrected them. But I found I wanted a stock of words, or a readiness in recollecting and using them, which I thought I should have acquired before that time if I had gone on making verses; since the continual occasion for words of the same import, but of different length to suit the measure, or of different sound for the rhyme, would have laid me under a constant necessity of searching for variety and also have tended to fix that variety in my mind and make me master of it. Therefore, I took some of the tales and turned them into verse; and,

From *Autobiography*, by Benjamin Franklin.

after a time, when I had pretty well forgotten the prose, turned them back again. I also sometimes jumbled my collections of hints into confusion, and after some weeks endeavored to reduce them into the best order, before I began to form the full sentences and complete the paper. This was to teach me method in the arrangement of thoughts. By comparing my work afterwards with the original, I discovered many faults and amended them; but I sometimes had the pleasure of fancying that in certain particulars of small import I had been lucky enough to improve the method or the language, and this encouraged me to think I might possibly in time come to be a tolerable English writer, of which I was extremely ambitious. My time for these exercises and for reading was at night, after work, or before it began in the morning, or on Sundays.

[3] While I was intent on improving my language, I met with an English grammar (I think it was Greenwood's), at the end of which there were two little sketches of the arts of rhetoric and logic, the latter finishing with a specimen of a dispute in the Socratic method; and soon after I procured Xenophon's *Memorable Things of Socrates,* wherein there are many instances of the same method. I was charmed with it, adopted it, dropped my abrupt contradition and positive argumentation, and put on the humble inquirer and doubter. And being then, from reading Shaftesbury and Collins, become a real doubter in many points of our religious doctrine, I found this method safest for myself and very embarrassing to those against whom I used it; therefore I took a delight in it, practiced it continually, and grew very artful and expert in drawing people, even of superior knowledge, into concessions, the consequences of which they did not foresee, entangling them in difficulties out of which they could not extricate themselves, and so obtaining victories that neither myself nor my cause always deserved. I continued this method some few years, but gradually left it, retaining only the habit of expressing myself in terms of modest diffidence; never using, when I advanced anything that may possibly be disputed, the words *certainly, undoubtedly,* or any others that give the air of positiveness to an opinion; but rather say, I conceive or apprehend a thing to be so or so; it appears to me, or I should think it so or so, for such and

such reasons; or I imagine it to be so; or it is so, if I am not mistaken. This habit, I believe, has been of great advantage to me when I have had occasion to inculcate my opinions and persuade men into measures that I have been from time to time engaged in promoting.

EXERCISES

In his *Autobiography* Franklin tells how his father discouraged his ambition to be a poet because of the poor quality of his verses. The "situation" to which he refers here was that he had no opportunity for a formal education. By the simple but arduous process here described and by continual practice he did become a master of English prose, both oral and written. He is best remembered for the *Autobiography* and *Poor Richard's Almanac*. But he wrote innumerable letters and influenced many people by his sound logic and winning style. His sage advice stood back of the Declaration of Independence and the Constitution. These were some of the "measures that I have been from time to time engaged in promoting."

1. When Franklin tried to imitate the style of the *Spectator,* he unwittingly used a very venerable method of education. Is that method used in this book of readings?
2. Franklin found that one requisite for a writer was a "stock of words," or a good vocabulary. Does this book attempt to increase your vocabulary? To make you aware of exactness of meaning? To make you aware that some words have similar but not identical "import"?
3. How did Franklin teach himself to organize and to outline?

The editor of this book cannot recommend turning prose into verse, or working at writing before and after all other work and on Sundays. But he does recommend Franklin's zeal and in general his method.

4. Distinguish among grammar, rhetoric, and logic. Why do you suppose the three were together in the book Franklin found? Are the three subjects still taught together?
5. One of the significant differences between the Socratic method which Franklin admired and his old method was in tone. The tone of his new method was modest and disarming, whereas his tone had formerly been belligerent and assured. Point out several passages in this selection which are modest, disarming, and unassuming.
6. Franklin says that after a time he discontinued the argumentative strategy of the new method, retaining only the modest tone. Rhetori-

cally, what was wrong with the embarrassment caused by his logical traps?

7. Explain the meaning of the following words as they are used in this selection:

instances	sentence
contradiction	concessions
argumentation	positiveness
sentiment	

Development by Example

An example is a particular, representative instance of a type, or a particular application of a principle. In composition, examples are used to illustrate a general statement. Some use of this method has occurred in earlier selections in this book. For example (and here the method is put to use), John Richard Green gave as some of Elizabeth's qualities brazenness, sensuousness, and vanity; to illustrate these qualities he gave specific acts as examples: she fondled her "sweet Robin" in the face of the court, "she loved to show off her rings," etc.

An example is clearly different from a detail or a component part, and its use is different. Examples of automobile heaters are Arvin, Mopar, and Southwind. Parts of an automobile heater are the housing, the motor, and the heat radiator. An Arvin is not a part, and a motor is not an example. One would explain an automobile heater by analyzing it, giving its main parts and its operation; examples would not explain it. But if one wished to write a theme on useless gadgets and ornaments for automobiles, he would need to use examples: red and blue lights, fake exhaust ports, altimeters, etc.

When examples are familiar to the reader and immediately clear to him, the writer usually gives several. This method serves well enough for easy material. But occasionally the writer needs to present one good example in some detail; in such cases he is of course developing his main theme by example, and developing the example itself by giving details or parts.

Example is a powerful force in life as well as in composition.

We follow the example of some other person in most of our actions: we want hair like Elizabeth Taylor's or Robert Taylor's; we want to be a nurse or a fireman because of early heroes. Benjamin Franklin taught himself to write by studying and imitating the example of the *Spectator*. This English book is designed to teach you by the same method. All your teachers use examples. Learn to recognize and use the method in your own writing in conversation.

The Gold Tooth

BERNARD LE BOVIER

[1] Let us be sure of our facts before we rack our wits to explain them. This cautious procedure may seem tedious to most people, who assume the truth of an alleged fact in their eagerness to understand its meaning. In the long run, however, it may spare us the absurdity of having accounted for what is not so.

[2] Such a misfortune drolly befell several German philosophers about a century ago. In 1593 it was widely rumored that in Silesia a child of seven, having cast its baby teeth, had cut a gold tooth, a molar. By 1595 Horstius, a professor of medicine at the University of Helmstad, had published a full account of this tooth, pointing out that it partook both of the natural and of the supernatural and explaining that God had decreed it to the gums of this baby in order that the Christians languishing under Turkish persecution might be reassured of His power. We may imagine how the news of this miracle consoled the despondent Christians and dismayed their infidel oppressors. In the same year Rullandus contributed another history of the Silesian tooth to the store of human learning, and two years later Ingolsteterus, and equally competent scholar, disputed the opinions of Rullandus, who promptly defended his views in a reply no less eloquent than profound. The whole literature of the tooth was reviewed and summarized by another savant, named Libavius, who concluded with his independent interpretation of it. In these magnificent works every resource of philosophy and rhetoric had been brought to bear upon the tooth, excepting only its verification. When a goldsmith examined it, he found that one of the child's natural teeth had been covered with gold leaf, very adroitly. The pedants first made books; then they consulted the goldsmith.

[3] The blunder is congenial, easy to make on any subject. Human ignorance is revealed less in the number of existing things which man cannot account for than in the nonexistent things for which he

From *Histoire des oracles,* by Bernard Le Bovier, sieur de Fontenelle.

finds a satisfying explanation. For in his perplexity he wants a logic to discover the truth; his facile speculations show him encumbered with another kind of logic, which readily adapts itself to error. Renowned physicists have ingeniously explained why caverns are warm in winter and cold in summer; greater scientists have since determined that they are not so. Historical discussions are even more open to this kind of error. We confidently rest our arguments upon the narratives of historians, who may have been prejudiced, credulous, misinformed, or careless. An eyewitness impartial in his observations and scrupulous in his reporting is the only reliable authority.

EXERCISES

The organization of this selection is based upon one of the rational orders which we have not observed before: the general to the specific. The introduction, paragraph 1, states a general thesis; the body, paragraph 2, gives a specific case which illustrates the thesis; the conclusion, paragraph 3, suggests a general application of the thesis.

The body of this selection is really a little anecdote, a story used as an example.

1. Find a group of words in paragraph 1 which states the general theme illustrated by the anecdote in paragraph 2.
2. How is paragraph 2 developed?
3. How is paragraph 2 organized?
4. What phrase in the first sentence of paragraph 2 makes direct reference to an idea in paragraph 1?
5. Does the example in paragraph 2 *prove* the generalization in paragraph 1, or only illustrate it?
6. What is the author's purpose in paragraph 3?
7. Are any examples used in paragraph 3?

The tone of the selection is one of polite irony. The author is civil, but clearly intolerant of the kind of absurdity of which he writes. He makes his position evident by the use of *irony,* a figure of speech in which the clearly implied meaning is the opposite of the surface meaning of the words. We say "A fine state of affairs!" when we really mean that affairs are in a terrible state.

8. Find two examples of irony in paragraph 2.
9. Comment on the advisability of the following word changes: *slow*

for *tedious* (paragraph 1), *loafing* for *languishing* (paragraph 2), *dexterously* for *adroitly* (paragraph 2), *compatible* for *congenial* (paragraph 3).

10. Which of the following topic sentences would you develop by the use of example?
    a. Harriet is a pretty woman.
    b. Harriet is a very tactful woman.
    c. Happiness consists of many things.
    d. Packing took most of the afternoon.
    e. A boring person can spoil an entire party.

11. Write a theme on one of the following topics.
    a. One sometimes learns a great deal from an embarrassing experience.
    b. The hardships of today often become the pleasant memories of tomorrow.
    c. Sometimes a very lazy person is really very efficient.

Tips on Straight Thinking

STUART CHASE

[1] One swallow does not make a summer. By the same token, one or two examples are not enough to establish a sound generalization.

[2] You drive through a town and see a drunken man on the sidewalk. Presently you see another. You turn to your companion and say: "Nothing but drunks in this town!" Soon you are out in the open country, bowling along at 60. A car comes by as if you were parked. Whoosh! a second car does the same. Your companion turns to you and says: "All the drivers in this state are crazy!"

[3] This kind of thinking has been around for a long time. Aristotle called it "reasoning by example" (too few examples) and put it high on his list of fallacies that lead unwary minds to false

From *The Reader's Digest,* June, 1954. Reprinted by permission.

conclusions. The Romans called it *secundum quid*. What it boils down to is failing to count your swallows before you announce that summer is here.

[4] In a dinner-party discussion of Old Age Assistance somebody says: "I have it straight that this man has $18,000 under the mattress. Yet he pretends he is broke, and is drawing benefits. Old Age Assistance is a disgrace." The speaker may be correctly informed about the miser but he is basing a whopping generalization on the case of one chiseler.

[5] Two friends of mine were recently involved in a heated argument over the dangers of excessive drinking. One man cited statistics to the effect that heavy drinkers, *on the average,* live shorter lives. To which the other replied triumphantly, "Ah, but I had an uncle who drank a bottle of whisky every day, and he lived to be 93!" As far as he was concerned, that settled the question.

[6] Arguments conducted in this fashion can go on for hours without leading anywhere. For every example one person cites, his opponent can usually find a contradictory example. When you are faced with someone who pulls out a single example to "prove" his case, you might stop and ask, "How *typical* is this? Does it prove your point, or merely illustrate it?"

[7] A good deal of reasoning by example comes under the head of mere small talk; but it can be serious and dangerous. In Arizona I met a woman who said: "I've had to let Maria go, and I'll never hire another Mexican. You just can't trust *any* of them!" I tried to reason with her but she was too angry to listen. She had built up a nasty case of prejudice, based on one or two unfortunate experiences with Mexican maids.

[8] How much of the prejudice against Negroes, Yankees, Jews, "foreigners" and what-have-you is similarly built up? One or two disagreeable personal encounters are developed into rejection of a whole group. How much of the conflict and misery and persecution in the world today arises from this kind of overgeneralizing?

[9] Take the case of Mr. Smith of Muncie, Indiana, who spends two days in Greece on a package tour. On his return he tells the neighbors all about the Greeks. They are a very backward people, he says—they had no decent traffic lights and they spend all day drinking coffee in sidewalk cafés, and they don't properly repair

the Parthenon. Meanwhile Mr. Parnassos of Athens spends two days in Chicago on a tour, is insulted by a cab driver and returns to tell his friends at the sidewalk café that Americans are rude and uncivilized.

[10] Another kind of overgeneralization is called "extrapolation." It means establishing some points on a chart, drawing a curve through them and then continuing the curve beyond the data. A careless person may ride the curve to kingdom come.

[11] We take some cross-section paper, for instance, and plot the population of the United States from 1800 to 1860. We find that during this period it doubled about every twenty years. We then generalize that it will continue to double every twenty years, and extrapolate the curve on this basis. This shows that by 1940 the population of the United States would have been 503 million. Actually it was about 131 million—our statistical buggy ride has thrown us off by about 300 percent.

[12] We must remember that the human mind is built for generalizing. All progress would halt if we did not collect facts and generalize from them. But we should beware of beating the gun, of not waiting until enough facts are in to say something useful about swallows, or maids, or drunks, or Greeks, or population.

[13] Generalization should be built up from cases the way a house is built of stones, bricks and lumber. If we see masons fitting large stones into a foundation we are not likely to say, "This is going to be a stone house." If we see bricklayers starting a chimney we will hardly generalize, "This will be a brick house." Watching such operations, we have learned to wait until enough material is in place to warrant a reasonable inference about the kind of house it is going to be.

[14] The scientific method depends on collecting enough cases to provide a sound generalization, and then collecting more facts to check it. This is dependable thinking. This is using the mind to build useful knowledge.

EXERCISES

1. What is the general theme of this article?
2. Where is this theme first stated?

3. How does the author make his theme statement vivid?
4. By what method of development does he make his theme immediately clear?
5. What is the main difference between the development of the main idea in this selection and the development of the main idea in the preceding selection?
6. Are all of Chase's examples illustrative of exactly the same idea?
7. Does he have enough examples to prove that the fallacy which he is discussing is really a common one, or only that it can happen?
8. What different aspects of the problem does the author deal with?
9. Characterize the tone of the selection, and see if you can tell how the tone is related to the diction.

The Importance of Trade

BROOKS ATKINSON

[1] Although trade ranks below scholarship, art, and all the professions in all the ancient and many of the modern codes of social standing, it is the most civilizing of human occupations. It is the unrecognized agent of good will. It provides a solid basis for the peace of the world. Ideas moving across national boundaries raise suspicions and stir up trouble or resistance. Religions and customs divide the world into distrustful camps. But food and goods are the only things that can cross the borders of countries peacefully—arousing nothing more pernicious than curiosity and discussions about value. The manganese ore we import by the shipload from the Black Sea ports of Russia does not create political crises in America. The natural rubber that we buy from the Malays and the Javanese does not make Moslems out of Americans. Anyone in any part of the world, whatever his morals may be, will gladly eat a can of Columbia River salmon or wear a pair of U.S. Army boots.

From *Once Around the Sun,* copyright, 1951, by Brooks Atkinson. Reprinted by permission of Harcourt, Brace and Company, Inc.

[2] Trade has an honorable record in the history of civilization. It has been good for everyone. In the second century the Chinese gratefully learned from Persian traders how to cultivate alfalfa, grapevines and walnuts. The great hot, dangerous, sandy, tempestuous Gobi desert divided the Far East from the Near East and Europe. But traders, eager for a profit, crossed it and took glass to China from Greece and Rome and stimulated the art of porcelain there. From China Europe got peaches, apricots and medicinal herbs. The Arabs learned the art of making paper from the Chinese in the second century. Rome grew luxurious with silks brought from China, and the Old Silk Road into China is still traveled after all these centuries and still has an honored name.

[3] America could not exist without foreign goods. Although we like to think that we are independent, we are virtually dependent on foreign countries for coffee, bananas, cocoa, shellac, tin, antimony, cadmium, manganese, chrome, nickel, asbestos, mica, quartz crystals, natural rubber, silk, diamonds, burlap, and cordage fibers. Nor have we enough sugar, oil, wood pulp, lead, zinc, and copper to supply our own needs. To keep our industries running, and to pay our politicians and professional calamity-howlers, we need the cushion of exports to foreign markets—about 10 per cent of our total production. That is the margin between normal prosperity and anxiety in this country.

[4] Our automobiles and industrial goods are the soundest ambassadors we send abroad. The good trader will do business with anyone who will trade in return. Trade is the one thing both parties can agree on, and it is the soundest basis for wholesome foreign relations.

EXERCISES

1. Find the statement of the author's main idea, the statement which gives unity of subject and of purpose to the entire selection.
2. What particular aspects of this idea are taken up by paragraphs 1, 2, and 3, respectively?
3. What is the function of paragraph 4?
4. How are the examples used to illustrate the idea of paragraph 1

made especially appropriate as contrasts to the trouble-causing "ideas" and "religions" mentioned earlier?

5. Are the examples in paragraph 2 particularly appropriate to the idea of that paragraph?

6. Can you imagine aspects of the trading discussed in paragraph 2, or items traded but not mentioned here, which would seem to weaken the author's assertion?

7. Does the author need to prove his assertions, or only to illustrate them, or both?

8. Le Bovier used only one main example. Why does Atkinson use several examples for each main idea?

9. Point out some examples which seem especially vivid. Why do they seem vivid? Could the author have made some of the other examples ("coffee, bananas, cocoa, shellac, tin," etc.) equally vivid? Why did he not try to make them all vivid? Why did he make any of them vivid?

10. Point out several sentences which use parallel construction.

11. Write a paragraph on one of the following topics.
   a. Some of our most successful men have been self-educated.
   b. Our college buildings are in a variety of architectural styles.
   c. The most effective teachers ordinarily use some kind of dramatic or emotional presentation to make the student remember what he has been taught.
   d. College introduces one to new ideas and new kinds of people.

The Changing Climate

GEORGE H. T. KIMBLE

[1] The one point on which most people agree when they talk about the weather is that things were very different when they were young. Beyond that, differences of opinion begin to creep in quite rapidly, for memory plays queer tricks with all of us where the weather is concerned. We tend to be exceptionally good

From "The Changing Climate," *Scientific American*, April, 1950.

at recalling certain kinds of weather, because of the effect they may have had upon our outdoor sports or our rheumatism, and exceptionally bad at recalling other kinds that did not happen to matter to us.

[2] What, exactly, is happening to our climate? Is it merely fluctuating on a short-term basis or is it undergoing a major long-term change?

[3] Some investigators have been at considerable pains to show that the world's climate has remained essentially stable since early historical times. The late geologist J. W. Gregory argued convincingly that because the distribution of the date palm in the Levant was practically the same in Biblical times as it is today, the mean temperature has not altered materially. Others have argued that, because the olive can still be made to grow in North Africa near the margin of the desert, the climate has not deteriorated significantly since the days when the Roman settlers around Timgad carried on their highly profitable trade in olive oil. Moreover, it must be admitted that a change of landscape is no proof of a change of climate. The decay or disappearance of once-proud cities that stood in areas now barren does not necessarily mean a decrease in rainfall; it may have resulted, in part at least, from overgrazing of the surrounding pastures and the improvident use of the plow. Soil erosion was an empire-killer long before the 20th century.

[4] Nonetheless we do have evidence of marked changes in climate during recorded history. Consider the following three cases, taken more or less at random.

[5] The first concerns the climate of Egypt. In the second century A. D., Claudius Ptolemaeus of Alexandria, who on all counts was one of the greatest geographers of antiquity, kept a systematic diary of the Egyptian weather. He had no thermometer or rain gauge, but he faithfully recorded thunderstorms, rainy days, winds and so on. From this record it is possible to reconstruct the main features of the climate of his day. The difference 150 A. D. and 1950 A. D. could hardly be more striking. Nowadays Egyptian summers are rainless; then they had almost as many rainy days as the winters. Today thunderstorms are unknown; then they were

frequent in the hot season. Now the prevailing, almost the only, summer wind is from the north; then it alternated with winds from the south and west.

[6] The second illustration is even more dramatic. In the 11th century, almost 1,000 years ago, there was a flourishing Norse culture in Greenland. Its sagas relate that there were some 300 farmsteads along the west coast of the great island, supporting 10,000 people and large numbers of sheep and cattle. This colony continued to lead an almost self-supporting existence until the 14th century, when it appears to have fallen on grim days. By 1400 A. D. very few settlements were left, and these were fighting a losing battle. While we are not going to suggest that the depopulation of Greenland can be explained solely in terms of climatic change, archaeologists have provided irrefutable evidence that the climate did undergo a deterioration. There are ancient Norse graves in the southern part of the island, with tree roots intertwined among the bones, in soil that is now permanently frozen.

[7] The third illustration is taken from the British Isles. At the present time the summer season in England is not warm enough to ripen grapes except in a very few sheltered locations, and then only if the summer is unusually hot. But at the time of the Norman Conquest things were different. The Doomsday Book mentions no fewer than 38 vineyards, in addition to those of the Crown, in England. In the 12th century vine dressers are frequently mentioned in abbey chronicles as forming part of the normal staff of an ecclesiastical estate. One William of Malmesbury, writing about 1150 A. D., assures us that the vale of Gloucester "exhibits a greater number of vineyards than any other county in England, yielding abundant crops and of superior quality: nor are the wines made here by any means harsh or ungrateful to the palate, for in point of sweetness, they may almost bear comparison with the growths of France." A century later such references became much less common, and by the end of the 14th century they had disappeared almost completely. It would seem, then, that the English summers were distinctly warmer during the 12th and 13th centuries than they normally are today.

[8] We know for certain that important changes in the climate of the Northern Hemisphere are going on at the present time.

These are not merely short-term fluctuations. In Philadelphia the mean annual temperature has risen by four degrees in a century —from approximately 52 degrees F. in the 1830s to over 56 degrees in the 1930s. In Montreal the rise has been from 42 degrees F. in the 1880s, when observations began, to 44 degrees in the 1940s. In Spitzbergen the rise since 1912 has been approximately four degrees. In Scandinavia and the British Isles rises of the order of one to two degrees have been general over the period of the last 100 years or so.

[9] More emphatic than the rise in mean annual temperature has been the warming up of the winter half of the year. At Washington, D. C., during the 20-year period ending with 1892 there was a total of 354 days with freezing temperature during the spring months; for the 20 years ending with 1933 the corresponding total was 237. At Montreal subzero temperatures are now only half as common as they were 75 years ago, and the mean temperature for March has risen more than six degrees. In Spitzbergen the average December temperature nowadays is more than 10 degrees higher than it was 30 years ago!

[10] The upward trend in temperature has been accompanied in several parts of the world by a downward trend in precipitation. Particularly noticeable has been the decline in snowfall in parts of North America. At Montreal, for instance, the expectation now is not much more than 80 inches of snow in a season, as against 130 inches or so in the 1880s. Including both snowfall and rainfall, the total winter precipitation (in terms of water) has declined from 22.12 inches in the 1900s to 19.80 inches in the 1940s.

[11] These temperature and precipitation trends are far from being world-wide, however. It is the Arctic, sub-Arctic, and mid-latitude zones that have experienced the major increases of temperature; the tropical and subtropical zones have become a little cooler, if anything, in the past half-century. The decline in precipitation has occurred chiefly in North America, Africa, Australia and Brazil.

[12] Already some of these changes are clearly reflected in human affairs. For instance, shipping operations in the White Sea and the Gulf of Bothnia can frequently be continued three to four weeks longer into the winter than formerly. In parts of Siberia

the southern boundary of the zone of permanently frozen ground is receding poleward several dozen yards per annum. In Northern Hemisphere waters various kinds of commercially valuable fish have migrated northward. The common cod now is found as far north as the 73rd latitude off the west coast of Greenland; the cod catch off this coast amounted to 13,000 tons in 1946 as against five tons in 1913.

[13] On land the warming up of the climate has begun to make itself felt in the acceleration of plant and animal growth and the poleward extension of various plant and animal habitats. In Iceland there has been an extension of barley cultivation. The same is true of Norway, where there has been a noticeable spread of farming up the sides of some of the mountains. In Sweden, Finland, Alaska, and northern Quebec the coniferous forests are growing faster and are beginning to colonize new ground. In eastern Canada the northern limit of feasible cultivation for crops such as wheat has advanced 200 to 300 miles. Some farmers in southern Ontario are even beginning to experiment with raising cotton!

EXERCISES

1. What is the function of paragraph 1?
2. Paragraph 2 might well have been combined with paragraph 1. What effect does the author achieve by separating these two brief sentences from the rest? Exactly what is the issue stated?
3. Which side of the issue is dealt with in paragraph 3?
4. Point out the examples used to illustrate this point of view.
5. What is the function of paragraph 4? In what ways is it like paragraph 2?
6. Why does the author use three fully developed examples of the assertion made in paragraph 4? Would one have sufficed? Many others were no doubt available; why these three?
7. Paragraphs 8 through 10 give more examples of changes in climate. How do these examples differ from those given in paragraphs 5 through 7? Where is the general topic statement which introduces them?
8. What is the general topic of paragraphs 12 and 13? On what basis did the author divide this material into two paragraphs?
9. How are the sections of the body organized? Could they have been arranged differently?

10. Outline this selection, being sure to subdivide the body into its main divisions.
11. Diagram the last sentence in paragraph 1 to show the parallel construction.
12. Why would this selection be interesting to most readers?

Development by Comparison

Development by comparison is slightly more complicated than development by analysis or by example in that it may involve either or both of these methods. If one were comparing the communist state and the republic, he might after some general discussion compare Russia and the United States, as examples of states having those forms of government.

The uses of comparison are fairly obvious. By comparison one can point out important differences between two things which are much alike in other respects, such as communism and social democracy. Or one can explain something unfamiliar to the reader by comparing it with something familiar, as the Ohio State student explains that his football stadium has the shape of a horseshoe.

A special form of comparison is the analogy. The analogy explains something unfamiliar, and usually abstract, by comparing it with something familiar and concrete. Often the items being compared actually have more differences than similarities, and the explanation of the similarities is therefore dramatic and often entertaining. This imaginative and concrete quality of analogy makes it useful in persuasion as well as in explanation. The early English historian Bede, in his account of how Christianity came to be adopted in England, records a good analogy.

". . . Another of the king's chief men, approving of his words and exhortations, presently added: 'The present life of man, O king, seems to me, in comparison of that time which is unknown to us, like the swift flight of a sparrow through the room wherein you sit at supper in winter, with your commanders and ministers, and a good fire in the midst, whilst the storms of rain and snow prevail abroad; the sparrow, I say, flying in at one door, and immediately out at another, whilst he is within is safe from the wintry storm; but after a short space of fair weather, he immediately vanishes out of your sight, from one winter to another. So this life of man appears for a short space, but of what went before, or what is to follow, we are utterly ignorant. If, therefore, this new doctrine contains something more certain, it seems justly to deserve to be followed.' "

Science and Antiquarianism

EDWIN E. SLOSSON

[1] Science . . . had its origin in the effort to predict the future; and that remains its present purpose, its reason for existence. There is a strong contrast . . . between the temperament of the scientist and that of the historian or, let me say rather, the antiquarian; for a historian may have the scientific temperament. Both are inevitably confined to the study of what has happened. But the scientist picks out from the multitudinous records of the past only what seems to him likely to be repeated in some similar form in the future, while the antiquarian is interested especially in what can never happen again. The antiquarian values things according to their rarity. The scientist values things according to their commonness. The antiquarian values a book that is unique, an event that is unique. The scientist has no use at all for an event that is unique, if there can be such a thing. He is searching for the common element in the rare objects he is studying; the common factor in all happenings. Poincaré says that mathematics is the art of giving the same name to different things. The more universal a law, the more highly it is prized. Newton is esteemed one of the greatest scientists because he discovered the greatest commonplace, the law of gravitation that drops an apple on a man's head and pulls the planets into their orbits. Iron is the commonest thing in the world; that is why it is so valuable. Water is worth more than wine. The diamond is the least valuable form of carbon. Wisdom is more to be sought than rubies and fine gold, because when it is found there is always enough of it to go around. Nobody can monopolize it.

[2] The antiquarian seeks the exception. The scientist seeks the rule. The antiquarian wants a variety. The scientist wants the common weal. The antiquarian searches for a curiosity. The scientist has a curiosity that makes him search.

EXERCISES

1. You will notice that the author has used some examples here and there to clarify his statements. Do the examples pertain to science, or antiquarianism, or both?
2. What is an antiquarian, according to your dictionary?
3. Are science and antiquarianism compared as to method, training, value to society, interest to the public, remuneration of workers, or what? That is, what is the *basis* of the comparison?
4. Which is being explained primarily? Give reasons for your answer.
5. Which do you understand better as a result of reading this selection, science or antiquarianism? How could the other have been made equally clear to you?

In several of the preceding selections you have studied parallelism and its uses. When the parallel elements, especially clauses, are nearly equal in length as well as similar in structure, the construction is said to have *balance*. Even two adjacent sentences of equal length and similar structure are said to be balanced. An example of balance is "The longer we avoid the job, the harder we must work at it." Balance is very useful in comparisons in which two or more items are being considered simultaneously. When the items being compared are in contrast, balance is often combined with *antithesis*. The combination is very emphatic. An example of balanced sentences in antithesis is "The antiquarian values things according to their rarity. The scientist values things according to their commonness."

6. Find an example of parallelism without obvious balance. Find an example of a balanced sentence or a pair of balanced sentences, without antithesis. Find an example of balance and antithesis.

A figure of speech once popular and still much used is *regression,* a figure in which two words in the first of two clauses or sentences exchange positions in the second clause or sentence, with an arresting reversal of statement of course. An example is the familiar "He doesn't eat to live, he lives to eat." The figure is especially useful in comparisons.

7. Find an example of regression in this selection.
8. Explain the meaning of each of the following words as they are used in this selection: *unique, rare, common, universal.*
9. As a class exercise, write a paragraph in which you compare one of the following pairs of items on the basis of their respective advantages. Try to use some balanced sentences.

    a. City and village
    b. The heavy car and the light car
    c. College and university
    d. The supermarket and the old-fashioned grocery store
    e. Television and motion pictures
10. In another paragraph point out the differences between the items of one of the following pairs. Try to use some balance and antithesis. Regression will also be useful if in the comparison you use two words which lend themselves naturally to the figure.
    a. Methods of teaching and study in high school and in college
    b. Modernistic and conventional houses
    c. Old and new farming methods
    d. The jet plane and the propellor plane

Two Weddings

NATHANIEL HAWTHORNE

[1] I was once present at the wedding of some poor English people, and was deeply impressed by the spectacle, though by no means with such proud and delightful emotions as seem to have affected all England on the recent occasion of the marriage of its Prince. It was in the Cathedral at Manchester, a particularly black and grim old structure, into which I had stepped to examine some ancient and curious wood-carvings within the choir. The woman in attendance greeted me with a smile (which always glimmers forth on the feminine visage, I know not why, when a wedding is in question), and asked me to take a seat in the nave till some poor parties were married, it being the Easter holidays, and a good time for them to marry, because no fees would be demanded by the clergyman. I sat down accordingly, and soon the parson and his clerk appeared at the altar, and a considerable crowd of people made their entrance at a side-door, and ranged themselves in a long, huddled line across the chancel. They were my ac-

From *Our Old Home*, by Nathaniel Hawthorne.

quaintances of the poor streets, or persons in a precisely similar condition of life, and were now come to their marriage-ceremony in just such garbs as I had always seen them wear: the men in their loafers' coats, out at elbows, or their laborers' jackets, defaced with grimy toil; the women drawing their shabby shawls tighter about their shoulders, to hide the raggedness beneath; all of them unbrushed, unshaven, unwashed, uncombed, and wrinkled with penury and care; nothing virgin-like in the brides, nor hopeful or energetic in the bridegrooms;—they were, in short, the mere rags and tatters of the human race, whom some east-wind of evil omen, howling along the streets, had chanced to sweep together into an unfragrant heap. Each and all of them, conscious of his or her individual misery, had blundered into the strange miscalculation of supposing that they could lessen the sum of it by multiplying it into the misery of another person. All the couples (and it was difficult, in such a confused crowd, to compute exactly their number) stood up at once, and had execution done upon them in the lump, the clergyman addressing only small parts of the service to each individual pair, but so managing the larger portion as to include the whole company without the trouble of repetition. By this compendious contrivance, one would apprehend, he came dangerously near making every man and woman the husband or wife of every other; nor, perhaps, would he have perpetrated much additional mischief by the mistake; but, after receiving a benediction in common, they assorted themselves in their own fashion, as they only knew how, and departed to the garrets, or the cellars, or the unsheltered street-corners, where their honeymoon and subsequent lives were to be spent. The parson smiled decorously, the clerk and the sexton grinned broadly, the female attendant tittered almost aloud, and even the married parties seemed to see something exceedingly funny in the affair; but for my part, though generally apt enough to be tickled by a joke, I laid it away in my memory as one of the saddest sights I ever looked upon.

[2] Not very long afterwards, I happened to be passing the same venerable Cathedral, and heard a clang of joyful bells, and beheld a bridal party coming down the steps towards a carriage and four horses, with a portly coachman and two postilions, that waited

at the gate. One parson and one service had amalgamated the
wretchedness of a score of paupers; a Bishop and three or four
clergymen had combined their spiritual might to forge the golden
links of this other marriage-bond. The bridegroom's mien had a
sort of careless and kindly English pride; the bride floated along
in her white drapery, a creature so nice and delicate that it was
a luxury to see her, and a pity that her silk slippers should touch
anything so grimy as the old stones of the churchyard avenue.
The crowd of ragged people, who always cluster to witness what
they may of an aristocratic wedding, broke into audible admiration
of the bride's beauty and the bridegroom's manliness, and uttered
prayers and ejaculations (possibly paid for in alms) for the happiness of both. If the most favorable of earthly conditions could
make them happy, they had every prospect of it. They were going to live on their abundance in one of those stately and delightful English homes, such as no other people ever created or inherited, a hall set far and safe within its own private grounds, and
surrounded with venerable trees, shaven lawns, rich shrubbery,
and trimmest pathways, the whole so artfully contrived and tended
that summer rendered it a paradise, and even winter would hardly
disrobe it of its beauty; and all this fair property seemed more
exclusively and inalienably their own, because of its descent
through many forefathers, each of whom had added an improvement or a charm, and thus transmitted it with a stronger stamp
of rightful possession to his heir. And is it possible, after all, that
there may be a flaw in the title-deeds? Is, or is not, the system
wrong that gives one married pair so immense a superfluity of
luxurious home, and shuts out a million others from any home
whatever? One day or another, safe as they deem themselves, and
safe as the hereditary temper of the people really tends to make
them, the gentlemen of England will be compelled to face this
question.

EXERCISES

1. Is the purpose of the comparison mainly to show the dramatic
   differences between the two weddings, or mainly to make a statement about one of them? How do you know?

2. Which sentence most nearly expresses Hawthorne's purpose?

3. List in parallel columns details which are selected for each description because they have a counterpart in the other.

4. Why does Hawthorne not need to give a detailed description of the wedding of the wealthy people?

5. For the sake of increasing the contrast, why should he not have had the poor wedding occur on a cold, windy day and the wealthy one on a bright, warm day?

6. Pick out the details which make the contrast equally sharp without actual references to the weather.

7. What part does metaphor play in this contrast?

8. Why is so little attention given to the actual appearance of the cathedral?

9. What would be the effect of including in the first description a mention of the stained-glass windows with the morning sun coming through them?

10. Could the second paragraph be divided? Explain your answer.

What Kind of People Are We?

R. P. T. COFFIN

[1] Before we start rearranging the rest of the world after this war, we had better find out what kind of people we are ourselves. Nations and families often do not know what they are like until some outsider, say an aunt, comes along and tells them.

[2] I had a New England aunt whose chief business in life was telling our family our strong points and our weak points, especially our weak. She came twice a year and straightened us all out, with herb remedies and moral precepts. Some of our worst features, we discovered from Aunt Emma, were minor habits that gave a wrong impression of us to the outside world.

[3] Minor peculiarities and odd ways of doing things can exasperate one's neighbors more than major sins. It has always been so

From *The American Mercury*, November, 1943. Reprinted by permission.

among nations, since history began. The old Akkadians mortally estranged the people of Ur by wearing beards. The people of Ur ate fat meat, and the Akkadians hated them for that habit and did their best to exterminate them. Underneath these superficial differences these nations had many sterling traits in common. And if they had been able to see these, they would have built up a civilization that would have defied the Chaldeans and Babylonians for centuries. But they could not see their common humanity for the whiskers and fat meat. So they fought each other and perished. And the Babylonians and Chaldeans—who wore whiskers and ate fat meat also, by the way—came and possessed their lands.

[4] It is good to have a chance to see ourselves through other nations' eyes. For maybe we Americans have some ways of doing things that conceal our good points from our neighbors across the water. If it isn't whiskers, maybe it is something just as obscuring.

[5] I have been lucky. Twice I have lived for long periods in countries oversea and so have been able to get a perspective on Americans I never would have got in any other way. First time, it was France, and I was a soldier, in World War I. It was a terrific shock to me to discover what the French thought of their American allies. It wasn't the grownup French who shocked me. They were too polite and careful of my feelings. It was the French children—girls in black dresses and boys in pinafores so you couldn't be sure they were boys till they turned around and showed they had a fork in their clothes after all. The French children thought all Americans were gluttons, drunkards, and overgrown boys. Not just one or another of these, but all three. That was their frank opinion. And nobody can be franker than children. Or wiser. Mind you, the French children loved the American soldiers. That was partly why they were so frank. They always poured out and got underfoot when our band played, and they shared all our meals with us while we were in their villages. I ate many a meal with a pair of Gallic breeches, yearning to be filled, straddling each of my knees.

[6] I know why those French children thought us all gluttons and drunkards and boys. They trusted their eyes. To their eyes we were all three. For we were not used to their wine. A drink that a five-year-old French boy could swallow without batting a bru-

nette eyelash knocked the strong blond men in my regiment gal-ley-west. Therefore all Americans were habitually flattened by drink. And we had meat three times a day in our mess. The French children saw it with their own beady eyes. They helped us eat it. French people had meat only once or twice a week. Therefore Americans were all gluttons. And we played with the French children as their fathers and older brothers and uncles never did. We came down to their level and played tag and pitched pennies with them. With only a few of their words, we got on with them splendidly. So all Americans must be overgrown boys.

[7] Out of those three French impressions, two are grounded upon superficialities. But the third is pure gold. We *are* a nation of people who can play easily with our children. We play more with our children than any other people on earth except maybe the Chinese. That is one of the greatest achievements of our civilization and one of our best assets as a nation. I see by the pictures from Sicily that American doughboys are still taking children on their knees and feeding them and teaching them to smile again in spite of war. We discovered children in our pioneer days, when they were the most important crop that men who had states to settle could raise. We go on paying a lot of attention to that crop. We should thank those French children for calling our attention to our wealth.

[8] Then I had a chance to set up housekeeping, when my wife and I were brand-new to each other, in England. It was in a village eight hundred years old. My wife and I got to know everybody in it from Schoolmistress Bley to the Lady of the Manor and on to the red-faced man who swept the street clean with a fagot-broom and slept an hour each noon on his wheelbarrow under our cottage window. We cooked over an open hearth. We played whist and tennis at the Village Institute. We kept hens and part of a pig. We got to know a lot about the English, and they got to know a lot about us in return. For though I was in the Uni-versity, I was also a father and a householder and so got to know the older and younger English people who are outside the Uni-versity family. Older English people are a revelation in warmth,

after the rather icy undergraduates. The English mellow late. My wife and I got a thorough education in British democracy such as only those who buy their own breakfast kippers and keep their own house can acquire.

[9] It is what the English taught us about ourselves that I want to talk about.

[10] Of course, after a year or so of being neighbors to us, our English friends took to regarding us as creatures very much like themselves. It came as a surprise to them that fundamentally we were like them. It was amazing, but we were. It makes me think of what one small Englishman, in breeches only as long as a man's hand, said of our first baby. He had been let out of school, in company with all his schoolmates, to see an American infant. And he was bitterly disappointed. I heard him voicing his disappointment under our cottage window. "Why," said he to another boy, "it's just like any baby!" He had expected a swarthy papoose, with feathers and a tomahawk maybe. The pink and gold skin and hair had been a great shock.

[11] But it was because our neighbors did come to regard us as much the same kind of people as themselves that they became sharp enough to notice and frank enough to tell us what it was that they found in Americans that was fundamentally different from characteristics that are English. And no one can be franker than a cousin, when he gets to know you.

[12] First off, the English agreed with the French children. We paid too much attention to our children. They saw my wife and me with our first-born. They caught me bathing it. They caught me wheeling my first-born in a pram. They caught us building our future life around that infant of ours. It was not an incident. It was a future. So they told us that Americans humor children too much, play with them too much, dress them too well, keep them at home too long—especially if they are boys—and work their fingers to the bone to build security for them. It was too bad. Life went by and left parents just parents.

[13] Guilty, say I! And I am sure most Americans would be proud to plead guilty, too. If Americans overdo things, it is in the best of causes. Children are the most real of real property. My father had ten, and he slaved all his life as a free man, and had

a righteous good time, educating us and building a house or fixing up a farm for each one of us. Of course, none of us living has needed the inheritance. We have been too busy acquiring farms and houses for our own offspring, who probably won't need them.

[14] Our English neighbors were shocked at our doing so much for ourselves, too, and with our own hands. Our passion for labor worried them. I don't know how often they blushed at seeing me bringing parcels on my bike or on the bus. English gentlemen never carried things, they finally blurted out. They never pushed them, either, I discovered. For I scandalized our village by wheeling our baby in the perambulator all through the lanes and to Oxford and beyond. No British father since Hengist and Horsa had ever done such a thing. It was woman's work. Why shouldn't I wheel my own baby? I asked my frank friends who told me it just wasn't done. In England there are two sets of human beings: those who work with their hands and carry things; those who work with their heads and have things brought to them.

[15] The beauty of American history is that we have combined the two sets. Our Yankee sea captains helped build their own ships with hammers and adzes, and helped sail them by using their hands on lines and gear. The wives who sailed with them could be the fine ships' ladies and yet do a good day's housework, too. It is a new woman in civilization who can write in a ship's diary: *Done a big washing and ironing and mended John's pants and went on board of Capt. Thurlow this evening and took tea.* As pioneers, we had to be carpenters and plowers, even when we were law-makers and teachers. We have never got over these basic occupations. Our women sew and wash dishes and children, and then go out and hold their own in cultured conversation. They have always done so. Our men, no matter what estates they have achieved, have never got over Thomas Jefferson's love of making gadgets and doing a little carpentering here and a little plumbing there, for themselves, in between business conferences or state papers.

[16] We are a nation in shirt-sleeves. We like to put our hands in dirt and get it on our trousers, as our ancestors did. We take our coats off and sail into the weeds in the garden, and we lose

no caste in the eyes of our neighbor. He is up to the eyes in the "innerds" of his Ford and couldn't see us if he tried.

[17] Oh yes, our English friends took us to task for Americans' taking their coats off in public and going in shirt and trousers. I had the right come-back for that. Our shirts are finished as decorous outside garments, unlike the frankly night-shirt-like British. Our trousers are outside ones, too. They are not ones that come up to the shoulder blades in unsightly bedroom style. If I wore British pants, I would die before I took my coat off in public!

[18] We Americans are too apt to take chances in matrimony also, we discovered from our English friends. We plunge into matrimony without any adequate preparations, in the way of career or income. We marry young. We marry at first sight, or second. We make mistakes. Again I plead guilty. Our divorce rate is shocking. We marry right out of college often. And even in. We marry on a shoestring. But it is something of a comfort to point out to the world that we Americans, who are so often dubbed crass materialists by the Europeans, have never had the dowry system of Europe or the long-deferred engagements of the English people, who wish to be sure of the economic basis of marriage before they rush into it. We have always divorced marriage from money. We have let affection, and even passion, take the place of a settlement of money on a wife as the proper foundation for raising a family. We fall in love, rather than fall into a fortune, when we do our leaping. Of course, we make mistakes. But we show more courage and idealism, on the whole, I think, in our daring to rush, young and empty-handed, into the greatest adventure of them all.

[19] And Americans travel too much. Our English villagers were pretty unanimous on that point. Not one of the 463 English adults in our village had even been to Stratford-on-Avon, forty-two miles to the north. Of course, when one considers what the commercialization of culture has done for Shakespeare's home town, one can sympathize a little with the English. But the villagers had not been to other places much either. They stayed at home pretty much all the time. They had never seen their own cathedrals, or Devon, or Wordsworth's lakes.

[20] Somehow or other, in pleading guilty to this charge of loving to be on the go, I think Americans are to be praised for their

desire to broaden themselves by seeing the old cradles in Europe from which their fathers sprang. Of course, there is a lot of lost motion with us. We travel too much for travel's sake. We make too much of mere sightseeing. Yet hungry-eyed schoolmarms drinking in castles and churches have somehow drunk in a lot of glory and strength that have borne fine fruit in high school courses and made better citizens of lots of young Americans. We have always believed in travel as an educator, just as we have believed in education by lectures. The English have mistrusted both. But naïve as we may seem to them to be, I think we have learned a good deal and grown a good deal towards world citizenship by going over the battlefield of Gettysburg, the Alps, seeing the Grand Canyon and Winchester Cathedral. Odysseus learned a lot that made him a better citizen from travel. George Washington and Thomas Jefferson did, too.

[21] Yes, and we make too much of saying *hello* to everybody and being friendly at the least chance. Our English neighbors were sure of that. We depend too much on a surface neighborliness.

[22] Maybe we do. Especially in the states west of the Appalachians. But from having lived in the Hoosier State, I should say that friendliness—even casual surface friendliness—is a good thing to make too much of. Again it is a pioneer failing, if it is a failing. It is a poetic thing, this going out of ourselves to meet strangers more than halfway. It is the best way to find poems, I have discovered. For, chances are, if you go out of your shell halfway, the stranger will come out of his, sparkling over with poetry. It seems to me that this poetry of human sympathy is a pretty fair foundation for the democracy in the world at large we want to build tomorrow.

[23] And, lastly, we Americans, according to our English neighbors, are forever wanting to change our *status quo,* wanting to get somewhere else from where we are, wanting to become something else. Fishermen's sons want to become mechanics, professors' sons want to become fishermen. Farmers' sons yearn to become railroad men. We are a restless and tiring people. We love change.

[24] We do love change. We are restless. But it seems to me to be

a kind of noble restlessness that eats us, and we do want to better ourselves, usually, want to go up in the world, make something more of ourselves, mentally as well as financially, than our fathers left us. Almost every American city is a monument to America's divine discontent. Our cities change shape faster than any other cities on earth. And usually they do not grow merely in the direction of material improvement. Our tall ugly buildings become the taller lovelier ones of New York's skyline today. Our architecture, our art, our literature, our music, are constantly on the make, as well as our railroads and automobiles. Improvement on one plane very often induces improvement on others.

[25] *Every son must rise above his father.* That is the New World physics to which we heartily subscribe. It isn't the physics of the Old World. *No river ever rises higher than its source.* That is the physics Europe believed in for two thousand years. But some Europeans would not subscribe to that physics. So they packed up and came over the sea. They wanted a new physics. For that reason men of totally different bloods and religions and political theories came into this wilderness that was America and tried the experiment of mingling bloods and brains. To escape that physics of their ancestors, Englishmen, Scotsmen, Irish, Dutch, French, and Germans bled themselves white, worked their fingers to the bone, fought Philistines more terrible than insectmen from another planet, hungered, thirsted, starved. They believed in the new physics of a man's improving on the politics and culture and noses and foreheads of his fathers. For this they lived in log huts, plowed among stones and roots, drained marshes, overturned mountains, knew vast loneliness for years and lives on end, endured polar cold, wore out their shoes, put on deerskin, felled forests, built churches and courthouses and state capitols and hospitals and colleges by the thousands to Europe's hundreds. For this they dared the dangerous experiment of giving schooling to all, of making rail-splitters and farmers the leaders of the people, of making fast, fine vehicles the property of every family. For this they moved mountains and sweat blood.

[26] It was not enough for us to believe in common man. We have believed in him from the beginning of our history. The "century of the common man" has been about three centuries

long so far. It was an extra belief that kept us going through Indian wars and Civil War—the belief that the common man can become an uncommon man. We have already produced a lot of him. Jefferson, born to silks and daring to make farmers and day-laborers into the cornerstones of the state, was one. So was the man who dared give the black people equality with the white. So were the ministers of the gospel and bankers who dared put college education into the poorest man's reach. So were the millionaires who dared spread free libraries and museums over the country. So were the benefactors who built great foundations in medicine and scientific research. We are a nation built squarely on the risk of improving ourselves to the limit of the blue sky.

[27] I am mighty glad my neighbors in France and England, through their criticism of our outside appearance, called my attention to the possibilities we Americans have as potential leading citizens in the world democracy to come. Great love for children, eagerness to learn by travel, daring in social experiments, friendliness, and a profound passion for improving ourselves ought to stand us in good stead in the new turn history will take after this war.

EXERCISES

This and the next three pieces are full-length essays, not merely selections which illustrate one method of development. They do rely heavily upon comparison for their effectiveness and so fulfill their purpose in this section of the book. But they also show how, in mature practice, a writer uses all methods of development, according to his needs. Some ideas are best developed by one method, some by another. This essay is mainly an analysis, a setting forth of some particular qualities of the American people which stand out distinctly to foreigners. But if the author merely listed the qualities, his readers might well wonder why he had chosen these qualities and whether his list was really a good one. So he compares us with others, the British mainly; and we easily see that these are the points of difference. And throughout the essay are several ideas developed by example. In this essay, then, we can see all the methods we have previously observed separately.

1. Which paragraphs serve as the introduction? The conclusion?
2. Which sentence in the introduction states the purpose of the entire

essay? Which sentence or sentences indicate the method the author expects to use?

3. What is the topic sentence of paragraph 3? By what method is the paragraph developed?

4. The account of the French children's opinions of Americans might be considered unnecessary, since the author thought only one of their three beliefs was correct and that one was shared by the British. But the account is a vivid illustration by example of one of the assertions made in the introduction. What is that assertion?

5. List the American traits discussed by the author.

6. Is there any recognizable order in the list? Could the traits have been presented in a different order?

7. Where does the author explain that these qualities are only the points of difference, and that in most ways we are like the British?

The two outstanding qualities in the style of this essay are its vividness and its informality. Vividness is always good, of course; informality may be at times. The language of this essay is really on a rather familiar colloquial level; it is the language of a man puffing on a pipe and talking away to some friends around a fireside. It is too informal for most writing, as the author, a professor of English at Bowdoin College, very well knew. But he wanted to reach as many readers as possible, including those who read little and best understand the spoken word. So the style is appropriate.

8. The author achieves vividness by using many concrete pictures, such as the French girls in black dresses and the boys in pinafores, and the "red-faced man who swept the street clean with a fagot-broom and slept an hour each noon on his wheelbarrow under our cottage window." Find several other pictures of this sort, which win the reader's goodwill as well as his understanding.

9. The customs of usage class some words as usually inappropriate to written English, even on an informal level. Ordinarily one would not use *pants, maybe, straddling,* or *innerds,* but would write instead *trousers, perhaps, astride,* and *engine* (of a Ford). There is nothing inherently wrong with writing the words in the first series except that, as the British told Professor Coffin of his pram-pushing, it isn't done. (Professor Coffin knew this too: he used *trousers* three times and *pants* only once.)

List several words which you would expect to hear in conversation but not to read in *Harper's.* Find several more of these words in the essay.

10. Another informal element is the use of homely figures of speech

such as "knocked . . . galley-west" and "a nation in shirt-sleeves." Find several other figures of this sort.

11. Some of the sentences are short and even fragmentary. Find examples in paragraph 5.

12. College dictionaries either include historical names in their alphabetical order or list them separately in a biographical appendix. In your dictionary look up Hengist and Horsa. Who were they, and why is the reference to them in paragraph 14 appropriate?

The Lost Art of Oratory

MAX EASTMAN

[1] You rarely hear a man described as an orator these days. We pay tribute to Demosthenes and Cicero, to Patrick Henry and Daniel Webster; but if warned that somebody is going to "orate," we run, not walk, to the nearest exit. There is wisdom in this, if "orate" means to spout. None of the great orators ever spouted, but there *aren't* any great orators left. The very idea of oratory, in these busy and businesslike times, is dying out.

[2] Oratory at its best is a dramatic art; it is the art of speaking lines you have written and acting the part of yourself. It might be revived, it seems to me, if the factors hostile to it were recognized.

[3] Chief among them, perhaps, is the microphone. I remember when this mechanical drag was first attached to me. I was lecturing in the Sinai Temple in Chicago, a vast cavern of a place, which, like a giant's mouth, possesses excellent acoustics. I walk around a good deal when talking to an audience; I want to talk to them all. But this time the chairman had planted me in front of an iron post quite a little way off to one side of the lectern. I stood there obediently for a while, and then forgetting myself walked over to the other side. The chairman stepped briskly up behind

From *The Saturday Review,* March 6, 1954.

me, seized my shoulders, and to the amusement of the audience led me back to the microphone. Pretty soon I forgot again, and found myself leaning over the lectern. Again the chairman seized my shoulders and brought me back. When it happened a third time the audience was hilarious, and I said into the microphone:

[4] "Demosthenes declared that there were three essentials of good oratory: action—and action—and action—and you're losing all three of them!"

[5] The next time I forgot myself the chairman did not come after me. But the triumph was temporary. The microphone had come to stay.

[6] Robert Ingersoll, whom Henry Ward Beecher described as "the most brilliant speaker of the English tongue of all men on this globe," used to start talking the minute he emerged from the wings, and he would have the audience in his arms—not the palm of his hands!—by the time he reached the center of the stage. He traveled back and forth as he talked, and if he ran into a speaker's stand he would pick it up and carry it out of the way of his motion. Walt Whitman described him as "tremendously, almost lethargically forceful, like a law of nature." Imagine tying a man like that to a hitching post!

[7] It is not only the delivery of a speech that is killed by this modern invention, but the preparation of it. Nobody is going to memorize an oration in order to stand stockstill and recite it into a microphone. He might just as well read it. And since he is only going to read it, why should he bother to write it? Let somebody else write the essay according to his specifications. That is what a large part of our political oratory has come down to in this day of the nationwide broadcast. Our second president, John Adams, in recommending to Congress the setting up of an academy for "correcting, improving and ascertaining the English language," said: "The constitutions of all the states are so democratical that eloquence will become the instrument for recommending men to their fellow-citizens, the principal means of advancement through the various ranks and offices of society." Our sixth president, John Quincy Adams, was for a time a professor of rhetoric and oratory at Harvard. Daniel Webster's orations have been

described as holding a place in the early history of our country similar to that of the Homeric poems in the history of ancient Greece. How far we have traveled from those resounding days!

[8] A more subtle foe of great oratory, especially in America, is our "inspirational" conception of it. We imagine that a great speech is caused by some mysterious afflatus that descends into a man from on high—or ascends into him from his "Unconscious." Many will object to my statement that oratory at its best is written out and learned by heart. And yet this is obvious from the fact that speeches of the great orators have been preserved to us throughout history. There were no stenographers in Athens to take down what Demosthenes said. And Cicero himself declared that "careful and assiduous composition . . . is the true source of the admiration and applause that is bestowed on eminent speakers."

[9] To jump a long way across the ages, Mark Twain said the same thing: "A person who is to make a speech at any time or anywhere on any topic whatever owes it to himself and to his audience to write the speech out and memorize it." He once attended a dinner where he was supposed to speak, and when his turn came got up and said that he had written and learned a speech, but was so tired out that he couldn't remember a word of it. With that candid apology he sat down.

[10] All the great orators have had a gift for remembering words like that of a musician for remembering music. When Daniel Webster was a boy his teacher held up one Saturday morning a shiny new jackknife and promised it to the boy who would commit the most Bible verses to memory by Monday. Daniel came back Monday and rattled off seventy verses before the astonished teacher handed him the jackknife—much to Daniel's disgust, for he still had several chapters to go.

[11] The story is told that once when he had delivered a short speech in the Senate, winding up with a magnificent peroration, an admirer asked him how he could think up such language on the spur of the moment. Webster drew out of his pocket a piece of notepaper on which the peroration had been neatly written out in advance.

[12] Bliss Perry tells how Wendell Phillips once delivered a lecture at Harvard, "leaning gracefully on the desk and talking for an hour and fifty minutes as though he were extemporizing." So perfectly did he create the illusion of spontaneity that everybody in the audience was deceived except President Eliot, who had with him a copy of the speech, and noted that Phillips did not depart from it by a syllable. This is significant because Phillips was famous as an extemporaneous speaker.

[13] Only a man who had trained himself by "careful and assiduous composition" could rise on the spur of the moment to such heights as Phillips did. Of this he was evidently aware, for he wrote and learned his speeches whenever he had time. He knew what Cicero again pointed out: that when the occasion for impromptu speech arises, if the main discourse has been carefully composed, its style has a momentum that will carry the orator forward with the same eloquence, "just as a boat moving at high speed keeps her course and motion when the oarsmen rest on their oars."

[14] Abraham Lincoln wrote out his addresses, John Hays tells us, from the age of fifteen, when he made them to the "nodding corn rows and the stolid pumpkins that lay between them." "His memory was exceedingly retentive," says his law-partner, Herndon. "He could write out a speech, as in the Cooper Institute speech, and repeat it word for word without any effort. This I know about the 'house divided against itself' speech; he wrote that fine effort . . . in slips, put those slips in his hat, numbering them, and when he was done with the ideas, gathered up the scraps, put them in the right order and wrote out his speech, read it to me before it was delivered, and in the evening delivered it just as written without notes."

[15] Winston Churchill is our sole surviving orator and comes near to being a great one, although his voice lacks resonance. Like Daniel Webster, Churchill won a prize as a schoolboy with a feat of memory, astonishing his teacher by reciting 1,200 lines of Macaulay's "Lays of Ancient Rome" without an error. He built up to the great war speeches by taking infinite pains with his

speeches in the House of Commons, "sometimes working on them as long as six weeks," his friend and biographer Virginia Cowles tells us; and "he always wrote them out and learned them by heart." (She adds that once a speech was ready to be delivered he took care that the newspapers received a copy in advance, and the editors often were surprised to see that the author had confidently punctuated his script with "cheers.")

[16] People who dread to memorize a speech for fear they will forget it and break down may comfort themselves with the fact that some of the greatest orators in history have broken down. John Pym, the great orator of the English revolution, lost the track of his argument and shuffled miserably and fumbled among his papers, in the greatest speech of his career, if not of English history—the one in which he cried (with the king himself present): "Shall it be treason to embase the king's coin, though but a piece of sixpence, and not a greater treason to embase the spirit of his subjects, to set a stamp and character of servitude upon them?"

[17] Winston Churchill broke down and quit altogether in what was to have been the critical speech of his early career in the Commons. This breakdown occurred in 1904 in the speech which was to make known his departure from the Conservative Party, his going over to the Liberals. "It lies with the Government," he cried in a climax, "to satisfy the working classes that there is no justification . . ." He paused, hesitated, then began the sentence again, but the words would not come. "It lies with them . . . What?" he ejaculated to someone who suggested a word. But it was the wrong word. He lifted a slip of paper from the bench but the cue was not there. He searched the deep pockets of his frock coat but found no help. A neighbor picked up torn scraps of paper from the floor, but the words were not there either. It was all over. He sat down murmuring thanks to the House for its kindness.

[18] This might seem an argument against learning speeches by heart, but the cause was opposite to that. Churchill was trying for the first time to give up memorizing and deliver a speech from notes on which his paragraph headings were written. Thereafter he combined the two methods, and arrived at what, to my thinking, is the best solution of this problem: to learn a speech by para-

graphs, but have on hand such headings, or sentence-beginnings, as will set you back on the track if you get lost.

[19] Not everybody, of course, can memorize a speech. And not everybody, having memorized one, can say it naturally. This requires a peculiar talent, or a special training, akin to that of an actor. I am not, therefore, giving advice to every amateur who has to make a speech. I am discussing the great art of oratory. And I think the failure to distinguish it from the gift of gab is a chief cause of the decline of this noble art.

[20] Another disastrous notion is that to be impressive one must speak slowly. Most Americans who consider themselves important speak more slowly when they address an audience than they do in lively conversation. And a good half of them retard the action still further by inserting an "ur" between every third or fourth word. This is supposed to suggest heavy meditation, a portentous feeling-of-the-way toward some original and portentous idea. What it does suggest to an audience brought up on lullabies is sleep. Nothing is more fatal to lucid communication than to allow your listener to run circles in the surrounding brush while waiting for each step in your argument to be taken.

[21] "Compel yourself to talk fast" is the motto with which lessons in oratory should begin. There are two reasons for this. One is that it will keep the audience awake. (The amount of energy wasted trying to keep awake at public meetings in America would turn all the dynamos in the country.) The other is that it will keep the orator awake. And that, after all, is the principal thing.

[22] The great speech is a feat of intellect, action, literary art, and practised memory. It cannot be performed in a lethargy, or by one who thinks the wholehearted performance of it is beneath his dignity. It cannot be performed impromptu except on the rarest occasions and by those trained in the careful preparation of it. And it cannot be performed by a man talking into a tin cup at the top of a hitching post.

[23] If these three facts were generally acknowledged there might be a revival under new conditions of the dying art of oratory. There would at least be an occasional relief from the excruciating boredom suffered by people who attend public meetings.

EXERCISES

1. What two things are being compared?
2. Are both elements of the comparison necessary to the meaning, or is one mainly for emphasis of the other, by contrast?
3. What does the author consider the main enemies of good oratory?
4. What qualities does he consider essential to great oratory?
5. Which of these does he evidently consider most essential? How do you know?
6. To what extent does he rely on examples to illustrate his statements? Point out some examples.
7. Where are all the main points briefly presented?
8. Does the author use any very informal diction?
9. Point out some effective metaphors and similes.

Feeding the Mind

LEWIS CARROLL

[1] Breakfast, dinner, tea; in extreme cases, breakfast, luncheon, dinner, tea, supper, and a glass of something hot at bedtime. What care we take about feeding the lucky body! Which of us does as much for his mind? And what causes the difference? Is the body so much the more important of the two?

[2] By no means; but life depends on the body being fed, whereas we can continue to exist as animals (scarcely as men) though the mind be utterly starved and neglected. Therefore Nature provides that, in case of serious neglect of the body, such terrible consequences of discomfort and pain shall ensue as will soon bring us back to a sense of our duty; and some of the functions necessary to life she does for us altogether, leaving us no choice in the matter. It would fare but ill with many of us if we were left to superintend our own digestion and circulation. "Bless me!" one would cry,

From *Harper's Magazine,* May, 1906.

"I forgot to wind up my heart this morning! To think that it has been standing still for the last three hours!" "I can't walk with you this afternoon," a friend would say, "as I have no less than eleven dinners to digest. I had to let them stand over from last week, being so busy—and my doctor says he will not answer for the consequences if I wait any longer!"

[3] Well it is, I say, for us, that the consequences of neglecting the body can be clearly seen and felt; and it might be well for some if the mind were equally visible and tangible—if we could take it, say, to the doctor and have its pulse felt.

[4] "Why, what have you been doing with this mind lately? How have you fed it? It looks pale, and the pulse is very slow."

[5] "Well, doctor, it has not had much regular food lately. I gave it a lot of sugar-plums yesterday."

[6] "Sugar-plums! What kind?"

[7] "Well, they were a parcel of conundrums, sir."

[8] "Ah! I thought so. Now just mind this: if you go on playing tricks like that, you'll spoil all its teeth, and get laid up with mental indigestion. You must have nothing but the plainest reading for the next few days. Take care now! No novels on any account!"

[9] Considering the amount of painful experience many of us have had in feeding and dosing the body, it would, I think, be quite worth our while to try to translate some of the rules into corresponding ones for the mind.

[10] First, then, we should set ourselves to provide for our mind its *proper kind* of food; we very soon learn what will, and what will not, agree with the body, and find little difficulty in refusing a piece of the tempting pudding or pie which is associated in our memory with that terrible attack of indigestion, and whose very name irresistibly recalls rhubarb and magnesia; but it takes a great many lessons to convince us how indigestible some of our favorite lines of reading are, and again and again we make a meal of the unwholesome novel, sure to be followed by its usual train of low spirits, unwillingness to work, weariness of existence—in fact by mental nightmare.

[11] Then we should be careful to provide this wholesome food in *proper amount*. Mental gluttony, or overreading, is a dangerous

propensity, tending to weakness of digestive power, and in some cases to loss of appetite; we know that bread is a good and wholesome food, but who would like to try the experiment of eating two or three loaves at a sitting?

[12] I have heard of a physician telling his patient—whose complaint was merely gluttony and want of exercise—that "the earliest symptom of hypernutrition is a deposition of adipose tissue," and no doubt the fine long words greatly consoled the poor man under his increasing load of fat.

[13] I wonder if there is such a thing in nature as a *fat mind?* I really think I have met with one or two minds which could not keep up with slowest trot in conversation, could not jump over a logical fence to save their lives, always got stuck fast in a narrow argument, and, in short, were fit for nothing but to waddle helplessly through the world.

[14] Then, again, though the food be wholesome and in proper amount, we know that we must not consume *too many kinds at once.* Take the thirsty haymaker a quart of beer, or a quart of cider, or even a quart of cold tea, and he will probably thank you (though not so heartily in the last case!). But what think you his feelings would be if you offered him a tray containing a little mug of beer, a little mug of cider, another of cold tea, one of hot tea, one of coffee, one of cocoa, and corresponding vessels of milk, water, brandy-and-water, and buttermilk? The sum total might be a quart, but would it be the same thing to the haymaker?

[15] Having settled the proper kind, amount, and variety of our mental food, it remains that we should be careful to allow *proper intervals* between meal and meal, and not swallow the food hastily without mastication, so that it may be thoroughly digested; both which rules for the body are also applicable at once to the mind.

[16] First as to the intervals: these are as really necessary as they are for the body, with this difference only, that while the body requires three or four hours' rest before it is ready for another meal, the mind will in many cases do with three or four minutes. I believe that the interval required is much shorter than is generally supposed, and from personal experience I would recommend anyone who has to devote several hours together to one subject of

thought to try the effect of such a break, say once an hour—leaving off for five minutes only, each time, but taking care to throw the mind absolutely "out of gear" for those five minutes, and to turn it entirely to other subjects. It is astonishing what an amount of impetus and elasticity the mind recovers during those short periods of rest.

[17] And then as to the mastication of the food: the mental process answering to this is simply *thinking over* what we read. This is a very much great exertion of mind than the mere passive taking in the contents of our author—so much greater an exertion is it, that, as Coleridge says, the mind often "angrily refuses" to put itself to such trouble—so much greater, that we are far too apt to neglect it altogether, and go on pouring in fresh food on the top of the undigested masses already lying there, till the unfortunate mind is fairly swamped under the flood. But the greater the exertion, the more valuable, we may be sure, is the effect; one hour of steady thinking over a subject (a solitary walk is as good an opportunity for the process as any other) is worth two or three of reading only.

[18] And just consider another effect of this thorough digestion of the books we read; I mean the arranging and "ticketing," so to speak, of the subjects in our minds, so that we can readily refer to them when we want them. Sam Slick tells us that he has learned several languages in his life, but somehow "couldn't keep the parcels sorted" in his mind; and many a mind that hurries through book after book, without waiting to digest or arrange anything, gets into that sort of condition, and the unfortunate owner finds himself far from fit really to support the character all his friends give him.

[19] "A thoroughly well-read man. Just you try him in any subject, now. You can't puzzle him!"

[20] You turn to the thoroughly well-read man: you ask him a question, say, in English history (he is understood to have just finished reading Macaulay); he smiles good-naturedly, tries to look as if he knew all about it, and proceeds to dive into his mind for the answer. Up comes a handful of very promising facts, but on examination they turn out to belong to the wrong century, and are pitched in again; a second haul brings up a fact much more

like the real thing, but unfortunately along with it comes a tangle of other things—a fact in political economy, a rule in arithmetic, the ages of his brother's children, and a stanza of Gray's "Elegy"; and among all these the fact he wants has got hopelessly twisted up and entangled. Meanwhile everyone is waiting for his reply, and as the silence is getting more and more awkward, our well-read friend has to stammer out some half-answer at last, not nearly so clear or so satisfactory as an ordinary schoolboy would have given. And all this for want of making up his knowledge into proper bundles and ticketing them!

[21] Do you know the unfortunate victim of ill-judged mental feeding when you see him? Can you doubt him? Look at him drearily wandering round a reading-room, tasting dish after dish —we beg his pardon, book after book—keeping to none. First a mouthful of novel—but, no, faugh! he has had nothing but that to eat for the last week, and is quite tired of the taste; then a slice of science, but you know at once what the result of that will be— ah, of course, much too tough for *his* teeth. And so on through the old weary round, which he tried (and failed in) yesterday, and will probably try, and fail in, tomorrow.

[22] Mr. Oliver Wendell Holmes, in his very amusing book *The Professor at the Breakfast-table,* gives the following rule for knowing whether a human being is young or old. "The crucial experiment is this. Offer a bulky bun to the suspected individual just ten minutes before dinner. If this is easily accepted and devoured, the fact of youth is established." He tells us that a human being, "if young, will eat anything at any hour of the day or night."

[23] To ascertain the healthiness of the *mental* appetite of a human animal, place in its hands a short, well-written, but not exciting treatise on some popular subject—a mental *bun,* in fact. If it is read with eager interest and perfect attention, *and if the reader can answer questions on the subject afterwards,* the mind is in first-rate working order; if it be politely laid down again, or perhaps lounged over for a few minutes, and then, "I can't read this stupid book! Would you hand me the second volume of *The Mysterious Murder?*" you may be equally sure that there is something wrong in the mental digestion.

[24] If this paper has given you any useful hints on the important subject of reading, and made you see that it is one's duty no less than one's interest to "read, mark, learn, and inwardly digest" the good books that fall in your way, its purpose will be fulfilled.

EXERCISES

1. Mark off the introduction, body, and conclusion.
2. What seem to be the two main purposes of the introduction?
3. Why can the essay be called an analogy?
4. What difficulties arise in any attempt to explain proper mental hygiene, or any other matter pertaining to the mind?
5. Why is it easier to talk about the body?
6. In "The Great Ravelled Knot" the author used a brief analogy when he compared the brain cortex to a holding corporation. For the purposes at hand, we may say that the cortex is the seat of the mind; so, in a general way, both authors are writing about the same thing. Do both analogies seem appropriate and useful? You can express the relation between the items being compared by a formula.

    The _____ of the mind is to the body as a holding corporation is to subsidiary companies.

    Reading is to the _____ of the mind as feeding is to the body.

7. What are the main points in the comparison, as presented in the body of the essay?
8. Find an example of parallel construction. Of balanced construction. Of balance and antithesis. How can you account for the scarcity of balance and antithesis?
9. As a class exercise, outline this essay according to the form recommended in your English handbook or taught you by your instructor.
10. Write a theme in which you further develop the idea of the fat mind, the mind heavily laden with knowledge but scarcely able to move about. For ease of clarification, you may wish to compare it with the muscular mind. For the sake of vividness, you may find it useful to give an example of each kind of mind from your own acquaintances.

Iron Filings and Magnetic Fields

ANDREW BONGIORNO

[1] I was struck several years ago by the following sentence in an article entitled "Reflections on Reading Acton" by H. S. A. Smith in the English review *Adelphi:* "History is like a pattern of iron filings formed by a magnetic field; the pattern is determined by the field, not by the particles, which are too numerous and tiny to fit together into any inevitable jig-saw puzzle." What is striking in the sentence is not only the idea but the manner in which an abstraction has been transmuted into something visible and tangible. What had before been a concept, true enough and yet somewhat pallid, has been given all the vividness and force of a visible phenomenon. The imagination has come to the aid of the reason and has served it in its peculiar way.

[2] But what of the idea which is here so vividly set forth? Let me point out that "history" in this context does not signify the complex of events that have occurred, but the account of them given by writers of histories; not the events that constitute the history of Rome, but the account of them set forth in, say, Gibbon's *Decline and Fall.* Gibbon's history is not a heap of details but a pattern; not an aggregate of random brush-strokes, but a picture, and in fact a *speaking* picture, for it conveys the message that Rome fell because it was invaded by Christianity, by "barbarism and religion," as Gibbon puts it. Whether this is what actually happened need not detain us here. Dante had surveyed the same phenomenon as Gibbon, but so far was he from seeing the corruption of a sound social order by a barbarous philosophy and theology that he saw neither a decline nor a fall, but only a transformation, and a transformation into something with infinitely greater possibilities for human happiness than any offered by pre-Christian civilizations. More recent historians have also surveyed Roman history and have agreed with Gibbon that what had once

From the series, "The Academic Procession," in the *Oberlin Review,* April 18, 1950.

been great ceased to be so, but many of them have attributed the fall to economic causes.

[3] How are we to explain the differences in these three conflicting accounts of the same historical phenomenon? The commonest way to do so is to point to the obvious fact that knowledge is a growing thing, that Gibbon knew more about the history of Rome than did Dante, and the modern historian more than Gibbon. The differences are the result of new excursions into unexplored regions of Roman civilization; new facts have been added to old, and as the mass of facts grows larger it reveals new explanations for the events in question. The contemporary historian's explanation is truer than Gibbon's because he knows more about Rome. But the economic interpretation of Roman history may yet prove not to be definitive. A definitive interpretation is in fact out of the question until the distant day when we shall have all or nearly all the knowledge which human industry can unearth. This explanation rests upon the assumption that facts speak for themselves, that if the historian will only fix his gaze upon the facts, the facts will tell him all that he can know.

[4] The positivist who speaks in this fashion would be more convincing if equally learned historians gave the same interpretation of the same historical phenomena. But we all know that they do not. If one twentieth-century historian ascribes the fall of Rome to economic causes, another, no less well informed than the first, may well ascribe it to a different cause, such as the failure of the old Roman stock to which Rome had owed its power. This can only be because different historians examine the facts with minds dominated by differing philosophies, theologies, psychologies, and even prejudices. Knowing this, another positivist will condemn the historian for bringing philosophy to bear upon the facts, asserting that philosophies are private possessions, that they are the products of the individual's temperament, of his private hopes and fears, and that in ideal circumstances they would not be brought into play in works of scholarship. Hence when reading history it is wise to disregard the interpretation, which is a purely subjective thing, and as far as possible to pay attention only to the facts. Man being what he is, a maker of philosophies and theologies, individuals will almost always arrange phenomena into patterns,

but since all philosophies and theologies are equally false, we are bound to acquaint ourselves with the historian's ideas not that we may test their validity, but that we may eliminate them from his account of historical events, which after all are the only realities.

[5] I have spoken of history and historians because the sentence which I have taken for my text inevitably leads one to think about them first. But the same thoughts must come to mind when we consider the writings of physicists or botanists or psychologists or economists or literary historians and critics. None of these writers deal in pure fact even when they are most certain that they do. Behind every presentation of natural phenomena stands the materialist or the mechanist or the vitalist or other philosopher of whatever school; and the same is to be said of every other human presentation of phenomena of other types. Are we compelled by the nature of things to hold that man's ineluctable impulse to philosophize is a regrettable perversion and that no individual can give us an interpretation of the facts that has more than a private validity?

[6] The author of the article from which I quoted asserts that the reason the filings do not spontaneously fall into a pattern is that they are "too numerous and tiny." Is not the true reason, rather, that they are inert things and therefore cannot move unless they receive an impulse from without? And are not facts equally inert, incapable of falling into a pattern unless they are subjected to the actions of the magnetic field which we call philosophy? The best that pure observation can do is to show us phenomena in juxtaposition with one another. The moment we assert that one of them is the effect of another we create a pattern, and the force that makes the pattern possible is the philosophy which asserts the reality of cause and effect. And whether our pattern does or does not correspond with reality depends not only upon the accuracy of our observation of facts, but upon the soundness of the philosophical principles invoked in arranging them.

[7] This being a newspaper column and not a treatise, I cannot explain at length why I have dared to speak of "sound philosophical principles." Briefly the reason is this. Philosophy is a discipline like physics and mathematics, i.e. a discipline that can arrive

at true conclusions. This proposition can be defended only if we admit two others: (1) that reality consists not only of entities that are observable by the senses, but of others that are not, and (2) that the human reason can come to grips with immaterial entities and learn much about their natures and their operations. These immaterial, or metaphysical, entities are always at work, creating, grouping, destroying, and no account of what happens in nature or human societies can be trustworthy which does not see observable fact in the light of a knowledge of unobservable events. The only true account of history of any period will be that in which the most extensive and accurate knowledge of the facts has been acted upon by the philosophy that most closely approximates the truth. Dante, Gibbon, and the Marxist give differing accounts of Roman history not so much because they are not equally learned as because they hold differing views about the nature of man and God. The Marxist historian is right if matter is the only reality, and if, in the words of his master, man is what he eats; Gibbon is right if man is a rational animal incapable of supernatural experience and living in a world completely cut off from God; Dante is right if man is both a natural and a supernatural being, living his brief life under the sway of Divine Providence.

[8] If this is so, there can be no sound study of the sciences, social sciences, or humanities unless it is accompanied by the study of philosophy. The techniques for observing facts can yield only inert masses of facts. But the human spirit demands meanings as well, and it will never refrain from arranging the facts into patterns. The choice we have to make is not between pure fact and interpretation, but between good interpretation and bad. And if we desire good interpretation we must face the fact that we cannot attain it unless we are willing to subject our minds to the discipline of philosophy. Modern education has a positivist bias, and as a result modern scholarship knows better how to collect facts than how to interpret them. We are all interested in educational reforms these days. The first reform we need is a revival of philosophy. We must come to realize that philosophy must pervade the study of every aspect of reality, as it must pervade the mind of every educated man.

EXERCISES

1. Mark off the introduction and conclusion of the essay.
2. What purposes are served by the introduction?
3. What are the two main divisions of the body of the essay?
4. Which of the following statements most accurately expresses the writer's main intention?
    a. To illustrate the idea that philosophy can give pattern to written history.
    b. To show that historical interpretations will vary but are unavoidable.
    c. To show that since various historical interpretations cannot all be true, we should not trust any.
    d. To assert the reality of non-material forces in world events and the consequent desirability and possible truth of interpretation in history.
5. Express the analogy upon which this essay is based in a formula like the one you used for "Feeding the Mind."
6. In commenting upon the arresting quality of the analogy which he uses, Professor Bongiorno perhaps explains the value of all analogies. What is that value, and which sentence in the essay best expresses it?
7. What fault does the author find with Smith's application of the analogy?
8. What method or methods of development does the author use to give meaning to his basic analogy before he goes on with his discussion?
9. Does the author believe that purely objective history is possible? Explain your answer.
10. Look for sentences using parallelism, balance, or antithesis, or any combination of these. Try to account for the author's use or non-use of these devices.
11. Explain the meaning of each of the following words as used in the essay: *pallid* (paragraph 1); *definitive* (paragraph 3); *positivist* (paragraph 4); *ineluctable* (paragraph 5); *bias* (paragraph 8).
12. Write a theme on one of the following analogies or on a similar one which occurs to you.
    a. Educating the mind is like tending a garden of many kinds of plants.

b. The word of the high school teacher, like the word of God in the parable, sometimes falls upon good soil and sometimes upon bad.

c. Learning to write well is like learning to play a musical instrument.

d. A person without an aim in life is like a ship without a rudder.

e. The influence of a very good teacher or parent or friend is like a leash that hangs loose and allows one to go his own pace on the right path but tightens if he begins to wander away from it.

Development by Definition

Definition is the most complicated and most exact, and consequently the most difficult, method of development. In addition to its own distinct technique, it may call to its aid detailed analysis, examples, and comparison. The purpose of definition is, as its Latin roots indicate, to mark off the limits, the exact area to which a given term applies.

Formal definition proceeds through two regular steps called *classification* and *differentiation*. The item to be defined is first classed within a general category of similar items, then differentiated from all other items in that category. The name of the main category and the qualities presented in differentiation are sometimes called by their Latin names, *genus* and *differentiae,* respectively.

Putting together the literal etymological meaning of *definition* and the required *genus* and *differentiae* of formal definition, we might define Indiana in this fashion:

Term	Genus	Differentiae
Indiana is	a state	bounded on the east by Ohio, on the south by the Ohio River, on the west by the Wabash River and Illinois, and on the north by Michigan and Lake Michigan.

So concise and formal a definition leaves a great deal unsaid about that fine state; but it demonstrates the literal meaning of *define*.

Another concise definition will demonstrate the ordinary use of
the method:

Term	*Genus*	*Differentiae*
A wrench is	a tool	designed to exert a twisting stress, usually in a plane parallel to its handle, or lever.

This definition also demonstrates the principles of economy
which ought to govern all concise definitions: the *genus* ought to
be as limited as possible, and the *differentiae* should be no more
numerous than necessary. The *genus* "tool" is about as narrow
as possible. "Mechanic's tool" would be too narrow, since carpenters, watchmakers and other workmen also use wrenches. On
the other hand "instrument" would be too broad, for it would
include such things as sextants, barometers, and dentists' drills.
The phrase "designed to exert a twisting stress" clearly sets
wrenches apart from hammers, saws, and in fact all tools but
screwdrivers. The other phrase, "usually in a plane parallel to
its handle, or lever," sets wrenches apart from screwdrivers.

The differentiation should be full enough to be absolutely clear
and unambiguous, however; and even in the definition of a simple
and concrete word like *wrench* an unabridged dictionary would
add such descriptive details as the head and the handle and such
examples of use as the turning of bolts and nuts. In an extended
definition the differentiation may run to considerable length and
present several kinds of the item being defined, or limitations of
meaning, or different meanings for different ages or places. Examples and comparisons are often used.

Although in daily writing definition is needed far less frequently
than other methods of development, it is indispensable in the
exact communication of thought. Parents, teachers, and older children use it continually in explaining words new to young children.
Employers and foremen use it in training employees. Much human unhappiness arises from lack of a clear understanding of
common terms. A tearful woman, in court, says, "When he said

I could have a career, I thought he meant . . ." Political abuse thrives on vagueness of terms. A leader promises "true democracy," and a whole nation is soon under a dictator. As with other kinds of writing, there seems to be no question as to whether we shall use definition or not, but only whether we shall define well or badly.

When definition is freed from the confines of its concise form but kept within its basic purpose, it may rise to the status of the true essay. What *is* democracy? What is love? What do we mean by "the good life"? What is the "spirit of Texas"? What was "the gilded age"? What is happiness? Definition, used both as an instrument of investigation and as a method of exposition, brings man some of his best answers to some of his best questions.

Two Definitions of Democracy

Dictionary Definition

de·moc'ra·cy (dē·mŏk'rȧ·sĭ), *n.; pl.* -CIES (-sĭz). [F. *démocratie,* fr. ML. *democratia,* fr. Gr. *dēmokratia,* fr. *dēmos* the people (akin to MIr. *dām* retinue, company, Ir. *dāmh* tribe, family, Gr. *daiomai* I divide) + *kratein* to rule, *kratos* authority. See TIDE; HARD. Cf. DEMAGOGUE, DEME, DEMOTIC, ENDEMIC, EPIDEMIC.] **1.** Government by the people; a form of government in which the supreme power is retained by the people and exercised either directly (*absolute,* or *pure, democracy*) or indirectly (*representative democracy*) through a system of representation and delegated authority periodically renewed, as in a constitutional representative government, or republic (which see). An *absolute democracy* is a government in which the sovereign powers are exercised theoretically by all the people, actually only by the electorate (voters). Even in the primitive forms, such as the Athenian democracy, where the governing powers were directly exercised by the assembled people, children and slaves, and usually women, were excluded. Specifically, and commonly in modern use, a *democracy* is a representative government where there is equality of rights without hereditary or arbitrary differences in rank or privilege, and is distinguished from *aristocracy.* In modern representative democracies, as the United States and France, the governing body comprises the qualified voters, and the basic principles of government are majority and plurality rule and popular sovereignty. **2.** A community or state so governed. **3.** Collectively, the people, esp. when regarded as the source of government. **4.** The principle or system of government by the people. The world must be made safe for *democracy.* *Woodrow Wilson.* **5.** [*cap.*] The principles and policy of the Democratic party; also, that party, or its members. *U.S.* **6.** Belief in or practice of social equality; disregard for social barriers, as of class; absence of snobbery.

By Permission. From Webster's New International Dictionary, Second Edition, Copyright, 1934, 1939, 1945, 1950, 1953, 1954, by G. & C. Merriam Co.

EXERCISES

1. A concise definition is given in lines 6 to 12. Write the parts of the definition under the three headings used for *wrench,* etc.

   The remainder of the entry is an elaboration of the basic definition.
2. What kinds of democracies are discussed and defined?
3. What terms in the basic definition are explained? Which are explained by limitation of their apparent meaning? Which are explained by extension of their apparent meaning?
4. What comparison or comparisons are used?
5. What examples are used?

Democracy As Defined by History

CARL BECKER

[1] Democracy, like liberty or science or progress, is a word with which we are all so familiar that we rarely take the trouble to ask what we mean by it. It is a term, as the devotees of semantics say, which has no 'referent'—there is no precise or palpable thing or object which we all think of when the word is pronounced. On the contrary, it is a word which connotes different things to different people, a kind of conceptual Gladstone bag, which, with a little manipulation, can be made to accommodate almost any collection of social facts we may wish to carry about in it. In it we can as easily pack a dictatorship as any other form of government. We have only to stretch the concept to include any form of government supported by a majority of the people, for whatever reasons and by whatever means of expressing assent, and before we know it the empire of Napoleon, the Soviet regime of Stalin, and the fascist systems of Mussolini and Hitler are all safely in the bag. But if this is what we mean by democracy, then virtually all forms of government are democratic, since virtually all governments, except in times of revolution, rest upon the explicit or implicit consent of the people. In order to discuss democracy intelligently it will be necessary, therefore, to define it, to attach to the word a sufficiently precise meaning to avoid the confusion which is not infrequently the chief result of such discussions.

[2] All human institutions, we are told, have their ideal forms laid away in heaven, and we do not need to be told that the actual institutions conform but indifferently to these ideal counterparts. It would be possible then to define democracy either in terms of the ideal or in terms of the real form—to define it as government of the people, by the people, for the people; or to define it as government of the people, by the politicians, for

From Carl Becker, *Modern Democracy,* 1940. By permission of Yale University Press.

whatever pressure groups can get their interests taken care of. But as a historian I am naturally disposed to be satisfied with the meaning which, in the history of politics, men have commonly attributed to the word—a meaning, needless to say, which derives partly from the experience and partly from the aspirations of mankind. So regarded, the term democracy refers primarily to a form of government by the many as opposed to government by the one—government by the people as opposed to government by a tyrant, a dictator, or an absolute monarch. This is the most general meaning of the word as men have commonly understood it.

[3] In this antithesis there are, however, certain implications, always tacitly understood, which give a more precise meaning to the term. Peisistratus, for example, was supported by a majority of the people, but his government was never regarded as a democracy for all that. Caesar's power derived from a popular mandate, conveyed through established republican forms, but that did not make his government any the less a dictatorship. Napoleon called his government a democratic empire, but no one, least of all Napoleon himself, doubted that he had destroyed the last vestiges of the democratic republic. Since the Greeks first used the term, the essential test of democratic government has always been this: the source of political authority must be and remain in the people and not in the ruler. A democratic government has always meant one in which the citizens, or a sufficient number of them to represent more or less effectively the common will, freely act from time to time, and according to established forms, to appoint or recall the magistrates and to enact or revoke the laws by which the community is governed. This I take to be the meaning which history has impressed upon the term democracy as a form of government.

EXERCISES

1. What do we usually call words like *democracy, liberty, science, progress,* which have no single tangible thing or object as a referent?
2. What is the meaning of *conceptual* as used in the phrase "conceptual Gladstone bag"?

3. Exactly which terms of the basic definition of *democracy,* and even of the commonly understood meaning, must be "stretched," and in what way, to make the word accommodate the totalitarian states mentioned in paragraph 1?
4. Find a very concise definition of *democracy* in the selection.
5. What condition does Becker consider the crucial test for democracy?
6. In what sense does the author use the words *ideal* and *real* in paragraph 2?
7. Why might this selection be called informal and the dictionary entry formal?
8. Are the two definitions in general agreement? Does the dictionary definition allow for Becker's distinction between "ideal" and "real" democracy?
9. Which definition is likely to remain vivid in your memory longer? Why?
10. For classroom practise, define one item in each of the following lists.
    a. (Concrete): pencil, tricycle, lipstick, cigarette, dance.
    b. (Abstract): love, political party, career, ambition, scorn.

Shagbark Hickory

DONALD CULROSS PEATTIE

[1] To everyone with a feeling for things American, and for American history, the Shagbark Hickory seems like a symbol of the pioneer age, with its hard, sinewy limbs and rude, shaggy coat, like the pioneer himself in fringed deerskin hunting shirt. The roaring heat of its fires, the tang of its nuts—the wild manna that it once cast down lavishly every autumn—stand for the days of forest abundance. With its marvelously strong and resilient fiber, it played a great part in our Age of Wood. Yet, tough and staunch though it is, Old Hickory is now retreating before its modern enemies.

From "Shagbark Hickory," *Scientific American,* September, 1948.

[2] A shagbark can usually be distinguished as far as it can be seen, by the smoke-gray bark which is forever warping away from its stem in great plates a foot or more long and six to eight inches wide. Frequently the strip is loose and curling at both ends, and is only more or less loosely attached at the middle. Its edges usually touch those of another strip of bark so that if one tries to pull it free from the trunk it is so engaged on both sides that one soon gives up the task. True, there are other trees with exfoliating bark, but none in our sylva with such great segments, so long or so thick. This shagginess begins to develop in comparatively young Hickories. Around the feet of old specimens the forest floor may be quite littered with the castoff heavy coat of armor. But the tree is not shedding its bark preparatory to some other condition— normally new shagginess simply thrusts the old away. Occasionally a tree has close, not shaggy, bark, and is called by lumbermen "Bastard Hickory."

[3] In rich, deep soil Shagbark attains heights of 120 feet, and under forest conditions it may form a columnar trunk, free of branches for the first 50 or 60 feet. It tends to have a narrow crown, with short branches and heavy drooping branchlets; against the winter sky the outline of form and twigs is uncouth and scraggly. But the winter gales may wrench at it as they will, for its very deep taproot makes it one of the most windfirm of trees. Spring is late in coming to the Hickory, and well after other trees have flowered or leafed out, this one stands forth, naked and massive, on the dry ridges and hillsides where it abounds. But about the first week in April the inner bud scales begin to open, arching out and twisting at the same time but with their tips at first still adhering in a pointed arch. Shining and pubescent on the inner surface, and yellow-green richly tinged with red, they part finally and curl back almost like magnolia petals, luminous as spring sunshine and with the downy look of young life. The new leaves and catkins are then seen standing up in a twist, like a skein of green wool. The catkins now rush into growth simultaneously with, but more swiftly than, the delicate, pale and lustrous young leaves.

[4] Dark, heavy, and aromatic is Hickory foliage all summer, but if the season is a dry ones the leaves may begin to turn a dull

brown even in August and drop, leaving the tree prematurely naked. Yet if they last through the summer, they join modestly in the autumn splendor of our middle-western woods, turning a soft dull gold that has a quiet beauty when the sun of Indian summer shines through them. To all who know the Shagbark, such memories are linked with visions of the violet smoke of asters curling low through drying grasses, with peeled October skies, with crow calls that telegraph your presence through the woods, and the shining of red haws, like little apples, on the thorn trees.

EXERCISES

1. What is the function of the first paragraph?
2. Can you find anywhere in the selection a concise definition of the hickory?
3. Is the *genus* of the formal definition anywhere specifically stated? What is it?
4. Why can the selection be called a definition?
5. List several qualities of the hickory which are self-sufficient as descriptive details, and several others which are involved in comparisons with the qualities of other trees. What is the value of the camparison in each case: to make clear, to make vivid, or both?
6. Peattie's style is vivid with similes and metaphors. List eight or ten good ones.
7. Why, presumably, does the author always capitalize Hickory? Does the language of the essay lend any support to your answer?
8. Find examples of parallel construction.
9. What is the most obvious difference between this selection and the dictionary definition of *democracy?* Between this and Becker's definition?
10. Develop one of the following topics into a full-length theme by definition. You need not make your definition formally complete, but fulfill the intention of definition.
    a. The official flower or tree of your native state
    b. A sloop (or other specific type of boat)
    c. Sport (general—not one specific sport)
    d. A home
    e. A friend
    f. Totalitarianism
    g. Imperialism

    h. War
    i. Religion
    j. Slang
    k. Kindness

What Is Teaching?

JACQUES BARZUN

[1] Since I am tackling the subject of teaching in a somewhat autobiographical manner, I had better say I taught my first class at the age of nine. All I remember about it is that it had to do with arithmetic and that the room seemed filled with thousands of very small children in black aprons. The explanation is that, with the shortage of teachers in France towards the middle of the last war, there were sporadic attempts at establishing the so-called Lancaster system of using older pupils to teach the younger. Lancaster, who lived a hundred years before, was only trying at first to meet the teacher shortage of the Napoleonic Wars, but he became an educational fanatic who believed that "any boy who can read can teach, although he knows nothing about it." I don't know what the "it" refers to, whether the art of teaching or the subject matter, but in any case this maxim, like so many others in education, is only half true.

[2] It served, however, to apprentice me to my trade. Not that I stayed very long in it that first time. Still I relapsed, not once but many times, into the habit of teaching. Having learned English and come to this country to rejoin my father, previously sent on a good-will mission, I found myself exchanging French lessons for further work in reading and speaking American. I had the good fortune to come in contact with a fine group of high school

teachers, and since advanced mathematics and beginning philosophy are taught earlier abroad, I was able to tutor boys of my own age in those subjects also.

[3] In my second year in college, I had my first academic offer. I was coaching two graduate students in the French educational theorists on whom they were to be examined—Rabelais, Montaigne, and Rousseau. My students, middle-aged men, apparently spoke of me to their sponsor and I received a note asking me to call on him. He was head of a department in a large university and I thought at the time that he scarcely lived up to the dignity of his position. For when I was announced by his secretary and he saw me, he laughed in my face. He had not been told that I was seventeen, and he was going to offer me an instructorship.

[4] This experience should have soured me against all academic entanglements, but circumstances prevailed. The period just before 1929 in this country, and particularly in the metropolis, offered the active-minded college man innumerable opportunities to achieve financial independence even before the bachelor's degree. So I found myself writing and tutoring in very profitable fashion before I thoroughly knew that I had chosen the two most backbreaking jobs in the whole world. A group of us students maintained a perfectly legal and honest tutoring mill, whose grist renewed itself as we put the backward rich through the entrance examinations of famous colleges not our own.

[5] School authorities smiled on our work and we ended by taking on all kinds of academic cases. No subjects were barred. If a retired minister came who wanted to read *Hamlet* in Esperanto (one did) we supplied an instructor who spoke the language like a native. As a subsidiary enterprise we undertook high-class literary hackwork. We compiled statistics, contributed to the lesser encyclopedias, and worked up the raw material for public addresses by public men. We referred to ourselves as Ghosts, Incorporated.

[6] When the time of my graduation came, in 1927, the die was cast. I knew I wanted to keep right on with both types of work, though no longer as piecework. Meanwhile I had formed an attachment to the Muse of History and was encouraged in it, chiefly by two men—Harry James Carman, now Dean of Columbia College, and Rexford Guy Tugwell, then Professor of Economics

in that institution and now President of the University of Puerto Rico. The ink on my diploma was not yet dry when the director of the Summer Session asked me whether I was willing to teach an introductory course. I said I should like nothing better. He wanted to know with whom I had taken that same course. I told him. "You can teach it anyway." That was my *hoc age*. I have been at it ever since, with breaks for study and travel and excursions into neighboring institutions. It is over a quarter of a century since I first obeyed the summons to teach, and I can only hope the habit has not become a compulsion.

[7] But I often wonder what originally made the impulse to teach take root. In the lives of so many good men one reads that they "drifted into teaching." They drift out again. It is clear that teachers are born, not made, and circumstances usually permit rather than compel. It is impossible to think of William James *not* teaching or of his brother Henry consenting to give a simple explanation.

[8] For many people, doing is far easier than talking about it. From which I conclude that the teaching impulse goes something like this: A fellow human being is puzzled or stymied. He wants to open a door or spell "accommodate." The would-be helper has two choices. He can open the door, spell the word; or he can show his pupil how to do it for himself. The second way is harder and takes more time, but a strong instinct in the born teacher makes him prefer it. It seems somehow to turn an accident into an opportunity for permanent creation. The raw material is what the learner can do, and upon this the teacher-artist builds by the familiar process of taking apart and putting together.

[9] The teacher must break down the new and puzzling situation into simpler bits and lead the beginner in the right order from one bit to the next. What the simpler bits and the right order are, no one can know ahead of time. They vary for each individual, and the teacher must grope around until he finds a "first step" that the particular pupil can manage. In any school subject, of course, this technique does not stop with the opening of a door. The need for it goes on and on—as it seems, forever—and it takes the stubbornness of a saint coupled with the imagination of a demon

for a teacher to pursue his art of improvisation gracefully, un-wearyingly, endlessly.

[10] Nor is this a purely mental task. All the while, the teacher must keep his charge's feelings in good order. A rattled student can do nothing, and a muddled teacher will rattle or dishearten almost any student. The teacher must not talk too much or too fast, must not trip over his own tongue, must not think out loud—must not forget, in short, that he is handling a pair of runaway horses: the pupil and a dramatic situation.

[11] It is obvious that the relation of teacher to pupil is an emotional one and most complex and unstable besides. To begin with, the motives, the forces that make teaching "go," are different on both sides of the desk. The pupil has some curiosity and he wants to know what grownups know. The master has curiosity also, but it is chiefly about the way the pupil's mind—or hand—works. Remembering his own efforts and the pleasure of discovery, the master finds a satisfaction which I have called artistic in seeing how a new human being will meet and make his own some part of our culture—our ways, our thoughts, even our errors and super-stitions.

[12] This interest, however, does not last forever. As the master grows away from his own learning period, he also finds that man-kind repeats itself. Hence young teachers are best; they are the most energetic, the most intuitive, and the least resented.

[13] For side by side with his eagerness, the pupil feels resent-ment arising from the fact that the grownup who teaches him appears to know it all. Even under the best conditions of fair play and deliberate spontaneity, the pupil, while needing and wanting knowledge, will hate and resist it. This resistance often makes one feel that the human mind is made of some wonderfully tough rub-ber, which you can stretch a little by pulling hard, but which snaps back into shape the moment you let go.

[14] The process may be exasperating for the teacher, but con-sider how the student feels, subjected to daily and hourly stretch-ing. "Here am I," he thinks, "with my brains nicely organized, —with everything, if not in its place, at least where I can find it, —and you come along with a new and strange item that you

want to force into my previous arrangement. Naturally I resist.
You persist. I begin to dislike you. But at the same time, you
show me aspects of this new fact or idea which in spite of myself
mesh in with my existing desires. You seem to know the contents of my mind. You show me the proper place for your contribution to my stock of knowledge. Finally, there is brooding over
us a vague threat of disgrace for me if I do not accept your offering and keep it and show you that I still have it when you—
dreadful thought!—*examine* me.

[15] "So I give in, I shut my eyes and swallow. I write little
notes about it to myself, and with luck the burr sticks: I have
learned something. Thanks to you? Well, not exactly. Thanks to
you and thanks to me. I shall always be grateful for your efforts,
but do not expect me to love you, at least not for a long, long
time. When I am fully formed and somewhat battered by the
world and yet not too displeased with myself, I shall generously
believe that I owe it all to you. It will be an exaggeration on the
other side, just as my present dislike is an injustice. Strike an
average between the two and that will be a fair measure of my
debt."

[16] If I have dwelt on the emotions of teaching and being taught,
it is because many people believe that schooling only engages
the mind—and only temporarily at that. "I've forgotten," says
the average man, "all I ever learned at school." And he mentally
contrasts this happy oblivion with the fact that he still knows how
to open oysters and ride a bicycle. But my description of teaching
applies equally to physical things and to metaphysical. We may
forget the substance of American History, but we are probably
scarred for life by the form and feeling of it as imparted by book
and teacher. Why is it that the business man's economics and the
well-bred woman's taste in art are normally twenty-five years
behind the times? It is that one's lifelong opinions are those
picked up before maturity—at school and college.

[17] This is why a "teacher's influence"—if he does exert one—
is not so big a joke as it seems. Notice in the lives of distinguished
men how invariably there is a Mr. Bowles or a Dr. Tompkins or
a Professor Clunk—whom no one ever heard of, but who is

"remembered" for inspiring, guiding, and teaching decisively at the critical time. We can all see the mark left by a teacher in physical arts like tennis or music. The pupils of Leopold Auer or Tobias Matthay can be recognized at forty paces by their posture and even in a dark room by the sound they make. For in these disciplines the teacher usually falls back on direct imitation: "Hold your hand like this," or, more simply, "Watch me." Well, much good teaching is of the "watch me" order; but the more abstract the knowledge, the less easy it is to imitate the teacher, and the genuine student wants to do the real thing in a real way *by himself.*

[18] Consequently, the whole aim of good teaching is to turn the young learner, by nature a little copycat, into an independent, self-propelling creature, who can not merely learn but study—that is, work as his own boss to the limit of his powers. This is to turn pupils into students, and it can be done on any rung of the ladder of learning.

[19] When I was a child, the multiplication table was taught from a printed sheet which had to be memorized one "square" at a time—the one's and the two's and so on up to nine. It never occurred to the teacher to show us how the answers could be arrived at also by addition, which we had already studied. No one said, "Look: if four times four is sixteen, you ought to be able to figure out, without aid from memory, what five times four is, because that amounts to four more one's added to the sixteen." This would at first have been puzzling, *more* complicated and difficult than memory work; but once explained and grasped, it would have been an instrument for learning and checking the whole business of multiplication. We could temporarily have dispensed with the teacher and cut loose from the printed table.[1]

[20] This is another way of saying that the only thing worth teaching anybody is a principle. Naturally principles involve facts and some facts must be learned "bare" because they do not rest on any principle. The capital of Alaska is Juneau and, so far as

[1] I find that General Grant complained of the same thing: "Both winters were spent in going over the same old arithmetic which I knew every word of before and repeating 'A noun is the name of a thing,' which I had also heard my Georgetown teachers repeat until I had come to believe it."— *Memoirs,* N. Y., 1894, p. 20.

I know, that is all there is to it; but a European child ought not
to be told that Washington is the capital of the United States without fixing firmly in his mind the relation between the city and
the man who led his countrymen to freedom. That would be missing an association, which is the germ of a principle. And just as a
complex athletic feat is made possible by rapid and accurate
coördination, so all valuable learning hangs together and *works*
by associations which make sense.

[21] Since associations are rooted in habit, and habits in feelings,
we can see that anything which makes school seem a nightmare
or a joke, which brands the teacher as a fool or a fraud, is the
archenemy of all learning. It so happens that there is one professional disease, or rather vice, which generates precisely this feeling and whose consequences are therefore fatal. I refer to Hokum
—and I hasten to explain what I mean. Hokum is the counterfeit
of true intellectual currency. It is words without meaning, verbal
filler, artificial apples of knowledge. From the necessities of the
case, nine tenths of all teaching is done with words, whence the
ever present temptation of hokum.

[22] Words should point to things, seen or unseen. But they can
also be used to wrap up emptiness of heart and lack of thought.
The student accepts some pompous, false, meaningless formula
and passes it back on demand, to be rewarded with—appropriately
enough—a passing grade. All the dull, second-rate opinions, all
the definitions that don't define, all the moral platitudes that "sound
good," all the conventional adjectives ("gentle Shakespeare"), all
the intimations that something must be learned because it has
somehow got lodged among learnable things (like the Binomial
Theorem or the date of Magna Charta)—all this in all its forms
gives off the atmosphere of hokum, which healthy people find
absolutely unbreathable.

[23] In a modern play, I think by A. A. Milne, this schoolmarm
vice has been caught and set down in a brief dialogue which goes
something like this:—

GOVERNESS: Recite.
PUPIL: "The Battle of Blenheim." (*Long pause.*)
GOVERNESS: By?
PUPIL: (*Silence.*)

GOVERNESS: By Robert Southey.
PUPIL: By Robert Southey.
GOVERNESS: Who was Robert Southey?
PUPIL: (*Pause.*) I don't know.
GOVERNESS: One of our greatest poets. Begin again.
PUPIL: The Battle of Blenheim by Robert Southey one of our greatest
poets.

[24] As this example shows, hokum is subtle and I will forbear
to analyze it. It hides in the porous part of solid learning and
vitiates it by making it stupid and ridiculous.

[25] "Any damn fool," said the Admiral with a friendly pat on
my shoulder, "can teach Naval History." I knew what he meant
by this subtle encouragement, but I disagreed. I had visited a
midshipmen's school and heard a petty officer, who was not a
damn fool but not a teacher either, instruct in the subject. He
had his nose in a book and was reading aloud: " 'On the eleventh
of February, Commodore Perry made for an anchorage twelve
miles farther up Yedo Bay.' This is important; take it down: 'On
the eleventh—of February—Commodore Perry—made for an
anchorage—' "
[26] This may have been the Admiral's idea of a lecture; certainly many people now alive have been taught in this fashion. But
it proves nothing except that anything may be done badly. What
is bad here is of course the absence of meaningful stress, of
drama. Given the three basic ways of conducting a class, success
will depend on the degree to which the chosen way has dramatic
form.
[27] Let me explain. The three basic ways are the lecture, the
discussion group, and the tutorial hour. In a lecture, a silent class
is addressed, more or less like a public meeting. In a discussion
group, comprising from five or six to not more than thirty students, the members of the class speak freely, putting or answering
questions on points which the teacher organizes so as to form a
coherent account of some topic. It may be that for this purpose
discussion by the class is broken at intervals by lecturettes from
him. In a tutorial hour, the instructor is really holding a conversation, usually with one student, certainly with not more than

three or four. This is in the best sense a free-for-all and it pre-supposes a good stock of knowledge on the part of the students. [28] I may seem to have left out the recitation class, common to the lower schools, in which every pupil in turn answers a part of the day's lesson. But this is really a form of examination. Its teaching value is that of any good examination.

[29] If, some few years back, I had listed lectures as a legitimate mode of teaching, I should have been set down by my progressive friends as an old mossback corrupted by university practice. But now several of the progressive colleges have officially restored lecturing—Bennington notably—and I suspect that unofficially they were unable at any time to do altogether without it. Lecturing comes so natural to mankind that it is hard to stop it by edict. It simply turns into bootleg form. Many teachers think that because they sit around a table with only a dozen students they are running a discussion group, but they are lecturing just the same if the stream of discourse flows in only one direction.

[30] Now what makes a lecture legitimate and good? The answer is—a combination of eloquence and personality. The petty officer reading aloud from a book was out of his element. But if Charles Dickens, famous for his public readings, had held that textbook of Naval History, the class would have *seen* Commodore Perry steaming up the bay in defiance of Japanese orders; they would have known without being told that it was important; they would not have had to take it down. And this is the justification of large-scale lecturing.

[31] The lecture room is the place where drama may properly become theater. This usually means a fluent speaker, no notes, and no shyness about "effects." In some teachers a large class filling a sloped-up amphitheater brings out a wonderful power of emphasis, timing, and organization. The speaker projects himself and the subject. The "effects" are not laid on; they are the meaningful stress which constitutes, most literally, the truth of the matter. This meaning—as against fact—is the one thing to be indelibly stamped on the mind, and it is this that the printed book cannot give. That is why their hearers never forgot Huxley lecturing, nor Michelet, nor William James. Plenty of facts can be conveyed, too—the more highly organized the better; but

in the hands of a great lecturer it is feelings and principles that illuminate the soul like a perfect play or concert.

[32] To try to abolish the varied forms of lecturing virtuosity in the name of a theory cut to fit more common gifts is surely a mistake. What led to the attempt was that formerly *all* college teaching was through lectures. Many were bad, and nothing is worse than a bad lecture. Everyone can conjure up from his own past the memory of incoherent mumblings that make time stand still and inspire suicidal thoughts.

[33] At the same time, it is also true that lectures alone will not suffice to teach, for the lecture method assumes that every member of the class comes in the same state of preparation and leaves with the same increment of knowledge. The fact is otherwise. Only individual attention to each student can keep the whole class abreast and truly teach. This is why a normal three-hours-a-week class is usually broken up into small groups for the "third hour" after the two lectures.

[34] Unfortunately, the third hour is too often entrusted to a "section man," usually a graduate student earning his keep by doing nothing else than this quiz and rehearsing work. This is bad practice. The lecturer should himself be available for questioning by his students; he should himself discover their failures and misconceptions; he should run his whole show as one enterprise and be responsible for conveying his subject to as many men, personally known to him, as possible. If we remember the axiom, Two Minds Sharing One Thought, we can see that teaching by proxy is as impossible as learning by proxy.

[35] The idea of breaking a large class into small groups gives us the second mode of teaching: by means of informal discussion. As a general rule, I believe that all introductory courses should be taught thus. It is expensive but worth it. Only in a small group can the student learn to marshal his thoughts, expose his weaknesses, argue out his beliefs, and gain that familiarity with a given subject which, if not learned early, will never be learned at all.

[36] Handling a discussion group requires a special talent, too. Here the drama is more subtle but equally imperative. The hour's discussion must not go off in all directions like a leaky hose. It must

have a pattern, beginning at a given point and logically reaching another, from which to start again the next day. Now it is relatively easy to impose a pattern on a lecture; the scheme of it can be written out beforehand and even memorized, because no one will interfere with it. But in a discussion, every one of twenty-five or thirty men has a right to shove the tiller in any direction he pleases. Since there must be an atmosphere of freedom, the instructor must not act like a priggish moderator with a gavel. He must be willing to go up side tracks and come back. His imagination must swarm with connecting links, factual illustrations, answers to unexpected questions.

[37] He must, moreover, know how to correct without wounding, contradict without discouraging, coax along without coddling. Every once in a while, a group of men will contain a crank or a fanatic: he must be turned to good teaching use without being made to feel a goat. Every once in a while, the class will want to take the bit in its teeth and hold a political or ethical debate, none too close to the issue. This must be tolerated. Every once in a while, the instructor will feel so strongly on a given matter that he will want to lecture. This must be nipped in the bud.

[38] An advanced discussion group—say twelve men in a senior colloquium in economics meeting for two consecutive hours—is a test of any discussion leader. His role is that of an orchestra conductor, except that neither he nor his men have a score before them. Yet the result of the evening's noise must be as intelligible as a symphony. Calling on the right man for the right thing, balancing opinions, drawing out the shy and backward, keeping silent so that the group itself will unwind its own errors,—and doing all this in the casual "colloquial" manner which the title of the course prescribes,—is an art that only comes with long practice.

[39] Compared with this the "tutorial" is far simpler though physically more exhausting. Two or three men can talk so fully that errors are quickly corrected and ground is covered faster. The students have probably studied the topic together anyway and they are reporting progress. The instructor usually finds little to amend and therefore feels bound to add, to fill out, to interpret the body of facts. This leads to more questions and he finds himself being

pumped absolutely dry. No matter how much he knows or how fully he has thought, he is relentlessly pushed until his back touches the wall of the great absolutes. For students are ever seeking final answers and they know how to ask questions which no wise man would dare answer.

[40] Not all tutors are wise, however, and the principal danger is that unprepared or malicious students will use a common trick to defeat the purpose of the meeting. If a man is known to have some pet view or favorite topic, he will be brought to the brink of it by artful dodges and then pushed over. While he climbs his way out, the students can respectfully daydream. I am told that one man at a Midwestern university can be wound up by his students like a grandfather clock. He runs down daily and hourly on the same topic like a weight on its chain, and no one is the worse, or the better, for the ticking.

[41] I do not know whether this is a saving of energy for him as well as the students, but I do know that the other and truer discharge of duty is a wearing process. At most progressive colleges, at least until recently, teachers were committed to whole days of half-hour tutorials, each with a single student. Every student was at work on a different phase of a given subject and, by virtue of the time and freedom allowed, was ravenous for knowledge. I can guarantee from experience that at the end of such a day the instructor is a gibbering idiot.

[42] The output of words alone, the quick modulations, the sense of multitudinous insistent claims of one's best thoughts, and what William James called "having to square oneself with others at every step" would in time surely kill the poor goose. One perceptive student, commenting on certain events at the time said to me: "At F—— (a progressive school) the teachers die young; at J—— (a nonprogressive one) the students hang themselves. That seems to be the basic difference between old-fashioned and progressive education."

[43] In all three modes of teaching—by lecture, by discussion, and by tutoring—it is evident that the effective agent is the living person. It is idle to talk about what could be done by gadgets— gramophone disks or sound films. We know just what they can do: the disk brings the music class a whole symphony; the film

can bring Chinese agriculture to students in Texas. But this will not replace the teacher, with his knowledge of subject matter and students, his power to lead them, and their response to his mind. Given a mastered subject and a person committed heart and soul to teaching it, a class accustomed to think, attend, and be led, the result will be, under God, as near to the discourse of men and angels as it is fit to go.

EXERCISES

1. Can you find anywhere in this selection a concise definition of teaching?
2. Write out, in your own words, a concise definition which includes the main elements of Professor Barzun's definition.
3. What are the main methods of teaching? Distinguish between them.
4. What are the main ingredients of good teaching, according to the author?
5. What are the main principles of teaching?
6. Professor Barzun's manner seems informal. Study his vocabulary and see how he achieves this effect of informality.
7. Point out several of the vivid examples by which the author emphasizes his main ideas.
8. Find some examples of hyperbole (see Glossary), or exaggeration.
9. Find an apparent paradox (see Glossary) in paragraph 9.

Quotation is often used as ornament, and, like other ornament, it is a form of emphasis because it attracts attention. Long quotations from books are usually not of this sort; they only illustrate points of view or give information. But brief and striking quotations are emphatic because they seem to bring living speech into the discourse.

10. Find some effective examples of this kind of quotation.

PART TWO

Essays, Articles, and Addresses

Definitions

This part of the book contains articles, essays, and addresses of greater length than most of the pieces in Part I. The words *essay* and *article* are frequently misunderstood or used interchangeably. Most periodicals publish both articles and essays; but some periodicals call them all articles, and others call them all essays. There is a useful distinction between them, however. An article is mainly an organized presentation of a body of fact; often it includes inferences or conclusions drawn from the facts, but the facts predominate. Ordinarily the tone is objective. An essay is based upon fact, but its emphasis is upon the author's analysis or interpretation. If the purpose is fairly serious, the interpretation logical, the tone objective, and the diction rather formal, we call the essay a formal one. If the purpose is merely to entertain, the interpretation whimsical, the tone highly subjective, and the diction informal or burlesque-formal, we call the essay an informal or personal one. But of course no law requires authors to write in pure types, or even to be aware of the distinctions among them; consequently some pieces seem to be half article and half essay, and there is a tendency toward informality in all types.

An *address* may resemble any of these written types, but both its content and its method may be influenced by the immediate presence of the audience. An audience of actual listeners, with no printed page before them, cannot carry in mind a great number of facts nor turn back a page to look up facts and study relationships. Therefore the speaker must state his plan clearly, concentrate on a few facts essential to his main topics, sometimes repeat and summarize, and if possible gain vividness by example, figurative language, and concrete detail; he must also be direct and concise. When an address is printed it of course retains these audience considerations, and the careful reader will make allowances whenever they seem inappropriate to written composition —as, for instance, repetition and extreme simplification often do; but they are virtues more often than they are faults. (These virtues might profitably be imitated, sometimes, by the writer who never sees his "audience." An old quail hunter once said that the greatest cause of misses was the shooter's knowledge that he had another barrel to fire. Very likely the knowledge that paper is plentiful encourages verbose and inexact writing, too.) T. H. Huxley's published addresses are notable for these qualities of simplicity and vividness required for effective oral delivery. On the other hand, some "addresses" were never meant to be presented except in writing; Milton's *Areopagitica* is called a speech, but it was never delivered orally. The distinctions among these types are meaningful, then; but they must not be overemphasized. Knowing them simply helps us to understand the author's purpose and his method.

These three types—the article, the essay, and the address— make up most of the non-fiction prose read or written by the educated person of the modern world; it is for that reason that they have been chosen as the substance for Part II. The ways in which these models may be studied are discussed specifically on page vii.

Section A: On Writing and Thinking

The selections in Section A are all concerned with logic and the logical use of language. Knowledge of the selection "Logic and Fallacies in Logic" is essential to understanding several of the pieces in later sections.

The exercises begin a rather intensive study of style which is continued in Section B.

The Method of Scientific Investigation

THOMAS HENRY HUXLEY

[1] The method of scientific investigation is nothing but the expression of the necessary mode of working of the human mind. It is simply the mode at which all phenomena are reasoned about, rendered precise and exact. There is no more difference, but there is just the same kind of difference, between the mental operations of a man of science and those of an ordinary person, as there is between the operations and methods of a baker or of a butcher weighing out his goods in common scales, and the operations of a chemist in performing a difficult and complex analysis by means of his balance and finely-graduated weights. It is not that the action of the scales in the one case, and the balance in the other, differ in the principles of their construction or manner of working; but the beam of one is set on an infinitely finer axis than the other, and of course turns by the addition of a much smaller weight.

[2] You will understand this better, perhaps, if I give you some familiar example. You have all heard it repeated, I dare say, that men of science work by means of Induction and Deduction, and that by the help of these operations, they, in a sort of sense, wring from Nature certain other things, which are called Natural Laws, and Causes, and that out of these, by some cunning skill of their own, they build up Hypotheses and Theories. And it is imagined by many, that the operations of the common mind can be by no means compared with these processes, and that they have to be acquired by a sort of special apprenticeship to the craft. To hear all these large words, you would think that the mind of a man of science must be constituted differently from that of his fellow-men; but if you will not be frightened by terms, you will discover that you are quite wrong, and that all these terrible apparatus are being used by yourselves every day and every hour of your lives.

[3] There is a well-known incident in one of Molière's plays,

From *Collected Essays,* by Thomas Henry Huxley, published by Appleton-Century-Crofts, Inc.

where the author makes the hero express unbounded delight on being told that he had been talking prose during the whole of his life. In the same way, I trust that you will take comfort, and be delighted with yourselves, on the discovery that you have been acting on the principles of inductive and deductive philosophy during the same period. Probably there is not one here who has not in the course of the day had occasion to set in motion a complex train of reasoning, of the very same kind, though differing of course in degree, as that which a scientific man goes through in tracing the causes of natural phenomena.

[4] A very trivial circumstance will serve to exemplify this. Suppose you go into a fruiterer's shop, wanting an apple,—you take up one, and, on biting it, you find it sour; you look at it, and see that it is hard and green. You take up another one, and that too is hard, green, and sour. The shopman offers you a third; but, before biting it you examine it, and find that it is hard and green, and you immediately say that you will not have it, as it must be sour, like those that you have already tried.

[5] Nothing can be more simple than that, you think; but if you will take the trouble to analyze and trace out into its logical elements what has been done by the mind, you will be greatly surprised. In the first place, you have performed the operation of Induction. You found that, in two experiences, hardness and greenness in apples went together with sourness. It was so in the first case, and it was confirmed by the second. True, it is a very small basis, but still it is enough to make an induction from; you generalize the facts, and you expect to find sourness in apples where you get hardness and greenness. You found upon that a general law, that all hard and green apples are sour; and that, so far as it goes, is a perfect induction. Well, having got your natural law in this way, when you are offered another apple which you find is hard and green, you say, "All hard and green apples are sour; this apple is hard and green, therefore this apple is sour." That train of reasoning is what logicians call a syllogism, and has all its various parts and terms,—its major premise, its minor premise, and its conclusion. And, by the help of further reasoning, which, if drawn out, would have to be exhibited in two or three other syllogisms, you arrive at your final determination, "I will not have

that apple." So that, you see, you have in the first place, established a law by Induction, and upon that you have founded a Deduction, and reasoned out the special conclusion of the particular case. Well now, suppose, having got your law, that at some time afterward, you are discussing the qualities of apples with a friend: you will say to him, "It is a very curious thing,—but I find that all hard and green apples are sour!" Your friend says to you, "But how do you know that?" You at once reply, "Oh, because I have tried them over and over again, and have always found them to be so." Well, if we were talking science instead of common sense, we should call that an Experimental Verification. And, if still opposed, you go further, and say, "I have heard from the people in Somersetshire and Devonshire, where a large number of apples are grown, that they have observed the same thing. It is also found to be the case in Normandy, and in North America. In short, I find it to be the universal experience of mankind wherever attention has been directed to the subject." Whereupon, your friend, unless he is a very unreasonable man, agrees with you, and is convinced that you are quite right in the conclusion you have drawn. He believes, although perhaps he does not know he believes it, that the more extensive verifications are,—that the more frequently experiments have been made, and results of the same kind arrived at,—that the more varied the conditions under which the same results are attained, the more certain is the ultimate conclusion, and he disputes the question no further. He sees that the experiment has been tried under all sorts of conditions, as to time, place, and people, with the same result; and he says with you, therefore, that the law you have laid down must be a good one, and he must believe it.

[6] In science we do the same thing,—the philosopher exercises precisely the same faculties, though in a much more delicate manner. In scientific inquiry it becomes a matter of duty to expose a supposed law to every possible kind of verification, and to take care, moreover, that this is done intentionally, and not left to a mere accident, as in the case of the apples. And in science, as in common life, our confidence in a law is in exact proportion to the absence of variation in the result of our experimental verifications. For instance, if you let go your grasp of an article you may have in your hand, it will immediately fall to the ground. That

is a very common verification of one of the best established laws of nature—that of gravitation. The method by which men of science establish the existence of that law is exactly the same as that by which we have established the trivial proposition about the sourness of hard and green apples. But we believe it in such an extensive, thorough, and unhesitating manner because the universal experience of mankind verifies it, and we can verify it ourselves at any time; and that is the strongest possible foundation on which any natural law can rest.

[7] So much, then, by way of proof that the method of establishing laws in science is exactly the same as that pursued in common life. Let us now turn to another matter (though really it is but another phase of the same question), and that is, the method by which, from the relations of certain phenomena, we prove that some stand in the position of causes toward the others.

[8] I want to put the case clearly before you, and I will therefore show you what I mean by another familiar example. I will suppose that one of you, on coming down in the morning to the parlor of your house, finds that a tea-pot and some spoons which had been left in the room on the previous evening are gone,—the window is open, and you observe the mark of a dirty hand on the window-frame, and perhaps, in addition to that, you notice the impress of a hob-nailed shoe on the gravel outside. All these phenomena have struck your attention instantly, and before two seconds have passed you say, "Oh, somebody has broken open the window, entered the room, and run off with the spoons and the tea-pot!" That speech is out of your mouth in a moment. And you will probably add, "I know there has; I am quite sure of it!" You mean to say exactly what you know; but in reality you are giving expression to what is, in all essential particulars, an Hypothesis. You do not *know* it at all; it is nothing but an hypothesis rapidly framed in your own mind! And, it is an hypothesis founded on a long train of inductions and deductions.

[9] What are those inductions and deductions, and how have you got at this hypothesis? You have observed, in the first place, that the window is open; but by a train of reasoning involving many Inductions and Deductions, you have probably arrived long before at the General Law—and a very good one it is—that windows do not open of themselves; and you therefore conclude

that something has opened the window. A second general law that you have arrived at in the same way is, that tea-pots and spoons do not go out of a window spontaneously, and you are satisfied that, as they are not now where you left them, they have been removed. In the third place, you look at the marks on the window-sill, and the shoemarks outside, and you say that in all previous experience the former kind of mark has never been produced by anything else but the hand of a human being; and the same experience shows that no other animal but man at present wears shoes with hob-nails in them such as would produce the marks in the gravel. I do not know, even if we could discover any of those "missing links" that are talked about, that they would help us to any other conclusion! At any rate the law which states our present experience is strong enough for my present purpose. You next reach the conclusion, that as these kinds of marks have not been left by any other animals than men, or are liable to be formed in any other way than by a man's hand and shoe, the marks in question have been formed by a man in that way. You have, further, a general law, founded on observation and experience, and that, too, is, I am sorry to say, a very universal and unimpeachable one,—that some men are thieves; and you assume at once from all these premises—and that is what constitutes your hypothesis—that the man who made the marks outside and on the window-sill, opened the window, got in the room, and stole your tea-pot and spoons. You have now arrived at a *Vera Causa;*—you have assumed a Cause which it is plain is competent to produce all the phenomena you have observed. You can explain all these phenomena only by the hypothesis of a thief. But that is a hypothetical conclusion, of the justice of which you have no absolute proof at all; it is only rendered highly probable by a series of inductive and deductive reasonings.

[10] I suppose your first action, assuming that you are a man of ordinary common sense, and that you have established this hypothesis to your own satisfaction, will very likely be to go off for the police, and set them on the track of the burglar, with the view to the recovery of your property. But just as you are starting with this object, some person comes in, and on learning what you are about, says, "My good friend, you are going on a great deal

too fast. How do you know that the man who really made the marks took the spoons? It might have been a monkey that took them, and the man may have merely looked in afterward." You would probably reply, "Well, that is all very well, but you see it is contrary to all experience of the way tea-pots and spoons are abstracted; so that, at any rate, your hypothesis is less probable than mine." While you are talking the thing over in this way, another friend arrives, one of that good kind of people that I was talking of a little while ago. And he might say, "Oh, my dear sir, you are certainly going on a great deal too fast. You are most presumptuous. You admit that all these occurrences took place when you were fast asleep, at a time when you could not possibly have known anything about what was taking place. How do you know that the laws of Nature were not suspended during the night? It may be that there has been some kind of supernatural interference in this case." In point of fact, he declares that your hypothesis is one of which you cannot at all demonstrate the truth, and that you are by no means sure that the laws of Nature are the same when you are asleep as when you are awake.

[11] Well, now, you cannot at the moment answer that kind of reasoning. You feel that your worthy friend has you somewhat at a disadvantage. You will feel perfectly convinced in your own mind, however, that you are quite right, and you say to him, "My good friend, I can only be guided by the natural probabilities of the case, and if you will be kind enough to stand aside and permit me to pass, I will go and fetch the police." Well, we will suppose that your journey is successful, and that by good luck you meet with a policeman; that eventually the burglar is found with your property on his person, and the marks correspond to his hand and of the shoes. Probably any jury would consider those facts a very good experimental verification of your hypothesis, touching the cause of the abnormal phenomena observed in your parlor, and would act accordingly.

[12] Now, in this suppositious case, I have taken phenomena of a very common kind, in order that you might see what are the different steps in an ordinary process of reasoning, if you will only take the trouble to analyze it carefully. All the operations I have described, you will see, are involved in the mind of any man

of sense in leading him to a conclusion as to the course he should take in order to make good a robbery and punish the offender. I say that you are led, in that case, to your conclusion by exactly the same train of reasoning as that which a man of science pursues when he is endeavoring to discover the origin and laws of the most occult phenomena. The process is, and always must be, the same; and precisely the same mode of reasoning was employed by Newton and Laplace in their endeavors to discover and define the causes of the movements of the heavenly bodies, as you, with your own common sense, would employ to detect a burglar. The only difference is, that the nature of the inquiry being more abstruse, every step has to be most carefully watched, so that there may not be a single crack or flaw in your hypothesis. A flaw or crack in many of the hypotheses of daily life may be of little or no moment as affecting the general correctness of the conclusions at which we may arrive; but in a scientific inquiry a fallacy, great or small, is always of importance, and is sure to be in the long run constantly productive of mischievous, if not fatal results.

[13] Do not allow yourselves to be misled by the common notion that an hypothesis is untrustworthy simply because it is an hypothesis. It is often urged, in respect to some scientific conclusion, that, after all, it is only an hypothesis. But what more have we to guide us in nine-tenths of the most important affairs of daily life than hypotheses, and often very ill-based ones? So that in science, where the evidence of an hypothesis is subjected to the most rigid examination, we may rightly pursue the same course. You may have hypotheses and hypotheses. A man may say, if he likes, that the moon is made of green cheese: that is an hypothesis. But another man, who has devoted a great deal of time and attention to the subject, and availed himself of the most powerful telescopes and the results of the observations of others, declares that in his opinion it is probably composed of materials very similar to those of which our own earth is made up: and that is also only an hypothesis. But I need not tell you that there is an enormous difference in the value of the two hypotheses. That one which is based on sound scientific knowledge is sure to have a corresponding value; and that which is a mere hasty, random guess, is likely to have but little value. Every great step in our progress in discovering causes has been made in exactly the same

way as that which I have detailed to you. A person observing the occurrence of certain facts and phenomena asks, naturally enough, what process, what kind of operation known to occur in nature applied to the particular case, will unravel and explain the mystery? Hence you have the scientific hypothesis; and its value will be proportionate to the care and completeness with which its basis had been tested and verified. It is in these matters as in the commonest affairs of practical life: the guess of the fool will be folly, while the guess of the wise man will contain wisdom. In all cases, you see that the value of the result depends on the patience and faithfulness with which the investigator applies to his hypothesis every possible kind of verification.

EXERCISES

1. Define the following terms as they are used in the essay:

induction	experimental verification
deduction	natural law
general law	*vera causa*
hypothesis	syllogism

2. Huxley is a scientist addressing a lay audience. One of his main purposes is to explain the nature of the scientific method. What common methods of development does he use to make clear his apparently complicated subject?
3. What is Huxley trying to do in addition to explaining the scientific method?
4. How is the tone of the introduction related to this second purpose?
5. Whatever Huxley's real attitude toward science and scientists may be, the tone of the address, especially in the introduction, is adapted to his immediate purposes. Of the following terms, tell which best designates this tone: *reverence, awe, distrust, mock friendliness, amiable condescension.*
6. What is the connotation of the following phrases from paragraph 2?
   some cunning skill
   all these large words
   all these terrible apparatus
7. Point out some instances of wit or humor. Explain how they are related to Huxley's purposes.
8. Find in the last paragraph a sentence which gains emphasis by a combination of balance and antithesis. How are the antithetical words given special emphasis?

9. In class discussion, see what inductions are generally accepted on one of the following topics:
   a. The "dressed up" car and the personality of its owner
   b. The relation of red hair to personality
   c. Southern cooking
   d. The relation between the shape of road signs and what they tell the driver
   e. Personality traits or physical qualities common to all members of the white race
   f. The quality of British motion pictures

10. Write a theme on some topic on which you have arrived at a generalization (or induction), and show how you have based deductions on that generalization (perhaps without knowing you were "deducing"). Here are some suggestions:
    a. Your attitude toward seafoods
    b. Your feeling about brunettes
    c. The practical value of a college education
    d. The relation between physical exposure and a cold
    e. The usual reaction of one of your friends to a certain kind of situation

---

Logic and Fallacies in Logic

W. ARTHUR TURNER

[1] Argument depends heavily upon exposition but differs from it in two important ways. Argument does not merely explain an idea or a plan but also tries to overcome an expected resistance to it. In consequence it must not merely develop but must give proof of its statements. These two features, *expected resistance* and *proof,* are the identifying marks of all argument.

[2] Here is part of a student theme which illustrates both points.

SCIENCE NEEDS YOUNG MEN AND WOMEN

There is an urgent need today for young men and women to enter scientific professions. There are two areas of scientific endeavor where

From *The Odyssey Handbook and Guide to Writing,* by George B. Woods and W. Arthur Turner, copyright, 1954, by The Odyssey Press, Inc.

this need is especially great. The first, and perhaps more glamorous of the two, is research work. Young people frequently underestimate this important field when choosing a life work; they sigh gloomily, "There's nothing more to be discovered." In six weeks of beginning zoölogy I have observed that the following facts are still unknown: (1) the position of the coronary artery in the frog's heart, (2) the action of the epithelial cells in the absorption of food, (3) the function and meaning of the nephrostomes in the frog's kidney, (4) the meaning of the nodes of Ranvier in nerve fibers, (5) the behavior of fat in the course of digestion, and (6) the basic reason for agglutination when different types of blood are mixed. In any science in which facts as basic as these are still unknown there is obviously an abundant field for investigation.

The assertion to be proved might be stated, "There is an urgent need for research workers in the scientific professions." The expected resistance is in the quoted "There's nothing more to be discovered." The proof of the writer's contention is then given in six telling examples. One example, of course, would not have been enough to prove so sweeping an assertion.

I. THE TWO MAIN KINDS OF ARGUMENT

Argument once flourished as a polite accomplishment; debating societies and college speakers kept many kinds of argument alive long past their periods of usefulness. Because some of the propositions were artificial and because we no longer care for debating for its own sake, we tend to neglect the study of argument today. But it is just as useful to us as it was to Cicero, Milton, Patrick Henry, or Disraeli. Our needs, however, are of two main kinds: supporting a conclusion, and establishing a cause-to-effect relationship.

A. SUPPORTING A CONCLUSION

The method of supporting a conclusion is to present the conclusion as a proposition at the beginning of the argument and to follow it with enough specific supporting material to convince the reader of its truth.

An article in a national magazine had as its thesis the proposition that white bread is unsatisfactory as a food. The writer could well expect resistance to the proposition. Bread is sold by the ton; everyone eats bread; bread is the staff of life. But, says the writer, the bread which earned this good reputation and the epithet "the staff of life" was not what we get today. It was an all-wheat bread as made fifty years ago or so. If we take that as the standard of good bread, then the commercially baked white bread we get today is not good bread. Here, in brief, are the reasons:

1. About twelve vitamins are removed in the flour refining process, and if the flour is "enriched" only two are put back.

2. Most of the minerals are removed in the same process.

3. Most of the proteins of natural wheat are removed.

4. Commercial bakeries use shortening "extenders" which, at best, are not nourishing.

5. Commercial bakeries use dough "conditioners" which hold water (thus adding weight) and make the loaf stand up well but contain no nourishment.

6. The finished loaf is mostly starch; it is a poor substitute for the all-wheat loaf, which contains proteins as well as starch.

Was the proof convincing? Since the article appeared thousands of people have demanded "the real thing," and bakeries all over the country have begun to supply the demand.

B. ESTABLISHING A CAUSE-TO-EFFECT RELATIONSHIP

The method of cause-to-effect argument is to present as a proposition the statement that a present (or proposed) cause will lead to a certain effect, then to show why the effect will result. This kind of argument usually either supports or attacks a proposed plan of action.

The late President Roosevelt proposed to Congress that the St. Lawrence Seaway Project would greatly aid the war effort and should therefore be undertaken immediately. In support he pointed out three expected results of the proposed seaway.

1. It would provide 2,200,000 horsepower of low-cost electricity for war production. Steam-powered electric plants could not substitute, for all facilities were needed to supply plants in areas remote from water power.

2. It would increase transportation along an important war-materials route. Railroads could not fill the need, and the production of new rolling stock was already competing with war production for facilities.

3. It would increase shipbuilding facilities on the coast by allowing much building of small ships to be shifted to the Great Lakes. There was, of course, no way to get such inland-built ships to sea except by the proposed seaway.

II. LOGIC

The two kinds of logical thinking which are used in argument are induction and deduction.

A. INDUCTION

Induction proceeds from specific instances to a general conclusion. For example, so many individual human beings have died that we can make the generalization "All men are mortal"; we expect no exceptions to occur. This is a commonplace induction. But let us watch an induction grow. Professor Lewis, of Hale College, observes that his income barely meets his expenses and that he has no luxuries and no savings. After some investigation he discovers that his colleagues are in the same plight. They conclude, "All Hale College professors are underpaid." They ask President Hope for a raise. But the president, lacking funds, conducts a survey of the salary level in several colleges and finds that his college pays as well as most; he does not give the raise. By this time Professor Lewis, an economics teacher, is professionally interested in the problem. He has talked to several of his friends in the town, bank clerks, office workers, insurance agents, and many others. He thinks he sees a generalization emerging, and he states it tentatively as a *hypothesis:* "All white-collar workers are underpaid." He must test it by answering three questions: (1) Is it true of all or nearly all examples? (2) What is the area of applicability? (3) Are there any notable exceptions? He sends out questionnaires to hundreds of people in all occupations in all parts of the country. From the results of these questionnaires and some other research he arrives at his final generalization: "Over a fifty-year period the income of the average white-collar worker in the United States has increased much less than that of other workers, so that in terms of buying power the average white-collar worker has suffered a comparative income loss so severe that in many instances he has fallen to substandard living conditions."

Professor Lewis has so far exercised logic only as an instrument of scholarship. He next turns to argument and writes an article entitled "The White-Collar Worker Is in a Sad Plight." In support of this proposition he offers statistics representing thousands of specific instances, all gleaned in his research. A few exceptions may be presented, but his conclusion stands.

Induction is used in argument chiefly to provide the proof necessary to support a conclusion. The steps by which the conclusion was drawn may or may not be given, and the conclusion is presented first instead of last; but the convincing logic is inductive.

B. DEDUCTION

Deduction, the opposite of induction, proceeds from the general to the specific. Professor Lewis's son decides to be a college professor. In view of his own recent researches, Professor Lewis asks, "Why?" The son replies, "Because college teachers have steady incomes, old-age security, a high life expectancy, cultural surroundings, and the respect of society; and they enjoy their work." The son has done a great deal of thinking, but the case which he finally builds to convince his father is based on a series of deductions, each something like this:

> College teachers have steady (if modest) incomes.
> I shall be a college teacher.
> Therefore I shall have a steady income.

This is a *syllogism,* the characteristic device of deduction. Too much can be said about the syllogism, but a few facts are essential. All syllogisms consist of a *major premise,* a *minor premise,* and a *conclusion.* The major premise names a class of individuals and gives an attribute common to all members of that class. The minor premise states that a certain individual is a member of the class or (in a negative syllogism) that the individual does not share the attribute named. The conclusion asserts that the individual therefore shares the attribute named or (in a negative syllogism) that the individual therefore is not a member of the class named. The class is called the *middle term,* the individual is called the *minor term,* and the attribute is called the *major term.* Each term appears twice, thus:

Positive Syllogism

MAJOR PREMISE: All *Phi Betta Kappa members* have *high averages,*
        A   B

MINOR PREMISE: *John* is a *Phi Beta Kappa member.*
       C   A

CONCLUSION: *John* must have a *high average.*
      C   B

Negative Syllogism

MAJOR PREMISE: All *Phi Beta Kappa members* have *high averages.*
        A   B

MINOR PREMISE: *He* does not have a *high average.*
       C   B

CONCLUSION: *He* cannot be a *Phi Beta Kappa member.*
     C   A

Logicians know many ways of stating valid syllogisms; but the two situations represented by syllogisms do not vary and, fortunately, can be shown schematically:

POSITIVE SYLLOGISM   NEGATIVE SYLLOGISM

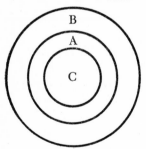
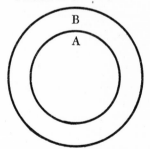

B—major term, "high average"
A—middle term, "Phi Beta Kappa members"
C—minor term, "John" or "He"

The positive form clearly shows that, since A is within B and C within A, C is inevitably within B. The negative form shows that, since C is not within B, it cannot possibly be within A.

The diagram can therefore be used as a test of soundness. Suppose the syllogism were

> All Phi Beta Kappa members have high averages.
> John has a high average.
> Therefore he must be a Phi Beta Kappa member.

This syllogism contains what is called a *fallacy,* an error in logic. Fallacies in form may occur in the statement of either of the premises or the conclusion. In this example the diagram would show:

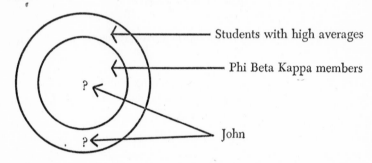

Students with high averages

Phi Beta Kappa members

? John

?

John may be among those with high averages who are members of Phi Beta Kappa, but he may not be. The fault is in the statement of the minor premise.

The following are some of the essential conditions of the syllogism:

1. The premises must be true. The major premise may be of two varieties: (1) an inductive generalization, such as "All insects have six legs," or (2) a commonly accepted assumption, such as "The death of a friend is cause for grief."

2. There must be three terms, and only three.

3. Each term must appear twice, and only twice.

4. Any qualifying word such as "usually" or "most" must appear in only one premise, and its qualification must be accounted for in the conclusion.

5. A negative premise requires a negative conclusion, and only one premise can be negative.

6. The middle term must be modified by "all" or "no" if the conclusion is to be an absolute statement. (Qualified conclusions are often useful, however.)

Deduction is the essential logic of cause-to-effect argument. The cause is actually the minor term as it appears in the minor premise, and the effect is the major term as it appears in the conclusion. The major premise is sometimes omitted, but it must be obvious and acceptable before the argument can be convincing. The first argument in Mr. Roosevelt's plea for the St. Lawrence Seaway Project would fall into this syllogism:

> Electric power aids the war effort. [Understood.]
> The proposed seaway would provide 2,200,000 horsepower of low-cost electricity.
> Therefore the proposed seaway would aid the war effort.

The reasoning seems sound, but each argument of this kind must be tested on three points: (1) Is the cause sufficient to bring about the desired effect? (2) Would another cause produce the same effect more satisfactorily? (3) Will the cause produce undesirable effects as well as the good ones expected? Mr. Roosevelt shows that over two million horsepower would result—surely a significant amount. He points out that steam power would serve as well, but that all facilities are needed elsewhere. And he anticipates the obvious question about resulting expense in his term "low-cost."

NOTE.—Deduction is also used, in a different way, in reasoning from effect back to cause. But this use is seldom involved in argument; it is essentially exposition—analysis of causes. It is therefore not discussed here.

III. ORGANIZATION

The organization of argument regularly falls into five main divisions.

1. The introduction attempts to put the reader into an agreeable frame of mind. It must convince him that the writer is a reasonable

person approaching him as another reasonable person on a problem of real importance.

2. The second part states the proposition and, if necessary, defines terms used in the proposition or conditions essential to the argument.

3. The next part (not always present) announces the basic issues into which the proposition is divided, the assertions which the writer feels he must prove in order to establish his proposition.

4. The main portion of the argument consists of the proof offered in support of the basic issues or assertions.

5. The conclusion, or peroration, summarizes the whole argument in such a way as to emphasize the main points made and asserts the writer's conviction that his case is proved.

IV. THE PROBLEM OF FAIRNESS

A study of unfair tactics is not so useful to the writer as to the reader, perhaps. Advertisements and political propaganda so bristle with abuses of logic and with emotional appeal that the citizen is hard pressed to keep either his money or his liberty. Yet the very honest writer, if uninformed, may involuntarily be unfair. Here are some common abuses.

1. The hasty generalization—jumping to a conclusion on too little evidence; "The cashier at X Market is dishonest. She short-changed me yesterday."

2. Assuming as true the proposition to be proved: "This well-qualified and honest man is the best candidate." Two well-known devices, *name-calling* and the *glittering generality,* partake of this fallacy. Name-calling: "I can prove that this thief must have taken the pearls." Glittering generality: "My improved tax system would benefit everyone."

3. Ignoring the question—diverting attention to a seemingly pertinent but actually irrelevant matter: "The principles that Washington and Jefferson fought for must not be compromised." We would rather support them because they are still good principles than because Washington and Jefferson fought for them. Three major fallacies are recognized as ignoring the question: *ad hominem, ad populum,* and *ad verecundiam. Ad hominem* diverts attention to the man and ignores the issue, as in "Come on now,

vote for Joey White. He's a local boy and a fine fellow." A candidate may be a local boy (all candidates are, somewhere) and a fine fellow, but still be a bad public servant. *Ad populum* appeals to known desires and likes of the public in general: desire for conformity, as in "Everybody's going to vote for Willie; make it a landslide"—the "bandwagon" device; liking for plain people, as in "Plain Hal, the farmer's pal"—the "plain folks" device; fondness for children, home, mother, and so on. *Ad verecundiam* transfers to the man or proposition the approval connected with something else. John Blank may publicize his church attendance—the "transfer" device, and the incumbent governor may give his approval of Blank—the "testimonial" device; neither does much to prove Blank would make a good governor.

4. *Non sequitur*—a conclusion which does not follow from the premises given or from the facts observed. This rather vague and carelessly used term is usually applied to any conclusion not well thought out. A teacher says, "Too many high grades on this examination: evidently it was too easy." His conclusion does not necessarily follow; the students might have studied harder than usual, or it may be that he has taught the material exceptionally well. A special form of the *non sequitur* is the *post hoc ergo propter hoc* (after this, therefore because of this) fallacy, in which a simple time relation is represented as causal. Mother says, "I knew you'd catch cold. You got your feet wet Saturday."

5. False analogy—the assumption of greater similarity between two situations than actually exists. The analogy implied in "Don't change horses in the middle of the stream" may well argue against changing typewriters in the middle of a thesis, but not against changing presidents in the middle of a war or a depression. The danger of changing horses is that the rider may fall into the stream (or make many errors on the unaccustomed typewriter), not that the new horse is untried. In changing presidents there is no danger that the country will fall during the election procedure, and the people are presumably engaged in judging the qualifications of the candidates before they make the change.

6. False dilemma—presenting only two alternatives when others are available: "The time has come when we must choose between free enterprise and a course which will lead to complete

socialization of industry and business." Not necessarily; we may continue to prefer our blend to either of the pure varieties.

EXERCISES

1. Analyze the following statements for logical validity or fallacy. Wherever possible, state carefully the implied inductions or deductions; use the syllogism when appropriate. Indicate the nature of all fallacies.

    a. I shot as soon as I saw the Swastika on his helmet.
    b. As Maine goes, so goes the nation.
    c. Join the Navy and see the world.
    d. I told you taxes would go up if we elected Doakes governor.
    e. I don't want to hear any more about him. I won't have any commies working for me.
    f. Senator Paul _____, like the apostle for whom he is named, wishes to improve the conditions of his fellow men.
    g. Boys, would you like to be the first in your neighborhood to have a regular Space-Suit?
    h. Eat Rox, the cereal of athletes.
    i. In college you have to choose between being a grind and being a good-time Harry.
    j. Henry Ford would have made an excellent President of the United States because of his years of experience as an extremely successful business executive.

2. Make up, and diagram, five valid syllogisms and five fallacious ones.
3. Examine Huxley's use of analogy, in the preceding selection, and decide why Huxley uses it and whether he uses it fairly.
4. Turner's subject is the same as Huxley's, but the two pieces are obviously different. Turner's article was originally a chapter in a composition handbook and Huxley's address was delivered to a lay audience. Exactly how, then, would their purposes differ?
5. How do the differences of purpose affect the tone?
6. How do the differences of purpose account for the greater detail in Turner? For instance, do Huxley's discussions of experimental verification and *vera causa* cover all points listed by Turner as necessary conditions of the syllogism and tests of a cause-to-effect argument?
7. What method of development used by Huxley does Turner also rely upon heavily?

Too Many Bad Boys

A STUDENT THEME

[1] Pittsfield, like cities everywhere, has always had bad boys, even in the "old days" when father was a boy and the city was a mere town of six thousand souls. But it was different then. Bad boys were rare enough to be known individually, by name and specialty. Some merely eschewed church and took to cigarettes at much too early an age. Some stole watermelons and even an occasional chicken. Now and then one actually stole his Uncle Hiram's six-shooter and high-tailed it for the West. But these severe aberrations occurred hardly one in a generation. Most youngsters were content to scalp, rob, and shoot each other down in sham battles along the levee. Larcenous spirits signed on pirate rafts and raided Jackson's Island. Those were days to be remembered.

[2] Today bad boys are not rare, and their escapades are not entertaining. Each year the courts handle over a thousand delinquency cases. The official cost is about $50,000, but the actual cost is much greater. Property damage and loss cannot be estimated, but it is considerable. When a boy is sent to reform school, the cost to the state rises nearly a thousand dollars. Many juvenile offenders become adult criminals and swell the total even more. And the greatest cost is not in dollars but in human character. Evil in a boy goes a long way.

[3] What has happened to make so many boys turn bad? Several things, but an important one is the loss of a place to play. Vacant lots are filled now, and there are too many children per square inch of lawn. And the levee and the river bottom have become the factory district. Today's men labor where yesterday's boys played Indian and scout. And nobody wants to raid the sewage disposal plant on Jackson's Island. Civilization has come.

[4] There is a solution, however. We can restore what we have taken away. A system of well-equipped, well-supervised play-

grounds would do much to alleviate our juvenile delinquency problem.

[5] Boys must have a place to play. They must be able to run, jump, and shout until they are tired. They must be able to throw things, make noise, and fight each other in some way. Whether these urges are innate or learned we may well leave to the investigations of psychologists, but we cannot await their findings. Boys *are* that way and seem always to have been. And, as the old saying has it, "The Devil finds work for idle hands." When there is nothing to do, a boy will find something. Too many boys find the wrong thing. On a good playground our boys could work off their excess energy and competitive urges in healthy play.

[6] Each playground must of course have good supervisors. In a way such men are professional fathers. They teach boys how to play different games, how to get along together, and how to take care of their equipment; they show sympathy and care for the injured, and they treat all boys alike. In these very teachings and actions they inculcate morality. There was a time when nearly all boys went to church on Sunday. The moral code they learned there might have been trite and even naive; but it was clear, and it seemed to work. On other days the home was a moral influence. Today churchgoing is not enforced by social pressure, and those who most need to go do not. And it is a sad but not seriously contested fact that in general the home is not as strong a moral influence as it once was. But boys are still boys, and they will still obey and imitate a man they admire. Good playground supervisors could more than repay their salaries, even on a dollar basis.

[7] Poverty is another cause of delinquency. Boys sometimes steal in order to buy play equipment or to buy entertainment in some form—not always a good form. Or they may simply feel angry and resentful of their poverty and want to be as "good" as other boys. Playgrounds will not remove the actual poverty of any poor boy, but they will alleviate the effects of it. On the playground the poor boy associates on equal terms with more fortunate youngsters and finds real friends among them. He resents his condition less. And he actually shares the use and ownership of the publicly owned playground and equipment. He has no need to steal.

[8] Finally, the playground provides a healthy social life. Boys are people; they must have social life. When they are on their own, the social life they find may not be good. The juvenile "athletic clubs" organized by boy gangs of our great cities are notorious. Boys who join simply for companionship are soon taught gambling and drawn into burglary by older boys, and the entertainment they find is not always purely athletic. The wholesome companionship of a public park or playground seems preferable.

[9] A public playground program, like any other public project, must be a good one. There must be enough play space, distributed so as to be available to all residents of the city; and there must be enough supervisors, chosen for their attractive personalities and known interest in the work. The cost of such a program would be great. But if the cost were as much as $100,000 a year, it would probably be cheaper in the long run than allowing delinquency to continue unchecked.

EXERCISES

1. Mark off the introduction. In what way does it serve as a general introduction to the subject? In what way is it specially designed as an introduction to argument? State the function of each paragraph in the introduction.
2. Where is the statement of the proposition? Is it clearly stated? Does it cover in general terms all issues raised later? Exactly what does "alleviate" (paragraph 4) mean?
3. Mark off the main body of the argument. Divide it into its four main parts, or items of proof.
4. Write out the syllogism implied in each part of the proof. Each syllogism can be stated in more than one way, but the situation represented will be the same.
5. Can you tell whether the major premises are inductive generalizations or common assumptions? Do they seem valid? How could you check them?
6. The minor premises are the crucial points in the proof (assuming that the major premises are acceptable). Do they seem to be sound? Which are obviously true? Which need support? Is the necessary support present?
7. Does the writer give adequate attention to the three tests of validity in cause-to-effect argument? Which concerns him most?

8. Do you find any instances of unfairness, conscious or unconscious?
9. Does the argument convince you, or do you wish more information on some points? Where could you find further information?
10. What objections to his plan has the writer anticipated?
11. Is the conclusion of the whole composition satisfactory? Either show why it is good or suggest improvements.
12. If you need practice in outlining you will find this selection easy to reduce to an orderly outline.

Declaration of Independence

In Congress, July 4, 1776

A declaration by the representatives of the United States of America, in Congress Assembled

[1] When, in the course of human events, it becomes necessary for one people to dissolve the political bands which have connected them with another, and to assume, among the powers of the earth, the separate and equal station to which the laws of nature and of nature's God entitle them, a decent respect to the opinions of mankind requires that they should declare the causes which impel them to the separation.

[2] We hold these truths to be self-evident:—That all men are created equal; that they are endowed by their Creator with certain unalienable rights; that among these are life, liberty, and the pursuit of happiness. That, to secure these rights, governments are instituted among men, deriving their just powers from the consent of the governed; that, whenever [3] any form of government becomes destructive of these ends, it is the right of the people to alter or to abolish it, and to institute a new government, laying its foundation on such principles, and organizing its powers in such form, as to them shall seem most likely to effect their safety and happiness. Prudence, indeed, will dictate, that governments long established should not be changed for light and

transient causes; and accordingly all experience hath shown that mankind are more disposed to suffer while evils are sufferable, than to right themselves by abolishing the forms to which they are accustomed. But when a long train of abuses and usurpations, pursuing invariably the same object, evinces a design to reduce them under absolute despotism, it is their right, it is their duty, to throw off such government, and to provide new guards for their future security.

[4] Such has been the patient sufferance of these colonies; and such is now the necessity which constrains them to alter their former systems of government. The history of the present King of Great Britain is a history of repeated injuries and usurpations, all having in direct object the establishment of an absolute tyranny over these states. To prove this, let facts be submitted to a candid world.

He has refused his assent to laws the most wholesome and necessary for the public good.

He has forbidden his governors to pass laws of immediate and pressing importance, unless suspended in their operation till his assent should be obtained; and when so suspended, he has utterly neglected to attend to them.

He has refused to pass other laws for the accommodation of large districts of people, unless those people would relinquish the right of representation in the legislature—a right inestimable to them, and formidable to tyrants only.

He has called together legislative bodies at places unusual, uncomfortable, and distant from the depository of their public records, for the sole purpose of fatiguing them into compliance with his measure.

He has dissolved representative houses repeatedly, for opposing, with manly firmness, his invasions on the rights of the people.

He has refused, for a long time after such dissolutions, to cause others to be elected, whereby the legislative powers, incapable of annihilation, have returned to the people at large for their exercise; the State remaining, in the mean time, exposed to all the dangers of invasions from without, and convulsions within.

He has endeavored to prevent the population of these States; for that purpose obstructing the laws for the naturalization of foreigners; refusing to pass others to encourage their migration hither, and raising the conditions of new appropriations of lands.

He has obstructed the administration of justice, by refusing his assent to laws for establishing judiciary powers.

He has made judges dependent on his will alone for the tenure of their offices, and the amount and payment of their salaries.

He has erected a multitude of new offices, and sent hither swarms of officers to harass our people and eat out their substance.

He has kept among us in times of peace, standing armies, without the consent of our legislatures.

He has affected to render the military independent of, and superior to, the civil power.

He has combined with others to subject us to a jurisdiction foreign to our constitutions, and unacknowledged by our laws; giving his assent to their acts of pretended legislation:

For quartering large bodies of armed troops among us;

For protecting them, by a mock trial, from punishment for any murders which they should commit on the inhabitants of these States;

For cutting off our trade with all parts of the world;

For imposing taxes on us without our consent;

For depriving us, in many cases, of the benefits of trial by jury;

For transporting us beyond seas, to be tried for pretended offences;

For abolishing the free system of English laws in a neighboring province, establishing therein an arbitary government, and enlarging its boundaries, so as to render it at once an example and fit instrument for introducing the same absolute rule into these colonies;

For taking away our charters, abolishing our most valuable laws, and altering, fundamentally, the forms of our governments;

For suspending our own legislatures, and declaring themselves invested with power to legislate for us in all cases whatsoever.

He has abdicated government here, by declaring us out of his protection, and waging war against us.

He has plundered our seas, ravaged our coasts, burned our towns, and destroyed the lives of our people.

He is at this time transporting large armies of foreign mercenaries to complete the works of death, desolation and tyranny, already begun with circumstances of cruelty and perfidy scarcely paralleled in the most barbarous ages, and totally unworthy the head of a civilized nation.

He has constrained our fellow-citizens, taken captive on the high seas, to bear arms against their country, to become the executioners of their friends and brethren; or to fall themselves by their hands.

He has excited domestic insurrection among us, and has endeavored to bring on the inhabitants of our frontiers the merciless Indian savages, whose known rule of warfare is an undistinguished destruction of all ages, sexes, and conditions.

In every stage of these oppressions we have petitioned for redress in the most humble terms; our repeated petitions have been answered only by repeated injury. A prince whose character is thus marked by every act which may define a tyrant, is unfit to be the ruler of a free people.

Nor have we been wanting in our attentions to our British brethren. We have warned them, from time to time, of attempts by their legislature to extend an unwarrantable jurisdiction over us. We have reminded them of the circumstances of our emigration and settlement here. We have appealed to their native justice and magnanimity; and we have conjured them, by the ties of our common kindred, to disavow these usurpations, which would inevitably interrupt our connections and correspondence. They, too, have been deaf to the voice of justice and consanguinity. We must, therefore, acquiesce in the necessity which denounces our separation, and hold them, as we hold the rest of mankind, enemies in war, in peace friends.

We, therefore, the Representatives of the United States of America, in General Congress assembled, appealing to the Supreme Judge of the world for the rectitude of our intentions, do, in the name and by the authority of the good people of these colonies, solemnly publish and declare, That these united Colonies are, and of right ought to be, free and independent states; that they are absolved from all allegiance to the British crown, and that all political connection between them and the state of Great Britain is, and ought to be, totally dissolved; and that, as free and independent states, they have full power to levy war, conclude peace, contract alliances, establish commerce, and do all other acts and things which independent states may of right do. And, for the support of this declaration, with a firm reliance on the protection of Divine Providence, we mutually pledge to each other our lives, our fortunes, and our sacred honor.

EXERCISES

1. What is the purpose of section 1?
2. Why is section 2 necessary? Were the "self-evident" truths probably acceptable to all men, even British, in 1776? Are they still? On what belief is the assumption of equal rights based? Can there be any other basis?
3. What syllogism is implied in sections 3 and 4? Indicate the three terms of the syllogism. Where is the term "these ends" elaborated?
4. To what part of the syllogism is the greatest resistance expected? (It is the strength of this expected resistance that makes necessary so much proof of the assertion and therefore makes the main body of the argument inductive.)
5. Where is the proposition stated?
6. Where is the proof? Would any single item of it warrant the generalization being proved? Does the whole body of evidence justify it?
7. Do you find any signs of unfairness or logical fallacy?

Words and Behaviour

ALDOUS HUXLEY

[1] Words form the thread on which we string our experiences. Without them we should live spasmodically and intermittently. Hatred itself is not so strong that animals will not forget it, if

From *The Olive Tree*, by Aldous Huxley, copyright, 1937, by Aldous Huxley. Reprinted by permission of Harper & Brothers.

distracted, even in the presence of the enemy. Watch a pair of cats, crouching on the brink of a fight. Balefully the eyes glare; from far down in the throat of each come bursts of a strange, strangled noise of defiance; as though animated by a life of their own, the tails twitch and tremble. What aimed intensity of loathing! Another moment and surely there must be an explosion. But no; all of a sudden one of the two creatures turns away, hoists a hind leg in a more than fascist salute and, with the same fixed and focussed attention as it had given a moment before to its enemy, begins to make a lingual toilet. Animal love is as much at the mercy of distractions as animal hatred. The dumb creation lives a life made up of discrete and mutually irrelevant episodes. Such as it is, the consistency of human characters is due to the words upon which all human experiences are strung. We are purposeful because we can describe our feelings in rememberable words, can justify and rationalize our desires in terms of some kind of argument. Faced by an enemy we do not allow an itch to distract us from our emotions; the mere word "enemy" is enough to keep us reminded of our hatred, to convince us that we do well to be angry. Similarly the word "love" bridges for us those chasms of momentary indifference and boredom which gape from time to time between even the most ardent lovers. Feeling and desire provide us with our motive power; words give continuity to what we do and to a considerable extent determine our direction. Inappropriate and badly chosen words vitiate thought and lead to wrong or foolish conduct. Most ignorances are vincible, and in the greater number of cases stupidity is what the Buddha pronounced it to be, a sin. For, consciously or sub-consciously, it is with deliberation that we do not know or fail to understand—because incomprehension allows us, with a good conscience, to evade unpleasant obligations and responsibilities, because ignorance is the best excuse for going on doing what one likes, but ought not, to do. Our egotisms are incessantly fighting to preserve themselves, not only from external enemies, but also from the assaults of the other and better self with which they are so uncomfortably associated. Ignorance is egotism's most effective defence against the Dr. Jekyll in us who desires perfection; stupidity, its subtlest stratagem. If, as so often happens, we choose to give continuity to our experience by means of words which falsify the facts, this is because the falsification is somehow to our advantage as egoists. [2] Consider, for example, the case of war. War is enormously discreditable to those who order it to be waged and even to those who merely tolerate its existence. Furthermore, to developed sensibilities the facts of war are revolting and horrifying. To falsify these facts, and by so doing to make war seem less evil than it really is, and our own responsibility in tolerating war less heavy, is doubly to our advantage. By suppressing and distorting the truth, we protect our sensibilities and preserve our self-esteem. Now, language is, among other things, a device which men use for suppressing and distorting the truth. Finding the reality of war too unpleasant to contemplate, we create a verbal alternative to that reality, parallel with it, but in quality quite different from it. That which we contemplate thenceforward is not that to which we react emotionally and upon which we pass our moral judgments, is not war as it is in fact, but the fiction of war as it exists in our pleasantly falsifying verbiage. Our stupidity in using inappropriate language turns out, on analysis, to be the most refined cunning.

[3] The most shocking fact about war is that its victims and its instruments are individual human beings, and that these individual human beings are condemned by the monstrous conventions of politics to murder or be murdered in quarrels not their own, to inflict upon the innocent and, innocent themselves of any crime against their enemies, to suffer cruelties of every kind.

[4] The language of strategy and politics is designed, so far as it is possible, to conceal this fact, to make it appear as though wars were not fought by individuals drilled to murder one another in cold blood and without provocation, but either by impersonal and therefore wholly non-moral and impassible forces, or else by personified abstractions.

[5] Here are a few examples of the first kind of falsification. In place of "cavalrymen" or "foot-soldiers" military writers like to speak of "sabres" and "rifles." Here is a sentence from a description of the Battle of Marengo: "According to Victor's report, the French retreat was orderly; it is certain, at any rate, that the regiments held together, for the six thousand Austrian sabres found no opportunity to charge home." The battle is between

sabres in line and muskets in échelon—a mere clash of iron-mongery.

[6] On other occasions there is no question of anything so vulgarly material as ironmongery. The battles are between Platonic ideas, between the abstractions of physics and mathematics. Forces interact; weights are flung into scales; masses are set in motion. Or else it is all a matter of geometry. Lines swing and sweep; are protracted or curved; pivot on a fixed point.

[7] Alternatively the combatants are personal, in the sense that they are personifications. There is "the enemy," in the singular, making "his" plans, striking "his" blows. The attribution of personal characteristics to collectivities, to geographical expressions, to institutions, is a source, as we shall see, of endless confusions in political thought, of innumerable political mistakes and crimes. Personification in politics is an error which we make because it is to our advantage as egotists to be able to feel violently proud of our country and of ourselves as belonging to it, and to believe that all the misfortunes due to our own mistakes are really the work of the Foreigner. It is easier to feel violently towards a person than towards an abstraction; hence our habit of making political personifications. A particular collectivity, the army or the warring nation, is given the name, and along with the name, the attributes of a single person, in order that we may be able to love or hate it more intensely than we could do if we thought of it as what it really is: a number of diverse individuals. In other cases personification is used for the purpose of concealing the fundamental absurdity and monstrosity of war. What is absurd and monstrous about war is that men who have no personal quarrel should be trained to murder one another in cold blood. By personifying opposing armies or countries, we are able to think of war as a conflict between individuals. The same result is obtained by writing of war as though it were carried on exclusively by the generals in command and not by the private soldiers in their armies. ("Rennenkampf had pressed back von Schubert.") The implication in both cases is that war is indistinguishable from a bout of fisticuffs in a bar room. Whereas in reality it is profoundly different. A scrap between two individuals is forgivable; mass murder, deliberately organized, is a

monstrous iniquity. We still choose to use war as an instrument of policy; and to comprehend the full wickedness and absurdity of war would therefore be inconvenient. For, once we understood, we should have to make some effort to get rid of the abominable thing. Accordingly, when we talk about war, we use a language which conceals or embellishes its reality. Ignoring the facts, so far as we possibly can, we imply that battles are not fought by soldiers, but by things, principles, allegories, personified collectivities, or (at the most human) by opposing commanders, pitched against one another in single combat. For the same reason, when we have to describe the processes and the results of war, we employ a rich variety of euphemisms. Even the most violently patriotic and militaristic are reluctant to call a spade by its own name. To conceal their intentions even from themselves, they make use of picturesque metaphors. We find them, for example, clamouring for war planes numerous and powerful enough to go and "destroy the hornets in their nests"—in other words, to go and throw thermite, high explosives and vesicants upon the inhabitants of neighbouring countries before they have time to come and do the same to us. And how reassuring is the language of historians and strategists! They write admiringly of those military geniuses who know "when to strike at the enemy's line" (a single combatant deranges the geometrical constructions of a personification); when to "turn his flank"; when to "execute an enveloping movement." As though they were engineers discussing the strength of materials and the distribution of stresses, they talk of abstract entities called "man power" and "fire power." They sum up the long-drawn sufferings and atrocities of trench warfare in the phrase, "a war of attrition;" the massacre and mangling of human beings is assimilated to the grinding of a lens.

[8] A dangerously abstract word, which figures in all discussions about war, is "force." Those who believe in organizing collective security by means of military pacts against a possible aggressor are particularly fond of this word. "You cannot," they say, "have international justice unless you are prepared to impose it by force." "Peace-loving countries must unite to use force against aggressive dictatorships." "Democratic institutions must be protected, if need be, by force." And so on.

[9] Now, the word "force," when used in reference to human relations, has no single, definite meaning. There is the "force" used by parents when, without resort to any kind of physical violence, they compel their children to act or refrain from acting in some particular way. There is the "force" used by attendants in an asylum when they try to prevent a maniac from hurting himself or others. There is the "force" used by the police when they control a crowd, and that other "force" which they use in a baton charge. And finally there is the "force" used in war. This, of course, varies with the technological devices at the disposal of the belligerents, with the policies they are pursuing, and with the particular circumstances of the war in question. But in general it may be said that, in war, "force" connotes violence and fraud used to the limit of the combatants' capacity.

[10] Variations in quantity, if sufficiently great, produce variations in quality. The "force" that is war, particularly modern war, is very different from the "force" that is police action, and the use of the same abstract word to describe the two dissimilar processes is profoundly misleading. (Still more misleading, of course, is the explicit assimilation of a war, waged by allied League-of-Nations powers against an aggressor, to police action against a criminal. The first is the use of violence and fraud without limit against innocent and guilty alike; the second is the use of strictly limited violence and a minimum of fraud exclusively against the guilty.)

[11] Reality is a succession of concrete and particular situations. When we think about such situations we should use the particular and concrete words which apply to them. If we use abstract words which apply equally well (and equally badly) to other, quite dissimilar situations, it is certain that we shall think incorrectly.

[12] Let us take the sentences quoted above and translate the abstract word "force" into language that will render (however inadequately) the concrete and particular realities of contemporary warfare.

[13] "You cannot have international justice, unless you are prepared to impose it by force." Translated, this becomes: "You cannot have international justice unless you are prepared, with a view to imposing a just settlement, to drop thermite, high explosives and vesicants upon the inhabitants of foreign cities and to

have thermite, high explosives and vesicants dropped in return upon the inhabitants of your cities." At the end of this proceeding, justice is to be imposed by the victorious party—that is, if there is a victorious party. It should be remarked that justice was to have been imposed by the victorious party at the end of the last war. But, unfortunately, after four years of fighting, the temper of the victors was such that they were quite incapable of making a just settlement. The Allies are reaping in Nazi Germany what they sowed at Versailles. The victors of the next war will have undergone intensive bombardments with thermite, high explosives and vesicants. Will their temper be better than that of the Allies in 1918? Will they be in a fitter state to make a just settlement? The answer, quite obviously, is: No. It is psychologically all but impossible that justice should be secured by the methods of contemporary warfare.

[14] The next two sentences may be taken together. "Peace-loving countries must unite to use force against aggressive dictatorships. Democratic institutions must be protected, if need be, by force." Let us translate. "Peace-loving countries must unite to throw thermite, high explosives and vesicants on the inhabitants of countries ruled by aggressive dictators. They must do this, and of course abide the consequences, in order to preserve peace and democratic institutions." Two questions immediately propound themselves. First, is it likely that peace can be secured by a process calculated to reduce the orderly life of our complicated societies to chaos? And, second, is it likely that democratic institutions will flourish in a state of chaos? Again, the answers are pretty clearly in the negative.

[15] By using the abstract word "force," instead of terms which at least attempt to describe the realities of war as it is to-day, the preachers of collective security through military collaboration disguise from themselves and from others, not only the contemporary facts, but also the probable consequences of their favourite policy. The attempt to secure justice, peace and democracy by "force" seems reasonable enough until we realize, first, that this non-committal word stands, in the circumstances of our age, for activities which can hardly fail to result in social chaos; and second, that the consequences of social chaos are in-

justice, chronic warfare and tyranny. The moment we think in concrete and particular terms of the concrete and particular process called "modern war," we see that a policy which worked (or at least didn't result in complete disaster) in the past has no prospect whatever of working in the immediate future. The attempt to secure justice, peace and democracy by means of a "force," which means at this particular moment of history, thermite, high explosives and vesicants, is about as reasonable as the attempt to put out a fire with a colourless liquid that happens to be, not water, but petrol.

[16] What applies to the "force" that is war applies in large measure to the "force" that is revolution. It seems inherently very unlikely that social justice and social peace can be secured by thermite, high explosives and vesicants. At first, it may be, the parties in a civil war would hesitate to use such instruments on their fellow countrymen. But there can be little doubt that, if the conflict were prolonged (as it probably would be between the evenly balanced Right and Left of a highly industrialized society), the combatants would end by losing their scruples.

[17] The alternatives confronting us seem to be plain enough. Either we invent and conscientiously employ a new technique for making revolutions and settling international disputes; or else we cling to the old technique and, using "force" (that is to say, thermite, high explosives and vesicants), destroy ourselves. Those who, for whatever motive, disguise the nature of the second alternative under inappropriate language, render the world a grave disservice. They lead us into one of the temptations we find it hardest to resist—the temptation to run away from reality, to pretend that facts are not what they are. Like Shelley (but without Shelley's acute awareness of what he was doing) we are perpetually weaving

> A shroud of talk to hide us from the sun
> Of this familiar life.

We protect our minds by an elaborate system of abstractions, ambiguities, metaphors and similes from the reality we do not wish to know too clearly; we lie to ourselves, in order that we may still have the excuse of ignorance, the alibi of stupidity and incomprehension, possessing which we can continue with a good conscience to commit and tolerate the most monstrous crimes:

> The poor wretch who has learned his only prayers
> From curses, who knows scarcely words enough
> To ask a blessing from his Heavenly Father,
> Becomes a fluent phraseman, absolute
> And technical in victories and defeats,
> And all our dainty terms for fratricide;
> Terms which we trundle smoothly o'er our tongues
> Like mere abstractions, empty sounds to which
> We join no meaning and attach no form!
> As if the soldier died without a wound:
> As if the fibres of this godlike frame
> Were gored without a pang: as if the wretch
> Who fell in battle, doing bloody deeds,
> Passed off to Heaven translated and not killed;
> As though he had no wife to pine for him,
> No God to judge him.

[18] The language we use about war is inappropriate, and its inappropriateness is designed to conceal a reality so odious that we do not wish to know it. The language we use about politics is also inappropriate; but here our mistake has a different purpose. Our principal aim in this case is to arouse and, having aroused, to rationalize and justify such intrinsically agreeable sentiments as pride and hatred, self-esteem and contempt for others. To achieve this end we speak about the facts of politics in words which more or less completely misrepresent them.

[19] The concrete realities of politics are individual human beings, living together in national groups. Politicians—and to some extent we are all politicians—substitute abstractions for these concrete realities, and having done this, proceed to invest each abstraction with an appearance of concreteness by personifying it. For example, the concrete reality of which "Britain" is the abstraction consists of some forty-odd millions of diverse individuals living on an island off the west coast of Europe. The personification of this abstraction appears, in classical fancy-dress and holding a very large toasting fork, on the backside of our copper coinage; appears in verbal form, every time we talk about international politics.

"Britain," the abstraction from forty millions of Britons, is endowed with thoughts, sensibilities and emotions, even with a sex —for, in spite of John Bull, the country is always a female.

[20] Now, it is of course possible that "Britain" is more than a mere name—is an entity that possesses some kind of reality distinct from that of the individuals constituting the group to which the name is applied. But this entity, if it exists, is certainly not a young lady with a toasting fork; nor is it possible to believe (though some eminent philosophers have preached the doctrine) that it should possess anything in the nature of a personal will. One must agree with T. H. Green that "there can be nothing in a nation, however exalted its mission, or in a society, however perfectly organized, which is not in the persons composing the nation or the society. . . . We cannot suppose a national spirit and will to exist except as the spirit and will of individuals." But the moment we start resolutely thinking about our world in terms of individual persons we find ourselves at the same time thinking in terms of universality. "The great rational religions," writes Professor Whitehead, "are the outcome of the emergence of a religious consciousness that is universal, as distinguished from tribal, or even social. Because it is universal, it introduces the note of solitariness." (And he might have added that, because it is solitary, it introduces the note of universality.) "The reason of this connection between universality and solitude is that universality is a disconnection from immediate surroundings." And conversely the disconnection from immediate surroundings, particularly such social surroundings as the tribe or nation the insistence on the person as the fundamental reality, leads to the conception of an all-embracing unity.

[21] A nation, then, may be more than a mere abstraction, may possess some kind of real existence apart from its constituent members. But there is no reason to suppose that it is a person; indeed, there is every reason to suppose that it isn't. Those who speak as though it were a person (and some go further than this and speak as though it were a personal god), do so because it is to their interest as egotists to make precisely this mistake.

[22] In the case of the ruling class these interests are in part material. The personification of the nation as a sacred being,

different from and superior to its constituent members, is merely
(I quote the words of a great French jurist, Léon Duguit) "a way
of imposing authority by making people believe it is an authority
de jure and not merely *de facto.*" By habitually talking of the
nation as though it were a person with thoughts, feelings and a
will of its own, the rulers of a country legitimate their own powers.
Personification leads easily to deification; and where the nation
is deified, its government ceases to be a mere convenience, like
drains or a telephone system, and, partaking in the sacredness of
the entity it represents, claims to give orders by divine right and
demands the unquestioning obedience due to a god. Rulers seldom
find it hard to recognize their friends. Hegel, the man who
elaborated an inappropriate figure of speech into a complete
philosophy of politics, was a favourite of the Prussian government.
"Es ist," he had written, *"es ist der Gang Gottes in der Welt, das
der Staat ist."* The decoration bestowed on him by Frederick
William III was richly deserved.

[23] Unlike their rulers, the ruled have no material interest in
using inappropriate language about states and nations. For them,
the reward of being mistaken is psychological. The personified and
deified nation becomes, in the minds of the individuals composing
it, a kind of enlargement of themselves. The superhuman qualities
which belong to the young lady with the toasting fork, the young
lady with plaits and a brass *soutiengorge,* the young lady in a
Phrygian bonnet, are claimed by individual Englishmen, Germans
and Frenchmen as being, at least in part, their own. *Dulce et
decorum est pro patria mori.* But there would be no need to die,
no need of war, if it had not been even sweeter to boast and swag-
ger for one's country, to hate, despise, swindle and bully for it.
Loyalty to the personified nation, or to the personified class or
party, justifies the loyal in indulging all those passions which good
manners and the moral code do not allow them to display in
their relations with their neighbours. The personified entity is a
being, not only great and noble, but also insanely proud, vain and
touchy; fiercely rapacious; a braggart; bound by no considerations
of right and wrong. (Hegel condemned as hopelessly shallow all
those who dared to apply ethical standards to the activities of
nations. To condone and applaud every iniquity committed in

the name of the State was to him a sign of philosophical pro-
fundity.) Identifying themselves with this god, individuals find relief from the constraints of ordinary social decency, feel themselves justified in giving rein, within duly prescribed limits, to
their criminal proclivities. As a loyal nationalist or party-man,
one can enjoy the luxury of behaving badly with a good conscience.

[24] The evil passions are further justified by another linguistic
error—the error of speaking about certain categories of persons
as though they were mere embodied abstractions. Foreigners and
those who disagree with us are not thought of as men and women
like ourselves and our fellow-countrymen; they are thought of as
representatives and, so to say, symbols of a class. In so far as
they have any personality at all, it is the personality we mistakenly
attribute to their class—a personality that is, by definition, intrinsically evil. We know that the harming or killing of men and
women is wrong, and we are reluctant consciously to do what we
know to be wrong. But when particular men and women are
thought of merely as representatives of a class, which has previously
been defined as evil and personified in the shape of a devil,
then the reluctance to hurt or murder disappears. Brown, Jones
and Robinson are no longer thought of as Brown, Jones and
Robinson, but as heretics, gentiles, Yids, niggers, barbarians,
Huns, communists, capitalists, fascists, liberals—whichever the
case may be. When they have been called such names and assimilated to the accursed class to which the names apply, Brown,
Jones and Robinson cease to be conceived as what they really
are—human persons—and become for the users of this fatally
inappropriate language mere vermin or, worse, demons whom it
is right and proper to destroy as thoroughly and as painfully as
possible. Wherever persons are present, questions of morality arise.
Rulers of nations and leaders of parties find morality embarrassing. That is why they take such pains to depersonalize their opponents. All propaganda directed against an opposing group has
but one aim: to substitute diabolical abstractions for concrete
persons. The propagandist's purpose is to make one set of people forget that certain other sets of people are human. By robbing
them of their personality, he puts them outside the pale of moral

obligation. Mere symbols can have no rights—particularly when that of which they are symbolical is, by definition, evil.

[25] Politics can become moral only on one condition: that its problems shall be spoken of and thought about exclusively in terms of concrete reality; that is to say, of persons. To depersonify human beings and to personify abstractions are complementary errors which lead, by an inexorable logic, to war between nations and to idolatrous worship of the State, with consequent governmental oppression. All current political thought is a mixture, in varying proportions, between thought in terms of concrete realities and thought in terms of depersonified symbols and personified abstractions. In the democratic countries the problems of internal politics are thought about mainly in terms of concrete reality; those of external politics, mainly in terms of abstractions and symbols. In dictatorial countries the proportion of concrete to abstract and symbolic thought is lower than in democratic countries. Dictators talk little of persons, much of personified abstractions, such as the Nation, the State, the Party, and much of depersonified symbols, such as Yids, Bolshies, Capitalists. The stupidity of politicians who talk about a world of persons as though it were not a world of persons is due in the main to self-interest. In a fictitious world of symbols and personified abstractions, rulers find that they can rule more effectively, and the ruled, that they can gratify instincts which the conventions of good manners and the imperatives of morality demand that they should repress. To think correctly is the condition of behaving well. It is also in itself a moral act; those who would think correctly must resist considerable temptations.

EXERCISES

1. Review the meaning of the words *concrete, abstract, specific,* and *general.* Look up the words *personification* and *metonymy.*
2. Restate what Huxley says in terms of the processes of abstraction, generalization, personification, and the use of metonymy.
3. Show how each of Huxley's main points is related to the first sentence of the essay.
4. Make an outline of the main headings and subheadings of this essay

and a similar outline of T. H. Huxley's address on the scientific method. Which has more detailed information to give? Which uses more space? Which is the more difficult subject? What conclusion can you draw about differences in conciseness of style? Make a similar study of the proportion of space which each writer devotes to each of his main topics.

5. What does Huxley mean by the statements "Most ignorances are vincible" and "Our stupidity . . . turns out . . . to be the most refined cunning"?

6. Explain the errors and dishonesties of language discussed by Huxley in terms of the fallacies in logic discussed by Turner.

7. How does Huxley make the first sentence of the essay especially emphatic? Why should he use such a device of emphasis in the very first sentence?

Cadence is a device of emphasis by sentence rhythm. The end of the sentence is naturally an emphatic position, and the emphasis seems to be increased when the interval between stressed syllables decreases toward the end and the sentence ends in only one unstressed syllable, or one stressed one, or two stressed ones. For example, a sentence in Carl Becker's *Heavenly City of the Eighteenth Century Philosophers* ends thus: "but the faithful would be gathered with God in the Heavenly City, there in perfection and felicity to dwell forever." Conscious stylists use this rhythm for important points, at the end of main divisions, and at the end of their compositions.

8. Mark the stressed and unstressed syllables in the last sentence of paragraph 2. Why should Huxley use a cadence in this sentence? Is there cadence in the first sentence of paragraph 10? Why? Is there a cadence in the last sentence of paragraph 13? Why?

Section B: The Logic of Freedom

Section B contains selections which will demonstrate in immediate and practical ways the use of the principles of logic and fallacies in logic elaborated by the selections in Section A. All the selections deal in one way or another with the logical bases of democracy. The two sections together can form the basis of a good study of practical logic.

The exercises also continue the study of sentence structure, diction, and figurative language, and lead to a comparative study of the widely different styles in Section B.

These pieces are also unified, in a different way, with those in Section C. Through Section B runs the theme of government control, and that is one of the main problems in Section C. Both sections involve the logical interpretation of unified bodies of facts; they may therefore serve as a background for the research paper.

The footnotes to *Areopagitica* are from Milton's *Prose Selections,* edited by Merritt Y. Hughes.

Areopagitica

A Speech for the Liberty of Unlicensed Printing, to the Parliament of England (November 1644)

JOHN MILTON

> *This is true liberty, when free-born men,*
> *Having to advise the public, may speak free,*
> *Which he who can, and will, deserves high praise;*
> *Who neither can, nor will, may hold his peace:*
> *What can be juster in a state than this?*
>   EURIPIDES, *The Suppliants*

[1] They who to states [1] and governors of the commonwealth direct their speech, High Court of Parliament, or, wanting such access in a private condition, write that which they foresee may advance the public good; I suppose them, as at the beginning of no mean endeavour, not a little altered and moved inwardly in their minds: some with doubt of what will be the success,[2] others with fear of what will be the censure;[3] some with hope, others with confidence of what they have to speak. And me perhaps each of these dispositions, as the subject was whereon I entered, may have at other times variously affected; and likely might in these foremost expressions now also disclose which of them swayed most, but that the very attempt of this address thus made, and the thought of whom it hath recourse to, hath got the power within me to a passion far more welcome than incidental to a preface.

[2] Which thought I stay not to confess ere any ask, I shall be blameless, if it be no other than the joy and gratulation [4] which it brings to all who wish and promote their country's liberty; whereof this whole discourse proposed will be a certain testimony, if not a trophy. For this is not the liberty which we can hope, that no grievance ever should arise in the commonwealth—that let no man in this world expect; but when complaints are freely heard,

---

[1] *states:* men of high estate, grandees.
[2] *success:* outcome, consequence.
[3] *censure:* judgment, estimate.
[4] *gratulation:* satisfaction, self-congratulation.

deeply considered, and speedily reformed, then is the utmost bound of civil liberty attained that wise men look for. To which if I now manifest, by the very sound of this which I shall utter, that we are already in good part arrived, and yet from such a steep disadvantage of tyranny and superstition grounded into our principles as was beyond the manhood of a Roman recovery, it will be attributed first, as is must due, to the strong assistance of God our deliverer, next, to your faithful guidance and undaunted wisdom, Lords and Commons of England. Neither is it in God's esteem the diminution of his glory, when honourable things are spoken of good men and worthy magistrates; which if I now first should begin to do, after so fair a progress of your laudable deeds, and such a long obligement upon the whole realm to your indefatigable virtues, I might be justly reckoned among the tardiest and the unwillingest of them that praise ye.

[3] Nevertheless there being three principal things, without which all praising is but courtship and flattery: first, when that only is praised which is solidly worth praise; next, when greatest likelihoods are brought that such things are truly and really in those persons to whom they are ascribed; the other, when he who praises, by showing that such his actual persuasion is of whom he writes, can demonstrate that he flatters not; the former two of these I have heretofore endeavoured, rescuing the employment from him who went about to impair your merits with a trivial and malignant encomium; the latter, as belonging chiefly to mine own acquittal, that whom I so extolled I did not flatter, hath been reserved opportunely to this occasion. For he who freely magnifies what hath been nobly done, and fears not to declare as freely what might be done better, gives ye the best covenant of his fidelity; and that his loyalest affection and his hope waits on your proceedings. His highest praising is not flattery, and his plainest advice is a kind of praising; for though I should affirm and hold by argument that it would fare better with truth, with learning, and the commonwealth, if one of your published orders, which I should name, were called in; yet at the same time it could not but much redound to the lustre of your mild and equal [5] government, whenas private persons are hereby animated to think ye

[5] *equal:* impartial.

better pleased with public advice than other statists [6] have been delighted heretofore with public flattery. And men will then see what difference there is between the magnanimity of a triennial parliament and the jealous haughtiness of prelates and cabin [7] counsellors that usurped of late, whenas they shall observe ye, in the midst of your victories and successes, more gently brooking written exceptions against a voted order than other courts, which had produced nothing worth memory but the weak ostentation of wealth, would have endured the least signified dislike at any sudden proclamation.

[4] If I should thus far presume upon the meek demeanour of your civil [8] and gentle greatness, Lords and Commons, as what your published order hath directly said, that to gainsay, I might defend myself with ease, if any should accuse me of being new or insolent, did they but know how much better I find ye esteem it to imitate the old and elegant humanity of Greece than the barbaric pride of a Hunnish and Norwegian stateliness. And out of those ages to whose polite wisdom and letters we owe that we are not yet Goths and Jutlanders, I could name him who from his private house wrote that discourse to the parliament of Athens, that persuades them to change the form of democracy which was then established. Such honour was done in those days to men who professed the study of wisdom and eloquence, not only in their own country but in other lands, that cities and seigniories heard them gladly and with great respect, if they had aught in public to admonish the state. Thus did Dion Prusaeus, a stranger and a private orator, counsel the Rhodians against a former edict; and I abound with other like examples, which to set here would be superfluous. But if from the industry of a life wholly dedicated to studious labours, and those natural endowments haply not the worst for two and fifty degrees of northern latitude, so much must be derogated as to count me not equal to any of those who had this privilege, I would obtain to be thought not so inferior as yourselves are superior to the most of them who received their counsel; and how far you excel them, be assured, Lords and Com-

---

[6] *statists:* statesmen.
[7] *cabin:* cabinet or council chamber.
[8] *civil:* civilized, polite.

mons, there can no greater testimony appear than when your prudent spirit acknowledges and obeys the voice of reason, from what quarter soever it be heard speaking; and renders ye as willing to repeal any act of your own setting forth as any set forth by your predecessors.

[5] If ye be thus resolved, as it were injury to think ye were not, I know not what should withhold me from presenting ye with a fit instance wherein to show both that love of truth which ye eminently profess, and that uprightness of your judgement which is not wont to be partial to yourselves; by judging over again that order which ye have ordained *to regulate printing: that no book, pamphlet, or paper shall be henceforth printed, unless the same be first approved and licensed by such,* or at least one of such, as shall be thereto appointed. For that part which preserves justly every man's copy [9] to himself, or provides for the poor, I touch not; only wish they be not made pretences to abuse and persecute honest and painful [10] men who offend not in either of these particulars. But that other clause of licensing books, which we thought had died with his brother *quadragesimal* [11] and *matrimonial* when the prelates expired, I shall now attend with such a homily as shall lay before ye, first, the inventors of it to be those whom ye will be loth to own; next, what is to be thought in general of reading, whatever sort the books be; and that this order avails nothing to the suppressing of scandalous, seditious, and libelous books, which were mainly intended to be suppressed; last, that it will be primely to the discouragement of all learning, and the stop of truth, not only by disexercising and blunting our abilities in what we know already, but by hindering and cropping the discovery that might be yet further made both in religious and civil wisdom.

[6] I deny not but that it is of greatest concernment in the church and commonwealth to have a vigilant eye how books demean themselves, as well as men, and thereafter to confine, imprison, and do sharpest justice on them as malefactors. For books are not absolutely dead things, but do contain a potency of life in them

---

[9] *copy:* copyright.
[10] *painful:* diligent, willing to take pains.
[11] *quadragesimal:* pertaining to the forty days of lent.

to be as active as that soul was whose progeny they are; nay, they do preserve as in a vial the purest efficacy and extraction of that living intellect that bred them. I know they are as lively, and as vigourously productive, as those fabulous dragon's teeth; and being sown up and down, may chance to spring up armed men. And yet, on the other hand, unless wariness be used, as good almost kill a man as kill a good book: who kills a man kills a reasonable creature, God's image; but he who destroys a good book, kills reason itself, kills the image of God, as it were, in the eye. Many a man lives a burden to the earth; but a good book is the precious life-blood of a master spirit, embalmed and treasured up on purpose to a life beyond life. 'Tis true, no age can restore a life, whereof, perhaps, there is no great loss; and revolutions of ages do not oft recover the loss of a rejected truth, for the want of which whole nations fare the worse. We should be wary, therefore, what persecution we raise against the living labours of public men, how we spill that seasoned life of man preserved and stored up in books; since we see a kind of homicide may be thus committed, sometimes a martyrdom; and if it extend to the whole impression, a kind of massacre, whereof the execution ends not in the slaying of an elemental life, but strikes at that ethereal and fifth essence, the breath of reason itself, slays an immortality rather than a life. But lest I should be condemned of introducing license, while I oppose licensing, I refuse not the pains to be so much historical as will serve to show what hath been done by ancient and famous commonwealths against this disorder, till the very time that this project of licensing crept out of the Inquisition, was catched up by our prelates, and hath caught some of our presbyters.

[7] In Athens, where books and wits were ever busier than in any other part of Greece, I find but only two sorts of writings which the magistrate cared to take notice of, those either blasphemous and atheistical, or libelous. Thus the books of Protagoras were by the judges of Areopagus commanded to be burnt, and himself banished the territory, for a discourse begun with his confessing not to know 'whether there were gods, or whether not.' And against defaming, it was decreed that none should be traduced by name, as was the manner of Vetus Comoedia, whereby we may

guess how they censured libeling; and this course was quick enough, as Cicero writes, to quell both the desperate wits of other atheists and the open way of defaming, as the event showed. Of other sects and opinions, though tending to voluptuousness, and the denying of divine Providence, they took no heed. Therefore we do not read that either Epicurus, or that libertine school of Cyrene, or what the Cynic impudence uttered, was ever questioned by the laws. Neither is it recorded that the writings of those old comedians were suppressed, though the acting of them were forbid; and that Plato commended the reading of Aristophanes, the loosest of them all, to his royal scholar Dionysius, is commonly known, and may be excused, if holy Chrysostom, as is reported, nightly studied so much the same author, and had the art to cleanse a scurrilous vehemence into the style of a rousing sermon.

[8] That other leading city of Greece, Lacedaemon, considering that Lycurgus their lawgiver was so addicted to elegant learning as to have been the first that brought out of Ionia the scattered works of Homer, and sent the poet Thales from Crete to prepare and mollify the Spartan surliness with his smooth songs and odes, the better to plant among them law and civility, it is to be wondered how museless [12] and unbookish they were, minding naught but the feats of war. There needed no licensing of books among them, for they disliked all but their own laconic apothegms, and took a slight occasion to chase Archilochus out of their city, perhaps for composing in a higher strain than their own soldierly ballads and roundels could reach to; or if it were for his broad verses, they were not therein so cautious, but they were as dissolute in their promiscuous conversing; whence Euripides affirms, in *Andromache,* that their women were all unchaste. Thus much may give us light after what sort books were prohibited among the Greeks.

[9] The Romans also, for many ages trained up only to a military roughness, resembling most the Lacedaemonian guise, knew of learning little but what their twelve tables and the pontific college with their augurs and flamens taught them in religion and law;

[12] *museless:* unfamiliar with the Muses, goddesses of poetry and the other arts.

so unacquainted with other learning that when Carneades and Critolaus, with the Stoic Diogenes, coming ambassadors to Rome, took thereby occasion to give the city a taste of their philosophy, they were suspected for seducers by no less a man than Cato the Censor, who moved it in the senate to dismiss them speedily, and to banish all such Attic babblers out of Italy. But Scipio and others of the noblest senators withstood him and his old Sabine austerity; honoured and admired the men; and the Censor himself at last, in his old age, fell to the study of that whereof before he was so scrupulous. And yet at the same time Naevius and Plautus, the first Latin comedians, had filled the city with all the borrowed scenes of Menander and Philemon. Then began to be considered there also what was to be done to libelous books and authors; for Naevius was quickly cast into prison for his unbridled pen, and released by the tribunes upon his recantation: we read also that libels were burnt, and the makers punished, by Augustus. The like severity, no doubt, was used, if aught were impiously written against their esteemed gods. Except in these two points, how the world went in books, the magistrate kept no reckoning. And therefore Lucretius, without impeachment, versifies his Epicurism to Memmius, and had the honour to be set forth the second time by Cicero, so great a father of the commonwealth; although himself disputes against that opinion in his own writings. Nor was the satirical sharpness or naked plainness of Lucilius, or Catullus, or Flaccus, by any order prohibited. And for matters of state, the story of Titus Livius, though it extolled that part [13] which Pompey held, was not therefore suppressed by Octavius Caesar of the other faction. But that Naso was by him banished in his old age, for the wanton poems of his youth, was but a mere covert of state over some secret cause; and besides, the books were neither banished nor called in. From hence we shall meet with little else but tyranny in the Roman empire, that we may not marvel if not so often bad as good books were silenced. I shall therefore deem to have been large enough in producing what among the ancients was punishable to write, save only which, all other arguments were free to treat on.

[10] By this time the emperors were become Christians, whose

[13] *part:* party or faction.

discipline in this point I do not find to have been more severe than what was formerly in practise. The books of those whom they took to be grand heretics were examined, refuted, and condemned in the general councils; and not till then were prohibited, or burnt, by authority of the emperor. As for the writings of heathen authors, unless they were plain invectives against Christianity, as those of Porphyrius and Proclus, they met with no interdict that can be cited, till about the year 400, in a Carthaginian council, wherein bishops themselves were forbid to read the books of Gentiles, but heresies they might read; while others long before them, on the contrary, scrupled more the books of heretics than of Gentiles. And that the primitive councils and bishops were wont only to declare what books were not commendable, passing no further, but leaving it to each one's conscience to read or to lay by, till after the year 800, is observed already by Padre Paolo, the great unmasker of the Trentine council. After which time the popes of Rome, engrossing what they pleased of political rule into their own hands, extended their dominion over men's eyes, as they had before over their judgments, burning and prohibiting to be read what they fancied not; yet sparing in their censures, and the books not many which they so dealt with; till Martin V, by his bull, not only prohibited, but was the first that excommunicated, the reading of heretical books; for about that time Wycliffe and Huss growing terrible, were they who first drove the papal court to a stricter policy of prohibiting. Which course Leo X and his successors followed, until the council of Trent and the Spanish Inquisition, engendering together, brought forth or perfected those catalogues and expurging indexes, that rake through the entrails of many an old good author, with a violation worse than any could be offered to his tomb.

[11] Nor did they stay in matters heretical, but any subject that was not to their palate, they either condemned in a prohibition, or had it straight into the new purgatory of an Index. To fill up the measure of encroachment, their last invention was to ordain that no book, pamphlet, or paper should be printed (as if St. Peter had bequeathed them the keys of the press also out of Paradise) unless it were approved and licensed under the hands of two or three glutton friars. For example:

Let the Chancellor Cini be pleased to see if in this present work be contained aught that may withstand the printing.

> Vincent Rabatta, Vicar of Florence.

I have seen this present work, and find nothing athwart the Catholic faith and good manners: in witness whereof I have given, &c.

> Nicolò Cini, Chancellor of Florence.

Attending the precedent relation, it is allowed that this present work of Davanzati may be printed.

> Vincent Rabatta, &c.

It may be printed, July 15.

> Friar Simon Mompei d'Amelia,
> Chancellor of the Holy Office in Florence.

Sure they have a conceit, if he of the bottomless pit had not long since broke prison, that this quadruple exorcism would bar him down. I fear their next design will be to get into their custody the licensing of that which they say Claudius intended, but went not through with. Vouchsafe to see another of their forms, the Roman stamp:

Imprimatur, If it seem good to the reverend master of the Holy Palace.

> Belcastro, Vicegerent.

Imprimatur.

> Friar Nicolò Rodolphi, Master of the Holy Palace.

[12] Sometimes five Imprimaturs are seen together, dialogue-wise, in the piazza of one titlepage, complimenting and ducking each to other with their shaven reverences, whether the author, who stands by in perplexity at the foot of his epistle, shall to the press or to the sponge. These are the pretty responsories,[14] these are the dear antiphonies,[15] that so bewitched of late our prelates and their chaplains with the goodly echo they made; and besotted us to the gay imitation of a lordly Imprimatur,[16] one from Lam-

---

[14] *responsories:* sections of the Psalms sung interspersed between readings from the missal in the mass.

[15] *antiphonies:* hymns or anthems sung in responsive parts by two choirs.

[16] *Imprimatur:* "let it be printed," the order stamped on manuscripts which are permitted by ecclesiastical authority to be sent to the press.

beth House, another from the west end of Paul's, so apishly Romanising that the word of command still was set down in Latin, as if the learned grammatical pen that wrote it would cast no ink without Latin; or perhaps, as they thought, because no vulgar tongue was worthy to express the pure conceit of an Imprimatur; but rather, as I hope, for that our English, the language of men ever famous and foremost in the achievements of liberty, will not easily find servile letters enow to spell such a dictatory presumption English.

[13] And thus ye have the inventors and the original of book-licensing ripped up and drawn as lineally as any pedigree. We have it not, that can be heard of, from any ancient state, or polity, or church, nor by any statute left us by our ancestors elder or later; nor from the modern custom of any reformed city or church abroad; but from the most antichristian council and the most tyrannous Inquisition that ever inquired. Till then books were ever as freely admitted into the world as any other birth; the issue of the brain was no more stifled than the issue of the womb: no envious Juno sat cross-legged over the nativity of any man's intellectual offspring; but if it proved a monster, who denies but that it was justly burnt, or sunk into the sea? But that a book, in worse condition than a peccant soul, should be to stand before a jury ere it be born to the world, and undergo yet in darkness the judgement of Rhadamanth and his colleagues, ere it can pass the ferry backward into light, was never heard before, till that mysterious iniquity, provoked and troubled at the first entrance of reformation, sought out new limbos [17] and new hells wherein they might include our books also within the number of their damned. And this was the rare morsel so officiously snatched up, and so ill-favouredly imitated by our inquisiturient bishops and the attendant minorities, their chaplains. That ye like not now these most certain authors of this licensing order, and that all sinister intention was far distant from your thoughts when ye were importuned the passing it, all men who know the integrity of your actions, and how ye honour truth, will clear ye readily.

[14] But some will say, 'What though the inventors were bad, the

---

[17] *limbos:* regions adjoining hell.

thing for all that may be good.' It may so; yet if that thing be no such deep invention, but obvious and easy for any man to light on, and yet best and wisest commonwealths through all ages and occasions have forborne to use it, and falsest seducers and oppressors of men were the first who took it up, and to no other purpose but to obstruct and hinder the first approach of reformation; I am of those who believe it will be a harder alchemy than Lullius ever knew to sublimate [18] any good use out of such an invention. Yet this only is what I request to gain from this reason, that it may be held a dangerous and suspicious fruit, as certainly it deserves, for the tree that bore it, until I can dissect one by one the properties it has. But I have first to finish, as was propounded, what is to be thought in general of reading books, whatever sort they be, and whether be more the benefit or the harm that thence proceeds.

[15] Not to insist upon the examples of Moses, Daniel, and Paul, who were skilful in all the learning of the Egyptians, Chaldeans, and Greeks, which could not probably be without reading their books of all sorts (in Paul especially, who thought it no defilement to insert into Holy Scripture the sentences of three Greek poets, and one of them a tragedian), the question was notwithstanding sometimes controverted among the primitive doctors, but with great odds on that side which affirmed it both lawful and profitable, as was then evidently perceived when Julian the Apostate, and subtlest enemy to our faith, made a decree forbidding Christians the study of heathen learning; for, said he, they wound us with our own weapons, and with our own arts and sciences they overcome us. And indeed the Christians were put so to their shifts by this crafty means, and so much in danger to decline into all ignorance, that the two Apollinarii were fain, as a man may say, to coin all the seven liberal sciences out of the Bible, reducing it into divers forms of orations, poems, dialogues, even to the calculating of a new Christian grammar. But, saith the historian Socrates, the providence of God provided better than the industry of Apollinarius and his son, by taking away that illiterate law with the life of him who devised it. So great an in-

---

[18] *sublimate:* in alchemy, to transform a base into a precious metal.

jury they then held it to be deprived of Hellenic learning; and thought it a persecution more undermining, and secretly decaying the church, than the open cruelty of Decius or Diocletian.

[16] And perhaps it was the same politic drift that the devil whipped St. Jerome in a Lenten dream, for reading Cicero; or else it was a phantasm bred by the fever which had then seized him. For had an angel been his discipliner, unless it were for dwelling too much upon Ciceronianisms, and had chastised the reading, not the vanity, it had been plainly partial, first, to correct him for grave Cicero and not for scurrile Plautus, whom he confesses to have been reading not long before; next to correct him only, and let so many more ancient fathers wax old in those pleasant and florid studies without the lash of such a tutoring apparition; insomuch that Basil teaches how some good use may be made of *Margites,* a sportful poem, not now extant, writ by Homer; and why not then of *Morgante,* an Italian romance much to the same purpose?

[17] But if it be agreed we shall be tried by visions, there is a vision recorded by Eusebius, far ancienter than his tale of Jerome to the nun Eustochium, and, besides, has nothing of a fever in it. Dionysius Alexandrinus was, about the year 240, a person of great name in the church for piety and learning, who had wont to avail himself much against heretics by being conversant in their books; until a certain presbyter laid it scrupulously to his conscience, how he durst venture himself among those defiling volumes. The worthy man, loth to give offence, fell into a new debate with himself what was to be thought; when suddenly a vision sent from God (it is his own epistle that so avers it) confirmed him in these words: 'Read any books, whatever come to thy hands, for thou art sufficient both to judge aright and to examine each matter.' To this revelation he assented the sooner, as he confesses, because it was answerable to that of the Apostle to the Thessalonians: 'Prove all things, hold fast that which is good.' And he might have added another remarkable saying of the same author: 'To the pure, all things are pure'; not only meats and drinks, but all kind of knowledge, whether of good or evil: the knowledge cannot defile, nor consequently the books, if the will and conscience be not defiled. For books are as meats and viands are, some of good, some of evil substance; and yet God in that un-

apocryphal vision said, without exception, 'Rise, Peter, kill and eat,' leaving the choice to each man's discretion. Wholesome meats to a vitiated stomach differ little or nothing from unwholesome, and best books to a naughty mind are not unappliable to occasions of evil. Bad meats will scarce breed good nourishment in the healthiest concoction; but herein the difference is of bad books, that they to a discreet and judicious reader serve in many respects to discover, to confute, to forewarn, and to illustrate. Whereof what better witness can ye expect I should produce than one of your own now sitting in parliament, the chief of learned men reputed in this land, Mr. Selden, whose volume of natural and national laws proves, not only by great authorities brought together, but by exquisite reasons and theorems almost mathematically demonstrative, that all opinions, yea, errors, known, read, and collated, are of main service and assistance towards the speedy attainment of what is truest.

[18] I conceive, therefore, that when God did enlarge the universal diet of man's body, saving ever the rules of temperance, he then also, as before, left arbitrary the dieting and repasting of our minds; as wherein every mature man might have to exercise his own leading capacity. How great a virtue is temperance, how much of moment through the whole life of man! Yet God commits the managing so great a trust, without particular law or prescription, wholly to the demeanour of every grown man. And therefore when he himself tabled the Jews from heaven, that omer, which was every man's daily portion of manna, is computed to have been more than might have well sufficed the heartiest feeder thrice as many meals. For those actions which enter into a man, rather than issue out of him, and therefore defile not, God uses not to captivate under a perpetual childhood of prescription, but trusts him with the gift of reason to be his own chooser; there were but little work left for preaching, if law and compulsion should grow so fast upon those things which heretofore were governed only by exhortation. Solomon informs us that much reading is a weariness to the flesh, but neither he nor other inspired author tells us that such or such reading is unlawful; yet certainly had God thought good to limit us herein, it had been much more expedient to have told us what was unlawful, than what was wearisome. As

for the burning of those Ephesian books by St. Paul's converts, 'tis replied the books were magic, the Syriac so renders them. It was a private act, a voluntary act, and leaves us to a voluntary imitation: the men in remorse burnt those books which were their own; the magistrate by this example is not appointed; these men practised the books, another might perhaps have read them in some sort usefully.

[19] Good and evil we know in the field of this world grow up together almost inseparably; and the knowledge of good is so involved and interwoven with the knowledge of evil, and in so many cunning resemblances hardly to be discerned, that those confused seeds which were imposed on Psyche as an incessant labour to cull out and sort asunder, were not more intermixed. It was from out the rind of one apple tasted that the knowledge of good and evil, as two twins cleaving together, leaped forth into the world. And perhaps this is that doom which Adam fell into of knowing good and evil, that is to say, of knowing good by evil. As therefore the state of man now is, what wisdom can there be to choose, what continence to forbear, without the knowledge of evil? He that can apprehend and consider vice with all her baits and seeming pleasures, and yet abstain, and yet distinguish, and yet prefer that which is truly better, he is the true warfaring [19] Christian. I cannot praise a fugitive and cloistered virtue, unexercised and unbreathed, that never sallies out and sees her adversary, but slinks out of the race where that immortal garland is to be run for, not without dust and heat. Assuredly we bring not innocence into the world, we bring impurity much rather; that which purifies us is trial, and trial is by what is contrary. That virtue therefore which is but a youngling in the contemplation of evil, and knows not the utmost that vice promises to her followers, and rejects it, is but a blank virtue, not a pure; her whiteness is but an excremental [20] whiteness; which was the reason why our sage and serious poet Spenser, whom I dare be known to think a better teacher than Scotus or Aquinas, describing true temperance under the person of Guyon, brings him in with his

---

[19] *wayfaring:* so in the first edition, but *warfaring* is suggested by the context and by a parallel passage in Lactantius.
[20] *excremental:* excrescential, external.

palmer through the cave of Mammon and the bower of earthly bliss, that he might see and know, and yet abstain. Since therefore the knowledge and survey of vice is in this world so necessary to the constituting of human virtue, and the scanning of error to the confirmation of truth, how can we more safely, and with less danger, scout into the regions of sin and falsity than by reading all manner of tractates and hearing all manner of reason? And this is the benefit which may be had of books promiscuously read. [20] But of the harm that may result hence, three kinds are usually reckoned. First is feared the infection that may spread; but then all human learning and controversy in religious points must remove out of the world, yea, the Bible itself; for that ofttimes relates blasphemy not nicely,[21] it describes the carnal sense of wicked men not unelegantly, it brings in holiest men passionately murmuring against Providence through all the arguments of Epicurus: in other great disputes it answers dubiously and darkly to the common reader; and ask a Talmudist what ails the modesty of his marginal Keri, that Moses and all the prophets cannot persuade him to pronounce the textual Chetiv. For these causes we all know the Bible itself put by the papist into the first rank of prohibited books. The ancientest fathers must be next removed, as Clement of Alexandria, and that Eusebian book of evangelic preparation, transmitting our ears through a hoard of heathenish obscenities to receive the gospel. Who finds not that Irenaeus, Epiphanius, Jerome, and others discover more heresies than they well confute, and that oft for heresy which is the truer opinion? [21] Nor boots it to say for these and all the heathen writers of greatest infection, if it must be thought so, with whom is bound up the life of human learning, that they writ in an unknown tongue, so long as we are sure those languages are known as well to the worst of men, who are both most able and most diligent to instil the poison they suck, first into the courts of princes, acquainting them with the choicest delights and criticisms[22] of sin. As perhaps did that Petronius whom Nero called his arbiter, the master of his revels; and that notorious ribald of Arezzo, dreaded and yet

[21] *nicely:* delicately.
[22] *criticisms:* critical refinements—here of an elegant connoisseur of the pleasures of vice.

dear to the Italian courtiers. I name not him, for posterity's sake, whom Harry VIII named in merriment his vicar of hell. By which compendious way all the contagion that foreign books can infuse will find a passage to the people far easier and shorter than an Indian voyage, though it could be sailed either by the north of Cataio eastward, or of Canada westward, while our Spanish licensing gags the English press never so severely.

[22] But, on the other side, that infection which is from books of controversy in religion is more doubtful and dangerous to the learned than to the ignorant; and yet those books must be permitted untouched by the licenser. It will be hard to instance where any ignorant man hath been ever seduced by papistical book in English, unless it were commended and expounded to him by some of that clergy; and indeed all such tractates, whether false or true, are as the prophecy of Isaiah was to the eunuch, not to be 'understood without a guide.' But of our priests and doctors how many have been corrupted by studying the comments of Jesuits and Sorbonists, and how fast they could transfuse that corruption into the people, our experience is both late and sad. It is not forgot, since the acute and distinct Arminius was perverted merely by the perusing of a nameless discourse written at Delft, which at first he took in hand to confute.

[23] Seeing therefore that those books, and those in great abundance, which are likeliest to taint both life and doctrine, cannot be suppressed without the fall of learning, and of all ability in disputation; and that these books of either sort are most and soonest catching to the learned (from whom to the common people whatever is heretical or dissolute may quickly be conveyed); and that evil manners are as perfectly learnt without books a thousand other ways which cannot be stopped; and evil doctrine not with books can propagate, except a teacher guide, which he might also do without writing, and so beyond prohibiting; I am not able to unfold how this cautelous enterprise of licensing can be exempted from the number of vain and impossible attempts. And he who were pleasantly disposed could not well avoid to liken it to the exploit of that gallant man who thought to pound up the crows by shutting his park gate.

[24] Besides another inconvenience, if learned men be the first

receivers out of books and dispreaders both of vice and error,
how shall the licensers themselves be confided in, unless we can
confer upon them, or they assume to themselves above all others
in the land, the grace of infallibility and uncorruptedness? And
again, if it be true that a wise man, like a good refiner, can gather
gold out of the drossiest volume, and that a fool will be a fool with
the best book, yea, or without book, there is no reason that we
should deprive a wise man of any advantage to his wisdom, while
we seek to restrain from a fool that which, being restrained, will
be no hindrance to his folly. For if there should be so much
exactness always used to keep that from him which is unfit for
his reading, we should, in the judgement of Aristotle not only,
but of Solomon and of our Saviour, not vouchsafe him good precepts, and by consequence not willingly admit him to good
books; as being certain that a wise man will make better use
of an idle pamphlet than a fool will do of sacred Scripture.

[25] 'Tis next alleged we must not expose ourselves to temptations
without necessity, and next to that, not employ our time in vain
things. To both these objections one answer will serve, out of the
grounds already laid, that to all men such books are not temptations nor vanities, but useful drugs and materials wherewith to
temper and compose effective and strong medicines, which man's
life cannot want.[23] The rest, as children and childish men, who
have not the art to qualify [24] and prepare these working minerals,
well may be exhorted to forbear, but hindered forcibly they cannot be by all the licensing that sainted Inquisition could ever yet
contrive. Which is what I promised to deliver next: that this order
of licensing conduces nothing to the end for which it was framed;
and hath almost prevented [25] me by being clear already while
thus much hath been explaining. See the ingenuity [26] of truth,
who, when she gets a free and willing hand, opens herself faster
than the pace of method and discourse can overtake her.

[26] It was the task which I began with, to show that no nation,
or well instituted state, if they valued books at all, did ever use

[23] *want:* do without, lack.

[24] *qualify:* fix the quality or nature of a drug by proper compounding.

[25] *prevented:* anticipated or "got ahead of" another person in arriving somewhere, or—as here—in doing something.

[26] *ingenuity:* ingenuousness, liberality.

this way of licensing; and it might be answered that this is a piece of prudence lately discovered. To which I return that, as it was a thing slight and obvious to think on, so if it had been difficult to find out, there wanted not among them long since who suggested such a course; which they not following, leave us a pattern of their judgement that it was not the not knowing, but the not approving, which was the cause of their not using it. Plato, a man of high authority indeed, but least of all for his commonwealth, in the book of his laws, which no city ever yet received, fed his fancy with making many edicts to his airy burgomasters, which they who otherwise admire him wish had been rather buried and excused in the genial cups of an Academic night-sitting. By which laws he seems to tolerate no kind of learning but by unalterable decree, consisting most of practical traditions, to the attainment whereof a library of smaller bulk than his own dialogues would be abundant. And there also enacts that no poet should so much as read to any private man what he had written, until the judges and lawkeepers had seen it and allowed it; but that Plato meant this law peculiarly to that commonwealth which he had imagined, and to no other, is evident. Why was he not else a lawgiver to himself, but a transgressor, and to be expelled by his own magistrates, both for the wanton epigrams and dialogues which he made, and his perpetual reading of Sophron Mimus and Aristophanes, books of grossest infamy; and also for commending the latter of them, though he were the malicious libeller of his chief friends, to be read by the tyrant Dionysius, who had little need of such trash to spend his time on? But that he knew this licensing of poems had reference and dependence to many other provisos there set down in his fancied republic, which in this world could have no place; and so neither he himself, nor any magistrate or city, ever imitated that course, which, taken apart from those other collateral injunctions, must needs be vain and fruitless.

[27] For if they fell upon one kind of strictness, unless their care were equal to regulate all other things of like aptness to corrupt the mind, that single endeavour they knew would be but a fond [27] labour—to shut and fortify one gate against corruption and be necessitated to leave others round about wide open. If we think

[27] *fond:* ineffective, foolish.

to regulate printing, thereby to rectify manners, we must regulate
all recreations and pastimes, all that is delightful to man. No
music must be heard, no song be set or sung, but what is grave
and Doric. There must be licensing dancers, that no gesture, motion, or deportment be taught our youth, but what by their allowance shall be thought honest; [28] for such Plato was provided of.
It will ask more than the work of twenty licensers to examine all
the lutes, the violins, and the guitars in every house; they must
not be suffered to prattle as they do, but must be licensed what
they may say. And who shall silence all the airs and madrigals
that whisper softness in chambers? The windows also, and the
balconies, must be thought on; *there* are shrewd [29] books, with
dangerous frontispieces,[30] set to sale: who shall prohibit them,
shall twenty licensers? The villages also must have their visitors [31]
to inquire what lectures the bagpipe and the rebeck [32] reads even
to the ballatry,[33] and the gamut of every municipal fiddler; for
these are the countryman's *Arcadias,* and his Montemayors.

[28] Next, what more national corruption, for which England
hears ill [34] abroad, than household gluttony? Who shall be the
rectors of our daily rioting? And what shall be done to inhibit the
multitudes that frequent those houses where drunkenness is sold
and harboured? Our garments also should be referred to the
licensing of some more sober work-masters, to see them cut into a
less wanton garb. Who shall regulate all the mixed conversation [35]
of our youth, male and female together, as is the fashion of this
country? Who shall still appoint what shall be discoursed, what
presumed, and no further? Lastly, who shall forbid and separate
all idle resort, all evil company? These things will be, and must
be; but how they shall be least hurtful, how least enticing, herein
consists the grave and governing wisdom of a state.

[29] To sequester out of the world into Atlantic and Utopian

---

[28] *honest:* honorable, decent.
[29] *shrewd:* mischievous, wicked.
[30] *frontispieces:* fronts or decorated pages at the beginning.
[31] *visitors:* inspectors.
[32] *rebeck:* a simple fiddle, originally with only two strings.
[33] *ballatry:* balladry.
[34] *hears ill:* hears unfavorably mentioned.
[35] *conversation:* social intercourse.

polities, which never can be drawn into use, will not mend our condition; but to ordain wisely as in this world of evil, in the midst
whereof God hath placed us unavoidably. Nor is it Plato's licensing of books will do this, which necessarily pulls along with it so
many other kinds of licensing as will make us all both ridiculous
and weary, and yet frustrate; but those unwritten or at least un-
constraining laws of virtuous education, religious and civil nurture,
which Plato there mentions as the bonds and ligaments of the
commonwealth, the pillars and the sustainers of every written
statute; these they be which will bear chief sway in such matters
as these, when all licensing will be easily eluded. Impunity and
remissness, for certain, are the bane of a commonwealth; but
here the great art lies, to discern in what the law is to bid restraint and punishment, and in what things persuasion only is to
work. If every action which is good or evil in man at ripe years
were to be under pittance [36] and prescription and compulsion,
what were virtue but a name, what praise could be then due to
well-doing, what gramercy [37] to be sober, just, or continent?

[30] Many there be that complain of divine Providence for suffering Adam to transgress. Foolish tongues! when God gave him
reason, he gave him freedom to choose, for reason is but choosing; he had been else a mere artificial Adam, such an Adam as
he is in the motions.[38] We ourselves esteem not of that obedience,
or love, or gift, which is of force; God therefore left him free,
set before him a provoking object, ever almost in his eyes; herein
consisted his merit, herein the right of his reward, the praise of
his abstinence. Wherefore did he create passions within us, pleasures round about us, but that these, rightly tempered, are the
very ingredients of virtue? They are not skilful considerers of
human things who imagine to remove sin by removing the matter
of sin; for, besides that it is a huge heap increasing under the
very act of diminishing, though some part of it may for a time be
withdrawn from some persons, it cannot from all, in such a
universal thing as books are; and when this is done, yet the sin
remains entire. Though ye take from a covetous man all his

[36] *pittance:* ration, allowance.
[37] *gramercy:* thanks.
[38] *motions:* puppet shows.

treasure, he has yet one jewel left—ye cannot bereave him of his covetousness. Banish all objects of lust, shut up all youth into the severest discipline that can be exercised in any hermitage, ye cannot make them chaste that came not thither so: such great care and wisdom is required to the right managing of this point.

[31] Suppose we could expel sin by this means: look how much we thus expel of sin, so much we expel of virtue, for the matter of them both is the same; remove that, and ye remove them both alike. This justifies the high providence of God, who, though he command us temperance, justice, continence, yet pours out before us even to a profuseness all desirable things, and gives us minds that can wander beyond all limit and satiety. Why should we then affect a rigour contrary to the manner of God and of nature, by abridging or scanting those means, which books freely permitted are, both to the trial of virtue and the exercise of truth?

[32] It would be better done to learn that the law must needs be frivolous which goes to restrain things uncertainly and yet equally working to good and to evil. And were I the chooser, a dram of well-doing should be preferred before many times as much the forcible hindrance of evil-doing. For God sure esteems the growth and completing of one virtuous person more than the restraint of ten vicious. And albeit whatever thing we hear or see, sitting, walking, travelling, or conversing, may be fitly called our book, and is of the same effect that writings are; yet grant the thing to be prohibited were only books, it appears that this order hitherto is far insufficient to the end which it intends. Do we not see, not once or oftener, but weekly, that continued court-libel against the parliament and city printed, as the wet sheets can witness, and dispersed among us, for all that licensing can do? Yet this is the prime service, a man would think, wherein this order should give proof of itself. If it were executed, you'll say. But certain, if execution be remiss or blindfold now, and in this particular, what will it be hereafter and in other books?

[33] If then the order shall not be vain and frustrate, behold a new labour, Lords and Commons. Ye must repeal and proscribe all scandalous and unlicensed books already printed and divulged,[39] after ye have drawn them up into a list, that all may know which

[39] *divulged:* publicly distributed, made generally available.

are condemned and which not; and ordain that no foreign books be delivered out of custody till they have been read over. This office will require the whole time of not a few overseers, and those no vulgar men. There be also books which are partly useful and excellent, partly culpable and pernicious; this work will ask as many more officials, to make expurgations and expunctions,[40] that the commonwealth of learning be not damnified. In fine, when the multitude of books increase upon their hands, ye must be fain to catalogue all those printers who are found frequently offending, and forbid the importation of their whole suspected typography. In a word, that this your order may be exact and not deficient, ye must reform it perfectly according to the model of Trent and Seville, which I know ye abhor to do.

[34] Yet though ye should condescend to this, which God forbid, the order still would be but fruitless and defective to that end whereto ye meant it. If to prevent sects and schisms, who is so un-read or so uncatechized in story that hath not heard of many sects refusing books as a hindrance, and preserving their doctrine unmixed for many ages, only by unwritten traditions? The Christian faith (for that was once a schism) is not unknown to have spread all over Asia, ere any gospel or epistle was seen in writing. If the amendment of manners be aimed at, look into Italy and Spain, whether those places be one scruple the better, the honester, the wiser, the chaster, since all the inquisitional rigour that hath been executed upon books.

[35] Another reason, whereby to make it plain that this order will miss the end it seeks, consider by the quality which ought to be in every licenser. It cannot be denied but that he who is made judge to sit upon the birth or death of books, whether they may be wafted into this world or not, had need to be a man above the common measure, both studious, learned, and judicious; there may be else no mean mistakes in the censure of what is passable or not, which is also no mean injury. If he be of such worth as behoves him, there cannot be a more tedious and unpleasing journey-work,[41] a greater loss of time levied upon his head, than to be made

---

[40] *expunctions:* expungings, excisions by the censor.
[41] *journey-work:* work by the day, or work done by a journeyman or day-laborer.

the perpetual reader of unchosen books and pamphlets, ofttimes huge volumes. There is no book that is acceptable unless at certain seasons; but to be enjoined the reading of that at all times, and in a hand scarce legible, whereof three pages would not down at any time in the fairest print, is an imposition which I cannot believe how he that values time and his own studies, or is but of a sensible [42] nostril, should be able to endure. In this one thing I crave leave of the present licensers to be pardoned for so thinking; who doubtless took this office up, looking on it through their obedience to the parliament, whose command perhaps made all things seem easy and unlabourious to them; but that this short trial hath wearied them out already, their own expressions and excuses to them who make so many journeys to solicit their license, are testimony enough. Seeing, therefore, those who now possess the employment, by all evident signs wish themselves well rid of it, and that no man of worth, none that is not a plain unthrift of his own hours, is ever likely to succeed them, except he mean to put himself to the salary of a press-corrector, we may easily foresee what kind of licensers we are to expect hereafter, either ignorant, imperious, and remiss, or basely pecuniary. This is what I had to show, wherein this order cannot conduce to that end whereof it bears the intention.

[36] I lastly proceed from the no good it can do, to the manifest hurt it causes, in being first the greatest discouragement and affront that can be offered to learning and to learned men. It was the complaint and lamentation of prelates, upon every least breath of a motion to remove pluralities and distribute more equally church revenues, that then all learning would be for ever dashed and discouraged. But as for that opinion, I never found cause to think that the tenth part of learning stood or fell with the clergy; nor could I ever but hold it for a sordid and unworthy speech of any churchman who had a competency left him. If therefore ye be loth to dishearten utterly and discontent, not the mercenary crew of false pretenders to learning, but the free and ingenuous sort of such as evidently were born to study and love learning for itself, not for lucre or any other end but the service of God and of truth, and perhaps that lasting fame and perpetuity of praise

[42] *sensible:* sensitive.

which God and good men have consented shall be the reward of those whose published labours advance the good of mankind; then know, that so far to distrust the judgement and the honesty of one who hath but a common repute in learning, and never yet offended, as not to count him fit to print his mind without a tutor and examiner, lest he should drop a schism or something of corruption, is the greatest displeasure and indignity to a free and knowing spirit that can be put upon him.

[37] What advantage is it to be a man over it is to be a boy at school, if we have only scaped the ferula to come under the fescue [43] of an Imprimatur; if serious and elaborate writings, as if they were no more than the theme of a grammar-lad under his pedagogue, must not be uttered without the cursory eyes of a temporizing and extemporizing licenser? He who is not trusted with his own actions, his drift not being known to be evil, and standing to the hazard of law and penalty, has no great argument to think himself reputed, in the commonwealth wherein he was born, for other than a fool or a foreigner. When a man writes to the world, he summons up all his reason and deliberation to assist him; he searches, meditates, is industrious, and likely consults and confers with his judicious friends; after all which done, he takes himself to be informed in what he writes, as well as any that writ before him. If in this, the most consummate act of his fidelity and ripeness, no years, no industry, no former proof of his abilities can bring him to that state of maturity as not to be still mistrusted and suspected (unless he carry all his considerate diligence, all his midnight watchings and expense of Palladian oil, to the hasty view of an unleisured licenser, perhaps much his younger, perhaps far his inferior in judgement, perhaps one who never knew the labour of book-writing), and if he be not repulsed or slighted, must appear in print like a puny [44] with his guardian, and his censor's hand on the back of his title to be his bail and surety that he is no idiot or seducer; it cannot be but a dishonour and derogation to the author, to the book, to the privilege and dignity of learning.

[38] And what if the author shall be one so copious of fancy as

---

[43] *ferula:* a schoolmaster's rod. The *fescue* is usually defined as a pointer.
[44] *puny:* a child, a person under the legal age of majority.

to have many things, well worth the adding, come into his mind after licensing, while the book is yet under the press, which not seldom happens to the best and diligentest writers; and that perhaps a dozen times in one book. The printer dares not go beyond his licensed copy; so often then must the author trudge to his leave-giver, that those his new insertions may be viewed; and many a jaunt will be made ere that licenser (for it must be the same man) can either be found, or found at leisure; meanwhile either the press must stand still, which is no small damage, or the author lose his accuratest thoughts, and send the book forth worse than he had made it, which to a diligent writer is the greatest melancholy and vexation that can befall.

[39] And how can a man teach with authority, which is the life of teaching, how can he be a doctor in his book, as he ought to be, or else had better be silent, whenas all he teaches, all he delivers, is but under the tuition, under the correction, of his patriarchal licenser, to blot or alter what precisely accords not with the hidebound humour which he calls his judgement? When every acute reader, upon the first sight of a pedantic license, will be ready with these like words to ding the book a quoit's distance from him: 'I hate a pupil teacher, I endure not an instructor that comes to me under the wardship of an overseeing fist. I know nothing of the licenser, but that I have his own hand here for his arrogance; who shall warrant me his judgement?' 'The state, sir,' replies the stationer, but has a quick return: 'The state shall be my governors, but not my critics; they may be mistaken in the choice of a licenser, as easily as this licenser may be mistaken in an author. This is some common stuff.' And he might add from Sir Francis Bacon, that 'such authorized books are but the language of the times.' For though a licenser should happen to be judicious more than ordinary (which will be a great jeopardy of the next succession), yet his very office and his commission enjoins him to let pass nothing but what is vulgarly received already.

[40] Nay, which is more lamentable, if the work of any deceased author, though never so famous in his lifetime and even to this day, come to their hands for license to be printed or reprinted, if there be found in his book one sentence of a venturous edge,

uttered in the height of zeal (and who knows whether it might not be the dictate of a divine spirit?), yet not suiting with every low decrepit humour of their own, though it were Knox himself, the reformer of a kingdom, that spake it, they will not pardon him their dash; the sense of that great man shall to all posterity be lost, for the fearfulness or the presumptuous rashness of a perfunctory licenser. And to what an author this violence hath been lately done, and in what book of greatest consequence to be faithfully published, I could now instance, but shall forbear till a more convenient season. Yet if these things be not resented seriously and timely by them who have the remedy in their power, but that such iron-moulds as these shall have authority to gnaw out the choicest periods of exquisitest books, and to commit such a treacherous fraud against the orphan remainders of worthiest men after death, the more sorrow will belong to that hapless race of men whose misfortune it is to have understanding. Henceforth let no man care to learn, or care to be more than worldly wise; for certainly in higher matters to be ignorant and slothful, to be a common steadfast dunce, will be the only pleasant life, and only in request.

[41] And as it is a particular disesteem of every knowing person alive, and most injurious to the written labours and monuments of the dead, so to me it seems an undervaluing and vilifying of the whole nation. I cannot set so light by all the invention, the art, the wit, the grave and solid judgement which is in England, as that it can be comprehended in any twenty capacities, how good soever; much less that it should not pass except their superintendence be over it, except it be sifted and strained with their strainers, that it should be uncurrent without their manual stamp. Truth and understanding are not such wares as to be monopolized and traded in by tickets and statutes and standards. We must not think to make a staple commodity of all the knowledge in the land, to mark and license it like our broadcloth and our woolpacks. What is it but a servitude like that imposed by the Philistines, not to be allowed the sharpening of our own axes and coulters, but we must repair from all quarters to twenty licensing forges?

[42] Had anyone written and divulged erroneous things and scandalous to honest life, misusing and forfeiting the esteem had

of his reason among men, if after conviction this only censure were adjudged him, that he should never henceforth write but what were first examined by an appointed officer, whose hand should be annexed to pass his credit for him, that now he might be safely read, it could not be apprehended less than a disgraceful punishment. Whence to include the whole nation, and those that never yet thus offended, under such a diffident and suspectful prohibition, may plainly be understood what a disparagement it is. So much the more whenas debtors and delinquents may walk abroad without a keeper, but unoffensive books must not stir forth without a visible jailer in their title. Nor is it to the common people less than a reproach; for if we be so jealous over them as that we dare not trust them with an English pamphlet, what do we but censure them for a giddy, vicious, and ungrounded people, in such a sick and weak estate of faith and discretion as to be able to take nothing down but through the pipe [45] of a licenser? That this is care or love of them we cannot pretend, whenas in those popish places where the laity are most hated and despised, the same strictness is used over them. Wisdom we cannot call it, because it stops but one breach of license, nor that neither, whenas those corruptions which it seeks to prevent, break in faster at other doors which cannot be shut.

[43] And in conclusion, it reflects to the disrepute of our ministers also, of whose labours we should hope better, and of the proficiency which their flock reaps by them, than that after all this light of the gospel which is and is to be, and all this continual preaching, they should be still frequented with such an unprincipled, unedified, and laic [46] rabble, as that the whiff of every new pamphlet should stagger them out of their catechism and Christian walking. This may have much reason to discourage the ministers, when such a low conceit is had of all their exhortations and the benefiting of their hearers, as that they are not thought fit to be turned loose to three sheets of paper without a licenser; that all the sermons, all the lectures preached, printed, vented in such numbers and such volumes as have now well-nigh made all other books unsaleable, should not be armour enough against one

[45] *pipe:* a tube for taking medicine.
[46] *laic:* belonging to the laity.

single enchiridion,[47] without the castle of St. Angelo of an Imprimatur.

[44] And lest some should persuade ye, Lords and Commons, that these arguments of learned men's discouragement at this your order are mere flourishes and not real, I could recount what I have seen and heard in other countries where this kind of inquisition tyrannizes, when I have sat among their learned men (for that honour I had), and been counted happy to be born in such a place of philosophic freedom as they supposed England was, while themselves did nothing but bemoan the servile condition into which learning amongst them was brought; that this was it which had damped the glory of Italian wits; that nothing had been there written now these many years but flattery and fustian. There it was that I found and visited the famous Galileo, grown old, a prisoner to the Inquisition, for thinking in astronomy otherwise than the Franciscan and Dominican licensers thought. And though I knew that England then was groaning loudest under the prelatical yoke, nevertheless I took it as a pledge of future happiness that other nations were so persuaded of her liberty.

[45] Yet was it beyond my hope that those worthies were then breathing in her air, who should be her leaders to such a deliverance as shall never be forgotten by any revolution of time that this world hath to finish. When that was once begun, it was as little in my fear that what words of complaint I heard among learned men of other parts uttered against the Inquisition, the same I should hear by as learned men at home uttered in time of parliament against an order of licensing; and that so generally, that when I had disclosed myself a companion of their discontent, I might say, if without envy, that he whom an honest quaestorship had endeared to the Sicilians was not more by them importuned against Verres, than the favourable opinion which I had among many who honour ye, and are known and respected by ye, loaded me with entreaties and persuasions that I would not despair to lay together that which just reason should bring into my mind towards the removal of an undeserved thraldom upon learning.

[46] That this is not therefore the disburdening of a particular

---

[47] *enchiridion:* a manual or small handbook.

fancy, but the common grievance of all those who had prepared their minds and studies above the vulgar pitch to advance truth in others, and from others to entertain it, thus much may satisfy. And in their name I shall for neither friend nor foe conceal what the general murmur is: that if it come to inquisitioning again, and licensing, and that we are so timorous of ourselves and so suspicious of all men as to fear each book and the shaking of every leaf, before we know what the contents are; if some, who but of late were little better than silenced from preaching, shall come now to silence us from reading, except what they please, it cannot be guessed what is intended by some but a second tyranny over learning; and will soon put it out of controversy that bishops and presbyters are the same to us, both name and thing.

[47] That those evils of prelaty, which before from five or six and twenty sees were distributively charged upon the whole people, will now light wholly upon learning, is not obscure to us; whenas now the pastor of a small unlearned parish on the sudden shall be exalted archbishop over a large diocese of books, and yet not remove, but keep his other cure too, a mystical pluralist. He who but of late cried down the sole ordination of every novice Bachelor of Art, and denied sole jurisdiction over the simplest parishioner, shall now at home in his private chair assume both these over worthiest and excellentest books and ablest authors that write them. This is not, ye covenants and protestations that we have made, this is not to put down prelaty; this is but to chop an episcopacy; this is but to translate the palace metropolitan [48] from one kind of dominion into another; this is but an old canonical [49] sleight of commuting our penance. To startle thus betimes at a mere unlicensed pamphlet will after a while be afraid of every conventicle,[50] and a while after will make a conventicle of every Christian meeting.

[48] But I am certain that a state governed by the rules of justice and fortitude, or a church built and founded upon the rock of faith and true knowledge, cannot be so pusillanimous. While things are yet not constituted in religion, that freedom of writing

[48] *metropolitan:* pertaining to an archbishop or to his power or property.
[49] *canonical:* pertaining to Canon Law or lawyers.
[50] *conventicle:* a religious meeting of any of the independent sects whose services were forbidden.

should be restrained by a discipline imitated from the prelates, and learnt by them from the Inquisition, to shut us up all again into the breast of a licenser, must needs give cause of doubt and discouragement to all learned and religious men. Who cannot but discern the fineness [51] of this politic drift, and who are the contrivers: that while bishops were to be baited down,[52] then all presses might be open—it was the people's birthright and privilege in time of parliament, it was the breaking forth of light? But now, the bishops abrogated and voided [53] out of the church, as if our reformation sought no more but to make room for others into their seats under another name, the episcopal arts begin to bud again; the cruse of truth must run no more oil; liberty of printing must be enthralled again, under a prelatical commission of twenty; the privilege of the people nullified; and, which is worse, the freedom of learning must groan again, and to her old fetters— all this the parliament yet sitting. Although their own late arguments and defences against the prelates might remember [54] them that this obstructing violence meets for the most part with an event utterly opposite to the end which it drives at: instead of suppressing sects and schisms, it raises them and invests them with a reputation. 'The punishing of wits enhances their authority,' saith the Viscount St. Albans, 'and a forbidden writing is thought to be a certain spark of truth that flies up in the faces of them who seek to tread it out.' This order, therefore, may prove a nursing mother to sects, but I shall easily show how it will be a stepdame to truth: and first by disenabling us to the maintenance of what is known already.

[49] Well knows he who uses to consider, that our faith and knowledge thrives by exercise, as well as our limbs and complexion.[55] Truth is compared in Scripture to a streaming fountain; if her waters flow not in a perpetual progression, they sicken into a muddy pool of conformity and tradition. A man may be a heretic in the truth; and if he believe things only because his pastor

[51] *fineness:* subtlety, cleverness.
[52] *baited down: i.e.,* like bears in the sport of bear-baiting.
[53] *voided:* emptied out, expelled.
[54] *remember:* remind.
[55] *complexion:* the balance of "humors" in the body, on which an individual's health and character were understood to depend.

says so, or the Assembly so determines, without knowing other
reason, though his belief be true, yet the very truth he holds becomes his heresy. There is not any burden that some would gladlier
post off to another than the charge and care of their religion.
There be—who knows not that there be?—of Protestants and
professors [56] who live and die in as arrant an implicit faith as any
lay papist of Loretto.

[50] A wealthy man, addicted to his pleasure and to his profits,
finds religion to be a traffic so entangled, and of so many piddling
accounts, that of all mysteries [57] he cannot skill [58] to keep a stock
going upon that trade. What should he do? Fain he would have
the name to be religious, fain he would bear up with his neighbours
in that. What does he, therefore, but resolves to give over toiling,
and to find himself out some factor to whose care and credit he
may commit the whole managing of his religious affairs; some
divine of note and estimation that must be. To him he adheres,
resigns the whole warehouse of his religion, with all the locks and
keys, into his custody; and indeed makes the very person of that
man his religion; esteems his associating with him a sufficient
evidence and commendatory of his own piety. So that a man may
say his religion is now no more within himself, but is become a
dividual [59] movable, and goes and comes near him, according
as that good man frequents the house. He entertains him, gives him
gifts, feasts him, lodges him; his religion come home at night,
prays, is liberally supped, and sumptuously laid to sleep; rises, is
saluted, and after the malmsey,[60] or some well-spiced brewage,
and better breakfasted than he whose morning appetite would
have gladly fed on green figs between Bethany and Jerusalem, his
religion walks abroad at eight, and leaves his kind entertainer in
the shop trading all day without his religion.

[51] Another sort there be, who, when they hear that all things
shall be ordered, all things regulated and settled, nothing written

---

[56] *professors:* persons professing religious (and presumably Protestant)
faith.

[57] *mysteries:* trades, skills—in the sense in which the terms were applied
to the trades which were organized into guilds.

[58] *skill:* contrive.

[59] *dividual:* separable.

[60] *malmsey:* a strong, sweet wine.

but what passes through the custom-house of certain publicans [61]
that have the tonnaging and the poundaging of all free-spoken
truth, will straight give themselves up into your hands, make 'em
and cut 'em out what religion ye please; there be delights, there
be recreations and jolly pastimes, that will fetch the day about
from sun to sun, and rock the tedious year as in a delightful dream.
What need they torture their heads with that which others have
taken so strictly and so unalterably into their own purveying?
These are the fruits which a dull ease and cessation of our knowledge will bring forth among the people. How goodly and how to be
wished were such an obedient unanimity as this, what a fine conformity would it starch us all into! Doubtless a staunch and solid
piece of framework as any January could freeze together.

[52] Nor much better will be the consequence even among the
clergy themselves. It is no new thing never heard of before, for
a parochial minister, who has his reward and is at his Hercules'
pillars in a warm benefice, to be easily inclinable, if he have nothing
else that may rouse up his studies, to finish his circuit in an
English concordance and a topic folio, the gatherings and savings
of a sober graduateship, a Harmony [62] and a Catena,[63] treading
the constant round of certain common doctrinal heads, attended
with their uses, motives, marks and means; out of which, as out of
an alphabet or sol-fa, by forming and transforming, joining and
disjoining variously, a little bookcraft and two hours' meditation
might furnish him unspeakably to the performance of more than
a weekly charge of sermoning; not to reckon up the infinite helps
of interlinearies, breviaries, synopses, and other loitering gear.
But as for the multitude of sermons ready printed and piled up,
on every text that is not difficult, our London trading St. Thomas
in his vestry, and add to boot St. Martin and St. Hugh, have not
within their hallowed limits more vendible ware of all sorts ready
made; so that penury he never need fear of pulpit provision, having where so plenteously to refresh his magazine. But if his rear and
flanks be not impaled,[64] if his back door be not secured by the

[61] *publicans:* tax-gatherers.
[62] *harmony:* a simple treatise bringing divergent scripture narratives, such
as those in the four gospels, into harmony with one another.
[63] *catena:* (in Latin) chain. The term was applied to compilations of texts.
[64] *impaled:* protected.

rigid licenser, but that a bold book may now and then issue forth and give the assault to some of his old collections in their trenches, it will concern him then to keep waking, to stand in watch, to set good guards and sentinels about his received opinions, to walk the round and counter-round with his fellow inspectors, fearing lest any of his flock be seduced, who also then would be better instructed, better exercised and disciplined. And God send [65] that the fear of this diligence, which must then be used, do not make us affect the laziness of a licensing church.

[53] For if we be sure we are in the right, and do not hold the truth guiltily (which becomes not), if we ourselves condemn not our own weak and frivolous teaching, and the people for an un-taught and irreligious gadding rout, what can be more fair than when a man judicious, learned, and of a conscience, for aught we know, as good as theirs that taught us what we know, shall not privily from house to house, which is more dangerous, but openly by writing, publish to the world what his opinion is, what his reasons, and wherefore that which is now thought cannot be sound? Christ urged it as wherewith to justify himself that he preached in public; yet writing is more public than preaching, and more easy to refutation if need be, there being so many whose business and profession merely it is to be the champions of truth; which if they neglect, what can be imputed but their sloth or unability?

[54] Thus much we are hindered and disinured [66] by this course of licensing towards the true knowledge of what we seem to know. For how much it hurts and hinders the licensers themselves in the calling of their ministry, more than any secular employment, if they will discharge that office as they ought, so that of necessity they must neglect either the one duty or the other, I insist not, because it is a particular, but leave it to their own conscience how they will decide it there.

[55] There is yet behind of what I purposed to lay open, the in-credible loss and detriment that this plot of licensing puts us to. More than if some enemy at sea should stop up all our havens

---

[65] *send:* the reading of the original, has been emended by some editors to *fend: i.e.,* prevent, forfend.

[66] *disinured:* diverted from a customary practice.

and ports and creeks, it hinders and retards the importation of our richest merchandise, truth. Nay, it was first established and put in practice by antichristian malice and mystery, on set purpose to extinguish, if it were possible, the light of reformation, and to settle falsehood; little differing from that policy wherewith the Turk upholds his Alcoran, by the prohibition of printing. 'Tis not denied, but gladly confessed, we are to send our thanks and vows to Heaven, louder than most of nations, for that great measure of truth which we enjoy, especially in those main points between us and the pope, with his appurtenances the prelates; but he who thinks we are to pitch our tent here, and have attained the utmost prospect of reformation that the mortal glass [67] wherein we contemplate can show us, till we come to beatific vision, that man by this very opinion declares that he is yet far short of truth. [56] Truth indeed came once into the world with her divine Master, and was a perfect shape most glorious to look on. But when he ascended, and his apostles after him were laid asleep, then straight arose a wicked race of deceivers, who (as that story goes of the Egyptian Typhon with his conspirators, how they dealt with the good Osiris) took the virgin Truth, hewed her lovely form into a thousand pieces, and scattered them to the four winds. From that time ever since, the sad friends of Truth, such as durst appear, imitating the careful search that Isis made for the mangled body of Osiris, went up and down gathering up limb by limb still as they could find them. We have not yet found them all, Lords and Commons, nor ever shall do, till her Master's second coming; he shall bring together every joint and member, and shall mould them into an immortal feature of loveliness and perfection. Suffer not these licensing prohibitions to stand at every place of opportunity, forbidding and disturbing them that continue seeking, that continue to do our obsequies to the torn body of our martyred saint. We boast our light; but if we look not wisely on the sun itself, it smites us into darkness. Who can discern those planets that are oft combust, and those stars of brightest magnitude that rise and set with the sun, until the opposite motion of their orbs bring them to such a place in the firmament where they may be seen evening or

[67] *glass:* mirror.

morning? The light which we have gained was given us, not to be ever staring on, but by it to discover onward things more remote from our knowledge. It is not the unfrocking of a priest, the unmitring of a bishop, and the removing him from off the Presbyterian shoulders, that will make us a happy nation; no, if other things as great in the church, and in the rule of life both economical and political, be not looked into and reformed, we have looked so long upon the blaze that Zuinglius and Calvin hath beaconed up to us, that we are stark blind.

[57] There be who perpetually complain of schisms and sects, and make it such a calamity that any man dissents from their maxims. 'Tis their own pride and ignorance which causes the disturbing, who neither will hear with meekness, nor can convince, yet all must be suppressed which is not found in their syntagma.[68] They are the troublers, they are the dividers of unity, who neglect and permit not others to unite those disservered pieces which are yet wanting to the body of Truth. To be still searching what we know not by what we know, still closing up truth to truth as we find it (for all her body is homogeneal and proportional), this is the golden rule in theology as well as in arithmetic, and makes up the best harmony in a church; not the forced and outward union of cold and neutral and inwardly divided minds.

[58] Lords and Commons of England, consider what nation it is whereof ye are, and whereof ye are the governors: a nation not slow and dull, but of a quick, ingenious, and piercing spirit, acute to invent, subtle and sinewy to discourse, not beneath the reach of any point the highest that human capacity can soar to. Therefore the studies of learning in her deepest sciences have been so ancient and so eminent among us, that writers of good antiquity and ablest judgement have been persuaded that even the school of Pythagoras and the Persian wisdom took beginning from the old philosophy of this island. And that wise and civil Roman, Julius Agricola, who governed once here for Caesar, preferred the natural wits of Britain before the labored studies of the French. Nor is it for nothing that the grave and frugal Transylvanian sends out yearly from as far as the mountainous borders of Russia and

[68] *syntagma:* collection, systematic compilation.

beyond the Hercynian wilderness, not their youth but their staid men, to learn our language and our theologic arts. Yet that which is above all this, the favour and the love of Heaven, we have great argument to think in a peculiar manner propitious and propending [69] towards us. Why else was this nation chosen before any other, that out of her, as out of Sion, should be proclaimed and sounded forth the first tidings and trumpet of reformation to all Europe? And had it not been the obstinate perverseness of our prelates against the divine and admirable spirit of Wycliffe, to suppress him as a schismatic and innovator, perhaps neither the Bohemian Huss and Jerome, no, nor the name of Luther or of Calvin had been ever known; the glory of reforming all our neighbours had been completely ours. But now, as our obdurate clergy have with violence demeaned [70] the matter, we are become hitherto the latest and the backwardest scholars, of whom God offered to have made us the teachers.

[59] Now once again by all concurrence of signs, and by the general instinct of holy and devout men, as they daily and solemnly express their thoughts, God is decreeing to begin some new and great period in his church, even to the reforming of reformation itself; what does he then but reveal himself to his servants and, as his manner is, first to his Englishmen? I say, as his manner is, first to us, though we mark not the method of his counsels, and are unworthy. Behold now this vast city, a city of refuge, the mansion-house of liberty, encompassed and surrounded with his protection; the shop of war hath not there more anvils and hammers waking to fashion out the plates and instruments of armed justice in defence of beleaguered truth, than there be pens and heads there, sitting by their studious lamps, musing, searching, revolving new notions and ideas wherewith to present, as with their homage and their fealty, the approaching reformation; others as fast reading, trying all things, assenting to the force of reason and convincement.

[60] What could a man require more from a nation so pliant and so prone to seek after knowledge? What wants there to such a towardly and pregnant soil but wise and faithful labourers, to

[69] *propending:* inclining.
[70] *demeaned:* conducted, handled.

make a knowing people, a nation of prophets, of sages, and of worthies? We reckon more than five months yet to harvest; there need not be five weeks, had we but eyes to lift up; the fields are white already. Where there is much desire to learn, there of necessity will be much arguing, much writing, many opinions; for opinion in good men is but knowledge in the making. Under these fantastic terrors of sect and schism, we wrong the earnest and zealous thirst after knowledge and understanding which God hath stirred up in this city. What some lament of, we rather should rejoice at, should rather praise this pious forwardness among men to reassume the ill-deputed care of their religion into their own hands again. A little generous prudence, a little forbearance of one another, and some grain of charity might win all these diligences to join and unite into one general and brotherly search after truth, could we but forgo this prelatical tradition of crowding free consciences and Christian liberties into canons and precepts of men. I doubt not, if some great and worthy stranger should come among us, wise to discern the mould and temper of a people and how to govern it, observing the high hopes and aims, the diligent alacrity of our extended thoughts and reasonings in the pursuance of truth and freedom, but that he would cry out as Pyrrhus did, admiring the Roman docility and courage, 'If such were my Epirots, I would not despair the greatest design that could be attempted to make a church or kingdom happy.'

[61] Yet these are the men cried out against for schismatics and sectaries; as if, while the temple of the Lord was building, some cutting, some squaring the marble, others hewing the cedars, there should be a sort of irrational man who could not consider there must be many schisms [71] and many dissections made in the quarry and in the timber ere the house of Gold can be built. And when every stone is laid artfully together, it cannot be united into a continuity, it can but be contiguous in this world; neither can every piece of the building be of one form; nay rather, the perfection consists in this, that out of many moderate varieties and brotherly dissimilitudes that are not vastly disproportional, arises the goodly and graceful symmetry that commends the whole pile and structure.

[71] *schisms:* Milton puns on the literal meaning of *schism*, cutting or division.

[62] Let us therefore be more considerate builders, more wise in spiritual architecture, when great reformation is expected. For now the time seems come wherein Moses, the great prophet, may sit in heaven rejoicing to see that memorable and glorious wish of his fulfilled, when not only our seventy elders, but all the Lord's people, are become prophets. No marvel then though some men, and some good men too perhaps, but young in goodness, as Joshua then was, envy them. They fret, and out of their own weakness are in agony, lest these divisions and subdivisions will undo us. The adversary again applauds, and waits the hour: when they have branched themselves out, saith he, small enough into parties and partitions, then will be our time. Fool! he sees not the firm root out of which we all grow, though into branches; nor will beware, until he see our small divided maniples [72] cutting through at every angle of his ill-united and unwieldy brigade. And that we are to hope better of all these supposed sects and schisms, and that we shall not need that solicitude, honest perhaps, though over-timorous, of them that vex in this behalf, but shall laugh in the end at those malicious applauders of our differences, I have these reasons to persuade me.

[63] First, when a city shall be as it were besieged and blocked about, her navigable river infested, inroads and incursions round, defiance and battle oft rumoured to be marching up even to her walls and suburb trenches; that then the people, or the greater part, more than at other times, wholly taken up with the study of highest and most important matters to be reformed, should be disputing, reasoning, reading, inventing, discoursing, even to a rarity and admiration, things not before discoursed or written of, argues first a singular goodwill, contentedness, and confidence in your prudent foresight and safe government, Lords and Commons; and from thence derives itself to a gallant bravery and well-grounded contempt of their enemies, as if there were no small number of as great spirits among us, as his was who, when Rome was nigh besieged by Hannibal, being in the city, bought that piece of ground at no cheap rate whereon Hannibal himself encamped his own regiment.

[64] Next, it is a lively and cheerful presage of our happy success

---

[72] *maniple:* a small company or unit of Roman soldiers.

and victory. For as in a body, when the blood is fresh, the spirits pure and vigourous not only to vital but to rational faculties, and those in the acutest and the pertest operations of wit and subtlety, it argues in what good plight and constitution the body is; so when the cheerfulness of the people is so sprightly up, as that it has not only wherewith to guard well its own freedom and safety, but to spare, and to bestow upon the solidest and sublimest points of controversy and new invention, it betokens us not degenerated nor drooping to a fatal decay, but casting off the old and wrinkled skin of corruption to outlive these pangs and wax young again, entering the glorious ways of truth and prosperous virtue, destined to become great and honourable in these latter ages. Methinks I see in my mind a noble and puissant nation rousing herself like a strong man after sleep, and shaking her invincible locks: methinks I see her as an eagle newing [73] her mighty youth, and kindling her undazzled eyes at the full midday beam, purging and unscaling her long-abused sight at the fountain itself of heavenly radiance; while the whole noise of timorous and flocking birds, with those also that love the twilight, flutter about, amazed at what she means, and in their envious gabble would prognosticate a year of sects and schisms.

[65] What should ye do then, should ye suppress all this flowery crop of knowledge and new light sprung up and yet springing daily in this city? Should ye set an oligarchy of twenty engrossers [74] over it, to bring a famine upon our minds again, when we shall know nothing but what is measured to us by their bushel? Believe it, Lords and Commons, they who counsel ye to such a suppressing do as good as bid ye suppress yourselves; and I will soon show how. If it be desired to know the immediate cause of all this free writing and free speaking, there cannot be assigned a truer than your own mild and free and humane government; it is the liberty, Lords and Commons, which your own valourous and happy counsels have purchased us, liberty which is the nurse of all great wits. This is that which hath rarefied and enlightened our spirits like the influence of heaven; this is that which hath en-

[73] *newing:* the original reads *muing,* probably an error for *newing,* an old word meaning *renewing.*

[74] *engrossers:* persons attempting to "corner" a market.

franchised, enlarged, and lifted up our apprehensions degrees above themselves. Ye cannot make us now less capable, less knowing, less eagerly pursuing of the truth, unless ye first make yourselves, that made us so, less the lovers, less the founders of our true liberty. We can grow ignorant again, brutish, formal, and slavish, as ye found us; but you then must first become that which ye cannot be, oppressive, arbitrary, and tyrannous, as they were from whom ye have freed us. That our hearts are now more capacious, our thoughts more erected to the search and expectation of greatest and exactest things, is the issue of your own virtue propagated in us; ye cannot suppress that unless ye reinforce an abrogated and merciless law, that fathers may dispatch at will their own children. And who shall then stick closest to ye and excite others? Not he who takes up arms for coat and conduct,[75] and his four nobles of Danegelt. Although I dispraise not the defence of just immunities, yet love my peace better, if that were all. Give me the liberty to know, to utter, and to argue freely according to conscience, above all liberties.

[66] What would be best advised, then, if it be found so hurtful and so unequal [76] to suppress opinions for the newness, or the unsuitableness to a customary acceptance, will not be my task to say. I only shall repeat what I have learned from one of your own honourable number, a right noble and pious lord, who had he not sacrificed his life and fortunes to the church and commonwealth, we had not now missed and bewailed a worthy and undoubted patron of this argument. Ye know him, I am sure; yet I for honour's sake, and may it be eternal to him, shall name him, the Lord Brooke. He, writing of episcopacy, and by the way treating of sects and schisms, left ye his vote,[77] or rather now the last words of his dying charge (which I know will ever be of dear and honoured regard with ye), so full of meekness and breathing charity that, next to his last testament who bequeathed love and peace to his disciples, I cannot call to mind where I have read or heard words more mild and peaceful. He there exhorts us to hear

---

[75] *coat and conduct:* an obsolete tax, originally levied to pay for clothing and transporting feudal troops in the king's service, and revived by Charles I in his effort to obtain funds without a parliamentary grant.

[76] *unequal:* unjust, inequitable.

[77] *vote:* solemn wish.

with patience and humility those, however they be miscalled, that
desire to live purely, in such a use of God's ordinances as the
best guidance of their conscience gives them, and to tolerate them,
though in some disconformity to ourselves. The book itself will
tell us more at large, being published to the world and dedicated
to the parliament by him who, both for his life and for his death,
deserves that what advice he left be not laid by without perusal.
[67] And now the time in special is, by privilege to write and
speak what may help to the further discussing of matters in
agitation. The temple of Janus, with his two controversal faces,
might now not unsignificantly be set open. And though all the
winds of doctrine were let loose to play upon the earth, so truth
be in the field, we do injuriously by licensing and prohibiting to
misdoubt her strength. Let her and falsehood grapple; who ever
knew truth put to the worse, in a free and open encounter? Her
confuting is the best and surest suppressing. He who hears what
praying there is for light and clearer knowledge to be sent down
among us, would think of other matters to be constituted beyond
the discipline of Geneva, framed and fabricked [78] already to our
hands.
[68] Yet when the new light which we beg for shines in upon us,
there be who envy and oppose, if it come not first in at their
casements. What a collusion is this, whenas we are exhorted by
the wise man to use dilligence, 'to seek for wisdom as for hidden
treasures' early and late, that another order shall enjoin us to
know nothing but by statute? When a man hath been labouring
the hardest labour in the deep mines of knowledge, hath furnished
out his findings in all their equipage, drawn forth his reasons as it
were a battle ranged, scattered and defeated all objections in his
way, calls out his adversary into the plain, offers him the advantage
of wind and sun, if he please, only that he may try the matter by
dint of argument; for his opponents then to skulk, to lay ambush-
ments, to keep a narrow bridge of licensing where the challenger
should pass, though it be valour enough in soldiership, is but
weakness and cowardice in the wars of truth. For who knows
not that truth is strong, next to the Almighty? She needs no
policies, nor stratagems, nor licensings to make her victorious;

[78] *fabriced:* fabricated.

those are the shifts and the defences that error uses against her power. 'Give her but room, and do not bind her when she sleeps, for then she speaks not true, as the old Proteus did, who spake oracles only when he was caught and bound, but then rather she turns herself into all shapes except her own, and perhaps tunes her voice according to the time, as Micaiah did before Ahab, until she be adjured into her own likeness.

[69] Yet is it not impossible that she may have more shapes than one. What else is all that rank of things indifferent, wherein truth may be on this side, or on the other, without being unlike herself? What but a vain shadow else is the abolition of 'those ordinances, that handwriting nailed to the cross'? What great purchase is this Christian liberty which Paul so often boasts of? His doctrine is that he who eats or eats not, regards a day or regards it not, may do either to the Lord. How many other things might be tolerated in peace and left to conscience, had we but charity, and were it not the chief stronghold of our hypocrisy to be ever judging one another? I fear yet this iron yoke of outward conformity hath left a slavish print upon our necks; the ghost of a linen decency yet haunts us. We stumble and are impatient at the least dividing of one visible congregation from another, though it be not in fundamentals; and through our forwardness to suppress, and our backwardness to recover, any enthralled piece of truth out of the gripe of custom, we care not to keep truth separated from truth, which is the fiercest rent and disunion of all. We do not see that while we still affect by all means a rigid external formality, we may as soon fall again into a gross conforming stupidity, a stark and dead congealment of 'wood and hay and stubble' forced and frozen together, which is more to the sudden degenerating of a church than many subdichotomies of petty schisms.

[70] Not that I can think well of every light separation; or that all in a church is to be expected 'gold and silver and precious stones.' It is not possible for man to sever the wheat from the tares, the good fish from the other fry; that must be the angels' ministry at the end of mortal things. Yet if all cannot be of one mind—as who looks they should be?—this doubtless is more wholesome, more prudent, and more Christian, that many be

tolerated, rather than all compelled. I mean not tolerated popery
and open superstition, which as it extirpates all religious and
civil supremacies, so itself should be extirpate, provided first that
all charitable and compassionate means be used to win and regain
the weak and the misled; that also which is impious or evil absolutely, either against faith or manners, no law can possibly permit that intends not to unlaw itself; but those neighbouring differences, or rather indifferences, are what I speak of, whether
in some point of doctrine or of discipline, which though they may
be many, yet need not interrupt the unity of Spirit, if we could but
find among us the bond of peace.

[71] In the meanwhile, if anyone would write and bring his helpful hand to the slow-moving reformation which we labour under,
if truth have spoken to him before others, or but seemed at least
to speak, who hath so bejesuited us that we should trouble that
man with asking license to do so worthy a deed; and not consider this, that if it come to prohibiting, there is not aught more
likely to be prohibited than truth itself, whose first appearance,
to our eyes bleared and dimmed with prejudice and custom, is more
unsightly and unplausible than many errors, even as the person is
of many a great man slight and contemptible to see to [79]? And
what do they tell us vainly of new opinions, when this very opinion
of theirs, that none must be heard but whom they like, is the worst
and newest opinion of all others; and is the chief cause why sects
and schisms do so much abound, and true knowledge is kept at
distance from us; besides yet a greater danger which is in it. For
when God shakes a kingdom with strong and healthful commotions
to a general reforming, 'tis not untrue that many sectaries and false
teachers are then busiest in seducing.

[72] But yet more true it is that God then raises to his own work
men of rare abilities and more than common industry, not only
to look back and revise what hath been taught heretofore, but to
gain further and go on some new enlightened steps in the discovery of truth. For such is the order of God's enlightening his
church, to dispense and deal out by degrees his beam, so as our
earthly eyes may best sustain it. Neither is God appointed and

---

[79] *to see to:* to look at.

confined where and out of what place these his chosen shall be first heard to speak; for he sees not as man sees, chooses not as man chooses, lest we should devote ourselves again to set places and assemblies, and outward callings of men; planting our faith one while in the old Convocation house, and another while in the Chapel at Westminster; when all the faith and religion that shall be there canonized is not sufficient, without plain convincement and the charity of patient instruction, to supple the least bruise of conscience, to edify the meanest Christian who desires to walk in the spirit and not in the letter of human trust, for all the number of voices that can be there made; no, though Harry VII himself there, with all his liege tombs about him, should lend them voices from the dead to swell their number.

[73] And if the men be erroneous who appear to be the leading schismatics, what withholds us but our sloth, our self-will, and distrust in the right cause, that we do not give them gentle meetings and gentle dimensions, that we debate not and examine the matter thoroughly with liberal and frequent audience, if not for their sakes yet for our own? Seeing no man who hath tasted learning but will confess the many ways of profiting by those who, not contented with stale receipts, are able to manage and set forth new positions to the world. And were they but as the dust and cinders of our feet, so long as in that notion they may yet serve to polish and brighten the armoury of truth, even for that respect they were not utterly to be cast away. But if they be of those whom God hath fitted for the special use of these times with eminent and ample gifts—and those perhaps neither among the priests nor among the pharisees—and we, in the haste of a precipitant zeal, shall make no distinction, but resolve to stop their mouths because we fear they come with new and dangerous opinions (as we commonly forejudge them ere we understand them), no less than woe to us while, thinking thus to defend the gospel, we are found the persecutors.

[74] There have been not a few since the beginning of this parliament, both of the presbytery and others, who by their unlicensed books, to the contempt of an Imprimatur, first broke that triple ice clung about our hearts, and taught the people to see day. I hope

that none of those were the persuaders to renew upon us this
bondage, which they themselves have wrought so much good by
contemning. But if neither the check that Moses gave to young
Joshua, nor the countermand which our Saviour gave to young
John, who was so ready to prohibit those whom he thought unlicensed, be not enough to admonish our elders how unacceptable
to God their testy mood of prohibiting is; if neither their own
remembrance what evil hath abounded in the church by this let
of licensing, and what good they themselves have begun by trans-
gressing it, be not enough, but that they will persuade and execute
the most Dominican part of the Inquisition over us, and are already with one foot in the stirrup so active at suppressing, it
would be no unequal distribution in the first place to suppress the
suppressors themselves, whom the change of their condition hath
puffed up more than their late experience of harder times hath
made wise.

[75] And as for regulating the press, let no man think to have
the honour of advising ye better than yourselves have done in
that order published next before this, 'that no book be printed,
unless the printer's and the author's name, or at least the printer's,
be registered.' Those which otherwise come forth, if they be found
mischievous and libelous, the fire and the executioner will be the
timeliest and the most effectual remedy that man's prevention
can use. For this authentic Spanish policy of licensing books, if I
have said aught, will prove the most unlicensed book itself within
a short while; and was the immediate image of a Star Chamber
decree to that purpose made in those very times when that court
did the rest of those her pious works, for which she is now fallen
from the stars with Lucifer. Whereby ye may guess what kind
of state prudence, what love of the people, what care of religion
or good manners there was at the contriving, although with
singular hypocrisy it pretended to bind books to their good behaviour. And how it got the upper hand of your precedent order
so well constituted before, if we may believe those men whose
profession gives them cause to inquire most, it may be doubted
there was in it the fraud of some old patentees and monopolizers
in the trade of bookselling; who, under pretence of the poor in

their Company not to be defrauded, and the just retaining of each man his several copy (which God forbid should be gainsaid), brought divers glozing colours to the House, which were indeed but colours, and serving to no end except it be to exercise a superiority over their neighbours; men who do not therefore labour in an honest profession, to which learning is indebted, that they should be made other men's vassals. Another end is thought was aimed at by some of them in procuring by petition this order, that having power in their hands, malignant books might the easier scape abroad, as the event shows. But of these sophisms and elenchs [80] of merchandise I skill not. This I know, that errors in a good government and in a bad are equally almost incident; for what magistrate may not be misinformed, and much the sooner, if liberty of printing be reduced into the power of a few? But to redress willingly and speedily what hath been erred, and in highest authority to esteem a plain advertisement [81] more than others have done a sumptuous bribe, is a virtue, honored Lords and Commons, answerable to your highest actions, and whereof none can participate but greatest and wisest men.

EXERCISES

Milton's *Areopagitica* was published in 1644 as a plea to Parliament to repeal an act requiring the licensing of all books before publication. Although its form is that of a classical oration, it was not actually delivered as a speech. *Areopagitica* itself was unlicensed, and Milton was not punished; but the licensing act was not repealed, either. However, for more than three hundred years Milton's eloquent plea has stood as a kind of manifesto for freedom of speech and the press, and in 1944 its tercentenary was celebrated around the world.

The three parts of rhetoric appropriate to the written oration, according to classical rhetoricians, were *elocutio, inventio,* and *dispositio. Elocutio* was largely what we study as style; *inventio,* or the finding of arguments, was what we speak of as development; and *dispositio* was about the same thing as organization; it was a prescribed order of more or less standard parts for each type of discourse. The *dispositio* for the written oration was soundly based on the needs of logical proof

---

[80] *elench:* "a fallacious answer to a sophistical question." (White.)
[81] *advertisement:* intimation, notification.

and explanation and is still followed by some of our best speakers and writers. The parts and their functions are these:

(1) *exordium*—to render the audience attentive and friendly
(2) *narratio*—to state the facts of the situation, in a light favorable to the speaker if possible
(3) *divisio*—to forecast the main points of the discourse
(4) *confirmatio*—to give affirmative proof or explanation of each point
(5) *refutatio*—to answer any expected or known objections
(6) *peroratio*—to summarize all points and make a final appeal

1. Locate all of these parts in *Areopagitica*.
2. Summarize all of Milton's main points in a sentence each.

We may discern three kinds of meaning in most prose: *explicit, implicit,* and *inferential.* Explicit meaning is that which is clearly and directly asserted; we have studied that kind of meaning from the first question on topic sentences. In *Areopagitica* Milton distinctly says that licensing of books is bad. Implicit meaning is that which is clearly implied, suggested, indirectly revealed; the author is usually conscious of it, and we can perceive it by his tone and by the assumptions he makes and the problems he is concerned about—his "climate of opinion." Milton clearly shows that he believes in God and God's active interest in man, and that he believes in truth as an active force in the world. Inferential meaning is that which the reader infers, or carries into the composition. We perceive it by the same means as those by which we perceive consciously implied meaning, but the author may or may not be aware of it. Sometimes implication and inference coincide, but sometimes they do not. We may perceive, for instance, by Milton's style and the way in which he attacks his problem that he is a vigorous spirit, even violent and prejudiced at times. Surely the communication of this personal quality was not one of his conscious intentions; it is our inference.

3. Summarize Milton's explicitly stated theory, in paragraph 19, of how virtue is achieved.
4. What attitude towards the authority of the ancients is implicit in paragraphs 15–17?
5. What inference may we make about national feeling in England in Milton's day, as reflected in paragraphs 58–59?
6. From Milton's statements in paragraph 19 we may infer that he thinks of virtue as more than simply a means to civic order. What is this additional use or value of virtue?
7. What syllogism is implied in paragraphs 10–13?

8. In the intellectual climate of Milton's day, what assumptions seem to have been made on the following topics:
   a. Religion and the church
   b. The aims of the individual life
   c. Ancient authorities
   d. The uses of knowledge
9. Does Milton use any analogies? Any name-calling? Are there any evidences of unfairness?
10. In paragraph 37 find an example of each of the following devices:
    a. Rhetorical question
    b. Periodic sentence
    c. Balance
    d. Alliteration for emphasis
    e. Repetition for emphasis
    f. Simile used to emphasize the ridiculousness of censorship
    g. Cadence

We can well begin the study of euphony at this point, for Milton is a master of English prose. *Euphony* means pleasantness of sound. It consists of a combination of the *rhythm, assonance,* and *consonance* of a sentence. (See all of these words and also *sound* in the Glossary.) Ordinarily euphony requires only that the sound be moderately pleasant or at least inoffensive. But sound may be suited to sense for emphatic effect; this is the same kind of concord between style and idea which we have already observed in the favorable and unfavorable connotation of words and figures of speech. Milton uses pleasant sound for a pleasant thought, for instance, in paragraph 70 when he writes of "the angels' ministry at the end of mortal things." His words spit and pop at an unpleasant thought in paragraph 37 when he writes of how an author is "not to be still mistrusted and suspected . . ." When the sound is thus unpleasant we call it *cacophony;* cacophony is to be avoided except as a means of emphasizing the unpleasantness of an idea.

11. Explain how the connotation of the words, metaphors, and allusions agree with the sense of the following passage from paragraph 66, and decide whether the sound also agrees with the sense. ". . . so full of meekness and breathing charity that, next to his last testament who bequeathed love and peace to his disciples, I cannot call to mind where I have read or heard words more mild and peaceful."
12. Explain similarly how the words, metaphors, and sound agree with the sense of the last sentence of paragraph 69.

13. Why does the rhythm seem unpleasant in the last clause of the last sentence in paragraph 37?
14. How is the sound appropriate to the sense of the last sentence in paragraph 71?

Essentials of the American System

CHARLES A. BEARD

[1] After an inquiry into our historical heritage, including the rise and growth of the democratic idea, it is appropriate that, in seeking a comprehensive view of our present situation, we try to get at the fundamental character of democracy, or, more properly speaking, the American system of government and polity. In a practical way this means trying to pick out those features of our system which are deemed essential, indispensable to its genius and its existence. The task is difficult. It must be undertaken, however, if we are to have a clear idea of what we are talking about when we speak of democracy or the American system.

[2] Never by solemn convention assembled has this nation proclaimed itself a democracy. Nowhere in law or decree is presented for our instruction a summary of the ideas and practices deemed essential components of democracy. The word is not found in the Declaration of Independence. Nor does it appear in the Constitution of the United States.

[3] In the early days of the nation, the term "democracy," when used, was generally applied to direct popular rule in small communities, such as the city-states of antiquity; and by a study of history leaders among the founders of our republic reached the conclusion that this type of government led inexorably to tumults, to attacks on persons and properties, and finally to the triumph

From *Public Policy and the General Welfare,* by Charles A. Beard. Reprinted by permission of Rinehart & Company, Inc.

of despotism. Scarcely less did they fear indirect popular rule through the representative assemblies of the American states, and especially the possibilities of full manhood suffrage. "Give the votes to the people who have no property," exclaimed Gouverneur Morris in the Constitutional Convention of 1787, "and they will sell them to the rich who will be able to buy them." Broadly speaking, these founders of the republic were as much alarmed by the specter of democracy in either form, direct or representative, as they were by the menace of monarchy or the dictatorial propensities of a military caste or of a plutocracy.

[4] Only by slow and halting processes have Americans arrived at the application of the word "democracy" to the government and society of the United States. Nothing like official sanction was given to this usage until 1917, when President Wilson declared that the war on the Central Powers of Europe was a war for democracy. Even now, amid all the florid eloquence about it, the term has no seal of national resolve, and awaits both comprehensive statement and formal adoption.

The Elements of Democracy

[5] Whence came the idea of democracy, so vaunted and so celebrated in our day? For an answer we must search; and our search carries us far back in time; beyond the Declaration of Independence into colonial and English history; beyond England to the Continent of Europe, through the Protestant Reformation, the Renaissance and medieval civilization; beyond the Christian doctrine of universal brotherhood, through the natural law of the Romans, to the social ideals of the Stoics; far beyond Stoicism into the very origins of primitive society, when man was the hunter and fighter and woman was the mother, originator of domestic arts, conservator of the humane spirit in mutual aid. And when we scan the horizon of the future, contemplate the coming fortunes of democracy, we find ourselves caught in the toils of this historical sweep. If we are bold enough and insistent enough, our search will carry us into a consideration of the nature of all things human—the ultimate design of the universe.

[6] When, however, we concentrate our thought upon experience in the United States, we find six enduring elements now inter-

twined under the prevalent conception of democracy: popular government within a span of time, efficiency in function, sustaining economy, civil liberty, appropriate education, and the spirit of humanity and enlightenment which lifts men and women above the beasts of the field and confers upon them moral rights and social duties. These six elements are closely related, are aspects of the same thing, are inseparable parts of the whole. The neglect or failure of one imperils the fortunes of all. Any conception of democracy in America less comprehensive would not correspond to irreducible facts in the case.

[7] It is true that democracy is often defined narrowly as the "form of government in which the sovereign power resides in the people as a whole and is exercised either directly by them . . . or by officers elected by them." But this definition is both exclusive and superficial. It fails to specify the concrete practices necessarily associated with the exercise of popular sovereignty in a span of time. Under this definition the despotism of Napoleon III might be called a democracy, for his elevation as emperor was approved by a popular vote of adult males, by a majority of ten to one. The definition omits all reference to society, in which every form of government must operate. In other words, it leaves out of account specific conditions of life and economy indispensable to the existence and functioning of democracy. It disregards the eternal oppositions of power and life, authority and liberty, public spirit and private interest, brute force and humanity, with which the institutions of democracy must cope if they are to endure.

[8] Both in conception and practice popular government in the United States transcends any superficial definition of form at a given moment. It is democratic in the sense that all high public authorities endowed with political power over lives and properties are chosen directly or indirectly by popular vote and that, in the long run, the sustained and matured will of the duly constituted majority is allowed to prevail. Here popular sovereignty and the time span are combined.

[9] Under this system, no mere majority of men and women at any momentary election of public authorities or in any given legislative assembly can immediately compel the enactment and

enforcement of any law they are pleased to demand amid the heats and tumults of a single campaign. If such immediacy is an essential element of democracy, then America has never been and is not now a democracy.

[10] Only in limited matters do simple majorities or pluralities control the decisions and actions of government. In all sovereign matters, as the Constitution of the United States prescribes, extraordinary majorities are required and a due process calling for an extension of actions in time must be followed. In no sovereign matter does the snap judgment of a majority or a plurality given at a mere moment have the force of law. Our system, in respect of great issues, allows for the time element and guarantees that prudence and daring, conservatism and radicalism, may each have its days in court, that discussion and education may intervene, that pleas and counterpleas may be heard, and that decision may be matured.

The Popular Will

[11] The declaration of popular will, even if matured, is only the beginning of democratic government. Government in action is function, the discharge of concrete duties. Government in action deals with issues of finance, economy, health, utilities, conservation of resources, human relations, national defense, foreign affairs, and the general welfare broadly and realistically conceived. If it is to endure, government must grapple with these issues competently, efficiently. Is popular government a guarantee that a democratic government can and will display this competence, this efficiency? If it were, then surely the elected parliaments of so many nations would not have vanished in our own time. Unless the agencies of popular will can legislate appropriately and administer efficiently, then democratic devices will perish, no matter what oceans of ink are spilt and what flowers of eloquence bloom in their defense. In ancient Rome men mouthed the grand phrase *Senatus Populusque Romanus* long after the assembly had degenerated into a farce and the Senate had become the home of gibbering ghosts. The wrecks of monarchies, tyrannies, aristocracies, dictatorships, and democracies scattered through fifty centuries are solemn demonstrations that varied forms of govern-

ment have failed at their tasks, in the discharge of their functions, under their symbols, in their times and places.

Efficiency in Function

[12] When, therefore, the test of efficiency is applied to democracy in the United States, an inescapable question arises: Is popular government, as now constituted, really competent to deal effectively with the general functions common to all governments, and more especially with the specific issues forced upon this government by giant technology, by the power of enormous private corporations, by huge urban aggregations unlike the cities of earlier times, by organized labor, by the decline in freehold agriculture, by periodic crises in economy, by the complications of international rivalries? Here is a question of the hour which challenges all talents and powers. Can popular government come to grips with these issues, overcome them, and efficiently administer its decisions?

[13] Already in our smaller laboratories of popular experimentation—cities and states—has appeared a profound conviction that many of our inherited institutions are not adapted to the requirements of the age, are in fact inefficient. In all our great cities the double-chamber council has been abolished, a single chamber installed, and the mayor endowed with broad powers in his own right. In 650 cities the mayor-and-council system has been discarded and the city-manager plan substituted for it. In a majority of the states the inherited scheme of administration has recently been abrogated, in whole or in part, and the power of the governor over finance and the conduct of public business has been materially increased. In several states an attack has been made on the weaknesses of legislatures, and a legislative council has been instituted for the purpose of concentrating research, knowledge, and imagination on public questions. More and more, the technical literature of competence in the field of state and local government is filled with doubt, inquiry, and a searching for constructive proposals.

[14] This quest for efficiency in government extends to national affairs. Already critics are saying that in the Congress of the United States a zeal for spending borrowed money, placating

special interests, and framing bills against dissident minorities outruns the capacity to concentrate powers of mind upon the supreme issues of the time. Already critics are saying that democracy cannot really act effectively in great matters, that party bickerings defeat the preparation, discussion, enactment, and administration of measures necessary to evoke creative energies, allay alarms, and bring our moral, industrial, and natural resources into wise and full use.

[15] In allowing some validity to these criticisms no aid and comfort need be given to the carping censors who fondly imagine that they can set the clock back to 1928 or 1898, or any other year in the past and thus find instantaneous solutions of our pressing problems of efficiency in government. Most of the measures now urged upon the federal administration by its detractors are the identical measures which were in full effect during the regime of golden prosperity, so called, which exploded with such devastating force in 1929. Why repeat the very origins of our present calamity? Both experience and reason suggest that the search for efficiency in government be turned to the invention of new devices for concentrating talents and wills on needs now clearly before us. The recitation of old phrases by a thousand specialists in propaganda will only add to the nation's confusion and delay the application of its abilities and energies to the attainment of efficiency in government.

A Sustaining Economy

[16] Bound up with popular government and its functioning is the economy of the people who are supposed to control the form and process. Nothing is truer than the old adage: An empty meal sack cannot stand up. All governments have economic foundations. This axiom of politics does not come from armchair philosophers or demagogues or agitators. It comes from the founders of the nation, builders of our institutions, from leaders of large vision, wide experience, and demonstrated capacity in great affairs. They made a revolution, waged a continental war for independence, offered their lives and property in defense of their cause, established a republic, and steered it through perilous times. As against the weight of their authority and achievement, the

axioms of private men pursuing private interests and of all petty phrasemakers in public affairs are as dust in the balance. Let those speak whose public accomplishments display the depth of their insight, the precision of their knowledge, the prowess of their minds, the invincibility of their courage.

[17] In words that admit of no equivocation these great of old who instruct us from their tombs declare that politics and economics are forever united. Ringing through their utterances like the tones of a clear bell is the warning thesis: A wide diffusion of property and a general equality of condition are the very foundation stones of popular government; a high concentration of wealth is incompatible with universal suffrage; a broad distribution of opportunity and assurance to labor is necessary to the security of republican institutions; the revolutions which have shaken other societies to pieces have sprung from the antagonism of private accumulations and popular power, fired by ambitious leaders. These findings, wrought out of hard experience, are set forth in many places by American statesmen of early times—nowhere more trenchantly than in the writings of James Madison, justly called the Father of the Constitution.

[18] Near the close of his long life, in the winter of 1829–30, Madison reviewed his rich experience and sought to lift the veil upon the future of his country. He prophesied that in 1930 the population of the United States would probably be 192,000,000 and that a majority of the people would be "without property or the hope of acquiring it." Then he asked: "What is to be done with this unfavored class of the community?"

[19] Madison confessed that he was unable to answer his own question. He thought that it would be unsafe to "admit them to a full share of political power." At the same time he declared that "it cannot be expedient to rest a republican government on a portion of the society having a numerical and physical force excluded from, and liable to be turned against it." This exclusion of whole masses from a share in government, Madison believed, "would lead to a standing military force, dangerous to all parties and to liberty itself." In this fateful conjecture of things, the Father of the Constitution saw the crucial test of popular government.

[20] Having arrived at the dilemma, Madison concluded: "How far this view of the subject will be affected by the republican laws of descent and distribution, in equalizing the property of the citizens . . . cannot be inferred from any direct and adequate experiment." But he foresaw the necessity of great alterations in public policy to meet the exigencies which he had predicted. "To the effect of these changes, intellectual, moral, and social," he said, "the institutions and laws of the country must be adapted; and it will require for the task all the wisdom of the wisest patriots."

[21] Although Madison overestimated the population of 1930, he did with amazing vision forecast the primary features of the economic scene as they appeared one hundred years later, in 1930. The proportion of farmers who were tenants had increased rapidly until it was more than 40 per cent of the total number; and at least one third of the nominal owners were heavily burdened by debts. In the great cities the major portion of the inhabitants were without property worthy of mention, if not entirely without hope of acquiring it. About ten million workers were unemployed and losing faith in the possibilities of employment. There had been grand gestures in the direction of economic security, but grave doubts were entertained respecting the underlying strength of that assurance. Our economic machine, on which all the people rely for sustenance and the government depends for its very existence, rumbled along in uncertainty at about one half of its full capacity—until the armament boom of 1941 gave it a temporary lift.

[22] Such are the axioms of experienced statesmen. Such are glaring economic facts of our present situation. The crisis in national life forecast long ago has arrived. This is the age in which the wisdom of the wisest patriots, as Madison warned us, is required for the resolution of the dilemma. Not curtailment but expansion of production is now a primary need of American democracy. Our output of wealth must be materially increased and there must be a distribution of employments, goods, and services wide enough to afford those opportunities and assurances upon which popular government rests and must ever rest. If the wisdom is lacking, force may be offered as a substitute. Nay, if

history is any guide, force will be offered and democracy may be started spinning swiftly on a downward spiral.

[23] In the light of this imperative, the policy of reduction applied generally to agriculture, however defensible as a temporary expedient in respect of certain commodities, is, in the long run, a peril to the economy of a democratic society. No less perilous is the apparent inability of leadership in business enterprise to prevent those periodical curtailments of production in industry which harrow the hearts of men and women with fear and despair. No less perilous is the apparent inability of that leadership to force or guarantee the expansion of industrial production toward the very borders of the capacity indicated by our plants, skills, and resources. Nor is the strife of organized labor over the crumbs that fall from a diminishing table any contribution to bringing about the economic arrangements necessary to the perpetuity of democratic institutions.

[24] If we are to learn from the instructions bequeathed to us by the founders and builders of this republic, it is idle gossip to speak of the long-term promise of democracy unless these essential factors of wealth production—government, industrial management, agriculture, and labor—can put aside their outworn formulas, rise to the occasion as did the creators of the republic, unite upon methods and measures that will expand production, enlarge and steady the domestic market, and assure the wide distribution of employment, goods, and services essential to the stability and progress of a democratic society.

Civil Liberties

[25] But at a given moment government may be popular in form, efficient in administration, competent to provide the conditions necessary for a wide economic security, and yet by its conduct of affairs undermine those civil liberties upon which democracy depends for its long-run existence. It may destroy that freedom which brings knowledge and wisdom to bear upon its operations, supplies criticism, and furnishes constructive thought for new occasions and measures. In operation popular government is government by public opinion and decision, enlightened by discussions that permit all causes and parties to be duly heard, even those

hateful to the majority. Without freedom of press, speech, and person from arbitrary power, popular election becomes a farce, government a tyranny, and administration an agency of personal vengeance.

[26] Hence indispensable to the functioning of a democratic system on its own principles are those constitutional safeguards which place restraints upon the regular operations of majorities and upon the irregular insolence of mobs: safeguards against press censorship, against interference with free speech, against arbitrary arrest, against secret trial and condemnation; safeguards against the enactment of ex post facto laws making crimes out of actions that are not crimes when committed; safeguards against depriving persons of life, liberty, and property without due process of law, against cruel and unusual punishments, against the suspension of the writ of habeas corpus, against the introduction of martial law, against assults upon the whole structure of civil rights so painfully built up through centuries of conflict and sacrifice. To permit the suppression of civil liberties by public agencies or private mobs is to cut away the intellectual foundations on which popular government rests in the long run, and to open the way for government by proscription and the firing squad, perhaps in the very name of the people.

[27] It is not enough that the maxims of civil liberty be spread upon paper and celebrated by sunshine patriots. They are futile unless made dynamic in government itself. They are mere trash unless supported by citizens in daily conduct. Again and again they have been flouted by the Congress of the United States, by state legislatures, by prosecuting attorneys, by judges sworn to administer justice under law, and by lawless crowds of rich and poor.

[28] Indeed so flagrant have been violations in recent years that the danger has become obvious even to careless and indifferent citizens, and a countermovement has been well launched. Defenders of liberty have come to its support. The Supreme Court, long heedless, has at length spoken out clearly and strongly against infractions. Once negligent, indeed apparently hostile, the American Bar Association has at last recovered the grand tradition of Erskine and Mackintosh, established a powerful committee on

civil liberty, and offered aid and counsel in the trial of causes involving personal rights. But more is needed: systematic instruction in the subject by the public schools and a deep-rooted respect for the tolerances of civil liberty among the people in whose hands rests the fate of their own government.

Education

[29] In connection with the functioning of democracy, in its public and private aspects, education may point the way upward or downward. It may prepare the people for the fulfillment of a great mission or for subjection to sheer force. If education is to be effective in strengthening all phases of democracy, it must be appropriate to the exigencies of American civilization. While it has a precious heritage to guard, education has a duty to assemble and diffuse the knowledge required by citizens and their leaders in operating popular institutions, in making them effective in every sphere, and in preserving civil liberties.

[30] No longer can education proceed safely on the assumption that by training youth for the successful pursuit of private interests it will automatically insure the general welfare and the perpetuity of democracy. Like other alluring illusions, that is highly dangerous. It is even now too widely cherished. Other conceptions of purpose and action are needed to counterbalance it. Only by a program of instruction that deals resolutely and realistically with the processes of democracy, with questions of sustaining economy and culture, and with the protection of civil rights can American education "defy powers that seem omnipotent" and span the full measure of its opportunity.

The Spirit of Democracy

[31] Universal suffrage, efficient government, material foundations, declarations of rights, and education alone cannot guarantee the safety of our civilization against the storms of passion and the lust of men for power. Behind all beneficent institutions of society, ever helping to sustain them, is that elusive but potent force known as the humane spirit. This spirit has ever been affiliated with, and expressed in, the noblest philosophies that have commanded the allegiance of hearts and minds since the beginnings

of society. It has been associated with all great religions. Trampled upon by power, crushed by the organization of interests, the humane spirit endures in many forms, under varied professions of faith, and offers the strength of justice and mercy against the effronteries of tyranny and the angers of brute destruction. Without it even democratic government is an empty shell—a numerical counting of heads that may be farcical in procedure and cruel in outcome.

[32] If our powers are to be effectively applied in sustaining the forms and achieving the ends of popular government, this humane spirit must be cherished and quickened, and ever brought to bear as a dynamic element in the enrichment of life. Knowledge is not enough. Science is not enough. Both may be employed to kill as well as to heal. Accumulated facts, though high as mountains, give us no instruction in human values and the choices of application. It is the humane spirit that points the way to the good life. To reiterate the maxims of this spirit, to restate them in terms of new times, to spread them through education and daily intercourse, to exemplify them in private conduct, to incorporate them in public practice, to cling to them despite our infirmities and hypocrisies—this, too, is a task of all who fain would make government by the people and for the people endure upon the earth.

[33] Such are the components of American democracy—all essential to its perpetuity and development. They are not figments of an imagination, fashioned in a philosopher's alcove. They are realities of experience, tried and tested in the fires of centuries. Such, too, are the challenges of dissolution and sheer might which threaten the existence and unfolding of all that is best in this democracy. These are the central points for our consideration; here is the conflict that engages our contemplation.

[34] Facing this antithesis, nay, caught in the turmoil of these contending forces, it will not do for us, as Carlyle warned America long ago, to sit idly caucusing the ballot-boxing upon the graves of our ancestors, saying "It is well, it is well." Rather is it for us to look with clear eyes upon the welter before us, to curb our little hates and loves, to forget our trivial slogans and party distempers, to clarify and purify our hearts and minds, to discover or invent,

by concerted effort, the best means for coping now with the central issues raised amid indubitable facts. It is for us to find the common denominators of a union necessary to success in applying the conclusions of our search, and, equipped with all the strong instruments of civilization, march upon the goal we have set before us, remembering that those who labor in so great a cause labor in a cause worthy of the finest and noblest talents.

EXERCISES

1. Compare Beard's method of defining democracy with the method used in defining the proper function of a good government in the Declaration of Independence (reprinted on page 146). What basic assumptions form the intellectual climate of the Declaration?

2. Where does Beard list his six main points? State each. Notice the correspondence of this list to the *divisio* of *Areopagitica*. Can you find other resemblances between the disposition of parts in Beard's discourse and in Milton's?

3. Find the places where some or all of these main points are repeated. Why are they repeated?

4. What figures of speech are involved in the expression "oceans of ink are spilt," in paragraph 11?

5. What figure of speech is involved in the expression "flowers of eloquence bloom in their defense," in the same paragraph?

6. What is the connotation of "mouthed the grand phrase" in paragraph 11?

7. What figure of speech is used in the first sentence of paragraph 13? What is the value of it?

8. In paragraph 11, in that part of the first sentence which follows the colon, is the parallel structure used for economy or for emphasis? Explain.

9. Is the parallel structure in the last sentence in paragraph 16 used for economy or for emphasis? Explain.

10. The phrase "alluring illusions" in paragraph 30 is surely an example of cacophony, or awkward sound. Why is this appropriate?

11. The sentence in paragraph 31 which begins "Trampled upon by power . . ." has a monotonous rhythm. Why is this appropriate?

12. Find examples of alliteration in paragraph 33. What is the effect of this alliteration?

13. Find two sentences in antithesis in paragraph 33. Explain why the

use of antithesis for these two statements at this point is effective composition.

14. What famous speech is alluded to at the close of paragraph 32? Why is the allusion appropriate? Would the paragraph have been equally effective without it?

15. Identify the allusion in the second sentence of paragraph 34. Explain why it is appropriate to the idea of the paragraph and what good effect it contributes to the composition.

16. Study the rhythm of the last sentence in paragraph 33. Mark the accented and unaccented syllables. Does the sentence end in a cadence? Is there any reason why it should? How many rhythmic units are there? Does the rhythm seem pleasant to you?

17. Write a theme on one of the following topics or a similar one. Make your introduction as attractive as possible, forecast your main points, develop each one adequately, and end your theme with as dramatic a conclusion as you can manage. Throughout the theme try to give special emphasis to important sentences (first and last sentences, sentences which state main points, sentences which end each section) by some of the devices of emphasis used by Milton and Beard or others which you find listed under *Emphasis* in the Glossary.

   a. The aims of education at your college
   b. The essential qualities of a good citizen
   c. Elements essential to any world government or federation which is to succeed
   d. The "natural rights" of man and how he came to have them

---

Address at Cooper Union

ABRAHAM LINCOLN

[1] Mr. President and Fellow-Citizens of New York: The facts with which I shall deal this evening are mainly old and familiar; nor is there anything new in the general use I shall make of them. If there shall be any novelty, it will be in the mode of presenting

Delivered on February 27, 1860.

the facts, and the inferences and observations following that presentation. In his speech last autumn at Columbus, Ohio, as reported in *The New-York Times,* Senator Douglas said:

[2] Our fathers, when they framed the government under which we live, understood this question just as well, and even better, than we do now.

[3] I fully indorse this, and I adopt it as a text for this discourse. I so adopt it because it furnishes a precise and an agreed starting-point for a discussion between Republicans and that wing of the Democracy headed by Senator Douglas. It simply leaves the inquiry: What was the understanding those fathers had of the question mentioned?

[4] What is the frame of government under which we live? The answer must be, "The Constitution of the United States." That Constitution consists of the original, framed in 1787, and under which the present government first went into operation, and twelve subsequently framed amendments, the first ten of which were framed in 1789.

[5] Who were our fathers that framed the Constitution? I suppose the "thirty-nine" who signed the original instrument may be fairly called our fathers who framed that part of the present government. It is almost exactly true to say they framed it, and it is altogether true to say they fairly represented the opinion and sentiment of the whole nation at that time. Their names, being familiar to nearly all, and accessible to quite all, need not now be repeated.

[6] I take these "thirty-nine," for the present, as being "our fathers who framed the government under which we live." What is the question which, according to the text, those fathers understood "just as well, and even better, than we do now"?

[7] It is this: Does the proper division of local from Federal authority, or anything in the Constitution, forbid our Federal Government to control as to slavery in our Federal Territories? [8] Upon this, Senator Douglas holds the affirmative, and Republicans the negative. This affirmation and denial form an issue; and this issue—this question—is precisely what the text declares our fathers understood "better than we." Let us now inquire

whether the "thirty-nine," or any of them, ever acted upon this question; and if they did, how they acted upon it—how they expressed that better understanding. In 1784, three years before the Constitution, the United States then owning the Northwestern Territory, and no other, the Congress of the Confederation had before them the question of prohibiting slavery in that Territory; and four of the "thirty-nine" who afterward framed the Constitution were in that Congress, and voted on that question. Of these, Roger Sherman, Thomas Mifflin, and Hugh Williamson voted for the prohibition, thus showing that, in their understanding, no line dividing local from Federal authority, nor anything else, properly forbade the Federal Government to control as to slavery in Federal territory. The other of the four, James McHenry, voted against the prohibition, showing that for some cause he thought it improper to vote for it.

[9] In 1787, still before the Constitution, but while the convention was in session framing it, and while the Northwestern Territory still was the only Territory owned by the United States, the same question of prohibiting slavery in the Territory again came before the Congress of the Confederation; and two more of the "thirty-nine" who afterward signed the Constitution were in that Congress, and voted on the question. They were William Blount and William Few; and they both voted for the prohibition—thus showing that in their understanding no line dividing local from Federal authority, nor anything else, properly forbade the Federal Government to control as to slavery in Federal territory. This time the prohibition became a law, being part of what is now well known as the ordinance of '87.

[10] The question of Federal control of slavery in the Territories seems not to have been directly before the convention which framed the original Constitution; and hence it is not recorded that the "thirty-nine," or any of them, while engaged on that instrument, expressed any opinion on that precise question.

[11] In 1789, by the first Congress which sat under the Constitution, an act was passed to enforce the ordinance of '87, including the prohibition of slavery in the Northwestern Territory. The bill for this act was reported by one of the "thirty-nine"—Thomas Fitzsimmons, then a member of the House of Representatives

from Pennsylvania. It went through all its stages without a word
of opposition, and finally passed both branches without ayes and
nays, which is equivalent to a unanimous passage. In this Congress there were sixteen of the thirty-nine fathers who framed the
original Constitution. They were John Langdon, Nicholas Gil-
man, Wm. S. Johnson, Roger Sherman, Robert Morris, Thos.
Fitzsimmons, William Few, Abraham Baldwin, Rufus King,
William Paterson, George Clymer, Richard Bassett, George Read,
Pierce Butler, Daniel Carroll and James Madison.

[12] This shows that, in their understanding, no line dividing
local from Federal authority, nor anything in the Constitution,
properly forbade Congress to prohibit slavery in the Federal territory; else both their fidelity to correct principle, and their oath
to support the Constitution, would have constrained them to
oppose the prohibition.

[13] Again, George Washington, another of the "thirty-nine,"
was then President of the United States and as such approved
and signed the bill, thus completing its validity as a law, and
thus showing that, in his understanding, no line dividing local
from Federal authority, nor anything in the Constitution, forbade
the Federal Government to control as to slavery in Federal territory.

[14] No great while after the adoption of the original Constitution, North Carolina ceded to the Federal Government the
country now constituting the State of Tennessee; and a few
years later Georgia ceded that which now constitutes the States
of Mississippi and Alabama. In both deeds of cession it was made
a condition by the ceding States that the Federal Government
should not prohibit slavery in the ceded country. Besides this,
slavery was then actually in the ceded country. Under these circumstances, Congress, on taking charge of these countries, did
not absolutely prohibit slavery within them. But they did interfere with it—take control of it—even there, to a certain extent.
In 1798 Congress organized the Territory of Mississippi. In the
act of organization they prohibited the bringing of slaves into
the Territory from any place without the United States, by fine,
and giving freedom to slaves so brought. This act passed both
branches of Congress without yeas and nays. In that Congress

were three of the "thirty-nine" who framed the original Constitution. They were John Langdon, George Read, and Abraham
Baldwin. They all probably voted for it. Certainly they would
have placed their opposition to it upon record if, in their understanding, any line dividing local from Federal authority, or anything in the Constitution, properly forbade the Federal Government to control as to slavery in Federal territory.

[15] In 1803 the Federal Government purchased the Louisiana
country. Our former territorial acquisitions came from certain of
our own States; but this Louisiana country was acquired from a
foreign nation. In 1804 Congress gave a territorial organization
to that part of it which now constitutes the State of Louisiana.
New Orleans, lying within that part, was an old and comparatively large city. There were other considerable towns and settlements, and slavery was extensively and thoroughly intermingled
with the people. Congress did not, in the Territorial Act, prohibit slavery; but they did interfere with it—take control of it—
in a more marked and extensive way than they did in the case
of Mississippi. The substance of the provision therein made in
relation to slaves was:

1st. That no slave should be imported into the Territory from
foreign parts.

2d. That no slave should be carried into it who had been imported into the United States since the first day of May, 1798.

3d. That no slave should be carried into it, except by the
owner, and for his own use as a settler; the penalty in all the
cases being a fine upon the violator of the law, and freedom to
the slave.

[16] This act also was passed without ayes or nays. In the Congress which passed it there were two of the "thirty-nine." They
were Abraham Baldwin and Jonathan Dayton. As stated in the
case of Mississippi, it is probable they both voted for it. They
would not have allowed it to pass without recording their opposition to it if, in their understanding, it violated either the line
properly dividing local from Federal authority, or any provision
of the Constitution.

[17] In 1819–20 came and passed the Missouri question. Many
votes were taken, by yeas and nays, in both branches of Con-

gress, upon the various phases of the general question. Two of
the "thirty-nine"—Rufus King and Charles Pinckney—were members of that Congress. Mr. King steadily voted for slavery prohibition and against all compromises, while Mr. Pinckney as
steadily voted against slavery prohibition and against all compromises. By this, Mr. King showed that, in his understanding, no
line dividing local from Federal authority, nor anything in the
Constitution, was violated by Congress prohibiting slavery in
Federal territory; while Mr. Pinckney, by his votes, showed that,
in his understanding, there was some sufficient reason for opposing such prohibition in that case.

[18] The cases I have mentioned are the only acts of the "thirty-
nine," or of any of them, upon the direct issue, which I have
been able to discover.

[19] To enumerate the persons who thus acted as being four in
1784, two in 1787, seventeen in 1789, three in 1798, two in 1804,
and two in 1819–20, there would be thirty of them. But this
would be counting John Langdon, Roger Sherman, William Few,
Rufus King, and George Read each twice, and Abraham Baldwin
three times. The true number of those of the "thirty-nine" whom
I have shown to have acted upon the question which, by the text,
they understood better than we, is twenty-three, leaving sixteen
not shown to have acted upon it in any way.

[20] Here, then, we have twenty-three out of our thirty-nine
fathers "who framed the government under which we live," who
have, upon their official responsibility and their corporal oaths,
acted upon the very question which the text affirms they "understood just as well, and even better, than we do now"; and twenty-
one of them—a clear majority of the whole "thirty-nine"—so
acting upon it as to make them guilty of gross political impropriety
and wilful perjury if, in their understanding, any proper division
between local and Federal authority, or anything in the Constitution they had made themselves, and sworn to support, forbade
the Federal Government to control as to slavery in the Federal
Territories. Thus the twenty-one acted; and, as actions speak
louder than words, so actions under such responsibility speak still
louder.

[21] Two of the twenty-three voted against congressional prohi-

bition of slavery in the Federal Territories, in the instances in which they acted upon the question. But for what reasons they so voted is not known. They may have done so because they thought a proper division of local from Federal authority, or some provision or principle of the Constitution, stood in the way; or they may, without any such question, have voted against the prohibition on what appeared to them to be sufficient grounds of expediency. No one who has sworn to support the Constitution can conscientiously vote for what he understands to be an unconstitutional measure, however expedient he may think it; but one may and ought to vote against a measure which he deems constitutional if, at the same time, he deems it inexpedient. It, therefore, would be unsafe to set down even the two who voted against the prohibition as having done so because, in their understanding, any proper division of local from Federal authority, or anything in the Constitution, forbade the Federal Government to control as to slavery in Federal territory.

[22] The remaining sixteen of the "thirty-nine," so far as I have discovered, have left no record of their understanding upon the direct question of Federal control of slavery in the Federal Territories. But there is much reason to believe that their understanding upon that question would not have appeared different from that of their twenty-three compeers, had it been manifested at all.

[23] For the purpose of adhering rigidly to the text, I have purposely omitted whatever understanding may have been manifested by any person, however distinguished, other than the thirty-nine fathers who framed the original Constitution; and, for the same reason, I have also omitted whatever understanding may have been manifested by any of the "thirty-nine" even on any other phase of the general question of slavery. If we should look into their acts and declarations on those other phases, as the foreign slave trade, and the morality and policy of slavery generally, it would appear to us that on the direct question of Federal control of slavery in Federal Territories, the sixteen, if they had acted at all, would probably have acted just as the twenty-three did. Among that sixteen were several of the most noted antislavery men of those times—as Dr. Franklin, Alexander Hamilton, and Gouver-

neur Morris—while there was not one now known to have been otherwise, unless it may be John Rutledge, of South Carolina.

[24] The sum of the whole is that of our thirty-nine fathers who framed the original Constitution, twenty-one—a clear majority of the whole—certainly understood that no proper division of local from Federal authority, nor any part of the Constitution, forbade the Federal Government to control slavery in the Federal Territories; while all the rest had probably the same understanding. Such, unquestionably, was the understanding of our fathers who framed the original Constitution; and the text affirms that they understood the question "better than we."

[25] But, so far, I have been considering the understanding of the question manifested by the framers of the original Constitution. In and by the original instrument, a mode was provided for amending it; and, as I have already stated, the present frame of "the government under which we live" consists of that original, and twelve amendatory articles framed and adopted since. Those who now insist that Federal control of slavery in Federal Territories violates the Constitution, point us to the provisions which they suppose it thus violates; and, as I understand, they all fix upon provisions in these amendatory articles, and not in the original instrument. The Supreme Court, in the Dred Scott case, plant themselves upon the Fifth Amendment, which provides that no person shall be deprived of "life, liberty, or property without due process of law"; while Senator Douglas and his peculiar adherents plant themselves upon the Tenth Amendment, providing that "the powers not delegated to the United States by the Consitution" "are reserved to the States respectively, or to the people."

[26] Now, it so happens that these amendments were framed by the first Congress which sat under the Constitution—the identical Congress which passed the act, already mentioned, enforcing the prohibition of slavery in the Northwestern Territory. Not only was it the same Congress, but they were the identical, same individual men who, at the same session, and at the same time within the session, had under consideration, and in progress toward maturity, these constitutional amendments, and this act prohibiting slavery in all the territory the nation then owned. The

consitutional amendments were introduced before, and passed after, the act enforcing the ordinance of '87; so that, during the whole pendency of the act to enforce the ordinance, the constitutional amendments were also pending.

[27] The seventy-six members of that Congress, including sixteen of the framers of the original Constitution, as before stated, were preëminently our fathers who framed that part of "the government under which we live" which is now claimed as forbidding the Federal Government to control slavery in the Federal Territories. [28] Is it not a little presumptuous in any one at this day to affirm that the two things which that Congress deliberately framed, and carried to maturity at the same time, are absolutely inconsistent with each other? And does not such affirmation become impudently absurd when coupled with the other affirmation, from the same mouth, that those who did the two things alleged to be inconsistent, understood whether they really were inconsistent better than we—better than he who affirms that they are inconsistent? [29] It is surely safe to assume that the thirty-nine framers of the original Constitution, and the seventy-six members of the Congress which framed the amendments thereto, taken together, do certainly include those who may be fairly called "our fathers who framed the government under which we live." And so assuming, I defy any man to show that any one of them ever, in his whole life, declared that, in his understanding, any proper division of local from Federal authority, or any part of the Constitution, forbade the Federal Government to control as to slavery in the Federal Territories. I go a step further. I defy any one to show that any living man in the whole world ever did, prior to the beginning of the present century (and I might almost say prior to the beginning of the last half of the present century), declare that, in his understanding, any proper division of local from Federal authority, or any part of the Constitution, forbade the Federal Government to control as to slavery in the Federal Territories. To those who now so declare I give not only "our fathers who framed the government under which we live," but with them all other living men within the century in which it was framed, among whom to search, and they shall not be able to find the evidence of a single man agreeing with them.

[30] Now, and here, let me guard a little against being misunderstood. I do not mean to say we are bound to follow implicitly in whatever our fathers did. To do so would be to discard all the lights of current experience—to reject all progress, all improvement. What I do say is that if we would supplant the opinions and policy of our fathers in any case, we should do so upon evidence so conclusive, and argument so clear, that even their great authority, fairly considered and weighed, cannot stand; and most surely not in a case whereof we ourselves declare they understood the question better than we.

[31] If any man at this day sincerely believes that a proper division of local from Federal authority, or any part of the Constitution, forbids the Federal Government to control as to slavery in the Federal Territories, he is right to say so, and to enforce his position by all truthful evidence and fair argument which he can. But he has no right to mislead others, who have less access to history, and less leisure to study it, into the false belief that "our fathers who framed the government under which we live" were of the same opinion—thus substituting falsehood and deception for truthful evidence and fair argument. If any man at this day sincerely believes "our fathers who framed the government under which we live" used and applied principles, in other cases, which ought to have led them to understand that a proper division of local from Federal authority, or some part of the Constitution, forbids the Federal Government to control as to slavery in the Federal Territories, he is right to say so. But he should, at the same time, brave the responsibility of declaring that, in his opinion, he understands their principles better than they did themselves, and especially should he not shirk that responsibility by asserting that they "understand the question just as well, and even better, than we do now."

[32] But enough! Let all who believe that "our fathers who framed the government under which we live understood this question just as well, and even better, than we do now," speak as they spoke, and act as they acted upon it. This is all Republicans ask —all Republicans desire—in relation to slavery. As those fathers marked it, so let it be again marked, as an evil not to be extended, but to be tolerated and protected only because of and so far as

its actual presence among us makes that toleration and protection a necessity. Let all the guaranties those fathers gave it be not grudgingly, but fully and fairly, maintained. For this Republicans contend, and with this, so far as I know or believe, they will be content.

[33] And now, if they would listen—as I suppose they will not —I would address a few words to the Southern people.

[34] I would say to them: You consider yourselves a reasonable and a just people; and I consider that in the general qualities of reason and justice you are not inferior to any other people. Still, when you speak of us Republicans, you do so only to denounce us as reptiles, or, at the best, as no better than outlaws. You will grant a hearing to pirates or murderers, but nothing like it to "Black Republicans." In all your contentions with one another, each of you deems an unconditional condemnation of "Black Republicanism" as the first thing to be attended to. Indeed, such condemnation of us seems to be an indispensable prerequisite— license, so to speak—among you to be admitted or permitted to speak at all. Now can you or not be prevailed upon to pause and to consider whether this is quite just to us, or even to yourselves? Bring forward your charges and specifications, and then be patient long enough to hear us deny or justify.

[35] You say we are sectional. We deny it. That makes an issue; and the burden of proof is upon you. You produce your proof; and what is it? Why, that our party has no existence in your section—gets no votes in your section. The fact is substantially true; but does it prove the issue? If it does, then in case we should, without change of principle, begin to get votes in your section, we should thereby cease to be sectional. You cannot escape this conclusion; and yet, are you willing to abide by it? If you are, you will probably soon find that we have ceased to be sectional, for we shall get votes in your section this very year. You will then begin to discover, as the truth plainly is, that your proof does not touch the issue. The fact that we get no votes in your section is a fact of your making, and not of ours. And if there be fault in that fact, that fault is primarily yours, and remains so until you show that we repel you by some wrong principle or practice. If we do repel you by any wrong principle or practice, the fault is ours; but this

brings you to where you ought to have started—to a discussion of the right or wrong of our principle. If our principle, put in practice, would wrong your section for the benefit of ours, or for any other object, then our principle, and we with it, are sectional, and are justly opposed and denounced as such. Meet us, then, on the question of whether our principle, put in practice, would wrong your section; and so meet us as if it were possible that something may be said on our side. Do you accept the challenge? No! Then you really believe that the principle which "our fathers who framed the government under which we live" thought so clearly right as to adopt it, and indorse it again and again, upon their official oaths, is in fact so clearly wrong as to demand your condemnation without a moment's consideration.

[36] Some of you delight to flaunt in our faces the warning against sectional parties given by Washington in his Farewell Address. Less than eight years before Washington gave that warning, he had, as President of the United States, approved and signed an act of Congress enforcing the prohibition of slavery in the Northwestern Territory, which act embodied the policy of the government upon that subject up to and at the very moment he penned that warning; and about one year after he penned it, he wrote Lafayette that he considered that prohibition a wise measure, expressing in the same connection his hope that we should at some time have a confederacy of free States.

[37] Bearing this in mind, and seeing that sectionalism has since arisen upon this same subject, is that warning a weapon in your hands against us, or in our hands against you? Could Washington himself speak, would he cast the blame of that sectionalism upon us, who sustain his policy, or upon you, who repudiate it? We respect that warning of Washington, and we commend it to you, together with his example pointing to the right application of it.

[38] But you say you are conservative—eminently conservative —while we are revolutionary, destructive, or something of the sort. What is conservatism? Is it not adherence to the old and tried, against the new and untried? We stick to, contend for, the identical old policy on the point in controversy which was adopted by "our fathers who framed the government under which we

live"; while you with one accord reject, and scout, and spit upon that old policy, and insist upon substituting something new. True, you disagree among yourselves as to what that substitute shall be. You are divided on new propositions and plans, but you are unanimous in rejecting and denouncing the old policy of the fathers. Some of you are for reviving the foreign slave trade; some for a congressional slave code for the Territories; some for Congress forbidding the Territories to prohibit slavery within their limits; some for maintaining slavery in the Territories through the judiciary; some for the "gur-reat pur-rinciple" that "if one man would enslave another, no third man should object," fantastically called "popular sovereignty"; but never a man among you is in favor of Federal prohibition of slavery in Federal Territories, according to the practice of "our fathers who framed the government under which we live." Not one of all your various plans can show a precedent or an advocate in the century within which our government originated. Consider, then, whether your claim of conservatism for yourselves, and your charge of destructiveness against us, are based on the most clear and stable foundations.

[39] Again, you say we have made the slavery question more prominent than it formerly was. We deny it. We admit that it is more prominent, but we deny that we made it so. It was not we, but you, who discarded the old policy of the fathers. We resisted, and still resist, your innovation; and thence comes the greater prominence of the question. Would you have that question reduced to its former proportions? Go back to that old policy. What has been will be again, under the same conditions. If you would have the peace of the old times, readopt the precepts and policy of the old times.

[40] You charge that we stir up insurrections among your slaves. We deny it; and what is your proof? Harper's Ferry! John Brown! John Brown was no Republican; and you have failed to implicate a single Republican in his Harper's Ferry enterprise. If any member of our party is guilty in that matter, you know it, or you do not know it. If you do know it, you are inexcusable for not designating the man and proving the fact. If you do not know it, you are inexcusable for asserting it, and especially for persisting in the assertion after you have tried and failed to make the proof.

You need not be told that persisting in a charge which one does not know to be true, is simply malicious slander.

[41] Some of you admit that no Republican designedly aided or encouraged the Harper's Ferry affair, but still insist that our doctrines and declarations necessarily lead to such results. We do not believe it. We know we hold no doctrine, and make no declaration, which were not held to and made by "our fathers who framed the government under which we live." You never dealt fairly by us in relation to this affair. When it occurred, some important State elections were near at hand, and you were in evident glee with the belief that, by charging the blame upon us, you could get an advantage of us in those elections. The elections came, and your expectations were not quite fulfilled. Every Republican man knew that, as to himself at least, your charge was a slander, and he was not much inclined by it to cast his vote in your favor. Republican doctrines and declarations are accompanied with a continual protest against any interference whatever with your slaves, or with you about your slaves. Surely, this does not encourage them to revolt. True, we do, in common with "our fathers who framed the government under which we live," declare our belief that slavery is wrong; but the slaves do not hear us declare even this. For anything we say or do, the slaves would scarcely know there is a Republican party. I believe they would not, in fact, generally know it but for your misrepresentations of us in their hearing. In your political contests among yourselves, each faction charges the other with sympathy with Black Republicanism; and then, to give point to the charge, defines Black Republicanism to simply be insurrection, blood, and thunder among the slaves.

[42] Slave insurrections are no more common now than they were before the Republican party was organized. What induced the Southampton insurrection, twenty-eight years ago, in which at least three times as many lives were lost as at Harper's Ferry? You can scarcely stretch your very elastic fancy to the conclusion that Southampton was "got up by Black Republicanism." In the present state of things in the United States, I do not think a general, or even a very extensive, slave insurrection is possible. The indispensable concert of action cannot be attained. The slaves

have no means of rapid communication; nor can incendiary free-men, black or white, supply it. The explosive materials are every-where in parcels; but there neither are, nor can be supplied, the indispensable connecting trains.

[43] Much is said by Southern people about the affection of slaves for their masters and mistresses; and a part of it, at least, is true. A plot for an uprising could scarcely be devised and com-municated to twenty individuals before some one of them, to save the life of a favorite master or mistress, would divulge it. This is the rule; and the slave revolution in Hayti was not an exception to it, but a case occurring under peculiar circumstances. The gunpowder plot of British history, though not connected with slaves, was more in point. In that case, only about twenty were admitted to the secret; and yet one of them, in his anxiety to save a friend, betrayed the plot to that friend, and, by consequence, averted the calamity. Occasional poisonings from the kitchen, and open or stealthy assassinations in the field, and local revolts extending to a score or so, will continue to occur as the natural results of slavery; but no general insurrection of slaves, as I think, can happen in this country for a long time. Whoever much fears, or much hopes, for such an event, will be alike disappointed.

[44] In the language of Mr. Jefferson, uttered many years ago, "It is still in our power to direct the process of emancipation and deportation peaceably, and in such slow degrees, as that the evil will wear off insensibly; and their places be, *pari passu,* filled up by free white laborers. If, on the contrary, it is left to force itself on, human nature must shudder at the prospect held up."

[45] Mr. Jefferson did not mean to say, nor do I, that the power of emancipation is in the Federal Government. He spoke of Vir-ginia; and, as to the power of emancipation, I speak of the slave-holding States only. The Federal Government, however, as we insist, has the power of restraining the extension of the institution —the power to insure that a slave insurrection shall never occur on any American soil which is now free from slavery.

[46] John Brown's effort was peculiar. It was not a slave insur-rection. It was an attempt by white men to get up a revolt among slaves, in which the slaves refused to participate. In fact, it was so absurd that the slaves, with all their ignorance, saw plainly

enough it could not succeed. That affair, in its philosophy, corresponds with the many attempts, related in history, at the assassination of kings and emperors. An enthusiast broods over the oppression of a people till he fancies himself commissioned by Heaven to liberate them. He ventures the attempt, which ends in little else than his own execution. Orsini's attempt on Louis Napoleon, and John Brown's attempt at Harper's Ferry, were, in their philosophy, precisely the same. The eagerness to cast blame on old England in the one case, and on New England in the other, does not disprove the sameness of the two things.

[47] And how much would it avail you, if you could, by the use of John Brown, Helper's book,* and the like, break up the Republican organization? Human action can be modified to some extent, but human nature cannot be changed. There is a judgment and a feeling against slavery in this nation, which cast at least a million and a half of votes. You cannot destroy that judgment and feeling—that sentiment—by breaking up the political organization which rallies around it. You can scarcely scatter and disperse an army which has been formed into order in the face of your heaviest fire; but if you could, how much would you gain by forcing the sentiment which created it out of the peaceful channel of the ballet-box into some other channel? What would that other channel probably be? Would the number of John Browns be lessened or enlarged by the operation?

[48] But you will break up the Union rather than submit to a denial of your constitutional rights.

[49] That has a somewhat reckless sound; but it would be palliated, if not fully justified, were we proposing, by the mere force of numbers, to deprive you of some right plainly written down in the Constitution. But we are proposing no such thing.

[50] When you make these declarations you have a specific and well-understood allusion to an assumed constitutional right of yours to take slaves into the Federal Territories, and to hold them there as property. But no such right is specifically written in the Constitution. That instrument is literally silent about any such right. We, on the contrary, deny that such a right has any existence in the Constitution, even by implication.

* H. R. Helper, *The Impending Crisis in the South.*

[51] Your purpose, then, plainly stated, is that you will destroy the government, unless you be allowed to construe and force the Constitution as you please, on all points in dispute between you and us. You will rule or ruin in all events.

[52] This, plainly stated, is your language. Perhaps you will say the Supreme Court has decided the disputed constitutional question in your favor.* Not quite so. But waiving the lawyer's distinction between dictum and decision, the court has decided the question for you in a sort of way. The court has substantially said, it is your constitutional right to take slaves into the Federal Territories, and to hold them there as property. When I say the decision was made in a sort of way, I mean it was made in a divided court, by a bare majority of the judges, and they not quite agreeing with one another in the reasons for making it; that it is so made as that its avowed supporters disagree with one another about its meaning, and that it was mainly based upon a mistaken statement of fact—the statement in the opinion that "the right of property in a slave is distinctly and expressly affirmed in the Constitution."

[53] An inspection of the Constitution will show that the right of property in a slave is not "distinctly and expressly affirmed" in it. Bear in mind, the judges do not pledge their judicial opinion that such right is impliedly affirmed in the Constitution; but they pledge their veracity that it is "distinctly and expressly" affirmed there—"distinctly," that is, not mingled with anything else—"expressly," that is, in words meaning just that, without the aid of any inference, and susceptible of no other meaning.

[54] If they had only pledged their judicial opinion that such right is affirmed in the instrument by implication, it would be open to others to show that neither the word "slave" nor "slavery" is to be found in the Constitution, nor the word "property" even, in any connection with language alluding to the things slave, or slavery; and that wherever in that instrument the slave is alluded to, he is called a "person"; and wherever his master's legal right in relation to him is alluded to, it is spoken of as "service or labor which may be due"—as a debt payable in service or labor. Also it would be open to show, by contemporaneous history, that this

* In the Dred Scott case.

mode of alluding to slaves and slavery, instead of speaking of them, was employed on purpose to exclude from the Constitution the idea that there could be property in man.

[55] To show all this is easy and certain.

[56] When this obvious mistake of the judges shall be brought to their notice, is it not reasonable to expect that they will withdraw the mistaken statement, and reconsider the conclusion based upon it?

[57] And then it is to be remembered that "our fathers who framed the government under which we live"—the men who made the Constitution—decided this same constitutional question in our favor long ago: decided it without division among themselves when making the decision; without division among themselves about the meaning of it after it was made, and, so far as any evidence is left, without basing it upon any mistaken statement of facts.

[58] Under all these circumstances, do you really feel yourselves justified to break up this government unless such a court decision as yours is shall be at once submitted to as a conclusive and final rule of political action? But you will not abide the election of a Republican president! In that supposed event, you say, you will destroy the Union; and then, you say, the great crime of having destroyed it will be upon us! That is cool. A highwayman holds a pistol to my ear, and mutters through his teeth, "Stand and deliver, or I shall kill you, and then you will be a murderer!"

[59] To be sure, what the robber demanded of me—my money —was my own; and I had a clear right to keep it; but it was no more my own than my vote is my own; and the threat of death to me, to extort my money, and the threat of destruction to the Union, to extort my vote, can scarcely be distinguished in principle.

[60] A few words now to Republicans. It is exceedingly desirable that all parts of this great Confederacy shall be at peace, and in harmony one with another. Let us Republicans do our part to have it so. Even though much provoked, let us do nothing through passion and ill temper. Even though the Southern people will not so much as listen to us, let us calmly consider their demands, and yield to them if, in our deliberate view of our duty, we possibly can.

Judging by all they say and do, and by the subject and nature of their controversy with us, let us determine, if we can, what will satisfy them.

[61] Will they be satisfied if the Territories be unconditionally surrendered to them? We know they will not. In all their present complaints against us, the Territories are scarcely mentioned. Invasions and insurrections are the rage now. Will it satisfy them if, in the future, we have nothing to do with invasions and insurrections? We know it will not. We so know, because we know we never had anything to do with invasions and insurrections; and yet this total abstaining does not exempt us from the charge and the denunciation.

[62] The question recurs, What will satisfy them? Simply this: we must not only let them alone, but we must somehow convince them that we do let them alone. This, we know by experience, is no easy task. We have been so trying to convince them from the very beginning of our organization, but with no success. In all our platforms and speeches we have constantly protested our purpose to let them alone; but this has had no tendency to convince them. Alike unavailing to convince them is the fact that they have never detected a man of us in any attempt to disturb them.

[63] These natural and apparently adequate means all failing, what will convince them? This, and this only: cease to call slavery wrong, and join them in calling it right. And this must be done thoroughly—done in acts as well as in words. Silence will not be tolerated—we must place ourselves avowedly with them. Senator Douglas's new sedition law must be enacted and enforced, suppressing all declarations that slavery is wrong, whether made in politics, in presses, in pulpits, or in private. We must arrest and return their fugitive slaves with greedy pleasure. We must pull down our Free-State constitutions. The whole atmosphere must be disinfected from all taint of opposition to slavery, before they will cease to believe that all their troubles proceed from us.

[64] I am quite aware they do not state their case precisely in this way. Most of them would probably say to us, "Let us alone; do nothing to us, and say what you please about slavery." But we do let them alone—have never disturbed them—so that, after

all, it is what we say which dissatisfies them. They will continue to accuse us of doing, until we cease saying.

[65] I am also aware they have not as yet in terms demanded the overthrow of our Free-State constitutions. Yet those constitutions declare the wrong of slavery with more solemn emphasis than do all other sayings against it; and when all these other sayings shall have been silenced, the overthrow of these constitutions will be demanded, and nothing be left to resist the demand. It is nothing to the contrary that they do not demand the whole of this just now. Demanding what they do, and for the reason they do, they can voluntarily stop nowhere short of this consummation. Holding, as they do, that slavery is morally right and socially elevating, they cannot cease to demand a full national recognition of it as a legal right and a social blessing.

[66] Nor can we justifiably withhold this on any ground save our conviction that slavery is wrong. If slavery is right, all words, acts, laws, and constitutions against it are themselves wrong, and should be silenced and swept away. If it is right, we cannot justly object to its nationality—its universality; if it is wrong, they cannot justly insist upon its extension—its enlargement. All they ask we could readily grant, if we thought slavery right; all we ask they could as readily grant, if they thought it wrong. Their thinking it right and our thinking it wrong is the precise fact upon which depends the whole controversy. Thinking it right, as they do, they are not to blame for desiring its full recognition as being right; but thinking it wrong, as we do, can we yield to them? Can we cast our votes with their view, and against our own? In view of our moral, social, and political responsibilities, can we do this?

[67] Wrong as we think slavery is, we can yet afford to let it alone where it is, because that much is due to the necessity arising from its actual presence in the nation; but can we, while our votes will prevent it, allow it to spread into the national Territories, and to overrun us here in these free States? If our sense of duty forbids this, then let us stand by our duty fearlessly and effectively. Let us be diverted by none of those sophistical contrivances wherewith we are so industriously plied and belabored—contrivances such as groping for some middle ground between the right and the wrong: vain as the search for a man who should

be neither a living man nor a dead man; such as a policy of "don't care" on a question about which all true men do care; such as Union appeals beseeching true Union men to yield to Disunionists, reversing the divine rule, and calling, not the sinners, but the righteous to repentance; such as invocations to Washington, imploring men to unsay what Washington said and undo what Washington did.

[68] Neither let us be slandered from our duty by false accusations against us, nor frightened from it by menaces of destruction to the government, nor of dungeons to ourselves. Let us have faith that right makes might, and in that faith let us to the end dare to do our duty as we understand it.

EXERCISES

Abraham Lincoln's *Cooper Union Address,* delivered on February 27, 1860, has perhaps not achieved the status of Milton's *Areopagitica* among the world's great utterances on freedom; but it holds a high place, and its many reprintings bespeak its greatness. It was one of the speeches which drew into sharp issues the conflicts leading up to the Civil War.

1. What is Lincoln's main purpose?
2. What are the three main divisions of the speech?
3. Why does Lincoln concern himself about the issue of the first division when he does not believe that we are bound by the decisions of our ancestors?
4. What kind of logic is involved in Lincoln's proof of his assertion in the first part? Is the majority which he finds really enough to prove his point? Were the founding fathers for whom he could find no proof necessarily on the other side? Does he handle this matter fairly? Does he apply the necessary tests of logic?
5. Write out the syllogism implied in paragraph 42.
6. We have observed that the beginning and end are the most emphatic positions. How is this principle related to the way in which Lincoln disposes the three main parts of his speech?
7. What ideas or statements are emphasized by repetition in the first part of the address?
8. Does Lincoln make fair use of analogy?
9. Does he do any name-calling? (He shows in paragraph 34 that he is aware of the device.)
10. Are there any signs of unfairness?

11. What is the tone of the first part? Of the second part? How would the tone of part two have had to be changed if Lincoln had really expected to win over the South to his way of thinking?

12. What implications does Lincoln make about the reasonableness of the Southerners?

13. What does Lincoln imply about Douglas in such statements as "Senator Douglas holds the affirmative, and the Republicans the negative"? He makes similar statements in slightly different words.

14. What inferences can you make about (a) the degree to which the moral issue was a part of the slavery question, (b) the sincerity of Lincoln's avowed moral convictions, (c) Lincoln's ability as a logician and an orator, and (d) Lincoln's attitude toward mankind.

15. Does Lincoln use as much figurative language and allusion as Beard? As Milton? How does he emphasize his ridicule of the opposition in paragraph 63?

16. Lincoln's rhythm conveys a sense of great deliberateness. Part of this effect is achieved by "slow spondees," or at least a high proportion of accented syllables, as in paragraph 48: "But you will break up . . . ." Study some other sentences which seem especially slow and strong, and try to account for the effect. (See *Rhythm* in the Glossary.)

The Idea of Equality

ALDOUS HUXLEY

Sunday Faith and Weekday Faith

[1] That all men are created equal is a proposition to which, at ordinary times, no sane human being has ever given his assent. A man who has to undergo a dangerous operation does not act on the assumption that one doctor is just as good as another. Editors do not print every contribution that reaches them. And when they require civil servants, even the most democratic gov-

From *Proper Studies,* by Aldous Huxley, copyright 1927, 1955, by Aldous Huxley.

ernments make a careful selection among their theoretically equal subjects. At ordinary times, then, we are perfectly certain that men are not equal. But when, in a democratic country, we think or act politically, we are no less certain that men are equal. Or at any rate—which comes to the same thing in practice—we behave as though we were certain of men's equality. Similarly, the pious medieval nobleman who, in church, believed in forgiving enemies and turning the other cheek was ready, as soon as he had emerged again into the light of day, to draw his sword at the slightest provocation. The human mind has an almost infinite capacity for being inconsistent.

[2] The amount of time during which men are engaged in thinking or acting politically is very small when compared with the whole period of their lives; but the brief activities of man the politician exercise a disproportionate influence on the daily life of man the worker, man at play, man the father and husband, man the owner of property. Hence the importance of knowing what he thinks in his political capacity and why he thinks it.

The Equalitarian Axiom

[3] Politicians and political philosophers have often talked about the equality of man as though it were a necessary and unavoidable idea, an idea which human beings must believe in, just as they must, from the very nature of their physical and mental constitution, believe in such notions as weight, heat, and light. Man is "by nature free, equal, and independent," says Locke, with the calm assurance of one who knows he is saying something that cannot be contradicted. It would be possible to quote literally thousands of similar pronouncements. One must be mad, says Babeuf, to deny so manifest a truth.

Equality and Christianity

[4] In point of historical fact, however, the notion of human equality is of recent growth, and, so far from being a directly apprehended and necessary truth, is a conclusion logically drawn from preëxisting metaphysical assumptions. In modern times the Christian doctrines of the brotherhood of men and of their equality before God have been invoked in support of political democracy.

Quite illogically, however. For the brotherhood of men does not imply their equality. Families have their fools and their men of genius, their black sheep and their saints, their worldly successes and their worldly failures. A man should treat his brothers lovingly and with justice, according to the deserts of each. But the deserts of every brother are not the same. Neither does men's equality before God imply their equality as among themselves. Compared with an infinite quantity, all finite quantities may be regarded as equal. There is no difference, where infinity is concerned, between one and a thousand. But leave infinity out of the question, and a thousand is very different from one. Our world is a series of finite quantities, and where worldly matters are concerned, the fact that all men are equal in relation to the infinite quantity which is God is entirely irrelevant. The church has at all times conducted its worldly policy on the assumption that it was irrelevant. It is only recently that the theorists of democracy have appealed to Christian doctrine for a confirmation of their equalitarian principles. Christian doctrine, as I have shown, gives no such support.

Equality and the Philosopher

[5] The writers who in the course of the eighteenth century supplied our modern political democracy with its philosophical basis did not turn to Christianity to find the doctrine of human equality. They were, to begin with, almost without exception anticlerical writers, to whom the idea of accepting any assistance from the church would have been extremely repugnant. Moreover, the church, as organized for its worldly activities, offered them no assistance, but a frank hostility. It represented, even more clearly than the monarchical and feudal state, that medieval principle of hierarchical, aristocratic government against which, precisely, the equalitarians were protesting.

[6] The origin of our modern idea of human equality is to be found in the philosophy of Aristotle. The tutor of Alexander the Great was not, it is true, a democrat. Living as he did in a slaveholding society, he regarded slavery as a necessary state of affairs. Whatever is, is right; the familiar is the reasonable; and Aristotle was an owner of slaves, not a slave himself; he had no cause to

complain. In his political philosophy he rationalized his satisfaction with the existing state of things, and affirmed that some men are born to be masters (himself, it went without saying, among them) and others to be slaves. But in saying this he was committing an inconsistency. For it was a fundamental tenet of his metaphysical system that specific qualities are the same in every member of a species. Individuals of one species are the same in essence or substance. Two human beings differ from one another in matter, but are the same in essence, as being both rational animals. The essential human quality which distinguishes the species Man from all other species is identical in both.

Inconsistencies

[7] How are we to reconcile this doctrine with Aristotle's statement that some men are born to be masters and others slaves? Clearly, no reconciliation is possible; the doctrines are contradictory. Aristotle said one thing when he was discussing the abstract problems of metaphysics and another when, as a slave-owner, he was discussing politics. Such inconsistencies are extremely common, and are generally made in perfectly good faith. In cases where material interests are at stake, where social and religious traditions, inculcated in childhood, and consequently incorporated into the very structure of the mind, can exercise their influence, men will naturally think in one way; in other cases, where their interests and their early-acquired beliefs are not concerned, they will naturally and inevitably think in quite a different way. A man who thinks and behaves as an open-minded, unprejudiced scientist so long as he is repairing his automobile will be outraged if asked to think about the creation of the world or the future life except in terms of the mythology current among the barbarous Semites three thousand years ago; and though quite ready to admit that the present system of wireless telegraphy might be improved, he will regard anyone who desires to alter the existing economic and political system as either a madman or a criminal.

[8] The greatest men of genius have not been exempt from these curious inconsistencies. Newton created the science of celestial mechanics; but he was also the author of *Observations on the Prophecies of Daniel and the Apocalypse of Saint John,* of a

Lexicon Propheticum and a *History of the Creation*. With one part of his mind he believed in the miracles and prophecies about which he had been taught in childhood; with another part he believed that the universe is a scene of order and uniformity. The two parts were impenetrably divided one from the other. The mathematical physicist never interfered with the commentator on the Apocalypse; the believer in miracles had no share in formulating the laws of gravitation.

[9] Similarly, Aristotle the slave-owner believed that some men are born to command and others to serve; Aristotle the metaphysician, thinking in the abstract, and unaffected by the social prejudices which influenced the slave-owner, expounded a doctrine of specific essences, which entailed belief in the real and substantial equality of all human beings. The opinion of the slave-owner was probably nearer the truth than that of the metaphysician. But it is by the metaphysician's doctrine that our lives are influenced today.

Applied Metaphysics

[10] That all members of a species are identical in essence was still, in the Middle Ages, a purely metaphysical doctrine. No attempt was made to apply it practically in politics. So long as the feudal and ecclesiastical hierarchies served their purpose of government, they seemed, to all but a very few, necessary and unquestionable. Whatever is, is right; feudalism and Catholicism *were*. It was only after what we call the Reformation and the Renaissance, when, under the stress of new economic and intellectual forces, the old system had largely broken down, that men began to think of applying the metaphysical doctrine of Aristotle and his medieval disciples to politics. Feudalism and ecclesiastical authority lingered on, but as the merest ghosts of themselves. They had, to all intents and purposes, ceased to be, and not being, they were wrong.

[11] It was not necessary, however, for the political thinkers of the eighteenth century to go back directly to Aristotle and the Schoolmen. They had what was for them a better authority nearer home. Descartes, the most influential philosopher of his age, had reaffirmed the Aristotelian and Scholastic doctrine in the most positive terms. At the beginning of his *Discourse on Method* we

read that "what is called good sense or reason is equal in all men," and a little later he says, "I am disposed to believe that [reason] is to be found complete in each individual; and on this point to adopt the opinion of philosophers who say that the difference of greater or less holds only among the accidents, and not among the forms or natures of individuals of the same species." Descartes took not the slightest interest in politics, and was concerned only with physical science and the theory of knowledge. It remained for others to draw the obvious political conclusions from what was for him, as it had been for Aristotle and the Schoolmen, a purely abstract metaphysical principle. These conclusions might have been drawn at any time during the preceding two thousand years. But it was only in the two centuries immediately following Descartes's death that political circumstances in Europe, especially in France, were favorable to such conclusions being drawn. The forms of government current during classical antiquity and the Middle Ages had been efficient and well adapted to the circumstances of the times. They seemed, accordingly, right and reasonable. In the eighteenth century, on the other hand, particularly on the continent of Europe, the existing form of government was not adapted to the social circumstances of the age. At a period when the middle classes were already rich and well educated, absolute monarchy and the ineffectual remains of feudalism were unsuitable as forms of government. Being unsuitable, they therefore seemed utterly unreasonable and wrong. Middle class Frenchmen wanted a share in the government. But men are not content merely to desire; they like to have a logical or a pseudo-logical justification for their desires; they like to believe that when they want something, it is not merely for their own personal advantage, but that their desires are dictated by pure reason, by nature, by God Himself. The greater part of the world's philosophy and theology is merely an intellectual justification for the wishes and the daydreams of philosophers and theologians. And practically all political theories are elaborated, after the fact, to justify the interests and desires of certain individuals, classes, or nations. In the eighteenth century, middle class Frenchmen justified their very natural wish to participate in the government of the country by elaborating a new political philosophy from the metaphysical doctrine of Aristotle, the Schoolmen, and Descartes.

These philosophers had taught that the specific essence is the same in all individuals of a species. In the case of *Homo Sapiens* this specific essence is reason. All men are equally reasonable. It follows that all men have an equal capacity, and therefore an equal right, to govern; there are no born slaves nor masters. Hence, monarchy and hereditary aristocracy are inadmissible. Nature herself demands that government shall be organized on democratic principles. Thus middle class Frenchmen had the satisfaction of discovering that their desires were indorsed as right and reasonable, not only by Aristotle, St. Thomas, and Descartes, but also by the Creator of the Universe in person.

Making the Facts Fit

[12] Even metaphysicians cannot entirely ignore the obvious facts of the world in which they live. Having committed themselves to a belief in this fundamental equality of all men, the eighteenth century political philosophers had to invent an explanation for the manifest inequalities which they could not fail to observe on every side. If Jones, they argued, is an imbecile and Smith a man of genius, that is due, not to any inherent and congenital differences between the two men, but to purely external and accidental differences in their upbringing, their education, and the ways in which circumstances have compelled them to use their minds. Give Jones the right sort of training, and you can turn him into a Newton, a St. Francis, or a Caesar according to taste. "The diversity of opinions," says Descartes, "does not arise from some being endowed with a larger share of reason than others, but solely from this, that we conduct our thoughts along different ways, and do not fix our attention on the same objects." "Intelligence, genius, and virtue," says Helvétius, whose work, *De l'Esprit,* was published in 1758, and exercised an enormous contemporary influence, "are the products of education." And again (*De l'Esprit,* Discours III, Ch. 26): *"La grande inégalité d'esprit qu'on aperçoit entre les hommes dépend donc uniquement et de la différente éducation qu'ils reçoivent, et de l'enchaînement inconnu et divers dans lesquels ils se trouvent placés,"* [1] and so on.

---

[1] "The great inequality of intelligence which one perceives among men results, then, only from the different education which they receive and from the unknown and varied environment in which they are placed."

[13] The political and philosophical literature of the eighteenth century teems with such notions. It was only to be expected; for such notions, it is obvious, are the necessary corollaries of the Cartesian axiom that reason is the same and entire in all men. They followed no less necessarily from the *tabula rasa* theory of mind elaborated by Locke. Both philosophers regarded men as originally and in essence equal, the one in possessing the same specific faculties and innate ideas, the other in possessing no innate ideas. It followed from either assumption that men are made or marred exclusively by environment and education. Followers whether of Locke or of Descartes, the eighteenth century philosophers were all agreed in attributing the observed inequalities of intelligence and virtue to inequalities of instruction. Men were naturally reasonable and therefore good; but they lived in the midst of vice and abject superstition. Why? Because evil-minded legislators—kings and priests—had created a social environment calculated to warp the native reason and corrupt the morals of the human race. Why priests and kings, who, as human beings, were themselves naturally reasonable and therefore virtuous, should have conspired against their fellows, or why their reasonable fellows should have allowed themselves to be put upon by these crafty corruptors, was never adequately explained. The democratic religion, like all other religions, is founded on faith as much as on reason. The king-priest theory in its wildest and most extravagant form is the inspiration and subject of much of Shelley's finest poetry. Poor Shelley, together with large numbers of his less talented predecessors and contemporaries, seems seriously to have believed that by getting rid of priests and kings you could inaugurate the golden age.[2]

The Tests of Experiment

[14] The historical and psychological researches of the past century have rendered the theory which lies behind the practice of modern democracy entirely untenable. Reason is not the same in all men; human beings belong to a variety of psychological types separated one from another by irreducible differences. Men are

[2] For a magnificent expression of this idea, read the final speech of the Spirit of the Hour, in Act III of Shelley's *Prometheus Unbound*.

not the exclusive products of their environments. A century of growing democracy has shown that the reform of institutions and the spread of education are by no means necessarily followed by inprovements in individual virtue and intelligence. At the same time biologists have accumulated an enormous mass of evidence tending to show that physical peculiarities are inherited in a perfectly regular and necessary fashion. Body being indissolubly connected with mind, this evidence would almost be enough in itself to prove that mental peculiarities are similarly heritable. Direct observation on the history of families reinforces this evidence, and makes it certain that mental idiosyncrasies are inherited in exactly the same way as physical idiosyncrasies. Indeed, mind being in some sort a function of brain, a mental idiosyncrasy is also a physical one, just as much as red hair or blue eyes. Faculties are heritable: we are born more or less intelligent, more or less musical, mathematical, and so on. From this it follows that men are not essentially equal, and that human beings are at least as much the product of their heredity as of their education.

The Behaviorist Reaction

[15] Recently, it is true, Helvétius's doctrine of the all-effectiveness of nurture and the unimportance of nature and heredity has been revived by psychologists of the Behaviorist School. Unlike the philosophers of the eighteenth century, the Behaviorists have no political axe to grind and are not metaphysicians. If they agree with Helvétius, it is not because they want the vote (they have it), nor, presumably, because they accept the authority of Aristotle, the Schoolmen, and Descartes on the one hand, or of Locke on the other. They agree with Helvétius on what they affirm to be scientific grounds. Helvétius's theory, according to the Behaviorists, is in accordance with the observed facts. Before going further, let us briefly examine their claims.

[16] "The Behaviorist," writes Mr. J. B. Watson, the leader of the school, "no longer finds support for hereditary patterns of behavior nor for special abilities (musical, art, etc.), which are supposed to run in families. He believes that, given the relatively simple list of embryological responses which are fairly uniform in infants, he can build (granting that both internal and external

environment can be controlled) any infant along any specified line—into rich man, poor man, beggar man, thief." Taken literally, this last statement is merely silly. No one was ever such a fool as to suggest that riches and poverty were heritable in the sense that a Roman nose or a talent for music may be said to be heritable. Opulent fathers have long anticipated this great discovery of the Behaviorists, and have "built their children into rich men" by placing large cheques to their account at the bank. We must presume, in charity to Mr. Watson, that he does not mean what he says, and that when he says "rich man, poor man, beggar man, thief," he really means something like intelligent man, imbecile, mathematician and non-mathematician, musical person and unmusical person, etc. Presuming that this is what he does mean, let us examine the Behaviorists' hypothesis, which is identical with that of the philosophers who, in the eighteenth century, elaborated the theory of modern democracy. The first thing that strikes one about the Behaviorists' hypothesis is that the observations on which it is based are almost exclusively observations on small children, not on fully grown men and women. It is on the ground that all infants are very much alike that the Behaviorists deny the hereditary transmission of special aptitudes, attributing the enormous differences of mental capacity observable among grown human beings exclusively to differences in environment, internal and external. Now it is an obvious and familiar fact that the younger a child, the less individually differentiated it is. Physically, all newborn children are very much alike: there are few fathers who, after seeing their newborn infant once, could recognize it again among a group of other infants. Mr. Watson will not, I suppose, venture to deny that physical peculiarities may be inherited. Yet the son who at twenty will have his father's aquiline nose and his mother's dark, straight hair may be as snubnosed and golden at two as another child whose father is pugfaced and his mother blonde, and who will grow up to be like them. If the Behaviorists had made their observations on children a few months before they were born, they would have been able to affirm not only the psychological identity of all men and women, but also their physical identity. Three days after their respective conceptions, Pocahontas, Shakespeare, and a Negro congenital idiot would probably be indistinguishable from one another, even under the most powerful microscope. According to Behaviorist notions, this should be regarded as a conclusive proof of the omnipotence of nurture. Since they are indistinguishable at conception, it must be environment that turns the fertilized ova into respectively a Red Indian woman, an English man of genius, and a Negro idiot. [17] Mind and body are closely interdependent: they come to maturity more or less simultaneously. A mind is not fully grown until the body with which it is connected through the brain has passed the age of puberty. The mind of a young child is as much undifferentiated and unindividualized as its body. It does not become completely itself until the body is more or less fully grown. A child of two has neither his father's nose nor his maternal grandfather's talent for mathematics. But that is no argument against his developing both when he is a few years older. A young child looks and thinks like other children of the same age and not like his parents. Later on he will certainly look like his parents. What reason is there to suppose that his mind will not also be like theirs? If he has his father's nose, why not his father's brain, and with it his father's mentality? The Behaviorists give us no answers to these questions. They merely state, what we already knew, that small children are very much alike. But this is entirely beside the point. Two fertilized ova may be indistinguishable; but if one belongs to a Negress and the other to a Japanese, no amount of nurture will make the Japanese egg develop into a Negro, or vice versa. There is no more valid reason for supposing the two very similar infants who were to become Shakespeare and Stratford's village idiot could have been educated into exchanging their adult parts. To study human psychology exclusively in babies is like studying the anatomy of frogs exclusively in tadpoles. That environment may profoundly influence the course of mental development is obvious. But it is no less obvious that there is a hereditarily conditioned development to be modified. Environment no more creates a mental aptitude in a grown boy that it creates the shape of his nose.

Equality of Virtue

[18] We have dealt so far with the primary assumption from which the whole theory and practice of democracy flows: that all men are substantially equal; and with one of its corollaries: that the

observed differences between human beings are due to environment, and that education, in the widest sense of the term, is all-powerful. It is now necessary to touch briefly on one or two other corollaries. Men being in essence equally reasonable, it follows that they are also in essence equally moral. For morality (according to the philosophers who formulated the theory of democracy) is absolute and exists in itself, apart from any actual society of right- or wrong-doing individuals. The truths of morality can be apprehended by reason. All men are equally reasonable: therefore all are equally capable of grasping the absolute truths of moral science. They are therefore, in essence, equally virtuous, and if, in practice, they behave badly, that is merely an accident, due to corrupting surroundings. Man must be delivered from his corrupting surroundings (and for the most ardent and ruthlessly logical spirits all government, all law, and organized religion are corrupting influences). Finding himself once more in that idyllic "state of nature" from which he should never have tried to rise, man will become, automatically, perfectly virtuous. There are few people now, I suppose, who take the theories of Rousseau very seriously. But though our intellect may reject them, our emotions are still largely influenced by them. Many people still cherish a vague sentimental belief that the poor and uncultivated, who are nearer to the "state of nature" than the cultured and the rich, are for that reason more virtuous.

Democratic Pot and Catholic Kettle

[19] Pots have a diverting way of calling kettles black, and the prophets of the democratic-humanitarian religion have at all times, from the eighteenth century down to the present day, denounced the upholders of Christian orthodoxy as anti-scientific. In certain important respects, however, the dogmas and the practice of orthodox Catholic Christianity were and are more nearly in accordance with the facts than the dogmas and practice of democratic-humanitarianism. The doctrine of original sin is, scientifically, much truer than the doctrine of natural reasonableness and virtue. Original sin, in the shape of antisocial tendencies inherited from our animal ancestors, is a familiar and observable fact. Primitively, and in a state of nature, human beings were not,

as the eighteenth century philosophers supposed, wise and virtuous: they were apes.

[20] Practically, the wisdom of the church displays itself in a recognition among human beings of different psychological types. It is not every Tom, Dick, or Harry who is allowed to study the intricacies of theology. What may strengthen the faith of one may bewilder or perhaps even disgust another. Moreover, not all are called upon to rule; there must be discipline, a hierarchy, the subjection of many and the dominion of few. In these matters the theory and practice of the church is based on observation and long experience. The humanitarian democrats who affirm that men are equal, and who on the strength of their belief distribute votes to everybody, can claim no experimental justification for their beliefs and actions. They are men who have a faith, and who act on it, without attempting to discover whether the faith corresponds with objective reality.

The Relation of Theory to Action

[21] It is in the theory of human equality that modern democracy finds its philosophic justification and some part, at any rate, of its motive force. It would not be true to say that the democratic movement took its rise in the theories propounded by Helvétius and his fellows. The origin of any widespread social disturbance is never merely a theory. It is only in pursuit of their interests, or under the influence of powerful emotions, that large masses of men are moved to action. When we analyze any of the historical movements in favor of democracy and self-determination, we find that they derive their original impetus from considerations of self-interest on the part of the whole or a part of the population. Autocracy and the rule of foreigners are often (though by no means invariably) inefficient, cruel, and corrupt. Large masses of the subjects of despots or strangers find their interests adversely affected by the activities of their rulers. They desire to change the form of government, so that it shall be more favorable to their particular national or class interests. But the discontented are never satisfied with mere discontent and desire for change. They like, as I have already pointed out, to justify their discontent, to find exalted and philosophical excuses for their desires, to feel that

the state of affairs most agreeable to them is also the state of affairs most agreeable to Pure Reason, Nature, and the Deity. Violent oppression begets violent and desperate reaction. But if their grievances are only moderate, men will not fight whole-heartedly for their redress, unless they can persuade themselves of the absolute rightness, the essential reasonableness of what they desire. Nor will they be able, without some kind of intellectual rationalization of these desires, to persuade other men, with less immediate cause for discontent, to join them. Emotion cannot be communicated by a direct contagion. It must be passed from man to man by means of a verbal medium. Now words, unless they are mere onomatopoeic exclamations, appeal to the emotions through the understanding. Feelings are communicated by means of ideas, which are their intellectual equivalent; at the sound of the words conveying the ideas appropriate emotion is evoked. Thus, theory is seen to be doubly important: first, as providing a higher, philosophical justification for feelings and wishes; and second, as making possible the communication of feeling from one man to another. "The equality of all men" and "natural rights" are examples of simple intellectual generalizations which have justified emotions of discontent and hatred, and at the same time have rendered them easily communicable. The rise and progress of any democratic movement may be schematically represented in some such way as this: Power is in the hands of a government that injures the material interests, or in some way outrages the feelings, of all, or at least an influential fraction of its subjects. The subjects are discontented and desire to change the existing government for one which shall be, for their purposes, better. But discontent and desire for change are not in themselves enough to drive men to action. They require a cause which they can believe to be absolutely, and not merely relatively and personally, good. By postulating (quite gratuitously) the congenital equality of all men, by assuming the existence of certain "natural rights" (the term is entirely meaningless), existing absolutely, in themselves and apart from any society in which such rights might be exercised, the discontented are able to justify their discontent, and at the same time to communicate it by means of easily remembered intellectual formulas to their less discontented fellows.

Theory Gets Out of Hand

[22] The invention of transcendental reasons to justify actions dictated by self-interest, instinct, or prejudice would be harmless enough if the justificatory philosophy ceased to exist with the accomplishment of the particular action it was designed to justify. But once it has been called into existence, a metaphysic is difficult to kill. Men will not let it go, but persist in elaborating the system, in drawing with a perfect logic ever fresh conclusions from the original assumptions. These assumptions, which are accepted as axiomatic, may be demonstrably false. But the arguments by which conclusions are reached may be logically flawless. In that case, the conclusions will be what the logicians call "hypothetically necessary." That is to say that, granted the truth of the assumptions, the conclusions are necessarily true. If the assumptions are false, the conclusions are necessarily false. It may be remarked, in passing, that the hypothetical necessity of the conclusions of a logically correct argument has often and quite unjustifiably been regarded as implying the absolute necessity of the assumptions from which the argument starts.

[23] In the case of the theory of democracy the original assumptions are these: that reason is the same and entire in all men, and that all men are naturally equal. To these assumptions are attached several corollaries: that men are naturally good as well as naturally reasonable; that they are the product of their environment; that they are indefinitely educable. The main conclusions derivable from these assumptions are the following: that the state ought to be organized on democratic lines; that the governors should be chosen by universal suffrage; that the opinion of the majority on all subjects is the best opinion; that education should be universal, and the same for all citizens. The primary assumptions, as we have seen, are almost certainly false; but the logic by which the metaphysicians of democracy deduced the conclusions was sound enough. Given the assumptions, the conclusions were necessary.

[24] In the early stages of that great movement which has made the whole of the West democratic, there were only discontent and a desire for such relatively small changes in the mode of government as would increase its efficiency and make it serve the interests of the discontented. A philosophy was invented to justify the malcontents in their demand for change; the philosophy was elaborated; conclusions were relentlessly drawn; and it was found that, granted the assumptions on which the philosophy was based, logic demanded that the changes in the existing institutions should be, not small, but vast, sweeping, and comprehensive. Those who rationalize their desires for the purpose of persuading themselves and others that these desires are in accord with nature and reason find themselves persuading the world of the rightness and reasonableness of many ideas and plans of action of which they had, originally, never dreamed. Whatever is, is right. Becoming familiar, a dogma automatically becomes right. Notions which for one generation are dubious novelties become for the next absolute truths, which it is criminal to deny and a duty to uphold. The malcontents of the first generation invent a justifying philosophy. The philosophy is elaborated, conclusions are logically drawn. Their children are brought up with the whole philosophy (remote conclusion as well as primary assumption), which becomes, by familiarity, not a reasonable hypothesis, but actually a part of the mind, conditioning and, so to speak, canalizing all rational thought. For most people, nothing which is contrary to any system of ideas with which they have been brought up since childhood can possibly be reasonable. New ideas are reasonable if they can be fitted into an already familiar scheme, unreasonable if they cannot be made to fit. Our intellectual prejudices determine the channels along which our reason shall flow.

[25] Of such systems of intellectual prejudices some seem merely reasonable, and some are sacred as well as reasonable. It depends on the kind of entity to which the prejudices refer. In general it may be said that intellectual prejudices about non-human entities appear to the holder of them as merely reasonable, while prejudices about human entities strike him as being sacred as well as reasonable. Thus, we all believe that the earth moves round the sun, and that the sun is at a distance of some ninety million miles

from our planet. We believe, even though we may be quite incapable of demonstrating the truth of either of these propositions —and the vast majority of those who believe in the findings of modern astronomy do so as an act of blind faith, and would be completely at a loss if asked to show reasons for their belief. We have a prejudice in favor of modern astronomy. Having been brought up with it, we find it reasonable, and any new idea which contradicts the findings of contemporary astronomy strikes us as absurd. But it does not strike us as morally reprehensible. Our complex of what may be called astronomy-prejudices is only reasonable, not sacred.

The Nearer, the More Sacred

[26] There was a time, however, when men's astronomy-prejudices were bound up with a great human activity—religion. For their contemporaries the ideas of Copernicus and Galileo were not merely absurd, as contradicting the established intellectual prejudices; they were also immoral. The established prejudices were supported by high religious authority. For its devotees, the local and contemporary brand of religion is "good," "sacred," "right," as well as reasonable and true. Anything which contradicts any part of the cult is therefore not only false and unreasonable, but also bad, unholy, and wrong. As the Copernican ideas became more familiar, they seemed less frightful. Brought up in a heliocentric system, the religious folk of ensuing generations accepted without demur the propositions which to their fathers had seemed absurd and wicked. History repeated itself when, in the middle of the nineteenth century, Darwin published his *Origin of Species*. The uproar was enormous. The theory of natural selection seemed much more criminal than the Copernican theory of planetary motion. Wickedness in these matters is proportionate to the distance from ourselves. Copernicus and Galileo had propounded unorthodox views about the stars. It was a crime, but not a very grave one; the stars are very remote. Darwin and the Darwinians propounded unorthodox views about man himself. Their crime was therefore enormous. The dislike of the Darwinian hypothesis is by no means confined to those who believe in the literal truth of the Book of Genesis. One does not have to be an orthodox

Christian to object to what seems an assault on human dignity, uniqueness, and superiority.

Democracy as a Religion

[27] The prejudices in favor of democracy belong to the second class; they seem, to those who cherish them, sacred as well as reasonable, morally right as well as true. Democracy is natural, good, just, progressive, and so forth. The opponents of it are reactionary, bad, unjust, antinatural, etc. For vast numbers of people the idea of democracy has become a religious idea, which it is a duty to try to carry into practice in all circumstances, regardless of the practical requirements of each particular case. The metaphysic of democracy which was in origin the rationalization of certain French and English men's desires for the improvement of their governments, has become a universally and absolutely true theology which it is all humanity's highest duty to put into practice. Thus, India must have democracy, not because democratic government would be better than the existing undemocratic government —it would almost certainly be incomparably worse—but because democracy is everywhere and in all circumstances right. The transformation of the theory of democracy into theology has had another curious result: it has created a desire for progress in the direction of more democracy among numbers of people whose material interests are in no way harmed, and are even actively advanced, by the existing form of government which they desire to change. This spread of socialism among the middle classes, the spontaneous granting of humanitarian reforms by power-holders to whose material advantages it would have been to wield their power ruthlessly and give none of it away—these are phenomena which have become so familiar that we have almost ceased to comment on them. They show how great the influence of a theory can be when by familiarity it has become a part of the mind of those who believe in it. In the beginning is desire; desire is rationalized; logic works on the rationalization and draws conclusions; the rationalization, with all these conclusions, undreamed of in many cases by those who first desired and rationalized, becomes one of the prejudices of men in the succeeding generations; the prejudice determines their judgment of what is right and

wrong, true and false; it gives direction to their thoughts and desires; it drives them into action. The result is that a man whose interests are bound up with the existing order of things will desire to make changes in that order much more sweeping than those desired by his grandfather, though the latter's material interests were genuinely injured by it. Man shall not live by bread alone. The divine injunction was unnecessary. Man never has lived by bread alone, but by every word that proceeded out of the mouth of every conceivable God. There are occasions when it would be greatly to man's advantage if he did confine himself for a little exclusively to bread.

EXERCISES

1. Why is Huxley's opening sentence rhetorically good?
2. By what method does he quickly demonstrate the apparent truth of his statement?
3. What inferences can you make about (a) Huxley's learning, (b) his religion, and (c) his attitude toward man?
4. Is the term "natural rights" meaningless? How is the concept related to the Creator, as mentioned in the Declaration of Independence? (The Declaration is reprinted on page 146.) *The Encyclopedia of the Social Sciences* will be helpful on this.
5. Does Huxley's interpretation of the philosophy of democracy, in paragraphs 1–4, represent the philosophy in sections [1] and [2] of the Declaration of Independence?
6. What parable seems to be alluded to in paragraph 4?
7. Did Jefferson (the main composer of the Declaration) believe that all men are equally wise? Did Jesus? In what way did they believe that all men are equal?
8. What error in logic does Huxley impute to the philosophers of democracy in paragraph 12?
9. What kind of logic is referred to in paragraph 14?
10. In pararaph 24 Huxley says "Whatever is, is right," meaning that it seems right. Could this statement be turned against Huxley and others of his philosophical and religious views?
11. What would be the political implications of Huxley's views?
12. What figure of speech are the words "madman" and "criminal" as used in the last sentence of paragraph 7?
13. In paragraph 7, what connotation does Huxley's expression "the

mythology current among the barbarous Semites three thousand
years ago" give to the Biblical concepts of the creation of the world
and the immortality of the soul?

14. What is the difference in meaning between "false" and "wrong"
in the 4th sentence of paragraph 26?

15. In the second sentence of paragraph 27, what connotation does the
phrase "and so forth" give to the adjectives before it?

16. Find some examples of wit and humor.

17. Analyze one paragraph for variety of sentence structure.

18. A special sentence construction called *gradation,* or *progression,*
technically a figure of speech, consists of a series of phrases or
clauses in which each builds upon the preceding one, thus: "Care-
lessness made him poor, poverty made him borrow, borrowing
made him worry, and worry drove him insane." The figure is a
rather striking one, and it is particularly useful in summaries. Find
an example of graduation in paragraph 27.

Liberty—For What?

ALEXANDER MEIKLEJOHN

[1] The principle of liberty, as we Americans interpret it, forbids interference with certain of our activities. But it also requires
or implies that we do not interfere with certain other activities.
And the major problem of the defining of freedom, both in theory
and in practice, is that of separating these two fields of human
action. Our fundamental question is, "To what human enterprises does the demand for liberty apply: in which of our ventures is the demand for it preposterous, contrary to all good social
policy?"

[2] At this point we encounter one of the strangest vagaries of our
national mind. In the course of three hundred years many Americans have come to believe that the liberty which we love is the
liberty to buy and sell without hindrance. In recent years a great

In *Harper's Magazine,* August, 1935.

array of practical men and scholars have interpreted for us the Spirit of America. And their conclusion can be summed up very briefly. The freedom which Americans worship, in terms of which they live, for the sake of which they are willing to die, is, these men tell us, the freedom to manage their own property without interference from their fellows. The freedom of the spirit is the freedom of the marketplace.

[3] The interpretation, as it stands, is so grotesquely untrue, so contradictory to the human intentions which it explains, that one can deal with it only by taking account of the peculiarities and the aberrations of the mind that makes it. In that mind, something has broken loose. Some fundamental ideas have gone wrong. Nonsense has taken the place of sense. Let me try then to break down the interpretation to show its falsity.

[4] The distinction which I have in mind is clearly suggested if we place side by side two familiar provisions of the Constitution. In the Bill of Rights, two sets of "liberties" are dealt with; but they are dealt with in exactly opposite ways. One of them is declared to be outside the field of interference or control by the government. The other is deliberately subjected to control and to interference. Under the term "liberty" then as the Constitution uses it, there are covered two very different kinds of liberty. It is that difference of kind to which I wish to call attention.

[5] The First Amendment to the Constitution reads as follows:

"Congress shall make no law respecting an establishment of religion, or prohibiting the free exercise thereof: or abridging the freedom of speech or of the press: or the right of the people peaceably to assemble, and to petition the government for a redress of grievances."

[6] The Fifth Amendment, adopted at the same time, reads in part as follows:

No person shall "be deprived of life, liberty, or property without due process of law: nor shall private property be taken without due process of law."

[7] Now the significance of these statements for our argument lies in the sharpness of the difference which they establish between two sets of human interests. We are trying in our defining of liberty to separate those activities which may properly be hindered

and restrained from those which, in our judgment, brook no inter-ference. And the Amendments to the Constitution which I have quoted tell us, in clear words, what, in the structure of our govern-ment, that separation is. On the one hand, Religion, Speech, the Press, Assemblage, Protest—these the Federal Congress may not touch. They are free. On the other hand, Life, Liberty, and Property—these are to be regulated and restrained by Congress: they may even be taken away provided that the action by which this is done is justly and properly performed.

[8] Our constituted authorities are forbidden—they forbid them-selves—to lay hands upon a man's religion. They may, however, deprive him of his life—by due process of law. No authority, pub-lic or private, may take from a citizen his freedom of speech. But the liberty of his body, his freedom of external physical action, may be limited and controlled as the public welfare may require. The unhindered integrity of the press is one of the highest ideals of our civilization: the Federal government may not limit it, may not subordinate it to other purposes. But as for the holding and managing of property—the regulation and restraint of these is the primary and engrossing occupation of every established governing body. Nothing could be further from the intention of the Constitution than to say that with respect to these restraint and limitation by the State are improper and unjustified, contrary to our ideals.

[9] This is, if I am not mistaken, the division of human interests upon which a proper understanding of liberty in America rests. In the field of Religion, Speech, Press, Assemblage a government finds itself facing activities which are beyond, above the level of its authority. It is their servant. It owes them allegiance. In re-lation to them its one legitimate activity is to see that they are kept free from interference, that no agency, public or private, shall establish control over them. Here the law reads, "Congress shall make no law . . . prohibiting . . . or abridging . . ."

[10] But in the other field, that of external possessions and pur-poses and actions, a radically different dictum is enacted. Here our government says, in effect, "Men desire life: they crave liberty of external action: they fight and strive for property. No State can allow them to pursue without hindrance or control these

multifarious and conflicting desires. It is, however, essential that
any government which exercises such control shall do so with
justice, with due regard for all men, in ways which will deserve
the confidence and respect of all who are affected by the decisions
made." Over against the "Congress shall make no law" of the first
field, stands the "not without due process of law" of the second
field. And these two phrases mark off for us, on the one hand, the
field of spiritual activities in which our institutions provide that
men shall be free and, on the other hand, the field of external
activities in which men must be regulated and restrained.

[11] Here, then, are two sets of liberties, one of which is granted,
the other of which is, under our government, denied. Men are free
to worship or not to worship. They are not, under the law, free
in the management of their property. And the argument which
concludes that freedom of external action is guaranteed by the
Constitution is sheer confusion as between these two differing
spheres of liberty. I do not like the phrase "wishful thinking" but,
if ever it should be applied, it is applicable here. The American
mind has, in terms of its desires, a powerful predisposition toward
free competition in business. For three hundred years we have
been busily engaged in taking possession of the resources, the
opportunities of a new country, a new industry. Out of the rush
of these external activities, out of our driven and, at times, frantic
preoccupation with them, we have developed habits of mind,
forms of belief, judgments of expediency as to the ways in which
the getting and distributing of wealth may best be carried on. But
these beliefs and impulses are not our spiritual love of liberty.
They express desires rather than admirations, expedients rather
than principles. No one can doubt their strength; but one may
challenge their meaning. And when that is done, the guarantees
of the Constitution are, I think, clear and unmistakable. The Fifth
and, with it, the Fourteenth Amendment, dealing with the ownership and management of external possessions, give assurance in
that field, not of freedom from restraint, but of justice and regularity in the imposing of restraints. They tell us, not that the State
is bound, as in the case of freedom of speech, to withhold all
regulation, but that, in the making of its regulations, the State
must do so justly, by orderly and trustworthy procedure. Justice,

rather than liberty, is the principle by which the regulation of property transactions is determined. And justice is not freedom. There is a close and necessary relation between these two, but they are not identical.

[12] The appeal to historical documents is not, however, decisive for our argument. And from this it follows that we must not press too hard even an argument from the Constitution of the United States. This point becomes all too clear if, for example, we compare with the provisions quoted from the Bill of Rights the corresponding statements from the Declaration of Independence. The two documents are on the question at issue so flatly contradictory of each other that the situation is almost ludicrous. The Constitution provides that the rights of life, liberty, and property are to be kept within regulation by orderly and just procedure. The Declaration proclaims that men are "endowed by their creator with certain inalienable rights: that among these are life, liberty and the pursuit of happiness." Now it is of course dangerous to interpret any statement of "natural rights" too literally. When the decrees of a Creator are introduced into discussion of the meaning of laws which men are themselves making, there is abundant room for misunderstanding. And yet, as they stand, the two statements do seem to be in direct opposition to each other. For one of them life, property, and liberty of action are inalienable: no government may take them away. For the other, the explicit task of government is that of determining in what ways and under what conditions life and liberty and property may be alienated, may be limited or taken away. One cannot help suspecting that many of those who interpret the Constitution as in favor of free competition in business are deriving their conviction, not from the Constitution itself, but from the Declaration, which is quite at variance with it. They have mistaken the highly emotional and unclear proclamation with which thirteen colonies flung themselves into a war of revolution for the deliberate and reasoned formulation of principles with which a new nation prepared itself for the organization of the activities of a society at peace.

[13] It is time, however, that we turn from the interpretation of documents to the examination of the actual procedures and attitudes which those documents were attempting to formulate.

Here we shall find a sounder basis for deciding as between the Declaration and the Constitution. Here, if anywhere, we shall be able to tell whether or not it is true that our American scheme of life requires and provides that the management of property shall be free from interference by the government.

[14] First, it is very clear that in the actual procedure of our government we do regulate and control the holding and management of property. Ever since the first group of Americans settled in the wilderness there has poured out from every village, district, county, town, city, State, as well as from the Federal authority itself, an increasing stream of ordinances, laws, statutes, regulations, codes which have told men what they may and may not do with respect to their property and that of their fellows. Thus in recent years we have regulated the railroads. We have fixed the hours and conditions and wages of labor. We have taken from men and corporations whatever part of their annual income we deemed just and necessary. We have, by changing the currency, determined what part of his debt a borrower need not pay when the time of settlement comes. We have seized for public use a share of the inheritance of the widow and the orphan. In these and in a multitude of other ways we have hindered the free use by a man of his own possessions. In the face of these actions, what can it mean to say that the Spirit of America is committed to the view that the public control of business is a denial of rightful freedom? To say that is to say that liberty and government are opposites. Do we mean to say that? The makers of our Constitution did not intend to say it. Nor do we.

[15] And, second, when we examine our own motives it is clear that we do intend to regulate the buying and selling of goods. Why should we not regulate them? Why, if a business practice is deemed to be harmful to the general welfare, should we allow it to go on? If a trader in seeking for profit is causing loss to his fellows there is, so far as I can see, no reason why they should allow him to continue doing so. Why in this field should we let a man do as he likes if we do not like what he does? The truth is, I fear, that some of us are trying by appeal to the general principle of liberty to find settlement of a current issue to which that principle does not apply. America is at present, like every other industrial

society, facing the issue as between individualism and collectivism in the management of business. With respect to that issue there are, with us as elsewhere, two sets of opposing opinions. Some of us believe that the methods of free competition are more promising that those of its rival. The business freedom of each, we say, is to the advantage of all. Others of us, however, are persuaded that the system of free competition will not work. We are convinced that if the stronger, the more fortunate, the more unscrupulous are left unhindered in their pursuit of wealth, other men will be enslaved and impoverished rather than helped by their successes.

[16] As between these two sets of opinions America is just now trying to make up her mind. What decision she may make no one can yet tell. She may go back to the ways of relatively free enterprise. She may move on into expedients of corporate control. In the latter case we face the practical problem as to whether the activities of regulation and control shall be given to the Federal government or whether they shall be reserved to State and municipal authorities. But in either case the essential point is that the spiritual liberty of America does not mean the freedom of its property holding. In the conflict between individualism and collectivism in business, the issue of the freedom of the human spirit is not at stake. In our scheme of life and government it is agreed, it is established, both in theory and in practice, that the management of business shall so far as needful be regulated and controlled. But to say that is not to say that the activities of the spirit are to be limited and restrained.

[17] To identify the freedom of the human spirit with the absence of legislative control of commerce and industry is then to deny both the theory and the practice of our institutions. As seen in the light of our history, in the face of our obligations and commitments, such an identification is absurd. Only a social system which has built up the external view of human living to the exclusion of the inner view, which has identified business activity with spiritual activity, which has come to regard the creation and distribution of wealth as the primary concern of a society, could create such an illusion as that. I know no deeper ground of reproach against our present social order than that so many of

its leaders in scholarship and in affairs have fallen, have led their followers, into that blunder. With the blind thus leading the blind it is little wonder that we totter on the edge of the ditch. With the realms of freedom and justice thus confused, there is little hope for either of them.

[18] To many of our scholars and practical men of affairs, this economic view of liberty has made strong appeal. These are the men who especially think of themselves as "realists," as hardheaded, as rising above sentimentalities and popular illusions. I should like now to point out how disastrously these men are cutting at the roots of the convictions by which our common life is nourished. They are bringing us to such confusion about the nature of freedom that no issue can be clearly seen, no practical situation clearly dealt with.

[19] It is commonly said in our current discussions of social policy that if the principle of liberty is accepted by us then the principles of equality and fraternity must be abandoned. "Liberty and equality," we have many times been told, "are incompatible." We must choose between them. And in fact, as the argument commonly runs, we have already chosen. As a people, our preference is registered for liberty. Therefore, it would be well if we would stop talking of such demands as those of equality and fraternity. These demands are outworn and outmoded. They do not fit into our "free" scheme of life. We moderns take our freedom straight. We ask only for liberty. Let each man be himself. Let each man take and keep what he can get. As for the belief that men are equal, the aspiration that men shall live like brothers, these are the yearnings of dreamers, of "idealists." They have no place in daily planning. It is better to leave them, either to private virtue or to some "Fate" which is so just and kind that free and independent men need not concern themselves with justice or with kindness.

[20] Now the revolutionary drift of this argument will be seen if we recall that the notion of liberty, when first accepted by us, was inextricably bound up with the ideas of equality and fraternity. These three demands were, in fact, so closely linked together that they were in effect parts of a single idea—that of democracy. Here again liberty was seen as only a fragment of a meaning. We did not take it alone. It was the liberty of equals and brothers which we

established as the guiding formula of our society. And so damaging is this attempt to tear liberty out of its setting that I am tempted once more to resort to epithets—to use the terms "revolutionary" and "un-American" in describing it. I would protest that except as men are regarded as "equals," except as they are treated as "brothers," the attempt to make them free, even to think of them as free, is a hopeless and futile one. If it has been found true that for the sake of liberty we must give up equality and fraternity, then that constitutes a radical revolution in the theory and practice of American life. To say that is to deny the beliefs and intentions out of which our scheme of life and of government sprang. In my opinion it denies what are at present our deepest and most cherished convictions. These three principles are still for us, I am sure, three different aspects of one mode of life which we choose as our own. To tear them apart is to tear our spirit to shreds. It is such violence as this that sets us at war with ourselves, that brings upon us the tragic sense of disloyalty to our own integrity. It is essential then that we examine closely this view of liberty which, once accepted, makes equality impossible and fraternity ridiculous. I am sure that we shall find that it is both untrue in principle and disastrous in its consequences.

[21] The arguments by which liberty as a principle has been seen to drive equality and fraternity out of our tradition are not hard to follow. They are distinctly of the rough and ready type. Their essence is the interpretation of all three principles as economic in meaning.

[22] Those who would give up equality as a principle incompatible with liberty argue from two premises. First, it is observed that men are not equal in capacity. That this is true in every phase of human living, no one can sensibly deny. To say that all men are equal in their abilities is not democracy: it is plain nonsense, plain disregard of obvious fact. Just as men differ in height, in speed, in digestion, in color of eyes, so do they differ in ability to think, ability to appreciate, ability to act, ability to lead and dominate their fellows. And, this being true, it is idle to build a social theory on the assumption that men are, or can be made, equal in business capacity. Some men are more shrewd than others. Men differ much in industriousness and perseverance; and even in such qualities

as unscrupulousness, the passionate, overbearing desire to get a bigger share of worldly goods and power, we human beings are not all alike. There are diversities of gifts among us.

[23] Second, it is asserted, liberty and equality are economic principles. They refer to the getting and having of material things. By liberty we mean that, just so far as possible, men shall be unhindered in their business affairs. The principle of freedom is the principle of free competition in financial and industrial life. So too, equality is, for this argument, economic in meaning. Equality would mean—if it were not too nonsensical to mean anything—that all the members of a society share equally in the having of goods. It is equality of getting, of possessing what one wants.

[24] Now when these two premises are combined, the conclusion in question follows from them as inevitably as does four from two plus two. If in an open market men are free to compete with one another, each being free to get and keep what he can, and if these competitors are different in the capacity for getting and keeping, it follows, by a logic which no one can deny, that liberty will and must destroy equality. If unequals strive in conflict, the stronger must win, the weaker must lose. And so—*Quod erat demonstrandum*—if men are free they are not equal. A social order must choose between these two. And we Americans, the argument says, have chosen liberty. Therefore, we have abandoned equality.

[25] The expulsion of fraternity, on grounds of liberty, has been far less consciously done. We have not argued brotherhood away. Rather, under heavy pressure, it has drifted out of sight. Few men have spoken against it, except perhaps in the form of vague and uneasy deductions from "liberty" as seen in the process of "the survival of the fittest." In fact, the fate of fraternity has been very much like that of the Devil in modern Protestant theology. No one has demonstrated its non-existence. We have simply ceased to think about it seriously. How can we think of it if the principle of free economic competition holds true? What, in a world defined by that principle, can the Brotherhood of Man mean? On the docks of San Francisco, in the summer of 1934, who was so silly as to make appeal to fraternity as between longshoremen and ship-owners? Are makers of munitions of war called to their trade by the love of their fellow-men? Do they

play with governments, contrive and scheme for the national murder of peoples because all men are brothers? No, that is not the theory. The theory of liberty which we are now discussing is very simple. It is that men are free to seek for profits. Under that principle each man is justified in getting what he can, as other men are doing. Our human living is a conflict. Men are not brothers. Liberty, as we construe it, has put an end to our fraternity. We are "free." Therefore fraternity is meaningless.

[26] Now the trouble with this double argument is that the conclusion at which it arrives is false. By a process of shrewd, logical deduction from its premise, it discovers that Americans do not care about equality or fraternity. But that statement is not true. It denies two of our deepest convictions. It contravenes two of our deepest passions. We will not have it as an account of ourselves. And this being the case, an equally savage logic will drive us to the only solution of which the situation admits. It is that the premise from which we started must be abandoned.

[27] Any belief which, directly or by implication, tells us that we have no interest in treating our fellows as equals and brothers we repudiate as denying the things of which we are most certain. Liberty, in its primary sense, is not then the liberty to buy and sell. That liberty we will restrain and diminish whenever the demands of our social order require it. It is our servant, not our master. It is one of our devices, not one of our principles. We find it a sorry substitute for the liberty on which the foundations of our individual and social living are established. The liberty for which we care is that of a fellowship of equals and brothers.

[28] But here, I know, I shall be sharply challenged on the question of fact. What evidence is there, I shall be asked, that Americans have loved, and still love, equality and fraternity? In reply may I say that the evidence, though not of the "laboratory" type, seems to me strong and convincing. I will try at least to suggest what it has been and is.

[29] In the days when the nation was being formed, our devotion to equality found characteristic expression in the Declaration of Independence. The first sentence in that document, after the preamble, begins as follows: "We hold these truths to be self-evident: that all men are created equal; . . ." I suppose that among the

great sentences which have determined human destiny no one was ever more muddled than this. At every turn of its meaning one's mind gasps at its unclearness. And yet, as registering a nation's commitment to the cause of equality, its import is clear and unmistakable. Our first pronouncement, as a united people, unanimously made by our representatives was: "All men are created equal." We meant it then as, I am sure, we mean it now.

[30] The evidence of our early commitment to fraternity is not to be found primarily in political documents. It appears rather in the influence of the Christian Church during our early history. "Thou shalt love thy neighbor as thyself" was a principle which was recognized as basic to all our documents. And this was true of men who attacked the Church as well as of those who defended it. Strong and bitter assaults were, it is true, directed against the Church. But these were brought not against its principles but against its failures as an institution to hold and to manifest its loyalty to those principles. It seems to me idle to deny that, in its beginnings, ours was a Christian civilization, that it planned for human society in terms of the Brotherhood of Man.

[31] The contemporary evidence of our loyalty to equality and fraternity is not to be found either in political documents or in religious formulas. Our documents are to-day very equivocal and our formulas of belief vague and uncertain. And yet the evidence seems to me vast and sure. One finds it in a prevalent demand for social justice so widespread and powerful that no phase of our common life escapes its influence. In private conversation, in public discussion, in magazines and books, in painting and poetry and music, in theaters and churches, that theme is dominant and engrossing. We are, it is true, bewildered as to ways in which social justice may be done. But we are to an amazing degree united in the conviction that the doing of it is the primary issue of current American life. When, for example, through the breakdown of our economic machinery, millions of families are brought to destitution, no theory of economic liberty can hold us to the view that these men and women and children shall be consigned to the care of natural economic laws. They are our equals, our brothers, and we will deal with them as such.

[32] It is true that we can hide our intentions under formulas of

business self-interest. Men tell us that only as these indigents are given the power of purchasing will our markets be restored. They warn us too that if large masses of people are left to starve they will break out into violence, will bring down about our ears the whole economic structure which shelters all of us. But these external arguments are poor and shoddy as compared with the present spirit of our people. One has only to put them side by side with Whitman's "By God! I will accept nothing which all men cannot have the counterpart of on the same terms" to see how poor and superficial they are. And we, as a people, are taking our stand with Whitman. We are not clear as to ways and means, but we are resolute in purpose.

[33] The man who does not see that is, in my opinion, blind to the most powerful forces now at work in the American scene. We have been hoping that an existing economic order which talks much of "liberty" would serve our purpose. Now we are ready to modify that order. And if mere modifying is not enough, we will transform it to suit our needs. Economic disaster and calamity have revealed us to ourselves, have shown us our own purposes. We are a just and friendly people. To say that we love liberty without regard for justice and kindness, to say that liberty, once accepted, has driven equality and fraternity out of our scheme of life, is simply to say that liberty is un-American. The men who think those thoughts have slipped. They do not know themselves nor us. The liberty which we demand is the liberty of equals and of brothers.

[34] I have dwelt at length upon this argument because it reveals so clearly the spiritual tragedy which has come upon America. Here again, our "practical men of affairs" have with an unfailing inaccuracy missed the point when dealing with essential things. They have taken the most fundamental motive in our social life and twisted it into a meaning which is hostile, not only to itself but to all the other deeper principles to which we are committed. They do not tell us—perhaps they have not noticed—that justice too must go the way of equality and fraternity if once their logic is admitted. What can justice mean in a social order defined in terms of free and unrestricted competition? The liberty of such an order is the liberty of men to prey one upon another. And

in that conflict, justice is simply what a man can get. Liberty, as
so defined, becomes, not the reasonable principle of a free society,
but an all-devouring dogma which destroys other meanings or
drives them out. It has become, not a principle, but a fetish of
the economic mind.

[35] And the human tragedy which has ensued from the worship
of that fetish is all too clear in the mind of present-day America.
It is often urged to-day that our unrest of spirit is due to the fact
that we have tried to keep in a new and changing world old ideals
which no longer serve our purposes. Our major task, it is said, is
that of creating new ideals to replace those which, though good
enough in their own day, can no longer serve our changing purposes. There is something of truth in this statement, and yet it
seems to me to be comparatively a minor truth. Far more important is a statement which is almost its exact opposite. Our
deepest tragedy lies in the fact that our current institutions, our
current beliefs, our current practices fail to give recognition to old
ideals which are still the essential and fundamental cravings of
the American spirit. Our trouble is that we still believe in equality,
however much we may deny it. Our agony comes from the fact
that the social world which we are making is false to a fraternity
of men to which we are still committed with a passionate devotion. The truth is not that old ideals have disappeared. It is rather
that in spite of our mistakes about them they are still within us.

[36] Underneath all the superficialities and externalities of our
thinking and practice, the demands that men shall live together on
equal terms, that they shall be friends to one another, still dominate us, still hold us fast. And it is the torture of thus finding ourselves holding beliefs which deny our most cherished truths, the
agony of seeing our own acts, our own behavior bringing to destruction the causes for which we care—it is that cleavage, that contradiction within ourselves which has brought us into such be-
wilderment and self-condemnation. And the way of escape from
this tragedy lies not in the framing of new ideals for a new world,
but in the bringing of that new world under the control of
principles which have always been the primary spiritual forces in
the life of the American people—the principles of liberty, equality,
fraternity, and justice.

EXERCISES

This essay appeared in 1935, and some of its references to economic control relate to the various programs undertaken by the government to revive the country from what was then called "the depression"; but many of the issues are still matters of contention, although on different grounds, twenty years later.

1. Exactly what is the distinction which Meiklejohn makes in paragraphs 1–17?
2. If this distinction is valid, does its validity make Huxley's argument in the preceding selection wrong, confused, incomplete, sound, irrelevant, or what? State the relationship between the two arguments.
3. Meiklejohn uses a great deal of antithesis. Why is this appropriate to this particular subject?
4. By what device, chiefly, does the author give emphasis to his main points throughout the essay?
5. Find one example of each of the following figures:
   a. A very short sentence apparently used for emphasis
   b. Regression
   c. A metaphor
   d. A rhetorical question
   e. Irony
6. Does the author use relatively few or many figures of speech?
7. Does the sentence which ends paragraph 12 have a smooth or a bumpy rhythm? Does the texture seem related to the sense?
8. Write a theme in which you give a brief analysis of the style of each selection in this section (B), basing your analyses on sentence structure, diction, ornament, and tone. Which style would you characterize as learned, ornate, artistic, and versatile? Which is direct and intellectual? Which is simple, direct, and strong? Which is skillful and sophisticated but "smart"? Which is clear and honest but relatively unskillful. You need not limit yourself to these terms, of course.
9. If you prefer to deal with the content of the selections, choose one of the following topics or a similar one.
   a. The basic issues facing modern democracy
   b. Are economic control and intellectual freedom compatible?

Section C: Man and His Resources

All selections in Section C deal with man's use and control of his resources—with the world of concrete things and specific facts. Ideas and values are involved, but subordinate. However, the series begins with Rorty's treatment of a very specific problem and ends with Vogt's proposal for future action, which involves general ideas and so leads naturally into Section D.

Beginning with Section C, the exercises are kept in general terms, mainly, to prompt the student to formulate his own specific problems and so begin to be independent of all study aids. Thus instead of three questions such as "What ideas are emphasized by repetition?" "What is the value of the metaphor in paragraph 3?" and "How does the sound of the last sentence support the meaning?", there may be one question such as "By what means does the author gain emphasis?"

Bread, and the Stuff We Eat

JAMES RORTY

I

[1] For many years, native and foreign gourmets have been hurling scurrilous epithets at American bread, and in response, spokesmen for our mass-production baking companies have roared with pained indignation. Have they not done their best, they ask, to give us the kind of bread we want? The sad and funny part of it is that to a degree, and after their own peculiar fashion, they undoubtedly have.

[2] How, then, does it happen that the cottony and tastless white bread of commerce, although officially "enriched" by the addition to the bread mix of the vitamins and minerals that are now mandatory in twenty-eight states, has in other respects tended to get worse and worse, both in flavor—as the gourmets have been insisting—and in nutritive value?

[3] How is it that after a century of progress our baking technologists are still running a couple of laps behind grandmother, both in the quality of their product, and in what it costs to make and distribute it?

[4] To understand what has happened, it will help if we recall what bread-making was like when grandmother—or was it great-grandmother?—did the job at home. Until well into the eighties of the past century, the housewife got her flour from one of the local grist mills whose ruins you can still see perched beside rural waterfalls. Grandmother's recipe combined this creamy "stone-ground" flour with yeast, water, lard or butter, sometimes milk and eggs. When the new "patent" flour produced by the steel roller mills of Minneapolis became available, she readily adopted it because it was finer and whiter and yielded a lighter loaf. But grandfather muttered that it didn't taste as good, and in fact it was much poorer nutritionally; many a village doctor noted that the whiter the bread, the more illness in the family.

In *Harper's Magazine,* March, 1950.

[5] Bread became worse when the commercial baker took over the job of bread-making for an increasingly urbanized America. He used bleached and inferior flour and less milk and butter; later he used chemical "yeast foods" to produce a lighter, fluffier loaf with "eye appeal." By this time physicians were urging a return to whole-wheat bread; when American nutritionists were polled just before World War I, a majority favored whole-wheat and only eight per cent approved of white bread.

[6] As the production of bread became more mechanized, more and more chemicals were added to the mix. To standardize the product and keep the belt line moving smoothly through the mechanical mixers, the dividers, the molders, the slicers, and the wrappers, it was necessary to "condition" the dough. The baking technologist worried more about feeding his machines than about feeding people; hence eventually it became necessary to condition the consumer too.

[7] Mass advertising took care of that. It also helped the big chain bakers to dominate the market and determine the price regardless of the changing costs of bread ingredients.

[8] This was the situation of the baking industry in 1939 when, with World War II impending and the public already vitamin-conscious, American nutritionists insisted that the Staff of Life had been badly bent by all this processing and chemicalizing; that it had to be repaired if our people were to get through the war without suffering malnutrition from thiamin and other vitamin and mineral deficiencies.

[9] The obvious solution, as the nutrition experts of the United States Public Health Service pointed out, was to make bread out of whole grain or undermilled 85 per cent extraction flour. This solution in one form or another was in fact adopted by every other country at war. But our own millers and bakers would have none of it. By this time they had got both themselves and their customers out on the end of a technological-distributive limb from which it was impossible to retreat—or so they insisted. Hence our unique "enrichment" program at which foreign—and many native—nutritionists raised, and continue to raise, incredulous and derisive eyebrows.

[10] By this program some twenty-odd natural vitamin and

mineral elements are expensively milled out of the wheat, after which four of them—thiamin, riboflavin, niacin, and iron—are expensively restored in the form of synthetic chemicals. That seemed a poor bargain to the majority of our nutritionists at the time, but they swallowed it—chiefly because, regardless of its merits or demerits, it was the only solution the industry was prepared to swallow.

[11] During the war, our baking industry prospered—more than did its product. Milk, fats, and eggs were scarce and expensive. Hence bakers tended to use less of them and more of the ersatz materials—emulsifiers and "shortening extenders"—that the war-stimulated chemical industry made increasingly available. Worried by this trend, the Food and Drug Administration attempted in 1941 to establish a legal "standard of identity" for white bread. Under the present law, this standard would have provided a list of officially approved, optional ingredients which the baker may use in his mix but need not disclose on the label.

[12] Some three thousand pages of testimony were accumulated. Then the hearings were suspended until after the war; in November 1948, they were resumed. More than 160 witnesses spoke and the record swelled to a total of over twenty thousand pages. On September 20 this past year [1949] the hearings were at last brought to an exhausted end, after most of the major issues had been kicked upstairs to current or prospective congressional inquiries.

[13] More is involved than bread. A thorough overhauling of the 1938 Food and Drug law is in prospect. It seems probable that in the end the Food and Drug Administration will be given authority to test and approve in advance the innumerable food preservatives, conditioners, and fortifiers that are now being tried out on our 150,000,000 human guinea pigs—just as, following the sulfanilamide-diethylene glycol disaster, the agency was given authority to censor in advance the introduction of new drugs. It is even possible that in the future bakers may not simply have to meet a legal "standard of identity" for bread, as at present—without disclosing on the label the exact contents of the loaf—but may have to adopt the explicit "open formula labeling" that

consumption economists have long advocated and that leading home economists are again demanding.

[14] Finally it is possible that the inadequacy of the emasculated 1938 Food and Drug law and the current stalemate of producer pressure groups may both be by-passed by the emergence of a powerful new factor in the situation. The new factor is a "yard-stick" bread of superior flavor and nutritional value, used for institutional feeding by hospitals and schools. Already, co-operatives and alert commercial bakers are beginning to produce and sell this bread, which costs only about a half cent more to make than the stuff we eat. But of this, more later.

[15] Friedrich Georg Juenger could not have asked for better documentation of his thesis of the "purposeless perfection" of modern technology than was produced at the bread hearings. Day after day the evidence accumulated that although the industry's product continues to be fervently endorsed by lady skiers and sportswear designers, neither disinterested nutritionists nor genuinely informed bread-eaters are likely to feel that way about it. On the contrary, it would appear that by the operation of a kind of nutritional Gresham's Law, a more and more phony kind of stage bread—with an increasing content of dubious chemical conditioners, softeners, shortening extenders, and other ersatzes—has been steadily driving good bread, made with honest, nutritionally valuable food ingredients, off the market.

[16] The manufacturers of some of these chemicals claim in their trade advertising that a pound of their product, mixed with five pounds of water, will replace six pounds of shortening; that milk solids can be eliminated almost entirely.•

[17] These claims, especially the last, have produced consternation among both public-health workers and farmers. For milk is probably our most valuable food, non-fat milk solids are its cheapest form, and bread has long been the most effective carrier for these precious animal proteins. Furthermore the stability of our whole dairy industry is dependent in considerable degree upon the use of milk solids in bread. Even so, our waste of milk is serious. In 1945 the Food and Agriculture Organization of the United Nations estimated that only 28 percent of the milk pro-

duced in this country was used for food, the rest being fed to domestic animals or thrown away. This compares poorly with 40 percent used for human consumption in the Netherlands and—believe it or not—60 per cent in Hungary.

[18] Does the American housewife expect her bread to contain milk solids? Or—as this question was phrased at the hearings—does the "consumer's concept" of white bread include milk solids? But how can the consumer have an intelligent concept of white bread if she is not permitted to know what is in it?

[19] Much of the time of the bread hearings was consumed with metaphysical pother about this "consumer's concept." Actually, what happens is that between them the baking technologists and the advertising men have been able to create their own concept of white bread almost at will and then impose it on the consumer. With chemical softeners and shortening extenders, white flour, yeast, salt, and water can be made to stand up, look pretty, and stay soft almost indefinitely to the testing finger of the housewife. She can't tell whether the loaf is stale or not and the label doesn't reveal its quantitative content of fat, milk, and eggs. Hence she may choose the glamorous stage bread over an honest loaf with superior nutritional value; in fact some of the "consumer surveys"—customarily conducted by more or less disguised advertising agencies—tended to show that this is what happens.

[20] When such evidence was introduced at the hearings, the attorneys for the industry were in a position to pound the table and defend passionately the right of the American woman to feed her family on chemicalized starch, wind, and water if that is her pleasure. Not that this fooled anybody, least of all the farmers, who became more and more alarmed as the hearings proceeded and who presumably confided their apprehensions to their representatives in Congress.

[21] At any rate, last March Congressman Frank B. Keefe of Wisconsin, our leading dairy state, introduced a resolution in the House calling for a congressional investigation of chemicals in food and of the effect on food of the improper use of insecticides and fertilizers. At this writing, the Keefe resolution is stalled in the House Rules Committee, but meanwhile hearings are being conducted by a subcommittee of the Senate Committee on Agricul-

ture and Forestry headed by Senator Guy M. Gillette of Iowa.
[22] In June, Senator Gillette and Senator Milton R. Young of
North Dakota sponsored a bill amending the present Food and
Drug law to read that a processed food must be considered adulter-
ated "if it is bread or pastry made in whole or in part from wheat
and it bears or contains less than four per cent of natural fat." In
September they introduced a further amendment that a processed
food must be considered misbranded "if it is any kind of bread or
rolls, unless it bears labeling stating the percentage therein of any
shortening, solids of milk, or milk products, and solids of egg or
egg products."

[23] While these proposed amendments are laudable in intent,
they have been justly objected to on the ground that they set a
precedent for legislating the content of a basic food under the pressure of competing producer lobbies; the potato growers, soybean
growers, and wheat growers might well be next in line. It cannot
be too strongly emphasized that the bread problem is primarily a
problem of consumer *and* producer education, which the law
should further, not obstruct. Certainly the problem will not be
solved by a fragmentary and fragile balancing of producer interests.

[24] That is why it is so important that we now have a satisfactory
loaf of bread which consumers can compare with the bakers'
current product.

II

[25] In a previous article in this magazine ("The Thin Rats Bury
the Fat Rats," May 1949), I referred to the flavorful and highly
nutritious "triple-rich" loaf of white bread developed by Dr. Clive
M. McCay and his associates at the Cornell School of Nutrition.
It is made with unbleached flour, 2 per cent wheat germ, 6 per
cent high fat soy flour, 8 per cent milk solids, and without any
softener, shortening extender, or other chemical substitute—all
this being clearly spelled out on the label.

[26] Laboratory rats fed this bread as their sole diet thrive and
grow. When they are restricted to run-of-the-market white bread,
they pine and die. Human beings like this "yardstick" bread—it
seems to express their concept of what white bread should be. In

a large co-operative supermarket in downtown Ithaca its sales rivaled the combined sales of seven commercial brands displayed on the same counter, although the co-op bread sold for three cents more per loaf.

[27] A year ago last November these facts were presented at the bread hearings by Dr. McCay himself. The object of his appearance, he explained, was to argue against the freezing of the bread formula around a rigid legal standard of identity based on the prevailing commercial product. If the standard put a ceiling on quality, which was what the industry's representative argued for, it might actually become illegal to sell *as white bread* a loaf that contained the percentages of basic food ingredients, such as soy flour, that nutritionists considered desirable. Why not open-formula labeling, asked Dr. McCay? Why shouldn't the urban consumer buy bread the way the farmer buys chicken feed?

[28] For an hour the baking industry's attorneys fumed around Dr. McCay in a vain attempt to discredit his qualifications. He was chief nutritionist for the Navy during the war and has done extensive work with bread.

[29] A year ago yardstick bread was only a vague threat to the baking industry. Today is it a *fait accompli* of formidable proportions. In the twenty-seven mental hospitals of New York state, bakers have been taught to bake this bread successfully, and both patients and staffs are eating it with enthusiasm. In Westchester County it has been adopted for use in the entire hospital and prison system. In the five boroughs of metropolitan New York, Colonel Harvey K. Allen, director of school lunches, is using it—temporarily without the wheat germ—to feed 110,000 school children. The city operates its own bakeries and gets dry skim milk free through the AAA program. Thus it is able to produce and distribute this superior bread for approximately five cents a pound—less than a third of the current price of ordinary bread.

[30] In a dozen upstate New York towns small bakers are making and selling the yardstick bread. A big interstate chain baker plans to feature it—at the competitive price of the standard white loaf—if the upshot of the bread hearings permits him to do so legally.

[31] This would at last put back into the bread picture the missing ingredient of price competition based on labeled standards. Al-

ways, in the larger cities at least, it has been possible to buy, at a premium price, good pumpernickel and whole-rye bread made by some technologically primitive but honest European immigrant. And ever since a Connecticut housewife put grandmother's product on the market it has been possible—again in the cities only—to buy good wheat bread, both white and whole-grain, made by a number of commercial bakers and by the co-ops. But these superior breads, including the co-op products, have been sold at premium prices, which limited their usefulness as yardsticks. Hence year after year over 95 per cent of the bread sold continued to be the stage stuff.

[32] Information about the new yardstick bread has spread like a grass fire. At a score of county fairs last summer crowds of housewives exclaimed over a graphic exhibit sponsored by the New York State Nutrition Committee and prepared by Miss Katharine Flack, chairman of the Committee and Director of Nutrition Service for the State Department of Health.

[33] The exhibit consists of a miniature revolving stage regulated by a stop-go mechanism. When the red light is on, a typical commercial white loaf appears. With it are presented the white rats, male and female, who have been trying to subsist on it. Despite the synthetic vitamins that enable the baker to call it "enriched," the rats are thin, mangy, despondent, and indifferent to each other and to their public. Then the green light flashes and a loaf of yardstick bread comes into view, as honestly labeled as a bag of dog food. Beside it are the happy rat couple who have been brought up on this bread as their sole food; fat, sleek, amative, and exhibitionistic.

[34] The big bread advertisers cannot be expected to applaud this exhibit, but small bakers and enterprising chain store operators, like the housewives, react quite differently. And they have the farmers on their side.

III

[35] Farm leaders were slow to realize the threat to their interests carried by the increasing chemicalization of staple processed foods. But they woke up with a jolt in 1945 when they read the text of the model state enrichment law with which the flour and

bread "enrichment" advocates in and out of government undertook to fasten the "take and put" policy permanently upon the
country.

[36] When the enrichment program was first proposed, during
the wartime emergency, its sponsors were forced to admit that it
was an expensive makeshift at best. But they argued that its
temporary adoption would be in the right direction since it would
help to increase the consumption of whole-wheat and superior
white breads, nutritionally improved by the addition of such natural food supplements as wheat germ, milk solids, yeast, and soy
flour.

[37] Nothing of the sort happened or was likely to happen under
the conditions set up by the model enrichment law. Bakers could
easily meet the jacked-up vitamin requirements of "enrichment"
by adding a few tablets of cheap synthetics to the mix, while it
was practically impossible for them to achieve the same result by
using the more costly natural food supplements. Nor could whole-
wheat bread call itself "enriched" even when strengthened by
the generous additions of milk solids that made it nutritionally a
better product.

[38] Yet with minor modifications the model law was passed in
state after state by the combined efforts of the Committee on
Cereals of the National Research Council, the Millers National
Federation, the American Bakers Association, and the Associated
Retail Bakers of America, aided by the lobbyists of the synthetic
vitamin manufacturers. The chemical industry was in and the
farmers were out.

[39] The dairy interests, representing one of the hardest hit farm
groups, got the point first and moved into action. By 1946 sponsors of the enrichment law in state legislatures faced increasing
resistance; and in 1949 the united front of the baking industry
was broken when the Associated Retail Bakers of America passed
a resolution saying that, while they favored the enrichment program, they would not support legislation making it compulsory.
Today, with twenty-eight states in the enrichment column and
twenty outside, the enrichment forces' campaign apparently has
been checked at least temporarily.

[40] Farm leaders are already contemplating looming surpluses of

milk solids, fats, soy flour, and other products. The revelation at the hearings of what the synthetic shortening extenders threaten to do to their remaining bread market was the last straw. The Council on Food and Nutrition of the American Medical Association also became alarmed and moved into the fight with notable vigor and effectiveness.

[41] At the May 20 session of the bread hearings, Dr. William J. Darby of Vanderbilt University presented a formal statement prepared by the American Medical Association's Council on Food and Nutrition. Confronting a stony-faced assemblage of baking and chemical industry executives and lawyers, Dr. Darby observed suavely that the current trend of baking practice left something to be desired, specifically with respect to the increasing use of the synthetic shortening extenders.

[42] "Available knowledge of the possible toxicity of these substances," he said, "is fragmentary. Particularly is evidence lacking as to chronic toxicity. . . . Unless the complete harmlessness of these agents can be demonstrated beyond a reasonable doubt, they should not, in the Council's opinion, be used in basic foods." And, he added, the reduction of natural food products in bread that might be entailed by the use of these extenders "is not desirable from a nutritional standpoint."

[43] Dr. Darby's statement was a turning point in the hearings. Three weeks later the organized baking industry officially repudiated the softeners. The American Bakers Association recommended that shortening extenders not be included as optional ingredients in the bread standard unless the Food and Drug Administration should subsequently find them harmless to human health. The Retail Bakers of America went even farther, omitting from their statement the escape clause regarding possible future use.

[44] Does this indicate the beginning of responsible action on the part of the organized baking industry? In justice, it must be said that a number of bakers testified that they had refused to take the easy route to sales and profits offered by the extenders, or that they had done so reluctantly under pressure of competition. In fact, the record of the hearings frequently gives the impression of an industry divided against itself. There was no such division,

and no lack of vigor, among the consumers' professional allies. At the August 4 session of the hearings Dr. Marion C. Pfund of the Cornell Home Economics staff made a powerful presentation on behalf of the American Home Economics Association.

[45] "The consumer," she said, "has a right to know all the ingredients that have been incorporated in a bread, the substances added to the ingredients used to make bread, the quantities of ingredients in excess of one per cent of flour weight, the weight of the loaf, the calorie value per pound, the minimum percentage of protein, and the maximum percentage of water in bread."

[46] That is approximately where the American Home Economics Association stood in 1933, when an earlier and much stronger draft of the 1938 Food and Drug law was defeated by a press and radio boycott and by a formidable lobby of food processors and their allies, the mass advertising media. The consumer advocates were right then, and they are right now, as an uninhibited congressional investigation would prove. Apparently the food processors fear this. They would prefer a commission of carefully picked "experts" instead of the seven-man investigating committee called for in the Keefe resolution.

[47] But it is precisely the role of the experts that Congress needs to examine. It was experts in and out of government who put through the flour and bread enrichment program in the first place —despite the protests and warnings of other equally qualified experts, including the chief nutritionist of the United States Public Health Service. And it was the experts on the Food and Nutrition Board of the National Research Council who missed a chance on at least one critical occasion to check the increasing use of chemicals.

[48] When the British nutritionist Lord Mellanby discovered that agene or nitrogen trichloride—used until recently to bleach and condition the bulk of the flour used in bread—gave running fits to dogs, the Food and Drug Administration referred the problem to the Food and Nutrition Board. Unhappily the Board's subcommittee on cereals has always been dominated by scientists who in their private capacities are or have been directly or indirectly connected with the milling, baking, and pharmaceutical industries. Even more unhappily it has been obliged, in order

to finance its work, to go with its hand out to industry or industry-supported foundations, such as the Nutrition Foundation. Since industry-employed and industry-financed scientists tend observably and doubtless quite honestly to become industry-minded, it was not surprising that the Board's recommendation was—another bleach. This went directly counter to the recommendation of the Army nutritionists. The latter pointed with approval to the findings of a 1925 British commission, to the effect that it would be best not to use *any* chemicals in bread.

[49] The bread hearings have put many of the facts on the record; the rest can be found in the Federal Trade Commission's three long and hair-raising studies of the industry. The Cornell nutritionists and their allies have proved that it is possible to produce good white bread and sell it, fully labeled, at a reasonable price. Why can't or won't our baking industry do it too? Would it help if we had a new Food and Drug law with teeth in it making full quantitative labeling compulsory? Just what is required to enable our marvelously equipped and fabulously prosperous baking industry, after fifty lagging years, to catch up with grandmother?

[50] The farmers would like to know, and so would the rest of us.

EXERCISES

1. Is this selection an article, an essay, or an address?
2. State the subject of the selection.
3. What main assertion does the author make about the subject?
4. What impression does the author apparently intend to make upon the reader?
5. In addition to the main explicit assertion there are several explicit statements on related matters. What, for instance, is said about the policy of other countries regarding nutrition during the war?
6. What, do you infer, is the factor which motivates the large baking companies to insist on one kind of bread and the farm interests to insist on a different kind?
7. What attitude toward the baking industry is implicit in the entire piece?

In answering these first seven questions you have arrived at something like the total meaning of the selection—the author's apparent purpose plus your own analysis of the material. If you will turn to the chart in the front of the book you will see how these larger aspects of composition are related to the various elements of rhetoric which you have been studying. Learn to use the chart to check your understanding of the relationships among the various elements of composition and to help you frame specific questions as you analyze and evaluate each selection.

8. How is the problem which is presented here related to the economic controls discussed by Meiklejohn?

9. What is the main source of the author's information, knowledge accumulated by experience or assembled by research on a given problem?

10. Does the organization seem appropriate to the purpose?

11. If the purpose had been to present only the conflicting interests involved, how would the organization have differed?

12. What is the value of the images, in paragraph 4, of the ruins of the old grist mill and of the steel roller mills of Minneapolis? Does all modern white flour come from Minneapolis?

13. List several words and figures of speech which show the author's attitude toward grandma's bread and his attitude toward modern white bread.

14. Why could the editors of *Harper's Magazine* assume that most readers would be interested in this piece? (See *Interest* in the Glossary.)

Ended: 400 Year Boom

WALTER PRESCOTT WEBB

I

[1] It is difficult to discuss the frontier with an American audience because the literate American assumes that he knows what you are going to say in advance. It is difficult to expound the subject to a foreign audience for the opposite reason: the foreigner knows little about the subject, and because he cannot see that it touches his life, he is pretty indifferent to it. My purpose here is

In *Harper's Magazine*, October, 1951.

to show the American a phase of the frontier which he has not yet considered, and show the European that the frontier has for more than four centuries affected his life and well-being most profoundly.

[2] The concept of the frontier as a factor in history was developed in the United States and has been applied primarily to American history. Though the word appears in similar form in nearly all European languages, it has a meaning and a set of connotations in the United States entirely different from those which obtain elsewhere. As used in Europe, it means the boundary between two nations and it is represented on the map by a thin line. That line is one to approach with caution, equipped with passports and permits. It is a place to stop at or to pass at national peril—"the sharp edge of sovereignty."

[3] In America the word frontier is hardly used to indicate the nation's limits. No American would refer to the line separating the United States from Canada or from Mexico as a "frontier." The American concept holds that the frontier lies *within,* and not at the edge of the country—not a line to stop at, but an area inviting entrance. In Europe the frontier is stationary and permanent; in America it was (note the past tense) transient and temporal. It is this American idea which we shall be concerned with, and which we shall apply to the enormous region that may be called the Great Frontier.

[4] The American concept of a moving frontier can be applied where a civilized people is advancing into a wilderness, an unsettled area, or one sparsely populated by primitive people. It was the sort of land into which the Boers moved in South Africa, the English in Australia, and the Americans and Canadians in their progress westward across North America. Likewise it was the land into which the Spaniards moved earlier in the New World. The frontier movement is an invasion of a land assumed to be vacant, as distinguished from an invasion of an occupied or civilized country. In view of the fact that from 1500 to about 1900 the European peoples were taking such lands on just such terms, it seems strange that the concept of the frontier as a force in human affairs should have hitherto been considered an American phenomenon. Actually the process was Western-world-wide.

[5] It is not strange that the expanded concept of the frontier should have had its origin in America because here history and circumstance conspired to present the frontier factor in clear outline. The American experience with home-making in the wilderness began very early, and went on continuously because the Americans were virtually sole proprietors of an unsettled and contiguous territory of enormous extent. Always, for some three centuries, to the west of the settlements there stretched an empty country inviting entrance, luring the venturesome toward the sunset. Of the immediately adjacent territory the United States usually had undisputed possession. When no foreign power contended for it, it did not present a problem of sovereignty, and movement into it was predominately civilian, not military. The territory was adjacent to the settled area, and the journey there did not involve a sea voyage, a long trek, or any considerable outlay of capital. The settlers were citizens moving into territory owned by the nation. It was understood on all sides that the status of the individual as a citizen was unchanged, and that within a short time the new territory would automatically become a state in the Union with rights no different from those of the oldest member.

[6] The absence of the military, the proximity of the new land to the old, the ease of migration, and the absence of any attempt on the part of the government to regulate or control the process made the American situation the last word in simplicity, so simple that it might seem to be chaotic. In these respects the movement of the American people into the frontier was unlike the movement of people from European nations into their equivalent frontier, and no doubt the simplicity of the American process explains why the historic force of the frontier was discovered first in the American context. Yet the American frontier was but a fragment of the Great Frontier, and the American process was but an example— the simplest and clearest, it is true—of a parallel but more complex development that was going on wherever European people were appropriating lands in the New Worlds.

[7] Since America led the way in evolving the frontier process, and leads the world in the study of that process, we have no choice but to examine the American experience and to note

briefly how scholars came to attend it as a field of study. American historians assume that the frontier process began with the English settlement at Jamestown in 1607, and the year 1890 is usually taken to mark the date when there was no more frontier available, when the new land was no longer new. There may be some quibbling about the dates, but they do bracket the three centuries of American frontier experience and experimentation. [8] It was the magnitude and the unbroken continuity of the experience that gave the frontier major importance in American life. It made no difference what other tasks the Americans had on their hands at a given time, there was the additional, ever-present one of moving into and settling new country. They did it while they fought for independence, before and after; they did it while they hammered out the principles of a democratic government shaped to the needs of frontiersmen; and they did not cease doing it in the period of civil strife. They never reached the limits of the vacancy they owned before they acquired another vacancy, by purchase, by treaty, by conquest, and in every case the frontiersmen infiltrated the country before the nation acquired it. Like locusts they swarmed, always to the west, and only the Pacific Ocean stopped them. Here in this movement beat the deep overtone of a nation's destiny, and to it all kept step unconsciously.
[9] To say that the people were unconscious of the force that moved them, and of the medium in which they moved, is to state a fact which is easy to prove but hard to explain. It may be said that they were emotionally aware of the frontier long before they were intellectually cognizant of it. People could not have as their main task for three centuries working with raw land without getting its dirt under their nails and deep into their skins. The effects were everywhere, in democratic government, in boisterous politics, in exploitative agriculture, in mobility of population, in disregard for conventions, in rude manners, and in unbridled optimism. Though these effects were present everywhere they were not understood anywhere by the people who felt and reflected them. The frontier still lacked its philosopher, the thinker who could view the whole dramatic experience and tell what was its meaning. This philosopher arrived three years after the experience

ended and told the American people that from the beginning the American frontier had been the dominant force, the determining factor, in their history thus far.

[10] This hypothesis was presented to the American Historical Association in a paper entitled "The Significance of the Frontier in American History." The date was 1893 and the author was a young and then little-known historian. That paper made Frederick Jackson Turner a scholar with honor in his own country; it altered the whole course of American historical scholarship, and it is recognized as the most influential single piece of historical writing ever done in the United States. The key to his thesis is found in this sentence: "The existence of an area of free land, its continuous recession, and the advance of American settlement westward, explain American development." The general acceptance of this frontier hypothesis, and the fame of its author, came about because the people in America were emotionally prepared to understand this rationalization and explanation of their own long experience. Turner's pupils—many of whom became disciples—flocked to the diggings and have worked out in every cove and valley the rich vein which he uncovered, but not one of them, not even the master himself, took the next step to point out or at least to emphasize that the American frontier was but a small fragment of the Great Frontier. On that Great Frontier was also an area of free land; it was in continuous recession; and the advance of European settlement into it should explain the development of Western civilization in modern times just as the American advance explains American development.

II

[11] What happened in America was but a detail in a much greater phenomenon, the interaction between European civilization and the vast raw lands into which it moved. An effort will be made here to portray the whole frontier, to suggest how it affected the life and institutions of Western civilization throughout the modern period; and as a basis for this exposition four propositions are submitted for consideration:

(1) Europe had a frontier more than a century before the United States was settled.

(2) Europe's frontier was much greater than that of the United States, or of any other one nation; it was the greatest of all time.

(3) The frontier of Europe was almost, if not quite, as important in determining the life and institutions of modern Europe as the frontier of America was in shaping the course of American history. Without the frontier modern Europe would have been so different from what it became that it could hardly be considered modern at all. This is almost equivalent to saying that the frontier made Europe modern.

(4) The close of the Great Frontier may mark the end of an epoch in Western civilization just as the close of the American frontier is often said to have marked the end of the first phase of American history. If the close of the Great Frontier does mark the end of an age, the modern age, then the institutions designed to function in a society dominated largely by frontier forces will find themselves under severe strain.

[12] If we conceive of Western Europe as a unified, densely populated region with a common culture and civilization—which it has long had basically—and if we see the frontier also as a unit, a vast and vacant land without culture, we are in position to view the interaction between the two as a simple but gigantic operation extending over more than four centuries, a process that may appear to be the drama of modern civilization.

[13] To emphasize the unity of western Europe, and at the same time set it off in sharp contrast to its opposite, the frontier, we may call it the Metropolis. Metropolis is a good name, implying what Europe really was, a cultural center holding within it everything pertaining to Western civilization. Prior to 1500 the Metropolis comprised all the "known" world save Asia, which was but vaguely known. Its area was approximately 3,750,000 square miles, and its population is estimated to have been about 100 million people.

[14] There is no need to elaborate the conditions under which these people lived, but it should be remembered that by modern standards the society was a static one with well-defined classes. The population pressed hard on the means of subsistence. There was not much food, practically no money, and very little freedom. What is more important, there was practically no means of escape

for those people living in this closed world. The idea of progress had not been born. Heaven alone, which could be reached only through the portals of death, offered any hope to the masses of the Metropolis.

[15] Then came the miracle that was to change everything, the emancipator bearing rich gifts of land and more land, of gold and silver, of new foods for every empty belly and new clothing stuffs for every half-naked back. Europe, the Metropolis, knocked on the door of the Great Frontier, and when the door was opened it was seen to be golden, for within there was undreamed-of treasure, enough to make the whole Metropolis rich. The long quest of a half-starved people had at last been rewarded with success beyond comprehension.

[16] Columbus has been accepted as the symbol, as the key that unlocked the golden door to a new world, but we know that he was only one of a group of curious investigators, Portuguese, Spanish, English, Dutch, and Scandinavian, men of the Metropolis and not of one country. Within a brief period, as history is told, Columbus and his prying associates pulled back the curtains of ignorance and revealed to the Metropolis three new continents, a large part of a fourth, and thousands of islands in oceans hitherto hardly known. They brought all of these—continents, oceans, and islands—and deposited them as a free gift at the feet of the impoverished Metropolis.

[17] The Metropolis had a new piece of property and the frontier had a new owner. The Metropolitans were naturally curious about their property, and quite naturally began to ask questions about it. How big is it? Who lives on it? What is its inherent worth? What can I get out of it? They learned that the frontier had an area five or six times that of Europe; that it was practically vacant, occupied by a few primitive inhabitants whose rights need not be respected; that its inherent worth could only be guessed at. As to what can I get out of it?, the answer came in time clear and strong: You can get everything you want from gold and silver to furs and foods, and in any quantity you want, provided only that you are willing to venture and work! And more faintly came the small voice, hardly audible: Something all of you can get as a by-product is some measure of freedom.

[18] The Metropolitans decided to accept the gifts. Instantly the divisions in Europe were projected into the frontier as each little European power that could man a ship seized a section of the frontier bigger than itself and tried to fight all the others off. Each nation wanted it all. The result was a series of wars lasting from 1689 to 1763 and from these wars England, France, and Spain emerged as chief owners of the frontier world. Their success was more apparent than real, for a spirit of freedom had been nurtured in the distant lands, and in less than fifty years England had lost her chief prize while Spain and France had lost practically everything.

[19] But their loss, like their previous gain, was more apparent than real. True, by 1820 the Metropolis had lost title to most of the new land, but it had not lost something more precious than title—namely, the beneficent effects that the frontier exerted on the older countries. The political separation of most of North and South America relieved the Metropolis of responsibility and onerous obligations, but it did not cut off the abundance of profits. Europe continued to share in the riches and the opportunity that the opening of the golden door had made visible.

III

[20] What was the essential character of the frontier? Was the direct force it exerted spiritual, intellectual, or was it material? The frontier was basically a vast body of wealth without proprietors. It was an empty land more than five times the size of western Europe, a land whose resources had not been exploited. Its first impact was mainly economic. Bathed in and invigorated by a flood of wealth, the Metropolis began to seethe with economic excitement.

[21] With all the ships coming and going, the wharves of Europe were piled high with strange goods, the tables were set with exotic foods of delightful flavors, and new-minted coins of gold and silver rattled in the coffers of the market place. The boom began when Columbus returned from his first voyage, and it continued at an ever-accelerating pace until the frontier that fed it was no more. Assuming that the frontier closed about 1890, it may be said that the boom lasted approximately four hundred

years. It lasted so long that it came to be considered the normal state, a fallacious assumption for any boom. It is conceivable that this boom has given the peculiar character to modern history, to what we call Western civilization.

[22] Assuming that there was such a boom and that it lasted four hundred years, it follows that a set of institutions, economic, political, and social, would in that time evolve to meet the needs of the world in boom. Insofar as they were designed to meet peculiar conditions, these institutions would be specialized boomward. It is accepted that a set of institutions has developed since 1500, and we speak of them as modern to distinguish them from medieval institutions. Therefore we may well inquire whether our modern institutions—economic, political, and social, constituting the superstructure of Western civilization—are founded on boom conditions.

[23] The factors involved, though of gigantic magnitude, are simple in nature and in their relation one to another. They are the old familiar ones of population, land, and capital. With the opening of the Great Frontier, land and capital rose out of all proportion to population, of those to share it, and therefore conditions were highly favorable to general prosperity and a boom. What we are really concerned with is an *excess* of land and an *excess* of capital for division among a relatively *fixed* number of people. The population did increase, but not until the nineteenth century did the extra population compare with the extra land and capital that had been long available.

[24] For example, in 1500 the Metropolis had a population of 100 million people crowded into an area of 3,750,000 square miles. The population density for the entire Metropolis was 26.7 persons per square mile. For each person there was available about twenty-four acres, a ratio that changed little from 1300 to 1650. The opening of the frontier upset the whole situation by destroying the balance that had been struck between land and man. A land excess of nearly 20 million square miles became available to the same number of people, reducing population density to less than five, increasing the average area per individual to 148 acres instead of 24.

[25] Capital may be considered in two forms, as gold and silver

and as capital goods or commodities. The Metropolis was short of both forms of wealth throughout the medieval period, and the dearth of coin prior to the discoveries was most critical. It has been estimated that the total amount of gold and silver in Europe in 1492 was less than 200 million dollars, less than two dollars per person. Certainly there was not enough to serve the needs of exchange, which was carried on by barter, or to give rise to erudite theories of money economy. Then very suddenly the whole money situation changed.

[26] By 1500 the Spaniards had cracked the treasure houses of the Great Frontier and set a stream of gold and silver flowing into the Metropolis, a stream that continued without abatement for 150 years, and that still continues. This flood of precious metals changed all the relations existing between man and money, between gold and a bushel of wheat or a *fanega* of barley. That changed relationship wrought the price revolution because temporarily—so fast did the metals come—there was more money than things, and so prices rose to the modern level. This new money was a powerful stimulus to the quest for more, and set the whole Metropolis into the frenzy of daring and adventure which gave character to the modern age.

[27] Since our concern here is with the excess of wealth over population, we may examine with interest the rise in the quantity of gold and silver. Taking the 200 million dollars of 1492 as a base, we find that by 1600 the amount had increased eightfold, by 1700 it had risen nearly twentyfold, by 1800 it stood at thirty-sevenfold, and by 1900 at a hundred-and-fourfold over what was on hand when the frontier was opened. Obviously this increase of precious metals was out of all proportion to the increase in population. If we grant that an excess of money makes a boom, then here in this new treasure was the stuff a boom needed. It is safe to say that out of each $100 worth of precious metals produced in the world since 1493, not less than $85 have been supplied by the frontier countries and not more than $15 by the Metropolis, including Asia. The bearing of these facts on the rise of a money economy, of modern capitalism, is something for the economists to think about.

[28] The spectacular influx of precious metals should not obscure

the fact that they constituted but the initial wave of wealth rolling into the Metropolis from the Great Frontier. Wave followed wave in endless succession in the form of material things, and each deposit left the Metropolis richer than before. Unfortunately the quantity of material goods cannot be measured, but we know it was enormous. South America sent coffee, Africa, cocoa, and the West Indies sent sugar to sweeten them. Strange and flavorsome fruits came from the tropics. From primeval forests came ship timbers, pitch, and tar with which to build the fleets for merchants and warriors. North America sent furs for the rich and cotton for the poor so that all could have more than one garment. The potato, adapted to the Metropolis, became second to bread as the staff of life. The New World gave Indian corn or maize, and the rich lands on which to grow it, and in time hides and beef came from the plains and pampas of two continents. Everywhere in Europe from the royal palace to the humble cottage men smoked American tobacco and under its soothing influence dreamed of far countries, wealth, and adventure. Scientists brought home strange plants and herbs and made plant experiment stations in scores of European gardens. In South America they found the bark of a tree from which quinine was derived to cure malaria and another plant which they sent to the East Indies to establish the rubber industry. No, it is not possible to measure the amount of goods flowing into Europe, but it can be said that the Great Frontier hung for centuries like the horn of plenty over the Metropolis and emptied out on it an avalanche of wealth.

[29] At this point let us turn to the growth of population, the number of people who in a rough sense shared the excess of land and of precious metals. As stated above the population in 1500 stood at about 100 million, and it did not increase appreciably before 1650. All the people of European origin, whether in the Metropolis or in the Great Frontier, had a little more than doubled by 1800. Not until the nineteenth century was the increase rapid. By 1850 the increase was more than threefold, by 1900 more than fivefold, but in 1940 population had increased eightfold over that of 1500. The significant fact is that between 1500 and 1850 the quantity of both land and capital stood high out of all proportion to the quantity of population. Equally significant, and somewhat

disturbing, is the fact that the excess of land incident to opening
the frontier disappeared in the world census of 1930. By 1940
the enlarged Western world was more crowded than the small
world of Europe was in 1500. It was the observation of this fact
which led Dean Inge to remark in 1938 that "the house is full."
Much earlier William Graham Sumner commented on the man-
land ratio: "It is this ratio of population to land which determines
what are the possibilities of human development or the limits of
what man can attain in civilization and comfort." To put the
matter in another way, if the boom rested on a four-century excess
of land over population, the land base of the boom disappeared
in 1930.

[30] The boom hypothesis of modern history may be summed
up by stating that with the tapping of the resources of the Great
Frontier there came into the possession of the Metropolis a body
of wealth consisting of land, precious metals, and commodities
out of all proportion to the number of people. . . .

IV

[31] If the opening of the Great Frontier did precipitate a boom
in Western civilization, the effects on human ideas and institutions
must have been profound and far-reaching. In general such a
boom would hasten the passing away of the ideas and institutions
of a static culture and the sure appearance of others adapted to
a dynamic and prospering society. There is no doubt that medieval
society was breaking up at the time of the discoveries, that men's
minds had been sharpened by their intellectual exercises, and that
their spirits had been stirred by doubt. The thinkers were restless
and inquiring, but what they lacked was room in which to try
out their innovations, and a fresh and uncluttered soil in which
some of their new ideas could take hold and grow. Their desires
had to be matched with opportunity before they could realize on
their aspirations, however laudable. The frontier offered them
the room and the opportunity. It did not necessarily originate ideas,
but it acted as a relentless sifter, letting some pass and rejecting
others. Those that the frontier favored prospered, and finally
matured into institutions; those it did not favor became recessive,
dormant, and many institutions based on these ideas withered

away. Feudal tenure, serfdom, barter, primogeniture, and the notion that the world was a no-good place in which to live are examples of things untenable in the presence of the frontier.

[32] Since we are dealing with the modern age, it would be very helpful if we could discover what it emphasized most. Where was the chief accent of modernity? What has been its focus? *Who* has held the spotlight on the stage of history since 1500? There can be little doubt, though there may be enough to start an argument, that the answer to all these questions is: the Individual. It is he who has been emphasized, accented; it is on him that the spotlight has focused; it is his importance that has been magnified. He is—or was—the common denominator of modern times, and an examination of any strictly modern institution such as democracy or capitalism will reveal an individual at the core, trying to rule himself in one case and make some money in the other. Not God nor the devil nor the state, but the ordinary man has been the favorite child of modern history.

[33] Did the Great Frontier, which was his contemporary, have any part in giving the individual his main chance, the triple opportunity of ruling himself, enriching himself, and saving his own soul on his own hook? These three freedoms were institutionalized in Protestantism, capitalism, and democracy—whose basic assumption is that they exist for the individual, and that the individual must be free in order to make them work. The desire for freedom men surely have always had, but in the old Metropolis conditions prevailed which made freedom impossible. Everywhere in Europe the individual was surrounded by institutions which, whether by design or not, kept him unfree. He was walled in by man-made regulations which controlled him from baptism to extreme unction.

[34] Then the golden door of the Great Frontier opened, and a way of escape lay before him. He moved out from the Metropolis to land on a distant shore, in America, Australia, South Africa. Here in the wild and empty land there was not a single institution; man had left them, albeit temporarily, far behind. Regardless of what befell him later, for an instant he was free of all the restrictions that society had put upon him. In short, he had escaped his

human masters only to find himself in the presence of another, a less picayunish one.

[35] The character of the new master, before whom he stood stripped of his institutions, was so in contrast with that of the old one as to defy comparison. Man stood naked in the presence of nature. On this subject, Alexander von Humbolt said, "In the Old World, nations and the distinction of their civilization form the principal point in the picture; in the New World, man and his production almost disappear amidst the stupendous display of wild and gigantic nature." The outstanding qualities of wild and gigantic nature are its impersonality and impassiveness. Nature broods over man, casts its mysterious spells, but it never intervenes for or against him. It gives no orders, issues no proclamations, has no prisons, no privileges; it knows nothing of vengeance or mercy. Before nature all men are free and equal.

[36] The important point is that the abstract man we have been following did not have to *win* his freedom. It was imposed upon him and he could not escape it. Being caught in the trap of freedom, his task was to adjust himself to it and to devise procedures which would be more convenient for living in such a state. His first task was to govern himself, for self-government is what freedom imposes.

[37] Of course there was not just one man on the frontier. In a short time the woods were full of them, all trained in the same school. As the years went by, they formed the habits of freedom, cherished it; and when a distant government tried to take from them that to which they had grown accustomed, they resisted, and their resistance was called the American Revolution. The American frontiersmen did not fight England to gain freedom, but to preserve it and have it officially recognized by the Metropolis. "Your nation," wrote Herman Melville, "enjoyed no little independence before your declaration declared it." Whence came this independence? Not from parliaments or kings or legislative assemblies, but from the conditions, the room, the space, and the natural wealth amidst which they lived. "The land was ours," writes Robert Frost, "before we were the land's."

[38] The other institution that magnified the importance of the

individual was capitalism, an economic system under which each person undertakes to enrich himself by his own effort. It is only in the presence of great abundance that such a free-for-all system of wealth-getting can long operate. There must be present enough wealth to go around to make such an economy practicable. We have seen that the tapping of the frontier furnished just this condition, a superabundance of land, of gold and silver, and of commodities which made the principle of *laissez faire* tenable. In the frontier the embryonic capitalists of the sixteenth and seventeenth centuries hit a magnificent windfall which set them up in business by demonstrating that the game of wealth-getting was both interesting and profitable. For four hundred years, to paraphrase Bernard DeVoto, "men stumbled over fortunes looking for cows." . . . Free homesteads in Kansas, free gold claims in California, and free grass on the Great Plains are examples of windfalls coming at the tag end of the frontier period, windfalls which come no more. In the larger sense the Great Frontier was a windfall for Europe.

[39] There is an unpleasant logic inherent in the frontier boom hypothesis of modern history. We come to it with the reluctance that men always have when they come to the end of a boom. They look back on the grand opportunities they had, they remember the excitement and adventure of it, they tot up their accounts and hope for another chance. Western civilization today stands facing a closed frontier, and in this sense it faces a unique situation in modern times.

[40] If we grant the boom, we must concede that the institutions we have, such as democracy and capitalism, were boom-born; we must also admit that the individual, this cherished darling of modern history, attained his glory in an abnormal period when there was enough room to give him freedom and enough wealth to give him independence. The future of the individual, of democracy and capitalism, and of many other modern institutions are deeply involved in this logic, and the lights are burning late in the capitals of the Western world where grave men are trying to determine what that future will be.

[41] Meantime less thoughtful people speak of new frontiers, though nothing comparable to the Great Frontier has yet been

found. The business man sees a business frontier in the customers he has not yet reached; the missionary sees a religious frontier among the souls he has not yet saved; the social worker sees a human frontier among the suffering people whose woes he has not yet alleviated; the educator of a sort sees the ignorance he is trying to dispel as a frontier to be taken; and the scientists permit us to believe that they are uncovering the real thing in a scientific frontier. But as yet no Columbus has come in from these voyages and announced: "Gentlemen, there is your frontier!" The best they do is to say that it is out beyond, that if you work hard enough and have faith enough, and put in a little money, you will surely find it. If you watch these peddlers of substitute frontiers, you will find that nearly every one wants you to buy something, give something, or believe in something. They want you to be a frontier for them. Unlike Columbus, they bring no continents and no oceans, no gold or silver or grass or forest to you.

[42] I should like to make it clear that mankind is really searching for a new frontier which we once had and did not prize, and the longer we had it, the less we valued it; but now that we have lost it, we have a great pain in the heart, and we are always trying to get it back again. It seems to me that historians and all thoughtful persons are bound by their obligation to say that there is no new frontier in sight comparable in magnitude or importance to the one that is lost. They should point out the diversity and heterogeneity, not to say the absurdity, of so-called new frontiers. They are all fallacies, these new frontiers, and they are pernicious in proportion to their plausibility and respectability. The scientists themselves should join in disabusing the public as to what science can be expected to do. It can do much, but, to paraphrase Isaiah Bowman, it is not likely soon to find a new world or make the one we have much bigger than it is. If the frontier is gone, we should have the courage and honesty to recognize the fact, cease to cry for what we have lost, and devote our energy to finding the solutions to the problems now facing a frontierless society. And when the age we now call modern is modern no longer, and requires a new name, we may appropriately call it the Age of the Frontier, and leave it to its place in history.

EXERCISES

1. Why is paragraph 1 arresting and therefore a good beginning?
2. What is the author's purpose in paragraphs 2–4?
3. State the main idea and the subdivisions of each section of the article. (Section IV really ends with paragraph 38; paragraphs 39–42 are a conclusion.) An outline would be helpful.
4. State the central idea, or thesis, of the article.
5. Write out the syllogism implied in paragraph 27, which states the relation between wealth and a boom.
6. Write out the syllogism implied in the conclusion, which states the reason for the end of the boom.
7. Exactly how are self-government and capitalism related to the frontier emphasis on the individual?
8. Why should this selection be called an article?
9. Is the content strictly factual, fact plus interpretation of the facts given, or mainly interpretation of meaning or experience?
10. How would one accumulate such a body of information?
11. Is the style appropriate to the content and the purpose?
12. Characterize the style. Is it plain or ornate? Clear or vague? Relatively concrete or relatively abstract? Formal or informal? Artistic or utilitarian?
13. Is the figurative language in paragraph 16 consistent?
14. What is rhetorically good about paragraph 21?
15. Write a paper on one of the following topics. Make specific reference to useful material in the sources involved.
    a. The economic implications of Meiklejohn's "Liberty—for What?", Rorty's "Bread, and the Stuff We Eat," and Webb's "Ended: 400 Year Boom."
    b. The implications for human ideals of Beard's "The Essentials of the American System," Meiklejohn's "Liberty—for What?", and Webb's "Ended: 400 Year Boom."

Insomnia in Whitehall

JOHN FISCHER

I

[1] Fifteen years ago I knew a nice revolutionist named Peter. He was an attractive specimen of the British upper middle class —blond, diffident, carefully tweeded, well drilled in Latin and cricket, and endowed with a modest inheritance. Like many similar young men in England about that time, he had dedicated his life to smashing capitalism (he called it ca*pit*alism) and building a chrome-bright socialist society on the ruins.

[2] Peter was, of course, an idealist. He had taken up revolution from the same religious impulse which might have sent him, fifty years earlier, into the clergy or off to India to civilize the barbarous Hindoo. Since we then lived in neighboring rooms in an Oxford college, he spent a good many evenings preaching his lofty and indignant gospel to me.

[3] It sounded pretty plausible. In those days of depression, capitalism obviously wasn't working too well—or, as Peter saw it, "the System is destroying itself with its own cruel and absurd contradictions." Once this *hara kiri* was complete, he had no doubts about what would follow. A horse-doctor's dose of state ownership would cure everything. Once the Workers' Government had taken over farms and factories, all the hard problems would evaporate out of hand. England would become a plump and shining realm, cleansed of parasites, peopled by happy laborers, and ruled by the wise and just—including, naturally, Peter himself.

[4] The last part of his vision, at least, eventually came true. Peter had inherited many of the traditional governing-class talents, and as soon as the Labor party came to power after the war he was given an inconspicuous but responsible job in Whitehall.

[5] When I looked him up there recently, I was surprised to find that he didn't look a bit like a successful revolutionist. He was

In *Harper's Magazine,* January, 1950.

slumped behind a mountainous deskload of papers, bound (literally) in red tape. His face was tense and his shirt collar was frayed. The evangelical high spirits with which he had started his rebel's career had been shed somewhere along the road. Nor had he picked up any of that triumphant assurance which one might expect in a minor prophet busily constructing the New Jerusalem. Instead he looked worried, uncertain, and pitifully tired.

[6] In the following weeks I saw a good deal of Peter, and of other old acquaintances in the same faith—minor bureaucrats, Labor journalists, and back-bench members of Parliament. Together they made up a fairly wide sample of the Labor party's junior officer class. I have no way of guessing at the temper of the high command—the Cabinet and the lords of the trade unions —but in these middle ranks, morale was curiously frazzled. All these were still devout socialists, but nearly every one exhibited the same hesitant lack of confidence.

[7] Peter himself finally summed it up. "We are just beginning to suspect," he said, "that socialism has some built-in contradictions of its own."

[8] The things that worried him turned out to be quite unexpected—to me, anyhow—and they are, I believe, matters of considerable importance to America. Before we examine them, however, it may be worth noting two items which were *not* causing much concern among the thirty-second degree socialists.

[9] For one thing, they weren't especially worried about the election coming this spring. Most of them were reasonably confident that Labor would get back in—if only because the Tories have not yet shown the public any alternative line of political drygoods. All the Conservatives are offering is a kind of diluted we-can-do-it-better socialism, plus their venerable war relic, Winston Churchill. Now, almost everybody in England seems to feel that Old Winnie is the best possible man to run a war, but that in peacetime he is about as useful as a beat-up Sherman tank. Even the younger members of his own party speak of him as an embarrassment, long overdue for glorious retirement.

[10] Neither were the Labor people I met much bothered about those features of their welfare state which have set so many

journalistic shirts afire in America. The National Health Service, to cite only one example, actually appeared to be working out slightly better than they had expected.

[11] Plenty of bugs still infest it, of course. It got under way with too few doctors, dentists, and hospitals, so that the professional staff is brutally overworked and patients often get second-rate treatment. In the beginning, too, a good many clients took advantage of the "free" service to wangle menstrual pain-killers, wigs, and lumbago plasters that they didn't strictly need, but the new charge of one shilling for each prescription presumably will curb some of that. Eventually, too, the shortage of physicians can be mended.

[12] Meanwhile, even second-rate medical care is a great comfort to many thousands of families that once couldn't afford *any* treatment for a serious illness. Mass Observation—a rough equivalent in Britain of the Gallup Poll—reported last summer that three-fifths of the people who had used the National Health Service spoke of it with approval. Only 26 per cent regarded it as an inconvenience, while 16 per cent thought it hadn't made much difference to them personally. In the face of such figures (and the bumptious health of English babies) the shrillest keening of the Scripps-Howard papers and the American Medical Association can hardly support an indictment of complete failure.

[13] It is scarcely necessary to add that nobody I talked to— Labor, Liberal, or Conservative—was sprouting gooseflesh over certain bugaboos which are occasionally paraded in the American press. They weren't afraid that free speech might be muffled, or scientists dragooned into a party line, or the London bobbies turned overnight into a Gestapo.

II

[14] What really worries a good many socialists is a failure of theory. They have run into a series of problems which they did not foresee, and their traditional doctrine provides no answers. In describing them as "contradictions," Peter was being quite precise, for they have usually cropped up in just that form. Perhaps the most pressing is—

[15] *Full Employment* vs. *Inflation*. Of course all good socialists

(like practically everybody else) believe in full employment. They also dread inflation, which is now the most dangerous threat confronting both the Labor party and Britain. For if the little island hopes to escape starvation, it must keep the prices of its manufactured goods low enough to compete in the world markets. Otherwise England can never pay for its indispensable imports of food and raw materials once the Marshall Plan spigot is turned off.

[16] Yet nobody has so far discovered any way to keep full employment in present-day Britain and to smother inflation at the same time.

[17] Remember that some 80 per cent of the economy is still run by private enterprisers. This means that thousands of individual business men are constantly bidding against each other for workmen and machinery and raw materials. They can bid handsomely, because—for reasons noted a little further on—most firms are raking in such whopping profits that they seldom have to think twice about costs.

[18] Well, in an economy where money is plentiful but manpower and all other resources are scarce, there can be only one result: a steady bidding-up of the prices of nearly everything, from stenographers and carbon paper to machine tools. This is what has been happening ever since the war, in spite of the partial controls on many items. This is why England was forced to devalue the pound, in a convulsive effort to lower prices for her customers overseas. This also is why there is grave danger that the benefits of that devaluation may be eroded away within a few months, as prices keep crawling upward.

[19] The old-fashioned remedy in any economy—from wide-open *laissez-faire* to communist—would be to tighten up the whole machine: put the screws on credit, throttle down construction and other capital investment, and trim public spending right to the quick. In short, deflation—an ugly word. It would mean a delay in many of Labor's pet projects, such as housing (which undeniably is badly needed). It would draw some blood from the sacred social services, because there's not much room in the budget for really big cuts anywhere else. Food subsidies might have to go;

people might have to pay a little more for their medical care and public housing.

[20] Worst of all, such a policy would mean some unemployment —not on a depression scale, but just enough to put a brake on rising wages and to squeeze some of the surplus man-power out of over-staffed industries. (There are a number—railroads, mining, building trades, ship repairing, for example—whose payrolls are stuffed way beyond the limits of efficiency.)

[21] Any unemployment is heresy to the Labor party, however—especially with an election in sight. Consequently, when the cabinet did announce a new economy program in late October, after weeks of agonized debate, it was not surprising that the London *Economist* had to describe it as "a catalogue of fleabites." The orthodox socialist simply cannot bring himself to tackle inflation by such means.

[22] Instead his thoughts turn to more and tighter controls. If he can't drain off the steam behind inflation, maybe he can sit harder on the safety valve. This answer is theologically acceptable, but it runs squarely into another contradiction—

[23] *Stability* vs. *Rigor Mortis.* In theory, enough controls—with enough inspectors to enforce them—might check inflation, and at the same time achieve Stability, one of the socialist's dearest idols. (One of his favorite pleasures is delivering a rousing lecture on "the chronic instability of the American economy.") To him, stability means something more than an end to the great tidal waves of boom and depression. It also means the ironing-out of those little dips and surges which make Rational Planning (another cherished idol) almost impossible. But the socialists are now discovering that when they "stabilize" prices, wages, profits, and markets, they also freeze up all the moving parts in the economic engine.

[24] This freeze-up already had gone pretty far before the Laborites came to power, for few English business men really believe in competition. Unhampered by anti-trusts, they started long before the war to spin a web of cartels, price agreements, divided markets, and "trade customs," with the happy purpose of eliminating most of the risk and discomfort from their operations.

[25] They also eliminated most of the hustle. Today the goal of many British industrialists apparently is to keep on selling the good old product, made on the old machines and displayed in the old packages, to the old customers at the old price (or a little higher) until the crack of doom. This is known as A Proud Tradition.

[26] One machine-tool manufacturer told me he is still using some equipment his grandfather installed seventy-five years ago. He has plenty of capital to retool, because the firm "has been paying at least a 25 per cent dividend ever since I was a lad, and still is." But his idea of the right moment to buy a new lathe is when grandpa's finally caves in like the one-hoss shay—not when somebody invents a better one.

[27] This attitude may have something to do with the fact that our tool and die shops are "twenty years ahead" of comparable British plants, as the head of Slater & Wakefield, a leading British concern in this industry, recently told a convention of his American colleagues. It certainly had a lot to do with the painful findings of an English productivity team which investigated American steel foundries last fall. The team reported that efficiency in American factories was 50 to 90 per cent higher than in their British counterparts—primarily because "productivity consciousness is to be found among all grades of employees, from executives to shop level."

[28] The Labor government's policies haven't done much to encourage this kind of "productivity consciousness" in England. After all, why should the average British manufacturer sprain his brain cells to find new ways to do it cheaper, faster, and better? He already can sell everything he turns out at a highly comforting profit, because he has two guaranteed markets of solid plush:

(1) *The home market,* floating high on the tide of inflation and dammed-up wartime demand. Here he is saved from any prod of competition by that cozy armor of "trade custom," plus rigid controls on imports from abroad. Similar controls—on raw materials, plant construction, and even on paper for advertising—make it difficult for new firms to enter his field or for old ones to expand.

(2) *The "sterling market,"* which means India, the Middle East, and all the other areas where England piled up huge debts during the war. These countries can collect only by taking payment in British goods—which they are now permitted to swallow at the rate of some two hundred million pounds a year. Since England gets nothing in return, this draining away of scarce goods increases the pressure of inflation very considerably. Because these sterling customers have, in effect, paid in advance, the British manufacturer doesn't have to worry about shaving his prices.

[29] Moreover, so long as this ready-made market is wide open, it is almost impossible for England to redirect her exports toward America, to earn those dollars she needs so desperately. When the government exhorts a bicycle maker, for example, to forget about his old and eager customers in Pakistan and fight for a toehold in the strange, highly competitive American market, he behaves like any sensible business man. He laughs.

[30] If Britain ever hopes to balance her foreign trade accounts, therefore, she will have to choke down on this flood of "free" exports to her sterling customers. Naturally her creditors will howl when their payments are slowed down, and some unemployment is bound to follow until the stream of trade can be diverted to new channels. So far, the government has found the task too painful to face.

[31] Meanwhile, the industrialist not only finds "the earning of profits as easy as falling off a stool," as the *Economist* recently put it. He also sees no point in risking a backache to earn more. After all, the tax collector would grab most of it—19½ shillings out of every 20, in the top brackets; 39 per cent of the entire national income. By the Treasury's own estimate, only 250 people in all Britain now enjoy an income, after taxes, above $14,000 a year. So why shouldn't everybody slide along in the same old grooves? There is no penalty if they do, no substantial reward if they try to change.

[32] But change—swift, deep-cutting change—is the only thing that can save Britain. The brutal needs of survival demand shifts throughout the whole economy—shifts from the easy sterling customers to the tough dollar market, shifts from high-cost pro-

ducers to the more efficient, shifts to meet the new pattern of demand caused by a massive redistribution of income, shifts to new products and new methods.

[33] The socialists know this, for most of them are intelligent men. They also realize that the controls they yearn for in the name of stability are certain to make any such shifts more difficult. At this writing, they are still wringing their hands in indecision; the dilemma remains unsolved.

III

[34] Their problem has been made tougher still by a third contradiction, which might be labelled—

Socialism vs. *Trade Unionism.* In theory, it ought to be possible to make all the needed shifts in the British economy by means of Socialist Planning. The wise men in Whitehall presumably could decide the proper level of wages in each industry and announce: This is it. They could figure how many men should be yanked out of the building trades, and send them packing to the undermanned textile mills. They could close down an exhausted coal pit in Scotland and ship both machinery and miners to a better site in Wales. Right now, in fact, the government has authority to do all these things.

[35] Unfortunately for theory, the Labor party is mostly made up of trade unionists. Their stubborn habit is to behave like good union men rather than socialist planners. For example, the British working man doesn't like to move. The footloose tradition of America, which can funnel thousands of families across the continent overnight, is simply unthinkable to him. In his mind, "full employment" means a permanent stranglehold on his present job. If the cabinet hints that it might actually use its power to direct labor, he cuts loose a bellow that even John L. Lewis would admire.

[36] Besides, the bitter years of unemployment are sharp in his memory. He can't quite believe that jobs-for-all will last. Labor-saving machinery is suspect, therefore, and any worker who sets a pace faster than a leisurely plod is a traitor to his class. (Penalty: nobody will drink a pint of ale with him, come evenings, at the Bricklayer's Arms.) Nor is he much tempted by higher pay for

higher output. He no longer has to save up for sickness, unemployment, or the education of his children—social services take care of that. And taxes would get a big bite of the extra earnings anyhow.

[37] Finally, he believes that the purpose of his union is to get him better wages and shorter hours, and that the duty of "his" government is to back up the union. Haven't Labor politicians been telling him for twenty years that once they got in power every laboring man would get more money for less work? Now, in office at last, they start to mutter about austerity, harder work, speedups, and tightened belts. Naturally the laboring man doesn't take them seriously.

[38] The union leaders can't do much about this. When they side with the government against their own members, the Communists are always waiting to scream "Betrayal!" The result has been a long series of wildcat strikes, many of them led by the Communists, who loathe socialists even more than they hate Churchill. Although these Communists are not very powerful at the moment, their persistent efforts to kidnap the unions away from the established leadership give nightmares to both the government and the trade union hierarchy. There is real danger that the workers might eventually look to the Communists as their only real spokesmen against their boss, the State.

[39] Indeed, the whole position of trade unions under a socialist regime has turned out to be a maze of contradictions. When the laborer's government becomes his employer as well, collective bargaining obviously doesn't make sense. And so long as it is attempted, Socialist Planning must remain a wistful fantasy.

[40] In the meantime, imagine what happens to the spirit of a revolution when its banner reads: "Come on boys, let's build a Brave New World—but don't work more than forty-five hours a week, insist on time-and-a-half for overtime, and never under any circumstances lay more than thirty bricks an hour."

IV

[41] Among all the curious puzzles which lie strewn about England's political scenery, perhaps the most baffling to an American is the conflict of—

Internationalism vs. *Isolation*. As everybody knows, the Socialists have been internationalists from way back. The Brotherhood of Man has always been their goal, nationalism their enemy. This article of faith, one might assume, would have been powerfully reinforced by the events of the past ten years.

[42] That decade surely has made it plain that Britain no longer can stand alone. By herself she can neither feed her people nor defend her shores. Since 1940 she has been kept alive only by repeated blood transfusions from the United States—lend-lease, Marshall aid, and loans which will never be repaid. Today she seems little more fit to stand on her own feet than she was when the treatment started. Even if all the problems noted above could somehow be magicked away overnight, there is little evidence that England will ever again be able to support forty million people at their accustomed living standard on her crowded little island.

[43] The reasons have been set forth in these pages from time to time by Barbara Ward, Kenneth Galbraith, and others, so there is no need to repeat them here. The conclusion has been underlined many times in the past few months by Paul Hoffman of ECA. Britain cannot survive unless she integrates her economy into some larger unit—a United States of Europe, or an English-Speaking Union, or perhaps a still broader Atlantic Community.

[44] Does this mean, then, that the socialists are hot and panting after some such federation? Not at all. On the contrary, they have made England the most isolationist country in the Western world. Every suggestion that they snuggle up a little closer has been repulsed with shudders of distaste.

[45] Their usual explanation is that England already belongs to one club—the British Commonwealth—and the Dominions might feel terribly upset if she joined another. There is some truth in this, but it isn't the whole story. The Labor people have stronger reasons, which they are usually too tactful to mention in public, for shrinking from any kind of economic union. They hold a different set of objections against each of the three kinds of merger commonly proposed.

[46] The most widely discussed of these is an "integration" of Western Europe. It has become an official aim of American policy, and several European governments at least pay it lip-service. So

do Mr. Churchill and a number of his Conservative colleagues. [47] The British socialists, however, want no part of it. They can foresee nothing but chaos if their economy—so austere, so delicately poised, so rigidly corseted—were linked to the disheveled and undisciplined societies of the continent. The wild men of France, for instance, can't even collect taxes, run a rationing system, or keep a cabinet in office for more than a few months. Switzerland and Belgium are crawling with unrepentant capitalists. Conservative Catholics rule Italy, and God knows what may emerge in a reviving Germany. If rational planning is hard for England by herself, it would become quite impossible in harness with such diverse and unpredictable teammates.

[48] Worse yet, British living standards might be pulled down to the level of the Continent. At the very least, a score of British industries would be disrupted by the competition of more efficient producers across the channel. In the long run, a more sensible, large-scale, productive pattern of industry might result. But meanwhile the shock of the operation might kill the patient. Almost certainly it would kill British socialism.

[49] Well, then, why not an English-Speaking Union—an economic merger of Britain, Canada, the other Dominions, and the United States? This arrangement would have certain obvious advantages over a European federation. It would solve England's dollar shortage once and for all, it would link her to areas producing food surpluses, and it would give her a chance to decant some of her excess population into relatively uncrowded countries.

[50] The customary argument against it—and it has considerable weight—is that such a step would split off Britain and America from the Continent. The Western Europeans might then conclude that they had been deserted, and sidle into the waiting arms of Moscow. Moreover, Englishmen of all shades of political opinion feel an understandable nervousness that they might be engulfed by their bigger partner. They have no desire to become a forty-ninth state.

[51] But the socialists—at least of the left-wing variety—are more than nervous; they shake with horror at the very thought. Many of these left-wingers are totally ignorant of America. Others—

such learned metaphysicians of the True Church as Harold Laski, Tom Driberg, and Kingsley Martin—are merely blinded by their own dogma. They see the United States as the stronghold of capitalism, and therefore the nest of all evil. In their eyes, it is a barbaric wilderness, addicted to bubble gum, lynching, and juke boxes, and ruled by bloated plutocrats who rejoice in stomping on the faces of the poor. They accept each dollar of American aid with sincere regret, like a penitent drunkard reaching for the bottle.

[52] Some even argue that America is turning imperialist and "proto-fascist" (because that is always supposed to happen to capitalism in its last stages). They expect our long overdue depression to overwhelm us any week now. They also fear that we may get "hysterical"—a favorite adjective for Americans—and start dropping atom bombs all over the lot. Marriage to such a monster clearly would be a fate worse than death.

[53] For a long while the sages of the left advocated a closer relationship with Russia, rather than the United States. Now even they are coming to realize that the Soviets would be interested only in the sense that a coyote is interested in closer relationships with a jackrabbit. At the moment, therefore, they have no coherent foreign policy. Yet they have a following, and their repugnance for the Beelzebubs of Wall Street must be taken into account by the more realistic leaders of the Labor party.

[54] The third alternative—a gradual welding of the Western Europeans and the English-speaking countries into a great Atlantic Community—is open to many of the objections brought against the two less ambitious schemes. Certainly the political difficulties are enormous. The economic strain and dislocation would be most painful, and Britain's socialism might get seriously diluted in the final mixture. Hence most Laborites are inclined to dismiss the idea as utopian and impractical.

[55] Of course it is equally utopian to expect the American taxpayer to go on subsidizing England indefinitely. Nevertheless, nobody in England, so far as I could discover, is drafting specific plans against the day when ECA money stops flowing. The Labor people are too busy, too tired, too harassed with their many crossgrained problems. They seem to be able to plan only from one

crisis to the next, like Eliza crossing the ice. Much like their counterparts in our old-fashioned capitalist parties, in fact.

v

[56] It would be a great mistake to imagine that all these skull-
popping dilemmas are causing much distress to ordinary Englishmen.
Aside from those like Peter, who are actively interested in
politics, hardly anyone seems conscious of them. Throughout the
devaluation crisis, most of the people I met in London took the
whole affair with aplomb, not to say indifference.

[57] And why not? These people have been living through one
crisis after another ever since 1939. Dunkirk, the blitz, V-bombs,
imminent bankruptcy—they all sounded terrible, but somehow
the country has always muddled through (up to now, anyway).
In spite of near-insolvency, moreover, the conditions of ordinary
living have been improving at an astonishing rate since the Labor
government came to power.

[58] London, which I had last seen in 1946, has been rebuilt and
repainted in a short three years more than I would thought possible
within an entire generation. Nearly a million families have moved
into new homes since the war; several million other houses have
been refurbished with government aid. (Because they are heavily
subsidized, rents average only about $2 a week.) Where the bomb
craters still gap, they have often been turned into tidy parking
lots. What rubble is still left has been stacked, with true British
neatness, into square mounds along the sidewalks.

[59] The people, too, look surprisingly better off. The gray,
drawn, slightly shabby look is gone. Crowds in the midtown streets
—largely made up of working people, naturally—seemed better
dressed, better fed, and somehow gayer than I had remembered
them even before the war. Rationing is still a genuine hardship;
fats and proteins, in particular, are probably too scarce to keep
the country's vigor up to the proper notch. Still there is plenty of
evidence that the ordinary laboring-class family is eating better
than ever before. Especially the children.

[60] The prostitutes who patrol Picadilly and Glass House Street
are gaudier than they used to be, and far fewer. One common
theory is that most of them retired on their wartime earnings,

bought stately mansions in the country, and now pour tea for the vicar every Thursday. A more prosaic, and more likely, explanation is that any girl can now take her pick of respectable daytime jobs.

[61] Although the upper classes are being gradually liquidated by ferocious taxes, they are marching to their doom with a certain style. Most Savile Row tailors are booked up for months in advance. Theaters do an SRO business, and swank cafés like the Caprice are crowded every night. In a single week I saw more champagne on restaurant tables than I have seen in five years in New York—and I didn't eat in fancy places, either. One reason is that Scotch is scarce, since practically all of it is shipped abroad; but another is that business men entertain each other generously. Sir William takes his solicitor to lunch today, and the solicitor returns the courtesy tomorrow; both bills can be deducted, wine and all, from their firms' income tax as business expense.

[62] Rolls Royces can be hired on the same basis, thus circumventing gasoline rationing. One evening I counted seven parked outside a modest home where a party evidently was under way. The pub around the corner was pretty gay, too. The truck drivers and charwomen who made up most of its clientele jammed the parlor bar right up to closing hour—and a surprising number seemed able to afford gin-and-orange in lieu of the traditional pint of bitter.

[63] What most people really got excited about last fall was the radiant weather: the warmest, sunniest autumn within living memory. It made the worries of bureaucrats and socialist pundits seem curiously unreal and far away. God obviously was in His heaven, looking after His chosen island just as He always has.

[64] The problems and contradictions of British socialism are real enough. Very possibly they are unsolvable. So far, however, I suspect that they have not even touched the great mass of Labor voters—and that these millions will not nourish any serious doubts about socialism so long as vague disasters merely darken the horizon. When the storm actually hits, when jobs get scarce and living standards begin to pinch, the story may change.

[65] Right now the barometer seems to be falling fast.

EXERCISES

1. What seems to be the author's general purpose?
2. Why are paragraphs 8–13, which deal with the achievements of socialism, placed where they are instead of at the end of the article?
3. Of what value is Fischer's "before and after" story of Peter? Why not just begin by showing Peter's present discouragement?
4. Why is the radiant weather introduced in paragraph 63?
5. Characterize the tone of the article.
6. How does the author use connotation? Notice especially such words as "infest" (paragraph 11) and "keening" (paragraph 12).
7. List several figures of speech. Does the author use many or few figures? Of what value are they?
8. Find an example of irony in paragraph 51.
9. Does the style seem especially appropriate to the subject, or is it used mostly as a means of gaining interest?
10. Why, according to the author, is British socialism not working? Look for a single factor which operates in all the conflicts. Specifically,
    a. Why do individual merchants keep raising wages and prices and so causing inflation?
    b. Why do they keep to the old and sure markets when avoiding competition for new markets is not good for the national economy?
    c. Why will the workers not shift jobs if a shift would benefit the national welfare?
    d. Why do the British not want to become a 49th state if that would benefit the national welfare?

The History of Our Future

WILLIAM VOGT

[1] By excessive breeding and abuse of the land mankind has backed itself into an ecological trap. By a lopsided use of applied science it has been living on promissory notes. Now, all over the world, the notes are falling due.

[2] Payment cannot be postponed much longer. Fortunately, we still may choose between payment and utterly disastrous bankruptcy on a world scale. It will certainly be more intelligent to pull in our belts and accept a long period of austerity and rebuilding than to wait for a catastrophic crash of our civilization. In hard fact, we have no other choice.

[3] When I write "we" I do not mean the other fellow. I mean every person who reads a newspaper printed on pulp from vanishing forests. I mean every man and woman who eats a meal drawn from steadily shrinking lands. Everyone who flushes a toilet, and thereby pollutes a river, wastes fertile organic matter and helps to lower a water table. Everyone who puts on a wool garment derived from overgrazed ranges that have been cut by the little hoofs and gullied by the rains, sending runoff and topsoil into the rivers downstream, flooding cities hundreds of miles away. Especially do I mean men and women in overpopulated countries who produce excessive numbers of children who, unhappily, cannot escape their fate as hostages to the forces of misery and disaster that lower upon the horizon of our future.

[4] If we ourselves do not govern our destiny, firmly and courageously, no one is going to do it for us. To regain ecological freedom for our civilization will be a heavy task. It will frequently require arduous and uncomfortable measures. It will cost considerable sums of money. Democratic governments are not likely to set forth on such a steep and rocky path unless the people lead the way. Nations with lower educational standards than ours, na-

tions that are technologically retarded, are still less likely to move. In our own interest we must accept the responsibility for this leadership, as we have in the spheres of economics and politics.

[5] Drastic measures are inescapable. Above everything else, we must reorganize our thinking. If we are to escape the crash we must abandon all thought of living unto ourselves. We form an earth-company, and the lot of the Indiana farmer can no longer be isolated from that of the Bantu. This is true, not only in John Donne's mystical sense, in the meaning of brotherhood that makes starving babies in Hindustan the concern of Americans; but in a direct, physical sense. An eroding hillside in Mexico or Yugoslavia affects the living standard and probability of survival of the American people. Irresponsible breeding makes amelioration of the condition of the Greeks—or the Italians or Indians or Chinese—difficult, if not impossible; it imposes a drain on the world's wealth, especially that of the United States, when this wealth might be used to improve living standards and survival chances for less people. We cannot escape our responsibility, since it is a responsibility to ourselves.

[6] We must equally abandon any philosophy of "Sufficient unto the day—." We are paying for the foolishness of yesterday while we shape our own tomorrow. Today's white bread may force a break in the levees, and flood New Orleans next spring. This year's wheat from Australia's eroding slopes may flare into a Japanese war three decades hence. Comic books from the flanks of the Nevado de Toluca in 1948 may close Mexico City's factories in 1955. The freebooting, rugged individualist, whose vigor, imagination, and courage contributed so much of good to the building of our country (along with the bad), we must now recognize, where his activities destroy resources, as the Enemy of the People he has become. The exploiting lumberman of Madagascar was beheaded; we should impose at least as effective, if kinder, controls. We must develop our sense of time, and think of the availability of beefsteaks not only for this Saturday but for the Saturdays of our old age, and of our children and grandchildren's youth. The day has long since passed when a senator may callously demand, "What has posterity ever done for me?" Posterity is of our making, as is the world in which it will have to live.

[7] Above all, we must learn to know—to feel to the core of our beings—our dependence upon the earth and the riches with which it sustains us. We can no longer believe valid our assumption that we live in independence. No longer can we rest secure in the certainty that somehow, from somewhere, our wants will be supplied. We, even we fortunate Americans, are pressing hard on our means of subsistence. Our neighbors on five continents know what it means to find their cupboards bare. There is no phase of our civilization that is not touched by wasting dearth. There is hardly an aspect of human activity, through all the complex span of our lives, that does not in some open or occult manner, feel the chill of scarcity's damp breath.

[8] We must—all of us, men, women, and children—reorient ourselves with relation to the world in which we live. We must learn to weigh the daily news in terms of man's subsistence. We must come to understand our past, our history, in terms of the soil and water and forests and grasses that have made it what it is. We must see the years to come in the frame that makes space and time one, that will keep us strong only as, like Antaeus, we draw our strength from the earth. Our education must be reshaped, as the story of our existence in an environment as completely subjected to physical laws as is a ball we let drop from our hands. Our philosophies must be rewritten to remove them from the domain of words and "ideas," and to plant their roots firmly in the earth. Above all, we must weigh our place in the society of nations and our future through the decades to come in the scale of our total environment.

[9] The history of our future is already written, at least for some decades. As we are crowded together, two and a quarter billions of us, on the shrinking surface of the globe, we have set in motion historical forces that are directed by our total environment.

[10] We might symbolize these forces by graphs. One of them is the curve of human populations that, after centuries of relative equilibrium, suddenly began to mount, and in the past fifty years has been climbing at a vertiginous rate.

[11] The other graph is that of our resources. It represents the area and thickness of our topsoil, the abundance of our forests, available waters, life-giving grasslands, and the biophysical web

that holds them together. This curve, except for local depressions, also maintained a high degree of regularity through the centuries. But it, too, has had its direction sharply diverted, especially during the past hundred and fifty years, and it is plunging downward like a rapid.

[12] These two curves—of population and the means of survival—have long since crossed. Ever more rapidly they are drawing apart. The farther they are separated the more difficult will it be to draw them together again.

[13] Everywhere, or nearly everywhere, about the earth we see the results of their divergence. The crumbling ruins of two wars mark their passing. The swollen bellies of hungry babies, from San Salvador to Bengal, dot the space between them. Parching fevers and racking coughs, from Osorno to Seoul, cry aloud the cleavage between these curves. The angry muttering of mobs, like the champing of jungle peccaries, is a swelling echo of their passing.

[14] The direction of these curves and the misery they write across the earth are not likely to be changed in the proximate future. Their direction is fixed for some decades. Great masses of people have a preponderantly young population; as they come into the breeding age we must, despite all possible efforts short of generalized slaughter, expect human members to increase for a time. The drag imposed by ignorance, selfishness, nationalism, custom, etc., is certain to retard, by some decades, any effective or substantial improvement of resource management.

[15] So that the people shall not delude themselves, find further frustration through quack nostrums, fight their way into blind alleys, it is imperative that this world-wide dilemma be made known to all mankind. The human race is caught in a situation as concrete as a pair of shoes two sizes too small. We must understand that, and stop blaming economic systems, the weather, bad luck, or callous saints. This is the beginning of wisdom, and the first step on the long road back.

[16] The second step is dual—the control of populations and the restoration of resources.

[17] Unless we take these steps and begin to swing into them soon—unless, in short, man readjusts his way of living, in its

fullest sense, to the imperatives imposed by the *limited* resources of his environment—we may as well give up all hope of continuing civilized life. Like Gadarene swine, we shall rush down a war-torn slope to a barbarian existence in the blackened rubble.

EXERCISES

This selection is the final chapter in William Vogt's book *Road to Survival*. In the body of the book he has given distressingly convincing bodies of fact in support of his assertions, and so he does not need to give more proof here. He needs only to summarize his main points as vividly as possible.

1. How does the author try to make his statements vivid?
2. What main points are emphasized?
3. What methods of emphasis are used?
4. Does the author recognize the fact that the uninformed or some-what irrational behavior which we call the "human element" (which we have seen interfering with the Rational Planning of the British socialists) will be the main impediment to remedial plans?
5. You have now read seven selections which deal with man and his relation to the soil, to money, and to government: those by Sears (in Part I), Beard, Meiklejohn, Rorty, Webb, Fischer, and Vogt. The material in these selections can provide substance for a source paper, or informal research paper; writing such a paper will give you practice for a full-scale research project which requires you to find your own material in the library. Using facts and opinions from these selections, write a paper on one of the topics below. Make specific acknowledgement, in footnotes, for all data and quotations which you borrow. (Your instructor may allow you to do supplementary reading in the library; if so, Vogt's book has a valuable bibliography.)

   Source paper topics:
   a. Man's relation to the soil
   b. The individual, his land, and his money
   c. The economic basis of human values
   d. The conflict between traditional values and present needs
   e. What we can do to preserve America's welfare within the American system
   f. Prosperity vs. conservation
   g. Security for the individual

Section D: The Nature and Uses of Knowledge

All the selections in Section D deal with abstract subjects such as the nature of knowledge, ways of acquiring or transmitting knowledge, and the values of knowledge to individual men. As Section C dealt with the world of physical reality, Section D deals with the world of the intellect—no less real. All the selections are essays or addresses in the nature of essays in that each presents the author's understanding and interpretation of some aspect of the subject.

Knowledge and Learning

JOHN HENRY NEWMAN

[1] I suppose the *primâ-facie* view which the public at large would take of a University, considering it as a place of Education, is nothing more or less than a place for acquiring a great deal of knowledge on a great many subjects. Memory is one of the first developed of mental faculties; a boy's business when he goes to school is to learn, that is, to store up things in his memory. For some years his intellect is little more than an instrument for taking in facts, or a receptacle for storing them; he welcomes them as fast as they come to him; he lives on what is without; he has his eyes ever about him; he has a lively susceptibility of impressions; he imbibes information of every kind; and little does he make his own in a true sense of the word, living rather upon his neighbors all around him. He has opinions, religious, political, and literary, and, for a boy, is very positive in them and sure about them; but he gets them from his schoolfellows, or his masters, or his parents, as the case may be. Such as he is in his other relations, such also is he in his school exercises; his mind is observant, sharp, ready, retentive; he is almost passive in the acquisition of knowledge. I say this in no disparagement of the idea of a clever boy. Geography, chronology, history, language, natural history, he heaps up the matter of these studies as treasures for a future day. It is the seven years of plenty with him: he gathers in by handfuls, like the Egyptians, without counting; and though, as time goes on, there is exercise for his argumentative powers in the Elements of Mathematics, and for his taste in the Poets and Orators, still, while at school, or at least, till quite the last years of his time, he acquires, and little more; and when he is leaving for the University, he is mainly the creature of foreign influences and circumstances, and made up of accidents, homogeneous or

From "Knowledge Viewed in Relation to Learning," *The Idea of a University*, 1873. Text taken from the edition of Longmans, Green and Company, 1901.

not, as the case may be. Moreover, the moral habits, which are a boy's praise, encourage and assist this result; that is, diligence, assiduity, regularity, despatch, persevering application; for these are the direct conditions of acquisition, and naturally lead to it. Acquirements, again, are emphatically producible, and at a moment; they are a something to show, both for master and scholar; an audience, even though ignorant themselves of the subjects of an examination, can comprehend when questions are answered and when they are not. Here again is a reason why mental culture is in the minds of men identified with the acquisition of knowledge.

[2] The same notion possesses the public mind, when it passes on from the thought of a school to that of a University: and with the best of reasons so far as this, that there is no true culture without acquirements, and that philosophy presupposes knowledge. It requires a great deal of reading, or a wide range of information, to warrant us in putting forth our opinions on any serious subject; and without such learning the most original mind may be able indeed to dazzle, to amuse, to refute, to perplex, but not to come to any useful result or any trustworthy conclusion. There are indeed persons who profess a different view of the matter, and even act upon it. Every now and then you will find a person of vigorous or fertile mind, who relies upon his own resources, despises all former authors, and gives the world, with the utmost fearlessness, his views upon religion, or history, or any other popular subject. And his works may sell for a while; he may get a name in his day; but this will be all. His readers are sure to find on the long run that his doctrines are mere theories, and not the expression of facts, that they are chaff instead of bread, and then his popularity drops as suddenly as it rose.

[3] Knowledge then is the indispensable condition of expansion of mind, and the instrument of attaining to it; this cannot be denied, it is ever to be insisted on; I begin with it as a first principle; however, the very truth of it carries men too far, and confirms to them the notion that it is the whole of the matter. A narrow mind is thought to be that which contains little knowledge; and an enlarged mind, that which holds a great deal; and what seems to put the matter beyond dispute is, the fact of the great number of studies which are pursued in a University, by its very

profession. Lectures are given on every kind of subject; examinations are held; prizes awarded. There are moral, metaphysical, physical Professors; Professors of languages, of history, of mathematics, of experimental science. Lists of questions are published, wonderful for their range and depth, variety and difficulty; treaties are written, which carry upon their very face the evidence of extensive reading or multifarious information; what then is wanting for mental culture to a person of large reading and scientific attainments? what is grasp of mind but acquirement? where shall philosophical repose be found, but in the consciousness and enjoyment of large intellectual possessions?

[4] And yet this notion is, I conceive, a mistake, and my present business is to show that it is one, and that the end of a Liberal Education is not mere knowledge, or knowledge considered in its *matter;* and I shall best attain my object, by actually setting down some cases, which will be generally granted to be instances of the process of enlightenment or enlargement of mind, and others which are not, and thus, by the comparison, you will be able to judge for yourselves, Gentlemen, whether Knowledge, that is, acquirement, is after all the real principle of the enlargement, or whether that principle is not rather something beyond it.

[5] For instance, let a person, whose experience has hitherto been confined to the more calm and unpretending scenery of these islands, . . . go for the first time into parts where physical nature puts on her wilder and more awful forms, whether at home or abroad, as into mountainous districts; or let one, who has ever lived in a quiet village, go for the first time to a great metropolis,—then I suppose he will have a sensation which perhaps he never had before. He has a feeling not in addition or increase of former feelings, but of something different in its nature. He will perhaps be borne forward, and find for a time that he has lost his bearings. He has made a certain progress, and he has a consciousness of mental enlargement; he does not stand where he did, he has a new centre, and a range of thoughts to which he was before a stranger.

[6] Again, the view of the heavens which the telescope opens upon us, if allowed to fill and possess the mind, may almost whirl it round and make it dizzy. It brings in a flood of ideas, and is

rightly called an intellectual enlargement, whatever is meant by the term.

[7] And so again, the sight of beasts of prey and other foreign animals, their strangeness, the originality (if I may use the term) of their forms and gestures and habits and their variety and independence of each other, throw us out of ourselves into another creation, and as if under another Creator, if I may so express the temptation which may come on the mind. We seem to have new faculties, or a new exercise for our faculties, by this addition to our knowledge; like a prisoner, who, having been accustomed to wear manacles or fetters, suddenly finds his arms and legs free.

[8] Hence Physical Science generally, in all its departments, as bringing before us the exuberant riches and resources, yet the orderly course, of the Universe, elevates and excites the student, and at first, I may say, almost takes away his breath, while in time it exercises a tranquilizing influence upon him.

[9] Again, the study of history is said to enlarge and enlighten the mind, and why? because, as I conceive, it gives it a power of judging of passing events, and of all events, and a conscious superiority over them, which before it did not possess.

[10] And in like manner, what is called seeing the world, entering into active life, going into society, travelling, gaining acquaintance with the various classes of the community, coming into contact wth the principles and modes of thought of various parties, interests, and races, their views, aims, habits and manners, their religious creeds and forms of worship,—gaining experience how various yet how alike men are, how low-minded, how bad, how opposed, yet how confident in their opinions; all this exerts a perceptible influence upon the mind, which it is impossible to mistake, be it good or be it bad, and is popularly called its enlargement.

[11] And then again, the first time the mind comes across the arguments and speculations of unbelievers, and feels what a novel light they cast upon what he has hitherto accounted sacred; and still more, if it gives in to them and embraces them, and throws off as so much prejudice what it has hitherto held, and, as if waking from a dream, begins to realize to its imagination that there is now no such thing as law and the transgression of law, that

sin is a phantom, and punishment a bugbear, that it is free to sin, free to enjoy the world and the flesh; and still further, when it does enjoy them, and reflects that it may think and hold just what it will, that "the world is all before it where to choose," and what system to build up as its own private persuasion; when this torrent of wilful thoughts rushes over and inundates it, who will deny that the fruit of the tree of knowledge, or what the mind takes for knowledge, has made it one of the gods, with a sense of expansion and elevation,—an intoxication in reality, still, so far as the subjective state of the mind goes, an illumination? Hence the fanaticism of individuals or nations, who suddenly cast off their Maker. Their eyes are opened; and, like the judgment-stricken king in the Tragedy, they see two suns, and a magic universe, out of which they look back upon their former state of faith and innocence with a sort of contempt and indignation, as if they were then but fools, and the dupes of imposture.

[12] On the other hand, Religion has its own enlargement, and an enlargement, not of tumult, but of peace. It is often remarked of uneducated persons, who have hitherto thought little of the unseen world, that, on their turning to God, looking into themselves, regulating their hearts, reforming their conduct, and meditating on death and judgment, heaven and hell, they seem to become, in point of intellect, different beings from what they were. Before, they took things as they came, and thought no more of one thing than another. But now every event has a meaning; they have their own estimate of whatever happens to them; they are mindful of times and seasons, and compare the present with the past; and the world, no longer dull, monotonous, unprofitable, and hopeless, is a various and complicated drama, with parts and an object, and an awful moral.

[13] Now from these instances, to which many more might be added, it is plain, first, that the communication of knowledge certainly is either a condition or the means of that sense of enlargement or enlightenment, of which at this day we hear so much in certain quarters: this cannot be denied; but next, it is equally plain, that such communication is not the whole of the process. The enlargement consists, not merely in the passive reception into

the mind of a number of ideas hitherto unknown to it, but in the mind's energetic and simultaneous action upon and towards and among those new ideas, which are rushing in upon it. It is the action of a formative power, reducing to order and meaning the matter of our acquirements; it is a making the objects of our knowledge subjectively our own, or, to use a familiar word, it is a digestion of what we receive, into the substance of our previous state of thought; and without this no enlargement is said to follow. There is no enlargement, unless there be a comparison of ideas one with another, as they come before the mind, and a systematizing of them. We feel our minds to be growing and expanding *then,* when we not only learn, but refer what we learn to what we know already. It is not the mere addition to our knowledge that is the illumination; but the locomotion, the movement onwards, of that mental centre, to which both what we know, and what we are learning, the accumulating mass of our acquirements, gravitates. And therefore a truly great intellect, and recognized to be such by the common opinion of mankind, such as the intellect of Aristotle, or of St. Thomas, or of Newton, or of Goethe, . . . is one which takes a connected view of old and new, past and present, far and near, and which has an insight into the influence of all these one on another; without which there is no whole, and no centre. It possesses the knowledge, not only of things, but also of their mutual and true relations; knowledge, not merely considered as acquirement, but as philosophy.

[14] Accordingly, when this analytical, distributive, harmonizing process is away, the mind experiences no enlargement, and is not reckoned as enlightened or comprehensive, whatever it may add to its knowledge. For instance, a great memory, as I have already said, does not make a philosopher, any more than a dictionary can be called a grammar. There are men who embrace in their minds a vast multitude of ideas, but with little sensibility about their real relations towards each other. These may be antiquarians, annalists, naturalists; they may be learned in the law; they may be versed in statistics; they are most useful in their own place; I should shrink from speaking disrespectfully of them; still, there is nothing in such attainments to guarantee the absence of narrowness of mind. If

they are nothing more than well-read men, or men of information, they have not what specially deserves the name of culture of mind, or fulfills the type of Liberal Education.

[15] In like manner, we sometimes fall in with persons who have seen much of the world, and of the men who, in their day, have played a conspicuous part in it, but who generalize nothing, and have no observation, in the true sense of the word. They abound in information in detail, curious and entertaining, about men and things; and, having lived under the influence of no very clear or settled principles, religious or political, they speak of every one and every thing, only as so many phenomena, which are complete in themselves, and lead to nothing, not discussing them, or teaching any truth, or instructing the hearer, but simply talking. No one would say that these persons, well informed as they are, had attained to any great culture of intellect or to philosophy.

[16] The case is the same still more strikingly where the persons in question are beyond dispute men of inferior powers and deficient education. Perhaps they have been much in foreign countries, and they receive, in a passive, otiose, unfruitful way, the various facts which are forced upon them there. Seafaring men, for example, range from one end of the earth to the other; but the multiplicity of external objects, which they have encountered, forms no symmetrical and consistent picture upon their imagination; they see the tapestry of human life, as it were on the wrong side, and it tells no story. They sleep, and they rise up, and they find themselves, now in Europe, now in Asia; they see visions of great cities and wild regions; they are in the marts of commerce, or amid the islands of the South; they gaze on Pompey's Pillar, or on the Andes; and nothing which meets them carries them forward or backward, to any idea beyond itself. Nothing has a drift or relation; nothing has a history or a promise. Every thing stands by itself, and comes and goes in its turn, like the shifting scenes of a show, which leave the spectator where he was. Perhaps you are near such a man on a particular occasion, and expect him to be shocked or perplexed at something which occurs; but one thing is much the same to him as another, or, if he is perplexed, it is as not knowing what to say, whether it is right to admire, or to ridicule, or to disapprove, while conscious that some expression of opinion is expected from him;

for in fact he has no standard of judgment at all, and no landmarks to guide him to a conclusion. Such is mere acquisition, and, I repeat, no one would dream of calling it philosophy.

[17] Instances, such as these, confirm, by the contrast, the conclusion I have already drawn from those which preceded them. That only is true enlargement of mind which is the power of viewing many things at once as one whole, of referring them severally to their true place in the universal system, of understanding their respective values, and determining their mutual dependence. Thus is that form of Universal Knowledge, of which I have on a former occasion spoken, set up in the individual intellect, and constitutes its perfection. Possessed of this real illumination, the mind never views any part of the extended subject-matter of Knowledge without recollecting that it is but a part, or without the associations which spring from this recollection. It makes every thing in some sort lead to every thing else; it would communicate the image of the whole to every separate portion, till that whole becomes in imagination like a spirit, every where pervading and penetrating its component parts, and giving them one definite meaning. Just as our bodily organs, when mentioned, recall their function in the body, as the word "creation" suggests the Creator, and "subjects" a sovereign, so, in the mind of the Philosopher, as we are abstractedly conceiving of him, the elements of the physical and moral world, sciences, arts, pursuits, ranks, offices, events, opinions, individualities, are all viewed as one, with correlative functions, and as gradually by successive combinations converging, one and all, to the true centre.

[18] To have even a portion of this illuminative reason and true philosophy is the highest state to which nature can aspire, in the way of intellect; it puts the mind above the influences of chance and necessity, above anxiety, suspense, unsettlement, and superstition, which is the lot of the many. Men, whose minds are possessed with some one object, take exaggerated views of its importance, are feverish in the pursuit of it, make it the measure of things which are utterly foreign to it, and are startled and despond if it happens to fail them. They are ever in alarm or in transport. Those on the other hand who have no object or principle whatever to hold by, lose their way, every step they take. They are

thrown out, and do not know what to think or say, at every fresh juncture; they have no view of persons, or occurrences, or facts, which come suddenly upon them, and they hang upon the opinion of others, for want of internal resources. But the intellect, which has been disciplined to the perfection of its powers, which knows, and thinks while it knows, which has learned to leaven the dense mass of facts and events with the elastic force of reason, such an intellect cannot be partial, cannot be exclusive, cannot be impetuous, cannot be at a loss, cannot but be patient, collected, and majestically calm, because it discerns the end in every beginning, the origin in every end, the law in every interruption, the limit in each delay; because it ever knows where it stands, and how its path lies from one point to another. It is the τετράγωνος of the Peripatetic, and has the "nil admirari" of the Stoic,—

> Felix qui potuit rerum cognoscere causas,
> Atque metus omnes, et inexorabile fatum
> Subjecit pedibus, strepitumque Acherontis avari.

There are men who, when in difficulties, originate at the moment vast ideas or dazzling projects; who, under the influence of excitement, are able to cast a light, almost as if from inspiration, on a subject or course of action which comes before them; who have a sudden presence of mind equal to any emergency, rising with the occasion, and an undaunted magnanimous bearing, and an energy and keenness which is but made intense by opposition. This is genius, this is heroism; it is the exhibition of a natural gift, which no culture can teach, at which no Institution can aim; here, on the contrary, we are concerned, not with mere nature, but with training and teaching. That perfection of the Intellect, which is the result of Education, and its *beau ideal,* to be imparted to individuals in their respective measures, is the clear, calm, accurate vision and comprehension of all things, as far as the finite mind can embrace them, each in its place, and with its own characteristics upon it. It is almost prophetic from its knowledge of history; it is almost heart-searching from its knowledge of human nature; it has almost supernatural charity from its freedom from littleness and prejudice; it has almost the repose of faith, because nothing can startle it; it has almost the beauty and harmony of heavenly contemplation, so intimate is it with the eternal order of things and the music of the spheres.

EXERCISES

1. Explain why this selection would be called an essay.
2. To what does Newman allude, in paragraph 1, when he speaks of "seven years of plenty"? Does understanding the allusion help to understand the meaning of the paragraph? Would all of Newman's audience have recognized the allusion, in spite of the fact that only two members of your class recognized it?
3. By what method (one seldom observed before) is paragraph 1 developed?
4. Distinguish between the "moral habits" (which we would call "mental habits") in paragraph 1.
5. What is the function of paragraph 4?
6. What difference is there between the examples in paragraphs 5–7 and those in paragraphs 11–12?
7. Why are the examples in paragraphs 5–12 arranged as they are?
8. What classes of men are represented by Aristotle, St. Thomas, Newton, and Goethe (paragraph 13)?
9. What distinction between mere acquisition of knowledge and true education does Newman make in paragraphs 13–14?
10. Do your college classes foster what Newman would regard as true "culture of the mind"?
11. Is Newman's diction specific or general? Concrete or abstract?
12. How does Newman try to make his abstract subject vivid?
13. Is Newman's style appropriate to his subject?
14. Does Newman seem to use rhythm with conscious artistry?
15. Is Newman discussing the humanities, the sciences, the studies which we have come to call the social sciences, or all three?
16. Write a theme on one of the following topics.
    a. Illustrate Newman's statement in paragraph 18, "Men, whose minds are possessed with some one object, take exaggerated views of its importance, are feverish in the pursuit of it, make it the measure of things which are utterly foreign to it   . . ."
    b. A character study of some person whom you consider learned but not educated.

Literature and Science

MATTHEW ARNOLD

[1] Practical people talk with a smile of Plato and of his absolute
ideas; and it is impossible to deny that Plato's ideas do often seem
unpractical and impracticable, and especially when one views
them in connection with the life of a great work-a-day world like
the United States. The necessary staple of the life of such a world
Plato regards with disdain; handicraft and trade and the working
professions he regards with disdain; but what becomes of the life
of an industrial modern community if you take handicraft and
trade and the working professions out of it? The base mechanic
arts and handicrafts, says Plato, bring about a natural weakness
in the principle of excellence in a man, so that he cannot govern
the ignoble growths in him, but nurses them, and cannot understand fostering any other. Those who exercise such arts and trades,
as they have their bodies, he says, marred by their vulgar businesses, so they have their souls, too, bowed and broken by them.
And if one of these uncomely people has a mind to seek self-
culture and philosophy, Plato compares him to a bald little tinker,
who has scraped together money, and has got his release from
service, and has had a bath, and bought a new coat, and is rigged
out like a bridegroom about to marry the daughter of his master
who has fallen into poor and helpless estate.
[2] Nor do the working professions fare any better than trade at
the hands of Plato. He draws for us an inimitable picture of the
working lawyer, and of his life of bondage; he shows how this
bondage from his youth up has stunted and warped him, and made
him small and crooked of soul, encompassing him with difficulties
which he is not man enough to rely on justice and truth as means
to encounter, but has recourse, for help out of them, to falsehood
and wrong. And so, says Plato, this poor creature is bent and
broken, and grows up from boy to man without a particle of sound-

From *Discourses in America,* 1885.

ness in him, although exceedingly smart and clever in his own esteem.

[3] One cannot refuse to admire the artist who draws these pictures. But we say to ourselves that his ideas show the influence of a primitive and obsolete order of things, when the warrior caste and the priestly caste were alone in honour and the humble work of the world was done by slaves. We have now changed all that; the modern majority consists in work, as Emerson declares; and in work, we may add, principally of such plain and dusty kind as the work of cultivators of the ground, handicraftsmen, men of trade and business, men of the working professions. Above all is this true in a great industrious community such as that of the United States.

[4] Now education, many people go on to say, is still mainly governed by the ideas of men like Plato, who lived when the warrior caste and the priestly or philosophical class were alone in honour, and the really useful part of the community were slaves. It is an education fitted for persons of leisure in such a community. This education passed from Greece and Rome to the feudal communities of Europe, where also the warrior caste and the priestly caste were alone held in honour and where the really useful and working part of the community, though not nominally slaves as in the pagan world, were practically not much better off than slaves, and not more seriously regarded. And how absurd it is, people end by saying, to inflict this education upon an industrious modern community, where very few indeed are persons of leisure, and the mass to be considered has not leisure, but is bound, for its own great good, and for the great good of the world at large, to plain labour and to industrial pursuits, and the education in question tends necessarily to make men dissatisfied with these pursuits and unfitted for them!

[5] That is what is said. So far I must defend Plato, as to plead that his view of education and studies is in the general, as it seems to me, sound enough, and fitted for all sorts and conditions of men, whatever their pursuits may be. 'An intelligent man,' says Plato, 'will prize those studies which result in his soul getting soberness, righteousness, and wisdom, and will less value the others.' I cannot consider *that* a bad description of the aim of

education, and of the motives which should govern us in the choice of studies, whether we are preparing ourselves for a hereditary seat in the English House of Lords or for the pork trade in Chicago.

[6] Still I admit that Plato's world was not ours, that his scorn of trade and handicraft is fantastic, that he had no conception of a great industrial community such as that of the United States, and that such a community must and will shape its education to suit its own needs. If the usual education handed down to it from the past does not suit it, it will certainly before long drop this and try another. The usual education in the past has been mainly literary. The question is whether the studies which were long supposed to be the best for all of us are practically the best now; whether others are not better. The tyranny of the past, many think, weighs on us injuriously in the predominance given to letters in education. The question is raised whether, to meet the needs of our modern life, the predominance ought not now to pass from letters to science; and naturally the question is nowhere raised with more energy than here in the United States. The design of abasing what is called 'mere literary instruction and education,' and of exalting what is called 'sound, extensive, and practical scientific knowledge,'[1] is, in this intensely modern world of the United States, even more perhaps than in Europe, a very popular design, and makes great and rapid progress.

[7] I am going to ask whether the present movement for ousting letters from their old predominance in education, and for transferring the predominance in education to the natural sciences, whether this brisk and flourishing movement ought to prevail, and whether it is likely that in the end it really will prevail. An objection may be raised which I will anticipate. My own studies have been almost wholly in letters, and my visits to the field of the natural sciences have been very slight and inadequate, although those sciences have always strongly moved my curiosity. A man of letters, it will perhaps be said, is not competent to discuss the comparative merits of letters and natural science as means of education. To this objection I reply, first of all, that his incom-

[1] From the instructions of Sir Josiah Mason for a college in Birmingham, England.

petence, if he attempts the discussion but is really incompetent for
it, will be abundantly visible; nobody will be taken in; he will have
plenty of sharp observers and critics to save mankind from that
danger. But the line I am going to follow is, as you will soon
discover, so extremely simple, that perhaps it may be followed
without failure even by one who for a more ambitious line of
discussion would be quite incompetent.

[8] Some of you may possibly remember a phrase of mine which
has been the object of a good deal of comment; an observation
to the effect that in our culture, the aim being *to know ourselves
and the world,* we have, as the means to this end, *to know the best
which has been thought and said in the world.*[2] A man of science,
who is also an excellent writer and the very prince of debaters,
Professor Huxley,[3] in a discourse at the opening of Sir Josiah
Mason's college at Birmingham, laying hold of this phrase, expanded it by quoting some more words of mine, which are these:
'The civilized world is to be regarded as now being, for intellectual
and spiritual purposes, one great confederation, bound to a joint
action and working to a common result; and whose members have
for their proper outfit a knowledge of Greek, Roman, and Eastern
antiquity, and of one another. Special local and temporary advantages being put out of account, that modern nation will in
the intellectual and spiritual sphere make most progress, which
most thoroughly carries out this programme.'

[9] Now on my phrase, thus enlarged, Professor Huxley remarks
that when I speak of the above-mentioned knowledge as enabling
us to know ourselves and the world, I assert *literature* to contain
the materials which suffice for thus making us know ourselves and
the world. But it is not by any means clear, says he, that after having learnt all which ancient and modern literatures have to tell us,
we have laid a sufficiently broad and deep foundation for that
criticism of life, that knowledge of ourselves and the world, which
constitutes culture. On the contrary, Professor Huxley declares that
he finds himself 'wholly unable to admit that either nations or
individuals will really advance, if their outfit draws nothing from

---

[2] From "The Function of Criticism at the Present Time" (1864).

[3] Thomas Henry Huxley, biologist. See "The Method of Scientific Investigation," page 124.

the stores of physical science. An army without weapons of precision, and with no particular base of operations, might more hopefully enter upon a campaign on the Rhine, than a man, devoid of a knowledge of what physical science has done in the last century, upon a criticism of life.'

[10] This shows how needful it is for those who are to discuss any matter together, to have a common understanding as to the sense of the terms they employ,—how needful, and how difficult. What Professor Huxley says, implies just the reproach which is so often brought against the study of *belles lettres,* as they are called: that the study is an elegant one, but slight and ineffectual; a smattering of Greek and Latin and other ornamental things, of little use for any one whose object is to get at truth, and to be a practical man. So, too, M. Renan talks of the 'superficial humanism' of a school-course which treats us as if we were all going to be poets, writers, preachers, orators, and he opposes this humanism to positive science, or the critical search after truth. And there is always a tendency in those who are remonstrating against the predominance of letters in education, to understand by letters *belles lettres,* and by *belles lettres* a superficial humanism the opposite of science or true knowledge.

[11] But when we talk of knowing Greek and Roman antiquity, for instance, which is the knowledge people have called the humanities, I for my part mean a knowledge which is something more than a superficial humanism, mainly decorative. 'I call all teaching *scientific,*' says Wolf, the critic of Homer, 'which is systematically laid out and followed up to its original sources. For example: a knowledge of classical antiquity is scientific when the remains of classical antiquity are correctly studied in the original languages.' There can be no doubt that Wolf is perfectly right; that all learning is scientific which is systematically laid out and followed up to its original sources, and that a genuine humanism is scientific.

[12] When I speak of knowing Greek and Roman antiquity, therefore, as a help to knowing ourselves and the world, I mean more than a knowledge of so much vocabulary, so much grammar, so many portions of authors in the Greek and Latin languages, I mean knowing the Greeks and Romans, and their life and genius,

and what they were and did in the world; what we get from them, and what is its value. That, at least, is the ideal; and when we talk of endeavouring to know Greek and Roman antiquity, as a help to knowing ourselves and the world, we mean endeavouring so to know them as to satisfy this ideal, however much we may still fall short of it.

[13] The same also as to knowing our own and other modern nations, with the like aim of getting to understand ourselves and the world. To know the best that has been thought and said by the modern nations, is to know, says Professor Huxley, 'only what modern *literatures* have to tell us; it is the criticism of life contained in modern literature.' And yet 'the distinctive character of our times,' he urges, 'lies in the vast and constantly increasing part which is played by natural knowledge.' And how, therefore, can a man, devoid of knowledge of what physical science has done in the last century, enter hopefully upon a criticism of modern life?

[14] Let us, I say, be agreed about the meaning of the terms we are using. I talk of knowing the best which has been thought and uttered in the world; Professor Huxley says this means knowing *literature*. Literature is a large word; it may mean everything written with letters or printed in a book. Euclid's *Elements* and Newton's *Principia* are thus literature. All knowledge that reaches us through books is literature. But by literature Professor Huxley means *belles lettres*. He means to make me say, that knowing the best which has been thought and said by the modern nations is knowing their *belles lettres* and no more. And this is no sufficient equipment, he argues, for a criticism of modern life. But as I do not mean, by knowing ancient Rome, knowing merely more or less of Latin *belles lettres,* and taking no account of Rome's military, and political, and legal, and administrative work in the world; and as, by knowing ancient Greece, I understand knowing her as the giver of Greek art, and the guide to a free and right use of reason and to scientific method, and the founder of our mathematics and physics and astronomy and biology,—I understand knowing her as all this, and not merely knowing certain Greek poems, and histories, and treatises, and speeches,—so as to the knowledge of modern nations also. By knowing modern na-

tions, I mean not merely knowing their *belles lettres,* but knowing also what has been done by such men as Copernicus, Galileo, Newton, Darwin. 'Our ancestors learned,' says Professor Huxley, 'that the earth is the centre of the visible universe, and that man is the cynosure of things terrestrial; and more especially was it inculcated that the course of nature had no fixed order, but that it could be, and constantly was, altered.' But for us now, continues Professor Huxley, 'the notions of the beginning and the end of the world entertained by our forefathers are no longer credible. It is very certain that the earth is not the chief body in the material universe, and that the world is not subordinated to man's use. It is even more certain that nature is the expression of a definite order, with which nothing interferes.' 'And yet,' he cries, 'the purely classical education advocated by the representatives of the humanists in our day gives no inkling of all this!'

[15] In due place and time I will just touch upon that vexed question of classical education; but at present the question is as to what is meant by knowing the best which modern nations have thought and said. It is not knowing their *belles lettres* merely which is meant. To know Italian *belles lettres,* is not to know Italy, and to know English *belles lettres* is not to know England. Into knowing Italy and England there comes a great deal more, Galileo and Newton amongst it. The reproach of being a superficial humanism, a tincture of *belles lettres,* may attach rightly enough to some other disciplines; but to the particular discipline recommended when I proposed knowing the best that has been thought and said in the world, it does not apply. In that best I certainly include what in modern times has been thought and said by the great observers and knowers of nature.

[16] There is, therefore, really no question between Professor Huxley and me as to whether knowing the great results of the modern scientific study of nature is not required as a part of our culture, as well as knowing the products of literature and art. But to follow the processes by which those results are reached, ought, say the friends of physical science, to be made the staple of education for the bulk of mankind. And here there does arise a question between those whom Professor Huxley calls with playful

sarcasm 'the Levites of culture,' and those whom the poor humanist is sometimes apt to regard as its Nebuchadnezzars.

[17] The great results of the scientific investigation of nature we are agreed upon knowing, but how much of our study are we bound to give to the processes by which those results are reached? The results have their visible bearing on human life. But all the processes, too, all the items of fact, by which those results are reached and established, are interesting. All knowledge is interesting to a wise man, and the knowledge of nature is interesting to all men. It is very interesting to know, that, from the albuminous white of the egg, the chick in the egg gets the materials for its flesh, bones, blood, and feathers; while from the fatty yolk of the egg, it gets the heat and energy which enable it at length to break its shell and begin the world. It is less interesting, perhaps, but still it is interesting, to know that when a taper burns, the wax is converted into carbonic acid and water. Moreover, it is quite true that the habit of dealing with facts, which is given by the study of nature, is, as the friends of physical science praise it for being, an excellent discipline. The appeal, in the study of nature, is constantly to observation and experiment; not only is it said that the thing is so, but we can be made to see that it is so. Not only does a man tell us that when a taper burns the wax is converted into carbonic acid and water, as a man may tell us, if he likes, that Charon is punting his ferry-boat on the river Styx, or that Victor Hugo is a sublime poet, or Mr. Gladstone the most admirable of statesmen; but we are made to see that the conversion into carbonic acid and water does actually happen. This reality of natural knowledge it is, which makes the friends of physical science contrast it, as a knowledge of things, with the humanist's knowledge, which is, say they, a knowledge of words. And hence Professor Huxley is moved to lay it down that, 'for the purpose of attaining real culture, an exclusively scientific education is at least as effectual as an exclusively literary education.' And a certain President of the Section of Mechanical Science in the British Association is, in Scripture phrase, 'very bold,' and declares that if a man, in his mental training, 'has substituted literature and history for natural science, he has chosen the less useful alternative.'

But whether we go these lengths or not, we must all admit that in natural science the habit gained of dealing with facts is a most valuable discipline, and that every one should have some experience of it.

[18] More than this, however, is demanded by the reformers. It is proposed to make the training in natural science the main part of education, for the great majority of mankind at any rate. And here, I confess, I part company with the friends of physical science, with whom up to this point I have been agreeing. In differing from them, however, I wish to proceed with the utmost caution and diffidence. The smallness of my own acquaintance with the disciplines of natural science is ever before my mind, and I am fearful of doing these disciplines an injustice. The ability and pugnacity of the partisans of natural science make them formidable persons to contradict. The tone of tentative inquiry, which befits a being of dim faculties and bounded knowledge, is the tone I would wish to take and not depart from. At present it seems to me, that those who are for giving to natural knowledge, as they call it, the chief place in the education of the majority of mankind, leave one important thing out of their account: the constitution of human nature. But I put this forward on the strength of some facts not at all recondite, very far from it; facts capable of being stated in the simplest possible fashion, and to which, if I so state them, the man of science will, I am sure, be willing to allow their due weight.

[19] Deny the facts altogether, I think, he hardly can. He can hardly deny, that when we set ourselves to enumerate the powers which go to the building up of human life, and say that they are the power of conduct, the power of intellect and knowledge, the power of beauty, and the power of social life and manners,—he can hardly deny that this scheme, though drawn in rough and plain lines enough, and not pretending to scientific exactness, does yet give a fairly true representation of the matter. Human nature is built up by these powers; we have the need for them all. When we have rightly met and adjusted the claims of them all, we shall then be in a fair way for getting soberness and righteousness, with wisdom. This is evident enough, and the friends of physical science would admit it.

[20] But perhaps they may not have sufficiently observed another thing: namely, that the several powers just mentioned are not isolated, but there is, in the generality of mankind, a perpetual tendency to relate them one to another in divers ways. With one such way of relating them I am particularly concerned now. Following our instinct for intellect and knowledge, we acquire pieces of knowledge; and presently, in the generality of men, there arises the desire to relate these pieces of knowledge to our sense for conduct, to our sense for beauty,—and there is weariness and dissatisfaction if the desire is baulked. Now in this desire lies, I think, the strength of that hold which letters have upon us.

[21] All knowledge is, as I said just now, interesting; and even items of knowledge which from the nature of the case cannot well be related, but must stand isolated in our thoughts, have their interest. Even lists of exceptions have their interest. If we are studying Greek accents it is interesting to know that *pais* and *pas,* and some other monosyllables of the same form of declension, do not take the circumflex upon the last syllable of the genitive plural, but vary, in this respect, from the common rule. If we are studying physiology, it is interesting to know that the pulmonary artery carries dark blood and the pulmonary vein carries bright blood, departing in this respect from the common rule for the division of labour between the veins and the arteries. But every one knows how we seek naturally to combine the pieces of our knowledge together, to bring them under general rules, to relate them to principles; and how unsatisfactory and tiresome it would be to go on forever learning lists of exceptions, or accumulating items of fact which must stand isolated.

[22] Well, that same need of relating our knowledge, which operates here within the sphere of our knowledge itself, we shall find operating, also, outside that sphere. We experience, as we go on learning that knowing,—the vast majority of us experience,—the need of relating what we have learnt and known to the sense which we have in us for conduct, to the sense which we have in us for beauty.

[23] A certain Greek prophetess of Mantineia in Arcadia, Diotima by name, once explained to the philosopher Socrates that love, and impulse, and bent of all kinds, is, in fact, nothing else but the

desire in men that good should forever be present to them. This desire for good, Diotima assured Socrates, is our fundamental desire, of which fundamental desire every impulse in us is only some one particular form. And therefore this fundamental desire it is, I suppose,—this desire in men that good should be forever present to them,—which acts in us when we feel the impulse for relating our knowledge to our sense for conduct and to our sense for beauty. At any rate, with men in general the instinct exists. Such is human nature. And the instinct, it will be admitted, is innocent, and human nature is preserved by our following the lead of its innocent instincts. Therefore, in seeking to gratify this instinct in question, we are following the instinct of self-preservation in humanity.

[24] But, no doubt, some kinds of knowledge cannot be made to directly serve the instinct in question, cannot be directly related to the sense for beauty, to the sense for conduct. These are instrument-knowledges; they lead on to other knowledges, which can. A man who passes his life in instrument-knowledges is a specialist. They may be invaluable as instruments to something beyond, for those who have the gift thus to employ them; and they may be disciplines in themselves wherein it is useful for every one to have some schooling. But it is inconceivable that the generality of men should pass all their mental life with Greek accents or with formal logic. My friend Professor Sylvester, who is one of the first mathematicians in the world, holds transcendental doctrines as to the virtue of mathematics, but those doctrines are not for common men. In the very Senate House and heart of our English Cambridge I once ventured, though not without an apology for my profaneness, to hazard the opinion that for the majority of mankind a little of mathematics, even, goes a long way. Of course this is quite consistent with their being of immense importance as an instrument to something else; but it is the few who have the aptitude for thus using them, not the bulk of mankind.

[25] The natural sciences do not, however, stand on the same footing with these instrument-knowledges. Experience shows us that the generality of men will find more interest in learning that, when a taper burns, the wax is converted into carbonic acid and water, or in learning the explanation of the phenomenon of dew, or in

learning how the circulation of the blood is carried on, than they
find in learning that the genitive plural of *pais* and *pas* does not take
the circumflex on the termination. And one piece of natural knowledge is added to another, and others are added to that, and at
last we come to propositions so interesting as Mr. Darwin's
famous proposition that 'our ancestor was a hairy quadruped
furnished with a tail and pointed ears, probably arboreal in his
habits.' Or we come to propositions of such reach and magnitude
as those which Professor Huxley delivers, when he says that the
notions of our forefathers about the beginning and the end of the
world were all wrong, and that nature is the expression of a
definite order with which nothing interferes.

[26] Interesting, indeed, these results of science are, important
they are, and we should all of us be acquainted with them. But
what I now wish you to mark is, that we are still, when they are
propounded to us and we receive them, we are still in the sphere
of intellect and knowledge. And for the generality of men there will
be found, I say, to arise, when they have duly taken in the proposition that their ancestor was 'a hairy quadruped furnished with a
tail and pointed ears, probably arboreal in his habits,' there will
be found to arise an invincible desire to relate this proposition
to the sense in us for conduct, and to the sense in us for beauty.
But this the men of science will not do for us, and will hardly even
profess to do. They will give us other pieces of knowledge, other
facts, about other animals and their ancestors, or about plants, or
about stones, or about stars; and they may finally bring us to those
great 'general conceptions of the universe, which are forced upon
us all,' says Professor Huxley, 'by the progress of physical science.'
But still it will be *knowledge* only which they give us; knowledge
not put for us into relation with our sense for conduct, our sense
for beauty, and touched with emotion by being so put; not thus
put for us, and therefore, to the majority of mankind, after a certain while, unsatisfying, wearying.

[27] Not to the born naturalist, I admit. But what do we mean
by a born naturalist? We mean a man in whom the zeal for
observing nature is so uncommonly strong and eminent, that it
marks him off from the bulk of mankind. Such a man will pass his
life happily in collecting natural knowledge and reasoning upon

it, and will ask for nothing, or hardly anything, more. I have heard it said that the sagacious and admirable naturalist whom we lost not very long ago, Mr. Darwin, once owned to a friend that for his part he did not experience the necessity for two things which most men find so necessary to them,—religion and poetry; science and the domestic affections, he thought, were enough.[4] To a born naturalist, I can well understand that this should seem so. So absorbing in his occupation with nature, so strong his love for his occupation, that he goes on acquiring natural knowledge and reasoning upon it, and has little time or inclination for thinking about getting it related to the desire in man for conduct, the desire in man for beauty. He relates it to them for himself as he goes along, so far as he feels the need; and he draws from the domestic affections all the additional solace necessary. But then Darwins are extremely rare. Another great and admirable master of natural knowledge, Faraday, was a Sandemanian. That is to say, he related his knowledge to his instinct for conduct and to his instinct for beauty, by the aid of that respectable Scottish sectary, Robert Sandeman. And so strong, in general, is the demand of religion and poetry to have their share in a man, to associate themselves with his knowing, and to relieve and rejoice it, that, probably, for one man amongst us with the disposition to do as Darwin did in this respect, there are at least fifty with the disposition to do as Faraday.

[28] Education lays hold upon us, in fact, by satisfying this demand. Professor Huxley holds up to scorn mediæval education, with its neglect of the knowledge of nature, its poverty even of literary studies, its formal logic devoted to 'showing how and why that which the Church said was true must be true.' But the great mediæval Universities were not brought into being, we may be sure, by the zeal for giving a jejune and contemptible education. Kings have been their nursing fathers, and queens have been their nursing mothers, but not for this. The mediæval Universities came into being, because the supposed knowledge, delivered by Scripture and the Church, so deeply engaged men's hearts, by so simply, easily, and powerfully relating itself to their desire for conduct,

---

[4] However, Darwin regretted his inability to enjoy poetry.

their desire for beauty. All other knowledge was dominated by this supposed knowledge and was subordinated to it, because of the surpassing strength of the hold which it gained upon the affections of men, by allying itself profoundly with their sense for conduct, their sense for beauty.

[29] But now, says Professor Huxley, conceptions of the universe fatal to the notions held by our forefathers have been forced upon us by physical science. Grant to him that they are thus fatal, that the new conceptions must and will soon become current everywhere, and that every one will finally perceive them to be fatal to the beliefs of our forefathers. The need of humane letters, as they are truly called, because they serve the paramount desire in men that good should be forever present to them,—the need of humane letters, to establish a relation between the new conceptions, and our instinct for beauty, our instinct for conduct, is only the more visible. The Middle Age could do without humane letters, as it could do without the study of nature, because its supposed knowledge was made to engage its emotions so powerfully. Grant that the supposed knowledge disappears, its power of being made to engage the emotions will of course disappear along with it,—but the emotions themselves, and their claim to be engaged and satisfied, will remain. Now if we find by experience that humane letters have an undeniable power of engaging the emotions, the importance of humane letters in a man's training becomes not less, but greater, in proportion to the success of modern science in extirpating what it calls 'mediæval thinking.'

[30] Have humane letters, then, have poetry and eloquence, the power here attributed to them of engaging the emotions, and do they exercise it? And if they have it and exercise it, *how* do they exercise it, so as to exert an influence upon man's sense for conduct, his sense for beauty? Finally, even if they both can and do exert an influence upon the senses in question, how are they to relate to them the results,—the modern results,—of natural science? All these questions may be asked. First, have poetry and eloquence the power of calling out the emotions? The appeal is to experience. Experience shows that for the vast majority of men, for mankind in general, they have the power. Next, do they ex-

ercise it? They do. But then, *how* do they exercise it so as to affect man's sense for conduct, his sense for beauty? And this is perhaps a case for applying the Preacher's words: 'Though a man labour to seek it out, yet he shall not find it; yea, farther, though a wise man think to know it, yet shall he not be able to find it.' Why should it be one thing, in its effect upon the emotions, to say, 'Patience is a virtue,' and quite another thing, in its effect upon the emotions, to say with Homer,

τλητὸν γὰρ Μοῖραι θυμὸν θέσαν ἀνθρώποισιν—

'for an enduring heart have the destinies appointed to the children of men'? Why should it be one thing, in its effect upon the emotions, to say with the philosopher Spinoza, *Felicitas in ea consistit quod homo suum esse conservare potest*—'Man's happiness consists in his being able to preserve his own essence,' and quite another thing, in its effect upon the emotions, to say with the Gospel, 'What is a man advantaged, if he gain the whole world, and lose himself, forfeit himself?' How does this difference of effect arise? I cannot tell, and I am not much concerned to know; the important thing is that it does arise, and that we can profit by it. But how, finally, are poetry and eloquence to exercise the power of relating the modern results of natural science to man's instinct for conduct, his instinct for beauty? And here again I answer that I do not know *how* they will exercise it, but that they can and will exercise it I am sure. I do not mean that modern philosophical poets and modern philosophical moralists are to come and relate for us, in express terms, the results of modern scientific research to our instinct for conduct, our instinct for beauty. But I mean that we shall find, as a matter of experience, if we know the best that has been thought and uttered in the world, we shall find that the art and poetry and eloquence of men who lived, perhaps, long ago, who had the most limited natural knowledge, who had the most erroneous conceptions about many important matters, we shall find that this art, and poetry, and eloquence, have in fact not only the power of refreshing and delighting us, they have also the power,—such is the strength and worth, in essentials, of their authors' criticism of life,—they have

a fortifying and elevating, and quickening, and suggestive power,
capable of wonderfully helping us to relate the results of modern
science to our need for conduct, our need for beauty. Homer's
conceptions of the physical universe were, I imagine, grotesque;
but really, under the shock of hearing from modern science that
'the world is not subordinated to man's use, and that man is not
the cynosure of things terrestrial,' I could, for my own part, desire
no better comfort than Homer's line which I quoted just now,

$$\tau\lambda\eta\tau\grave{o}\nu\ \gamma\grave{a}\rho\ \text{Μο}\hat{\iota}\rho\alpha\iota\ \theta\upsilon\mu\grave{o}\nu\ \theta\acute{\epsilon}\sigma\alpha\nu\ \grave{a}\nu\theta\rho\acute{\omega}\pi o\iota\sigma\iota\nu—$$

'for an enduring heart have the destinies appointed to the children
of men'!

[31] And the more that men's minds are cleared, the more that
the results of science are frankly accepted, the more that poetry
and eloquence come to be received and studied as what in truth
they really are,—the criticism of life by gifted men, alive and
active with extraordinary power at an unusual number of points;—
so much the more will the value of humane letters, and of art also,
which is an utterance having a like kind of power with theirs,
be felt and acknowledged, and their place in education be secured.

[32] Let us therefore, all of us, avoid indeed as much as possible
any invidious comparison between the merits of humane letters,
as means of education, and the merits of the natural sciences.
But when some President of a Section for Mechanical Science
insists on making the comparison, and tells us that 'he who in his
training has substituted literature and history for natural science
has chosen the less useful alternative,' let us make answer to him
that the student of humane letters only, will, at least, know also
the great general conceptions brought in by modern physical
science; for science, as Professor Huxley says, forces them upon
us all. But the student of the natural sciences only, will, by our
very hypothesis, know nothing of humane letters; not to mention
that in setting himself to be perpetually accumulating natural
knowledge, he sets himself to do what only specialists have in
general the gift for doing genially. And so he will probably be un-
satisfied, or at any rate incomplete, and even more incomplete
than the student of humane letters only.

[33] I once mentioned in a school-report, how a young man in one of our English training colleges having to paraphrase the passage in *Macbeth* beginning,

> Can'st thou not minister to a mind diseased?

turned this line into, 'Can you not wait upon the lunatic?' And I remarked what a curious state of things it would be, if every pupil of our national schools knew, let us say, that the moon is two thousand one hundred and sixty miles in diameter, and thought at the same time that a good paraphrase for

> Can'st thou not minister to a mind diseased?

was, 'Can you not wait upon the lunatic?' If one is driven to choose, I think I would rather have a young person ignorant about the moon's diameter, but aware that 'Can you not wait upon the lunatic?' is bad, than a young person whose education had been such as to manage things the other way.

[34] Or to go higher than the pupils of our national schools. I have in my mind's eye a member of our British Parliament who comes to travel here in America, who afterwards relates his travels, and who shows a really masterly knowledge of the geology of this great country and of its mining capabilities, but who ends by gravely suggesting that the United States should borrow a prince from our Royal Family, and should make him their king, and should create a House of Lords of great landed proprietors after the pattern of ours; and then America, he thinks, would have her future happily and perfectly secured. Surely, in this case, the President of the Section for Mechanical Science would himself hardly say that our member of Parliament, by concentrating himself upon geology and mineralogy, and so on, and not attending to literature and history, had 'chosen the more useful alternative.'

[35] If then there is to be separation and option between humane letters on the one hand, and the natural sciences on the other, the great majority of mankind, all who have not exceptional and overpowering aptitudes for the study of nature, would do well, I cannot but think, to choose to be educated in humane letters rather than in the natural sciences. Letters will call out their being at more points, will make them live more.

[36] I said that before I ended I would just touch on the question of classical education, and I will keep my word. Even if literature is to retain a large place in our education, yet Latin and Greek, say the friends of progress, will certainly have to go. Greek is the grand offender in the eyes of these gentlemen. The attackers of the established course of study think that against Greek, at any rate, they have irresistible arguments. Literature may perhaps be needed in education, they say; but why on earth should it be Greek literature? Why not French or German? Nay, 'has not an Englishman models in his own literature of every kind of excellence?' As before, it is not on any weak pleadings of my own that I rely for convincing the gainsayers; it is on the constitution of human nature itself, and on the instinct of self-preservation in humanity. The instinct for beauty is set in human nature, as surely as the instinct for knowledge is set there, or the instinct for conduct. If the instinct for beauty is served by Greek literature and art as it is served by no other literature and art, we may trust to the instinct of self-preservation in humanity for keeping Greek as part of our culture. We may trust to it for even making the study of Greek more prevalent than it is now. Greek will come, I hope, some day to be studied more rationally than at present; but it will be increasingly studied as men increasingly feel the need in them for beauty, and how powerfully Greek art and Greek literature can serve this need. Women will again study Greek, as Lady Jane Grey did; I believe that in that chain of forts, with which the fair host of the Amazons are now engirdling our English universities, I find that here in America, in colleges like Smith College in Massachusetts, and Vassar College in the State of New York, and in the happy families of the mixed universities out West, they are studying it already.

[37] *Defuit una mihi symmetria prisca,*—'The antique symmetry was the one thing wanting to me,' said Leonardo da Vinci; and he was an Italian. I will not presume to speak for the Americans, but I am sure that, in the Englishman, the want of this admirable symmetry of the Greeks is a thousand times more great and crying than in any Italian. The results of the want show themselves most glaringly, perhaps, in our architecture, but they show themselves, also, in all our art. *Fit details strictly combined, in view of a*

large general result nobly conceived; that is just the beautiful *symmetria prisca* of the Greeks, and it is just where we English fail, where all our art fails. Striking ideas we have, and well executed details we have; but that high symmetry which, with satisfying and delightful effect, combines them, we seldom or never have. The glorious beauty of the Acropolis at Athens did not come from single fine things stuck about on that hill, a statue here, a gateway there;—no, it arose from all things being perfectly combined for a supreme total effect. What must not an Englishman feel about our deficiencies in this respect, as the sense for beauty, whereof this symmetry is an essential element, awakens and strengthens within him! what will not one day be his respect and desire for Greece and its *symmetria prisca,* when the scales drop from his eyes as he walks the London streets, and he sees such a lesson in meanness, as the Strand, for instance, in its true deformity! But here we are coming to our friend Mr. Ruskin's province, and I will not intrude upon it, for he is its very sufficient guardian.

[38] And so we at last find, it seems, we find flowing in favour of the humanities the natural and necessary stream of things, which seemed against them when we started. The 'hairy quadruped furnished with a tail and pointed ears, probably arboreal in his habits,' this good fellow carried hidden in his nature, apparently, something destined to develop into a necessity for humane letters. Nay, more; we seem finally to be even led to the further conclusion that our hairy ancestor carried in his nature, also, a necessity for Greek.

[39] And, therefore, to say the truth, I cannot really think that humane letters are in much actual danger of being thrust out from their leading place in education, in spite of the array of authorities against them at this moment. So long as human nature is what it is, their attractions will remain irresistible. As with Greek, so with letters generally: they will some day come, we may hope, to be studied more rationally, but they will not lose their place. What will happen will rather be that there will be crowded into education other matters besides, far too many; there will be, perhaps, a period of unsettlement and confusion and false tendency; but letters will not in the end lose their leading place. If they lose it for a time, they will get it back again. We shall be brought back to

them by our wants and aspirations. And a poor humanist may possess his soul in patience, neither strive nor cry, admit the energy and brilliancy of the partisans of physical science, and their present favour with the public, to be far greater than his own, and still have a happy faith that the nature of things works silently on behalf of the studies which he loves, and that, while we shall all have to acquaint ourselves with the great results reached by modern science, and to give ourselves as much training in its disciplines as we can conveniently carry, yet the majority of men will always require humane letters; and so much the more, as they have the more and the greater results of science to relate to the need in man for conduct, and to the need in him for beauty.

EXERCISES

1. Why is the discussion of Plato appropriate to the introduction?
2. Exactly what is the issue with which Arnold is dealing?
3. What is Arnold's purpose in paragraphs 8–16?
4. Give a definition of humanism, in your own words, from Arnold's discussion of it.
5. What is Arnold's notion of the value of letters?
6. Explain in very specific terms what Arnold probably means by the terms "sense for conduct" and "sense for beauty."
7. Is he question-begging in paragraph 30?
8. On what conception of man does he base his contention that humane letters are necessary?
9. Do you believe that he is probably right?
10. Do you think that he has presented a convincing and moving case? Base your judgment on both content and style.
11. What are the prominent features of his style—both strengths and weaknesses?
12. Compare Arnold's address with Huxley's (pages 124–131). Which is more effective, and why?

The Value of History

GEORGE M. TREVELYAN

[1] What, then, are the various ways in which history can educate the mind?

[2] The first, or at least the most generally acknowledged educational effect of history, is to train the mind of the citizen into a state in which he is capable of taking a just view of political problems. But, even in this capacity, history cannot prophesy the future; it cannot supply a set of invariably applicable laws for the guidance of politicians; it cannot show, by the deductions of historical analogy, which side is in the right in any quarrel of our own day. It can do a thing less, and yet greater than all these. It can mould the mind itself into the capability of understanding great affairs and sympathising with other men. The information given by history is valueless in itself, unless it produce a new state of mind. The value of Lecky's Irish history did not consist in the fact that he recorded in a book the details of numerous massacres and murders, but that he produced sympathy and shame, and caused a better understanding among us all of how the sins of the fathers are often visited upon the children, unto the third and fourth generations of them that hate each other. He does not prove that Home Rule is right or wrong, but he trains the mind of Unionists and Home Rulers to think sensibly about that and other problems.

[3] For it is in this political function of history that the study of cause and effect is of some real use. Though such a study can be neither scientific nor exact, common sense sometimes points to an obvious causal connection. Thus it was supposed, even before the invention of scientific history, that Alva's policy was in some causal connection with the revolt of the Netherlands, that Brunswick's manifesto had something to do with the September

From "Clio, a Muse," in *Clio, a Muse and Other Essays Literary and Pedestrian* by George Macaulay Trevelyan. Reprinted by permission of Longmans, Green & Co., Inc.

Massacres, and the September Massacres with the spread of reaction. Such suggestions of cause and effect in the past help to
teach political wisdom. When a man of the world reads history,
he is called on to form a judgment on a social or political problem, without previous bias, and with some knowledge of the final
protracted result of what was done. The exercise of his mind
under such unwonted conditions, sends him back to the still unsettled problems of modern politics and society, with larger views,
clearer head and better temper. The study of past controversies,
of which the final outcome is known, destroys the spirit of prejudice. It brings home to the mind the evils that are likely to spring
from violent policy, based on want of understanding of opponents.
When a man has studied the history of the Democrats and Aristo-
crats of Corcyra, of the English and Irish, of the Jacobins and
anti-Jacobins, his political views may remain the same, but his
political temper and his way of thinking about politics may have
improved, if he is capable of receiving an impression.

[4] And so, too, in a larger sphere than politics, a review of
the process of historical evolution teaches a man to see his own
age, with its peculiar ideals and interests, in proper perspective
as one among other ages. If he can learn to understand that other
ages had not only a different social and economic structure but
correspondingly different ideals and interests from those of his
own age, his mind will have veritably enlarged. I have hopes that
ere long the Workers' Educational Association will have taught
its historical students not to ask, "What was Shakespeare's attitude
to Democracy?" and to perceive that the question no more admits of an answer than the inquiry, "What was Dante's attitude to
Protestantism?" or, "What was Archimedes' attitude to the steam-
engine?"

[5] The study of cause and effect is by no means the only, and
perhaps not the principal means, of broadening the mind. History does most to cure a man of political prejudice, when it enables him, by reading about men or movements in the past, to
understand points of view which he never saw before, and to
respect ideals which he had formerly despised. Gardiner's *History
of the Civil War* has done much to explain Englishmen to each
other, by revealing the rich variety of our national life, far nobler

than the unity of similitude. Forms of idealism, considerations of policy and wisdom, are acceptable or at least comprehensible, when presented by the historian to minds which would reject them if they came from the political opponent or the professed sage.

[6] But history should not only remove prejudice, it should breed enthusiasm. To many it is an important source of the ideas that inspire their lives. With the exception of a few creative minds, men are too weak to fly by their own unaided imagination beyond the circle of ideas that govern the world in which they are placed. And since the ideals of no one epoch can in themselves be suffi-cient as an interpretation of life, it is fortunate that the student of the past can draw upon the purest springs of ancient thought and feeling. Men will join in associations to propagate the old-new idea, and to recast society again in the ancient mould, as when the study of Plutarch and the ancient historians rekindled the breath of liberty and of civic virtue in modern Europe; as when in our own day men attempt to revive mediæval ideals of religious or of corporate life, or to rise to the Greek standard of the individual. We may like or dislike such revivals, but at least they bear witness to the potency of history as something quite other than a science. And outside the circle of these larger influ-ences, history supplies us each with private ideals, only too varied and too numerous for complete realisation. One may aspire to the best characteristics of a man of Athens or a citizen of Rome; a Churchman of the twelfth century, or a Reformer of the six-teenth; a Cavalier of the old school, or a Puritan of the Inde-pendent party; a Radical of the time of Castlereagh, or a public servant of the time of Peel. Still more are individual great men the model and inspiration of the smaller. It is difficult to appropri-ate the essential qualities of these old people under new condi-tions; but whatever we study with strong loving conception, and admire as a thing good in itself and not merely good for its pur-pose or its age, we do in some measure absorb.

[7] This presentation of ideals and heroes from other ages is perhaps the most important among the educative functions of history. For this purpose, even more than for the purpose of teaching political wisdom, it is requisite that the events should be both written and read with intellectual passion. Truth itself

will be the gainer, for those by whom history was enacted were in their day passionate.

[8] Another educative function of history is to enable the reader to comprehend the historical aspect of literature proper. Literature can no doubt be enjoyed in its highest aspects even if the reader is ignorant of history. But on those terms it cannot be enjoyed completely, and much of it cannot be enjoyed at all. For much of literature is allusion, either definite or implied. And the allusions, even of the Victorian age, are by this time historical. For example, the last half dozen stanzas of Browning's *Old Pictures in Florence,* the fifth stanza of his *Lovers' Quarrel,* and half his wife's best poems are already meaningless unless we know something of the continental history of that day. Political authors like Burke, Sydney Smith, and Courier, the prose of Milton, one-half of Swift, the best of Dryden, and the best of Byron (his satires and letters) are enjoyed *ceteris paribus,* in exact proportion to the amount we know of the history of their times. And since allusions to classical history and mythology, and even to the Bible, are no longer, as they used to be, familiar ground for all educated readers, there is all the more reason, in the interest of literature, why allusions to modern history should be generally understood. History and literature cannot be fully comprehended, still less fully enjoyed, except in connection with one another. I confess I have little love either for "Histories of Literature," or for chapters on "the literature of the period," hanging at the end of history books like the tail from a cow. I mean, rather, that those who write or read the history of a period should be soaked in its literature, and that those who read or expound literature should be soaked in history. The "scientific" view of history that discouraged such interchange and desired the strictest specialisation by political historians, has done much harm to our latter-day culture. The mid-Victorians at any rate knew better than that.

[9] The substitution of a pseudo-scientific for a literary atmosphere in historical circles, has not only done much to divorce history from the outside public, but has diminished its humanising power over its own devotees in school and university. Not a few university teachers are already conscious of this and are trying to remedy it, having seen that historical "science" for the under-

graduate means the text-book, that is, the "crammer" in print. At one university as I know, and at others I dare say, literature already plays a greater part in historical teaching and reading than it played some years ago. Historical students are now encouraged to read the "literary" historians of old, who were recently *taboo*, and still more to read the contemporary literature of periods studied. But for all that, there is much leeway to be made up.

[10] The value and pleasure of travel, whether at home or abroad, is doubled by a knowledge of history. For places, like books, have an interest or a beauty of association, as well as an absolute or æsthetic beauty. The garden front of St. John's, Oxford, is beautiful to every one; but, for the lover of history, its outward charm is blent with the intimate feelings of his own mind, with images of that same College as it was during the Great Civil War. Given over to the use of a Court whose days of royalty were numbered, its walks and quadrangles were filled, as the end came near, with men and women learning to accept sorrow as their lot through life, the ambitious abandoning hope of power, the wealthy hardening themselves to embrace poverty, those who loved England preparing to sail for foreign shores, and lovers to be parted forever. There they strolled through the garden, as the hopeless evenings fell, listening, at the end of all, while the siege-guns broke the silence with ominous iteration. Behind the cannon on those low hills to northward were ranked the inexorable men who came to lay their hands on all this beauty, hoping to change it to strength and sterner virtue. And this was the curse of the victors, not to die, but to live, and almost to lose their awful faith in God, when they saw the Restoration, not of the old gaiety that was too gay for them and the old loyalty that was too loyal for them, but of corruption and selfishness that had neither country nor king. The sound of the Roundhead cannon has long ago died away, but still the silence of the garden is heavy with unalterable fate, brooding over besiegers and besieged, in such haste to destroy each other and permit only the vile to survive. St. John's College is not mere stone and mortar, tastefully compiled, but an appropriate and mournful witness between those who see it now and those by whom it once was seen. And so it is, for the reader of history, with every ruined castle and ancient church throughout the wide, mysterious lands of Europe.

EXERCISES

1. Tell why this selection would be called an essay.
2. How is the factual content used?
3. What are the values of history, according to Trevelyan?
4. Do any of these values seem to be of a sort which Newman would call mere acquired facts, or do they all seem to be what he would call true learning?
5. By what means are the main ideas emphasized? Study the methods of emphasis especially in paragraph 2.
6. Would history, considered as Trevelyan presents it, be what Plato considers one of those studies which results in a man's "getting soberness, righteousness, and wisdom" (quoted by Arnold, paragraph 5)?
7. Analyze the style of the last paragraph as to rhythm and other elements of sound, diction, and figurative language.
8. Which is the better stylist, Arnold or Trevelyan? Justify your preference.

Liberal Education

NORMAN FOERSTER

[1] An education inspired by the humanistic ideal will be a liberal education. It alone is fully worthy of the dignity of man. Its object is clear: to liberate the young from ignorance, prejudice, foolishness, and the like; to aid them to attain freedom through realization of their capacities as men and women. An education aiming at something less than the human is in so far barbarous, for example the slavish education of the totalitarian state, or a vocational education which degrades men to tools. To be sure, men must have vocations, and therefore preparation ranging from a few weeks or months to a term of years, according to the calling

From *The Humanities and the Common Man*. Reprinted by permission of the University of North Carolina Press.

selected, but such preparation, whether narrowly or broadly conceived, is not what we mean by liberal education.

[2] When liberal education arose in ancient Greece, it was the discipline of free men—the unfree learned the vocations. Today the division is not between classes but within the individual. To make a living he works forty hours a week, more or less; to live he has all the rest, to live freely, as he chooses. Only a relatively few men can have vocations that exercise their full humanity. The vast majority can feel free only in their free time, and they want more and more free time. Whatever the value of their vocational work to themselves and to the state, the value of their free time is even greater both to themselves and to the state as well. For the state needs citizens even more than it needs shopkeepers, carpenters, bankers, lawyers, needs men who are more than instruments in the work of the world, who experience life in many ways, develop many interests, play a role in the formation of that public opinion which is the real government of the democratic state, and attain a morale high enough to sustain the state in peace and war. The most civilized state will, if resources and manpower are equal, be the strongest, happiest, and most memorable.

[3] From the point of view of the American state, therefore, the function of liberal education, as President Roosevelt said at Jefferson's alma mater, is that of 'training men for citizenship in a great republic.' 'This,' he went on to say, 'was in the spirit of the old America, and it is, I believe, in the spirit of the America of today. The necessities of our time demand that men avoid being set in grooves, that they avoid the occupational predestination of the older world . . . Every form of cooperative human endeavor cries out for men and women who, in their thinking processes, will know something of the broader aspects of any given problem.' Clearly, the states of the Union cannot afford, in their public universities, the multiplication of occupational curricula that offer what Edmund Burke somewhere calls 'tricking short-cuts and little fallacious facilities.' Even in the professions liberal training is gravely hindered by the motivation of the student, who, as another of our presidents—Woodrow Wilson—put it, 'will be immersed in the things that touch his profit and loss, and a man is not free to think inside that territory.'

[4] Liberal education is one thing and vocational education another, and no amount of sophistry about liberal education 'in a new sense of the term' will alter the fact. That they differ in principle has been recognized from ancient times to the present. As they were apart in ancient Greece, so they were in the Middle Ages, when an education in the seven liberal arts was prescribed for every student before he turned to his professional preparation. They were apart again in the Renaissance. In the Mantuan school of Vittorino, for instance, which merits a few words here because it blended so well the classical and Christian traditions, the aim, as stated by W. H. Woodward, was 'to lay foundations in liberal culture to serve as the necessary preliminaries to specific training for careers.' As a humanist educator, Vittorino da Feltre sought to create 'the complete citizen,' or, to say the same thing another way, 'to secure the harmonious development of mind, body, and character.' The curriculum was limited by the meagre scientific knowledge then available, but it supplemented the humanities with mathematics and some natural science (astrology was discarded for astronomy). Ancient culture was not pursued in abstraction but focused earnestly on the needs of the present. As for individual differences, Vittorino considered, 'almost with reverence, the tastes and bent of each of his pupils.' Before going on to professional study his pupils stayed with him 'until they had passed their twenty-first year.' On the whole, his school might well serve as a fruitful source of suggestion for the liberal college in modern America, as it has served for secondary education in modern Europe. Our high schools accomplish something in liberal education and could accomplish more, but under our system it is the responsibility of the college to complete the program, postponing occupational training till it *has* been completed—if necessary till the student has passed his twenty-first year.

[5] But the beguiling hope persists: Could not liberal education be attempted *through* vocational education? Many persons, like John Dewey in his article in *Fortune* in 1944, have argued that liberal education as we have known it from ancient till recent times is a relic of the pre-democratic and pre-scientific past, and that today the appropriate education must be technical and vocational. It is frankly admitted that our job-centered training has

been too narrow and mechanical. So we should set about 'liberalizing our technical and vocational education.' How this is to be done has not been made very clear. One might suppose, to take a concrete example, that a course in Advanced Clothing would be so taught as to lead the student back to earlier conceptions of costume, eventually to Greek costume and hence to Greek art and hence to the whole Greek view of life, perhaps attracting the student to an elective in ancient civilization which he would 'feed into' his vocational preparation. But this is not what Dr. Dewey means. His great object is to make the student modern, that is, scientific. The past, lingering in our conceptions and standards, is only a clog that prevents our going forward with undivided zeal toward 'the scientific way of life.' Vocational education must be liberalized by showing how modern industry rests on scientific processes. What this would seem to mean, in our course on Advanced Clothing, is that the student would be brought to 'awareness of the scientific processes embodied' in designing, constructing, and preserving clothing and in relating contemporary clothing to contemporary social forces. Whatever it means the net result might be the improvement of vocational education but could not be the improvement of liberal education.

[6] If liberal education is not concerned with vocational skills, it is profoundly concerned with other skills and abilities. There are many things which the student, as a human being, should be able to do. He should be able to care for his body, his physical welfare. He should be able to speak, to read, to write, on a plane suited to his college years and later life. He should know how to think: how to think in the concrete terms of science, how to think in the abstract manner of mathematics and philosophy, and how to think (and feel and will) in the humanistic realm of value-judgments. He should be able to relate his growing abilities and knowledge in the gradual development of a philosophy of life to which he is willing provisionally to commit himself. He should be able to relate his developing philosophy to active experience in living, to complete the revolving circle of thought and action. Through the discipline of his entire nature he will come into ever fuller possession of himself as a human being and as a particular person.

[7] Something like this set of skills and abilities is agreed upon by virtually all who profess belief in liberal education. The list may never be altogether the same, and differences in emphasis will appear, but on the whole the objectives are sufficiently agreed upon. There is a fundamental cleavage, however, between those who assert that liberal education is concerned only with abilities and those who assert that it involves both abilities and knowledge.

[8] The tendency has been especially marked among educationists to limit the objectives to abilities, using knowledge only as means. What sort of person, they ask, do we want the student to be when we are through with him? What do we want to have happen to him in consequence of his education? Once we have decided upon the end-product, it will be easy to plan a curriculum and hire and fire teachers according to their success in changing the student as we want him changed. The student is to be conditioned, the teacher is to be approved or purged. This totalitarian parody of liberal education—I have stated it crudely because I have heard it stated crudely—shows some signs of becoming a menace in a society floundering for lack of assured values. America today has more reason than England had in 1935 to heed the warning then sounded by John Murray, principal of University College, Exeter. 'Any dictator,' he cried, 'might see his chance in the present state of the universities that have sold themselves to utility. If the universities have lost their humanism, or the prophetic and magisterial tones in preaching it, need a dictator hesitate? From him that hath not shall be taken away even that which he hath.'

[9] Protection against this perversion is offered by those who assert that liberal education involves not only abilities but common knowledge, common knowledge not of anything at random but of the liberating best that man has said and done. Even if the goal were allowed to be abilities alone, it could be attained most effectively by the use of the best materials. After all is anyone so crass as to maintain that the history of Peru would do as well as the history of modern Europe, the literature of the Philippines as well as the literature of England, an African dialect as well as French, the science of numismatics as well as the science of biology? The knowledge to be learned may obviously be more or less relevant. Is there, then, a most relevant knowledge? Is

there an indispensable best? If so, who shall say what it is? At this point the specialist professor will break down in utter helplessness. But even he, if he could drop his pose or his politics, would quickly begin a list of essentials, or of things so important that they might as well be called essentials. There is a large area of general agreement as to the best that man has said and done, large enough for the planning of a curriculum. This best will guard the student against conditioning to the intellectual fashions and veering passions of the day, fashions and passions to which the faculty itself is not immune. He will have at hand a standard by which to measure the instruction he is receiving. Even if the knowledge opened to him is not necessarily the best, it will have high value as common knowledge, shared knowledge, tending to unite his and other students' minds in common experience, common duties, common memories. Liberal education based on common knowledge is social education; vocational education separating youth into groups according to special interests is unsocial education.

[10] When a common fund of knowledge has been selected, the liberal college will begin to take on a definiteness of type comparable to that of the professional schools. Once this definiteness of type has been fully established in terms of objectives, curriculum and teaching methods, the uniform requirement of specific knowledge will seem no more arbitrary than it does today in training for the professions. If something like half of the total Bachelor's program is made common, the other half will be available for election among advanced liberal studies, or for concentration upon a segment of the field of learning, to be chosen according to individual differences in interest and ability and to be studied in the same liberal manner.

The Great Curriculum

[11] What should the common studies be? In a humanistic reorientation, it goes without saying, the humanities will take on a new importance. But can we be satisfied with the thesis of President Conant that a general education must be based on literature, the arts, and philosophy, even if we add history, which he has elsewhere predicted will be the most widely required study in

the next fifty years? All these are humanities; is the humanistic spirit content to ignore science? The answer must be clear and unequivocal.

[12] Historically, the answer is plain: an education permeated with the humanistic spirit has always included science. In ancient Greece, science—mathematics, astronomy, some natural history—was a part of liberal education. In the Renaissance, in the school of Vittorino, for example, it was likewise included. That science was sometimes disparaged by the humanists of the Renaissance is not surprising, in view of the scant knowledge of nature then existing. Science was little more than a promise or a hope, while the humanities had attained a dazzling achievement as far back as the fifth century B. C., indeed still earlier in the greatest of all poets, Homer. By the late nineteenth century this contrast had disappeared: science had arrived, it too had attained a dazzling achievement, and it claimed and won its place in education. If the zeal of its opponents was occasionally excessive, so was the zeal of its proponents. One must regret the mutual hostility of the two sides that attended the arrival of science in education and that lingers with us to this day, because it was not and is not justified.

[13] The hostility is the result of mistaken attitudes. On the one side, scientists have often depreciated the humanities as not concerned with knowledge, on the assumption that there is only one kind of knowledge, scientific knowledge. They have believed that science is competent, and alone competent, to deal securely and fruitfully with everything natural and human. All fields of knowledge should be freed of unvalidated guesses, armchair philosophizing, the drag of superstition, and be duly scientized. 'What knowledge is of most worth?' 'The answer is always—Science.' This attitude, as I have already suggested, comes not from science but from philosophy, the philosophy of naturalism. On the other side: humanists have often depreciated the sciences as materialistic, as if they were responsible for the sordid world of the machine, of big business and little living, a world in which things are in the saddle and ride mankind. When this has been their attitude, humanists have forgotten that the source of what they term materialism is, as Michael Pupin rightly declared, not in 'any material

structure raised by the genius of man,' but 'in the deepest depths of the human soul where selfishness and greed, hatred and fear' have displaced 'beauty and goodness.' The evil from which we suffer lies in the realm of the humanities. It was not caused by scientists and engineers and will never be destroyed by them.

[14] Between a naturalistic philosophy reducing man wholly to the flux of nature and a humanistic philosophy emphasizing his distinctive humanity the conflict is real and, in the end, irreconcilable. But between science and the humanities there can be no real conflict whatever. That men in these two broad domains can come together in mutual respect was indicated, for instance, a number of years ago in a public statement. Fifteen distinguished American scientists (including such names as Walcott, Osborn, Conklin, Pupin, Mayo, Millikan) issued a joint statement with a similar group of religious leaders and men of affairs, regretting the antagonism between men in the domains of science and the humanities, specifically religion. They declared: *'The purpose of science is to develop, without prejudice or preconception of any kind, a knowledge of the facts, the laws, and the processes of nature. The even more important task of religion, on the other hand, is to develop the consciences, the ideals, and the aspirations of mankind.'* The province of the one is natural knowledge; the province of the other is human values. So long as each stays within its bounds there can be no conflict. They are complementary, and should be cooperative. We need to know *what is,* we need to know *what ought to be,* and we need to know how they may be related.

[15] To say that science is concerned with judgments of fact and not with judgments of value is not, however, to deny that implications of value enter into science. It is precisely because of the value implications of science that the humanistic spirit wholeheartedly supports science. The human values implied and presupposed by science are twofold.

[16] First, it is animated by the passion to know, the quest of knowledge for its own sake. There is no science save as men produce it, and men produce it because they value it as men. Among the 'aspirations of mankind' mentioned above, we must assign a high place to the desire for knowledge, including knowl-

edge of nature—the physical and biological constitution and environment of our species. To this aspiration science owes its existence, as Dr. Einstein reminds us in a passage I have quoted. To this aspiration science also owes its capacity to survive. Whenever the aspiration for truth for its own sake declines, science also declines. This happened, for instance, when a Nazi leadership sought to evoke the miracle of a 'German science.' American men of science were revolted by this perversion not as scientists (science revolts at nothing) but as humanists. The humanistic spirit has, as one of its first and finest attributes, a passion for the disinterested, impartial pursuit of truth. In the process of education it is communicated with difficulty, and demands time and hard work. Yet innumerable college graduates can say of some scientist what one of them, for example, said of his beloved teacher of zoology, Henry V. Wilson, who 'first revealed to my hazy young mind the fact that there was a vast field of knowledge where Truth, within certain recognizable limits, was not a matter of opinion, nor of taste, nor a recollection of historical facts, but a thing of demonstrable law . . . He is the embodiment of the scientific spirit which seeks Truth always, without prejudices, without preconceptions, not caring where the search leads but careful always that in the utmost detail the distinction be preserved between that which is known and that which is supposed.' Now, this distinction is one which is nowhere so impressively communicated as in the sciences of nature, which consequently merit an important place in liberal education.

[17] Secondly, science is animated by the desire for use. Knowledge is not only an end in itself, but a means to further ends. As Francis Bacon taught, knowledge is power, and may be aimed at 'the relief of man's estate,' 'inventions that may in some degree subdue and overcome the necessities and miseries of humanity' and also, we may add, contribute to man's chances of happiness. Science is thus instrumental in the achieving of values already defined by the humanistic spirit. For a hundred years the instrumental service of science has tended to obscure its intrinsic value, so that T. H. Huxley complained, as long ago as 1866, that science had been degraded to 'a sort of comfort-grinding machine.' On the intellectual plane the same tendency has led to a whole philosophy

of instrumentalism, associated with the name of John Dewey. The motivation of this philosophy is human purpose, action, advantage, working experimentally in the overcoming of difficulties, and by a strange inversion truth itself is conceived as serviceability. This conclusion is not acceptable to the disinterested pursuit of truth which we call science. As W. T. Stace has said, 'The ideal of the scientific mind has been, throughout the history of the west from Greek times to the present day, not to appraise theories by their capacity for helping human beings, but by their correspondence with the facts of the objective world. Of course science has sought, among other things, to discover truths which shall be of service to men. But it is a monstrous perversion to suggest that the quality of being serviceable to men is what, in the opinion of science, has rendered its discoveries true.'

[18] The humanistic spirit, believing in the pursuit of truth as an end in itself, believing also in the use of truth as a means to further ends, must hereafter give unstinted support to the great sciences of nature set in motion by the Hellenic mind and accelerated enormously by our own age. What is to be said of the so-called sciences of man?

[19] The social sciences are relatively new and undeveloped subjects. With the exception of political science, heir of a political philosophy already mature as far back as Plato and Aristotle, the sciences of man in society came into being only a century or two ago—economics in the eighteenth century, anthropology, sociology, and social psychology in the late nineteenth century. As a distinct group or academic division comparable to the natural sciences and the humanities, they date from the present century. They owe their existence, in the form in which we have them, mainly to a belief that the objectives and methods of the triumphant natural sciences should next be applied to the study of human society. In the words of a committee report, 'in social science, as in other sciences, an attempt is made to describe, rather than to evaluate, the subject matter. The goal is to understand the social order, to discover important concrete facts, and to find regularities that may be assumed to obtain beyond the cases observed and described.' A social scientist, emulating the impartiality of the natural scientist, is not in a position to choose, for

example, between democracy and fascism, either in his studies or
in his teaching. He is permitted no preferences, no fixed standards,
no absolute values. 'As a scientist,' says Robert M. MacIver, 'he
must be content with his world of relative values. Whatever his
own convictions may be, he must be constantly alert not to impose
them on the changeful order of things.'

[20] The impulse is admirable, but the results have been disap-
pointing, and the suspicion is growing that methods and concepts
drawn from natural science will not suffice for social science. The
'wavering and incalculable behavior' of man, in the phrase of
F. W. Taussig, suggests the enormous difficulty of a true science
of man. The concept of cause and effect, as it appears in natural
science, seems not to carry over to social science. Unlike other
animate beings man is purposive, with a will that seems like the
wind's will of the poet. Besides, while social behavior may be observed with a good deal of precision, the attempt to generalize
the facts in the form of hypotheses cannot lead to positive results
because the scientific method of controlled experiment and verification is not available. The result is a prevailing haziness and
sense of frustration. 'Twenty years hence,' said Torrens in regard
to political economy, 'there will scarcely exist a doubt respecting
any of its fundamental principles.' Twenty years passed, one
hundred and twenty years passed, and today the air is filled with
more doubts than ever. Perhaps the best summary of the struggle
of the social sciences to find themselves is that of Roscoe Pound,
who begins by saying that he has no quarrel with them, having
taught jurisprudence for forty years from the sociological standpoint. 'But I do not deceive myself,' he says, 'as to those so-called
sciences. So far as they are not descriptive, they are in continual
flux. In the nature of things they cannot be sciences in the sense
of physics or chemistry or astronomy. They have been organized
as philosophies, have been worked out on the lines of geometry,
have been remade to theories of history, have had their period
of positivism, have turned to social psychology, and are now in
an era of neo-Kantian methodology in some hands and of economic determinism or psychological realism or relativist skepti-
cism or phenomenonological intuitionism in other hands. They do
not impart wisdom; they need to be approached with acquired

wisdom . . . They are not foundation subjects. They belong in the superstructure.'

[21] How the social sciences are eventually to find themselves and to establish themselves as an essential part of liberal education, I shall not venture to suggest. One thing, however, seems very clear. They will have to derive their methodology from their own subject matter, rather than from the natural sciences. Since their subject matter is man, they may be expected to draw closer to the humanities. Even the 'dismal science' of economics—dismal in its vicious circle of 'producing wealth to produce more wealth'—is capable of taking on a profound human relevance in the hands of a man like John Ruskin, who does not look so foolish as he did in the good old days of classical political economy. A university professor wrote to me: 'We economists too often stress some mechanical adjustment of prices or production when the real need is men of character and insight who can direct and enlighten us.' Is there any reason why economists should not themselves be men of character and insight? In point of fact, the researches of our social scientists are largely directed by concepts of human values, despite professions of innocence. But the values are casually assumed, derived from the climate of opinion rather than earned by study and hard reflection. The social scientist of the future, one may venture to predict, will be obliged to bring his subject into more fruitful relation with the humanities, perhaps even to restore it to its humane matrix.

[22] The curriculum of foundation studies, then, will be drawn mainly from the natural sciences and the humanities: the physical and the biological sciences, history, literature, art, and philosophy. It will offer, not hasty encyclopedic surveys of these fields, but a rich and intimate knowledge and experience of the best that man has learned and said and done in them. It will address the student, not as a future technician and specialist, but as a human being interested in understanding himself and his world. In this new task it cannot be expected to succeed until scholars in each subject have reconceived their aims and methods in the manner proposed, for one subject, by a recent collaborative book on *Literary Scholarship: Its Aims and Methods*. Only then will it be possible for us

to undertake profitably the search for the concrete program of subjects and courses which will constitute the modern Great Curriculum equal in solidity and authority to the great curricula of past ages.

[23] Reform within the subjects, if it has not advanced far, has at least begun. While it continues, we may welcome serious reflection upon the more general problem, as in the article by William C. DeVane on 'American Education After the War,' the book entitled *Liberal Education Re-Examined* by a committee appointed by the American Council of Learned Societies, and the book on *The Rebirth of Liberal Education* written by Fred B. Millett for the Rockefeller Foundation. We may welcome the ferment of curricular thought working everywhere today in our colleges and universities even though so much of it seems only frivolously modish and leads only to a meaningless tinkering dictated by political motives. Yet there is a danger that our preoccupation with curricula and organization and teaching procedures, in a word with machinery, will obscure the real problem. That problem, as I have tried to show, is the spirit and aim of the men who do the teaching, the faculty's philosophy of life and of education, which should give direction to all the practical decisions that must be made. A naturalistic philosophy has led the modern world, in totalitarian and democratic nations alike, toward a materialistic chaos and a resurgence of barbarism. An age of science has become an age of the misuse of science. Whether the forces of darkness will be halted no man can say. But this one can affirm: that if America is to play a high and civilizing role in the rest of the twentieth century, it will need a humanistic philosophy of life based on the concept of the dignity of man, and a humanistic philosophy of education that will supply our democratic society with men and women of intelligence and character.

EXERCISES

1. What, according to Foerster, is the object of a liberal education?
2. Distinguish between the civic values and the personal values of a liberal education.

3. What is Foerster's attitude toward the natural sciences?
4. What is his attitude toward individual scientists who propose to base the student's entire education on science?
5. What is his attitude toward the social sciences?
6. How are these attitudes manifested?
7. Compare the styles of Foerster and Trevelyan as to their degree of artistry, especially conscious manipulation of sentence movement and rhythm, figurative language, and connotative diction.
8. Which writer is simply analyzing his subject, and which is analyzing his subject and also trying to win favor for it?
9. Does this difference of purpose help to account for the difference of styles?
10. Would history, taught according to the values given by Trevelyan, fulfill the object of a liberal education as Foerster defines it in paragraph 1?
11. Ernie Pyle's "Break-Through" (pages 30–33) may be taken as literature, and George W. Gray's "The Great Ravelled Knot" (pages 27–29) may be taken as a report of the results of scientific investigation, although it is a somewhat sophisticated report. Study both pieces in the light of the essays by Newman, Arnold, and Foerster. Then write an essay in which you state your own conclusions about the nature of literature and science, the objectives of each, the objectives of a liberal education, and the contributions which both literature and science can make. Use "Break-Through" and "The Great Ravelled Knot" to illustrate your essay, showing what literature can do that science cannot possibly do, and vice versa.

Section E: Human Values

The pieces in Section E are all, like those in Section D, expressions of opinion or interpretations of fact and experience. They are unified by a common interest in the values which direct human thought and action. That they reflect a similar interest in spiritual values is justified partly by the fact that political and material problems were dealt with in earlier sections, and partly by the fact that a return to spiritual values seems to be in progress.

Self-Reliance

RALPH WALDO EMERSON

[1] I read the other day some verses written by an eminent painter which were original and not conventional. The soul always hears an admonition in such lines, let the subject be what it may. The sentiment they instil is of more value than any thought they may contain. To believe your own thought, to believe that what is true for you in your private heart is true for all men,—that is genius. Speak your latent conviction, and it shall be the universal sense; for the inmost in due time becomes the outmost,—and our first thought is rendered back to us by the trumpets of the Last Judgment. Familiar as the voice of the mind is to each, the highest merit we ascribe to Moses, Plato, and Milton is, that they set at naught books and traditions, and spoke not what men, but what *they* thought. A man should learn to detect and watch that gleam of light which flashes across his mind from within, more than the lustre of the firmament of bards and sages. Yet he dismisses without notice his thought, because it is his. In every work of genius we recognize our own rejected thoughts: they come back to us with a certain alienated majesty. Great works of art have no more affecting lesson for us than this. They teach us to abide by our spontaneous impression with good-humored inflexibility then most when the whole cry of voices is on the other side. Else to-morrow a stranger will say with masterly good sense precisely what we have thought and felt all the time, and we shall be forced to take with shame our own opinion from another.

[2] There is a time in every man's education when he arrives at the conviction that envy is ignorance; that imitation is suicide; that he must take himself for better, for worse, as his portion; that though the wide universe is full of good, no kernel of nourishing corn can come to him but through his toil bestowed on that plot of ground which is given to him to till. The power which resides in him is new in nature, and none but he knows what that is which he can do, nor does he know until he has tried. Not for nothing

one face, one character, one fact, makes much impression on him, and another none. This sculpture in the memory is not without pre-established harmony. The eye was placed where one ray should fall, that it might testify of that particular ray. We but half express ourselves, and are ashamed of that divine idea which each of us represents. It may be safely trusted as proportionate and of good issues, so it be faithfully imparted, but God will not have his work made manifest by cowards. A man is relieved and gay when he has put his heart into his work and done his best; but what he has said or done otherwise, shall give him no peace. It is a deliverance which does not deliver. In the attempt his genius deserts him; no muse befriends; no invention, no hope.

[3] Trust thyself: every heart vibrates to that iron string. Accept the place the divine providence has found for you, the society of your contemporaries, the connection of events. Great men have always done so, and confided themselves childlike to the genius of their age, betraying their perception that the absolutely trustworthy was seated at their heart, working through their hands, predominating in all their being. And we are now men, and must accept in the highest mind the same transcendent destiny; and not minors and invalids in a protected corner, not cowards fleeing before a revolution, but guides, redeemers, and benefactors, obeying the Almighty effort, and advancing on Chaos and the Dark.

[4] What pretty oracles nature yields us on this text, in the face and behavior of children, babes, and even brutes! That divided and rebel mind, that distrust of a sentiment because our arithmetic has computed the strength and means opposed to our purpose, these have not. Their mind being whole, their eye is as yet unconquered, and when we look in their faces, we are disconcerted. Infancy conforms to nobody: all conform to it, so that one babe commonly makes four or five out of the adults who prattle and play to it. So God has armed youth and puberty and manhood no less with its own piquancy and charm, and made it enviable and gracious and its claims not to be put by, if it will stand by itself. Do not think the youth has no force, because he cannot speak to you and me. Hark! in the next room his voice is sufficiently clear and emphatic. It seems he knows how to speak to his contempo-

raries. Bashful or bold, then, he will know how to make us seniors very unnecessary.

[5] The nonchalance of boys who are sure of a dinner, and would disdain as much as a lord to do or say aught to conciliate one, is the healthy attitude of human nature. A boy is in the parlor what the pit is in the playhouse; independent, irresponsible, looking out from his corner on such people and facts as pass by, he tries and sentences them on their merits, in the swift, summary way of boys, as good, bad, interesting, silly, eloquent, troublesome. He cumbers himself never about consequences, about interests; he gives an independent, genuine verdict. You must court him: he does not court you. But the man is, as it were, clapped into jail by his consciousness. As soon as he has once acted or spoken with *éclat,* he is a committed person, watched by the sympathy or the hatred of hundreds, whose affections must now enter into his account. There is no Lethe for this. Ah, that he could pass again into his neutrality! Who can thus avoid all pledges, and having observed, observe again from the same unaffected, unbiassed, unbribable, unaffrighted innocence, must always be formidable. He would utter opinions on all passing affairs, which being seen to be not private, but necessary, would sink like darts into the ear of men, and put them in fear.

[6] These are the voices which we hear in solitude, but they grow faint and inaudible as we enter into the world. Society everywhere is in conspiracy against the manhood of every one of its members. Society is a joint-stock company, in which the members agree, for the better securing of his bread to each shareholder, to surrender the liberty and culture of the eater. The virtue in most request is conformity. Self-reliance is its aversion. It loves not realities and creators, but names and customs.

[7] Whoso would be a man must be a nonconformist. He who would gather immortal palms must not be hindered by the name of goodness, but must explore if it be goodness. Nothing is at last sacred but the integrity of your own mind. Absolve you to yourself, and you shall have the suffrage of the world. I remember an answer which when quite young I was prompted to make to a valued adviser, who was wont to importune me with the dear old doctrines of the church. On my saying, "What have I to do with

the sacredness of traditions, if I live wholly from within?" my friend suggested: "But these impulses may be from below, not from above." I replied: "They do not seem to me to be such; but if I am the Devil's child, I will live then from the Devil." No law can be sacred to me but that of my nature. Good and bad are but names very readily transferable to that or this; the only right is what is after my constitution, the only wrong what is against it. A man is to carry himself in the presence of all opposition, as if everything were titular and ephemeral but him. I am ashamed to think how easily we capitulate to badges and names, to large societies and dead institutions. Every decent and well-spoken individual affects and sways me more than is right. I ought to go upright and vital, and speak the rude truth in all ways. If malice and vanity wear the coat of philanthropy, shall that pass? If an angry bigot assumes this bountiful cause of Abolition, and comes to me with his last news from Barbados, why should I not say to him: "Go love thy infant; love thy wood-chopper: be good-natured and modest: have that grace; and never varnish your hard, uncharitable ambition with this incredible tenderness for black folk a thousand miles off. Thy love afar is spite at home." Rough and graceless would be such greeting, but truth is handsomer than the affectation of love. Your goodness must have some edge to it,—else it is none. The doctrine of hatred must be preached as the counteraction of the doctrine of love when that pules and whines. I shun father and mother and wife and brother, when my genius calls me. I would write on the lintels of the doorpost, *Whim*. I hope it is somewhat better than whim at last, but we cannot spend the day in explanation. Expect me not to show cause why I seek or why I exclude company. Then, again, do not tell me, as a good man did to-day, of my obligation to put all poor men in good situations. Are they *my* poor? I tell thee, thou foolish philanthropist, that I grudge the dollar, the dime, the cent, I give to such men as do not belong to me and to whom I do not belong. There is a class of persons to whom by all spiritual affinity I am bought and sold; for them I will go to prison, if need be; but your miscellaneous popular charities; the education at college of fools; the building of meeting-houses to the vain end to which many now stand; alms to sots; and the thousand-fold

Relief Societies;—though I confess with shame I sometimes suc-
cumb and give the dollar, it is a wicked dollar which by and by I
shall have the manhood to withhold.

[8] Virtues are, in the popular estimate, rather the exception than
the rule. There is the man *and* his virtues. Men do what is called
a good action, as some piece of courage or charity, much as they
would pay a fine in expiation of daily non-appearance on parade.
Their works are done as an apology or extenuation of their living in the world,—as invalids and the insane pay a high board.
Their virtues are penances. I do not wish to expiate, but to live.
My life is for itself and not for a spectacle. I much prefer that
it should be of a lower strain, so it be genuine and equal, than
that it should be glittering and unsteady. I wish it to be sound
and sweet, and not to need diet and bleeding. I ask primary
evidence that you are a man, and refuse this appeal from the man
to his actions. I know that for myself it makes no difference
whether I do or forbear those actions which are reckoned excellent. I cannot consent to pay for a privilege where I have intrinsic
right. Few and mean as my gifts may be, I actually am, and do
not need for my own assurance or the assurance of my fellows
any secondary testimony.

[9] What I must do is all that concerns me, not what the people
think. This rule, equally arduous in actual and in intellectual life,
may serve for the whole distinction between greatness and meanness. It is the harder, because you will always find those who think
they know what is your duty better than you know it. It is easy
in the world to live after the world's opinion; it is easy in solitude
to live after our own; but the great man is he who in the midst
of the crowd keeps with perfect sweetness the independence of
solitude.

[10] The objection to conforming to usages that have become
dead to you is, that it scatters your force. It loses your time and
blurs the impression of your character. If you maintain a dead
church, contribute to a dead Bible society, vote with a great party
either for the government or against it, spread your table like base
housekeepers,—under all these screens I have difficulty to detect the precise man you are. And, of course, so much force is
withdrawn from your proper life. But do your work, and I shall

know you. Do your work, and you shall reinforce yourself. A man must consider what a blind-man's-buff is this game of conformity. If I know your sect, I anticipate your argument. I hear a preacher announce for his text and topic the expediency of one of the institutions of his church. Do I not know beforehand that not possibly can he say a new and spontaneous word? Do I not know that, with all this ostentation of examining the grounds of the institution, he will do no such thing? Do I not know that he is pledged to himself not to look but at one side,—the permitted side, not as a man, but as a parish minister? He is a retained attorney, and these airs of the bench are the emptiest affectation. Well, most men have bound their eyes with one or another handkerchief, and attached themselves to some one of these communities of opinion. This conformity makes them not false in a few particulars, authors of a few lies, but false in all particulars. Their every truth is not quite true. Their two is not the real two, their four is not the real four; so that every word they say chagrins us, and we know not where to begin to set them right. Meantime nature is not slow to equip us in the prison-uniform of the party to which we adhere. We come to wear one cut of face and figure, and acquire by degrees the gentlest asinine expression. There is a mortifying experience in particular, which does not fail to wreak itself also in the general history; I mean "the foolish face of praise," the forced smile which we put on in company where we do not feel at ease in answer to conversation which does not interest us. The muscles, not spontaneously moved, but moved by a low usurping wilfulness, grow tight about the outline of the face with the most disagreeable sensation.

[11] For non-conformity the world whips you with its displeasure. And therefore a man must know how to estimate a sour face. The bystanders look askance on him in the public street or in the friend's parlor. If this aversion had its origin in contempt and resistance like his own, he might well go home with a sad countenance; but the sour faces of the multitude, like their sweet faces, have no deep cause, but are put on and off as the wind blows and a newspaper directs. Yet is the discontent of the multitude more formidable than that of the senate and the college. It is easy enough for a firm man who knows the world to brook the rage

of the cultivated classes. Their rage is decorous and prudent, for they are timid as being very vulnerable themselves. But when to their feminine rage the indignation of the people is added, when the ignorant and the poor are aroused, when the unintelligent brute force that lies at the bottom of society is made to growl and mow, it needs the habit of magnanimity and religion to treat it godlike as a trifle of no concernment.

[12] The other terror that scares us from self-trust is our consistency; a reverence for our past act or word, because the eyes of others have no other data for computing our orbit than our past acts, and we are loathe to disappoint them.

[13] But why should you keep your head over your shoulder? Why drag about this corpse of your memory, lest you contradict somewhat you have stated in this or that public place? Suppose you should contradict yourself; what then? It seems to be a rule of wisdom never to rely on your memory alone, scarcely even in acts of pure memory, but to bring the past for judgment into the thousand-eyed present, and live ever in a new day. In your metaphysics you have denied personality to the Deity: yet when the devout motions of the soul come, yield to them heart and life, though they should clothe God with shape and color. Leave your theory, as Joseph his coat in the hand of the harlot, and flee.

[14] A foolish consistency is the hobgoblin of little minds, adored by little statesmen and philosophers and divines. With consistency a great soul has simply nothing to do. He may as well concern himself with his shadow on the wall. Speak what you think now in hard words and to-morrow speak what to-morrow thinks in hard words again, though it contradict everything you said to-day.—"Ah, so you shall be sure to be misunderstood?"—Is it so bad, then, to be misunderstood? Pythagoras was misunderstood, and Socrates, and Jesus, and Luther, and Copernicus, and Galileo, and Newton, and every pure and wise spirit that ever took flesh. To be great is to be misunderstood.

[15] I suppose no man can violate his nature. All the sallies of his will are rounded in by the law of his being, as the inequalities of Andes and Himmaleh are insignificant in the curve of the sphere. Nor does it matter how you gauge and try him. A charac-

ter is like an acrostic or Alexandrian stanza;—read it forward, backward, or across, it still spells the same thing. In this pleasing, contrite wood-life which God allows me, let me record day by day my honest thought without prospect or retrospect, and, I cannot doubt, it will be found symmetrical, though I mean it not and see it not. My book should smell of pines and resound with the hum of insects. The swallow over my window should interweave that thread or straw he carries in his bill into my web also. We pass for what we are. Character teaches above our wills. Men imagine that they communicate their virtue or vice only by overt actions, and do not see that virtue or vice emit a breath every moment.

[16] There will be an agreement in whatever variety of actions, so they be each honest and natural in their hour. For of one will, the actions will be harmonious, however unlike they seem. These varieties are lost sight of at a little distance, at a little height of thought. One tendency unites them all. The voyage of the best ship is a zigzag line of a hundred tacks. See the line from a sufficient distance, and it straightens itself to the average tendency. Your genuine action will explain itself, and will explain your other genuine actions. Your conformity explains nothing. Act singly, and what you have already done singly will justify you now. Greatness appeals to the future. If I can be firm enough to-day to do right, and scorn eyes, I must have done so much right before as to defend me now. Be it how it will, do right now. Always scorn appearances, and you always may. The force of character is cumulative. All the foregone days of virtue work their health into this. What makes the majesty of the heroes of the senate and the field, which so fills the imagination? The consciousness of a train of great days and victories behind. They shed a united light on the advancing actor. He is attended as by a visible escort of angels. That is it which throws thunder into Chatham's voice, and dignity into Washington's port, and America into Adams's eye. Honor is venerable to us because it is no ephemeris. It is always ancient virtue. We worship it to-day because it is not of to-day. We love it and pay it homage, because it is not a trap for our love and homage, but is self-dependent, self-derived, and therefore of an old immaculate pedigree, even if shown in a young person.

[17] I hope in these days we have heard the last of conformity and consistency. Let the words be gazetted and ridiculous henceforward. Instead of the gong for dinner, let us hear a whistle from the Spartan fife. Let us never bow and apologize more. A great man is coming to eat at my house. I do not wish to please him; I wish that he should wish to please me. I will stand here for humanity, and though I would make it kind, I would make it true. Let us affront and reprimand the smooth mediocrity and squalid contentment of the times, and hurl in the face of custom, and trade, and office, the fact which is the upshot of all history, that there is a great responsible Thinker and Actor working wherever a man works; that a true man belongs to no other time or place, but is the centre of things. Where he is, there is nature. He measures you, and all men, and all events. Ordinarily, everybody in society reminds us of somewhat else, or of some other person. Character, reality, reminds you of nothing else; it takes place of the whole creation. The man must be so much, that he must make all circumstances indifferent. Every true man is a cause, a country, and an age; requires infinite spaces and numbers and time fully to accomplish his design;—and posterity seems to follow his steps as a train of clients. A man Cæsar is born, and for ages after we have a Roman Empire. Christ is born, and millions of minds so grow and cleave to his genius, that he is confounded with virtue and the possible of man. An institution is the lengthened shadow of one man; as Monachism, of the Hermit Antony; the Reformation, of Luther; Quakerism, of Fox; Methodism, of Wesley; Abolition, of Clarkson. Scipio, Milton called "the height of Rome"; and all history resolves itself very easily into the biography of a few stout and earnest persons.

[18] Let a man then know his worth, and keep things under his feet. Let him not peep or steal, or skulk up and down with the air of a charity-boy, a bastard, or an interloper, in the world which exists for him. But the man in the street, finding no worth in himself which corresponds to the force which built a tower or sculptured a marble god, feels poor when he looks on these. To him a palace, a statue, or a costly book have an alien and forbidding air, much like a gay equipage, and seem to say like that, "Who are you sir?" Yet they all are his suitors for his notice, petitioners

to his faculties that they will come out and take possession. The picture waits for my verdict: it is not to command me, but I am to settle its claims to praise. That popular fable of the sot who was picked up dead drunk in the street, carried to the duke's house, washed and dressed and laid in the duke's bed, and, on his waking, treated with all obsequious ceremony like the duke, and assured that he had been insane, owes its popularity to the fact, that it symbolizes so well the state of man, who is in the world a sort of sot, but now and then wakes up, exercises his reason and finds himself a true prince.

[19] Our reading is mendicant and sycophantic. In history, our imagination plays us false. Kingdom and lordship, power and estate, are a gaudier vocabulary than private John and Edward in a small house and common day's work; but the things of life are the same to both; the sum total of both are the same. Why all this deference to Alfred, and Scanderbeg, and Gustavus? Suppose they were virtuous; did they wear out virtue? As great a stake depends on your private act to-day, as followed their public and renowned steps. When private men shall act with original views, the lustre will be transferred from the actions of kings to those of gentlemen.

[20] The world has been instructed by its kings, who have so magnetized the eyes of nations. It has been taught by this colossal symbol the mutual reverence that is due from man to man. The joyful loyalty with which men have everywhere suffered the king, the noble, or the great proprietor to walk among them by a law of his own, make his own scale of men and things and reverse theirs, pay for benefits not with money but with honor, and represent the law in his person, was the hieroglyphic by which they obscurely signified their consciousness of their own right and comeliness, the right of every man.

[21] The magnetism which all original action exerts is explained when we inquire the reason of self-trust. Who is the Trustee? What is the aboriginal Self, on which a universal reliance may be grounded? What is the nature and power of that science-baffling star, without parallax, without calculable elements, which shoots a ray of beauty even into trivial and impure actions, if the least mark of independence appear? The inquiry leads us to that source,

at once the essence of genius, of virtue, and of life, which we call
Spontaneity or Instinct. We denote this primary wisdom as Intuition, whilst all later teachings are tuitions. In that deep force, the
last fact behind which analysis cannot go, all things find their
common origin. For, the sense of being which in calm hours rises,
we know not how, in the soul, is not diverse from things, from
space, from light, from time, from man, but one with them, and
proceeds obviously from the same source whence their life and
being also proceed. We first share the life by which things exist,
and afterwards see them as appearances in nature, and forget
that we have shared their cause. Here is the fountain of action
and of thought. Here are the lungs of that inspiration which giveth
man wisdom, and which cannot be denied without impiety and
atheism. We lie in the lap of immense intelligence, which makes us
receivers of its truth and organs of its activity. When we discern justice, when we discern truth, we do nothing of ourselves,
but allow a passage to its beams. If we ask whence this comes, if
we seek to pry into the soul that causes, all philosophy is at fault.
Its presence or its absence is all we can affirm. Every man discriminates between the voluntary acts of his mind, and his involuntary perceptions, and knows that to his involuntary perceptions a perfect faith is due. He may err in the expression of
them, but he knows that these things are so, like day and night,
not to be disputed. My wilful actions and acquisitions are but
roving;—the idlest revery, the faintest native emotion, command my curiosity and respect. Thoughtless people contradict as
readily the statements of perceptions as of opinions, or rather
much more readily; for, they do not distinguish between perception and notion. They fancy that I choose to see this or that thing.
But perception is not whimsical, it is fatal. If I see a trait, my
children will see it after me, and in course of time, all mankind,—
although it may chance that no one has seen it before me. For my
perception of it is as much a fact as the sun.

[22] The relations of the soul to the divine spirit are so pure,
that it is profane to seek to interpose helps. It must be that when
God speaketh he should communicate, not one thing, but all things;
should fill the world with his voice; should scatter forth light,
nature, time, souls, from the centre of the present thought; and

new date and new create the whole. Whenever a mind is simple, and receives a divine wisdom, old things pass away,—means, teachers, texts, temples, fall; it lives now, and absorbs past and future into the present hour. All things are made sacred by relation to it,—one as much as another. All things are dissolved to their centre by their cause, and, in the universal miracle, petty and particular miracles disappear. If, therefore, a man claims to know and speak of God, and carries you backward to the phraseology of some old mouldered nation in another country, in another world, believe him not. Is the acorn better than the oak which is its fulness and completion? Is the parent better than the child into whom he has cast his ripened being? Whence, then, this worship of the past? The centuries are conspirators against the sanity and authority of the soul. Time and space are but physiological colors which the eye makes, but the soul is light; where it is, is day; where it was, is night; and history is an impertinence and an injury, if it be anything more than a cheerful apologue or parable of my being and becoming.

[23] Man is timid and apologetic; he is no longer upright; he dares not say, "I think," "I am," but quotes some saint or sage. He is ashamed before the blade of grass or the blowing rose. These roses under my window make no reference to former roses or to better ones; they are for what they are; they exist with God to-day. There is no time to them. There is simply the rose; it is perfect in every moment of its existence. Before a leaf-bud has burst, its whole life acts; in the full-blown flower there is no more; in the leafless root there is no less. Its nature is satisfied, and it satisfies nature, in all moments alike. But man postpones or remembers; he does not live in the present, but with reverted eye laments the past, or, heedless of the riches that surround him, stands on tiptoe to foresee the future. He cannot be happy and strong until he too lives with nature in the present, above time.

[24] This should be plain enough. Yet see what strong intellects dare not yet hear God himself, unless he speak the phraseology of I know not what David, or Jeremiah, or Paul. We shall not always set so great a price on a few texts, on a few lives. We are like children who repeat by rote the sentences of grandames and tutors, and, as they grow older, of the men of talents and character

they chance to see,—painfully recollecting the exact words they spoke; afterwards, when they come into the point of view which those had who uttered these sayings, they understand them, and are willing to let the words go; for, at any time, they can use words as good when occasion comes. If we live truly, we shall see truly. It is as easy for the strong man to be strong, as it is for the weak to be weak. When we have new perception, we shall gladly disburden the memory of its hoarded treasures as old rubbish. When a man lives with God, his voice shall be as sweet as the murmur of the brook and the rustle of the corn.

[25] And now at last the highest truth on this subject remains unsaid; probably cannot be said; for all that we say is the far-off remembering of the intuition. That thought, by what I can now nearest approach to say it, is this. When good is near you, when you have life in yourself, it is not by any known or accustomed way; you shall not discern the footprints of any other; you shall not see the face of man; you shall not hear any name; the way, the thought, the good, shall be wholly strange and new. It shall exclude example and experience. You take the way from man, not to man. All persons that ever existed are its forgotten ministers. Fear and hope are alike beneath it. There is somewhat low even in hope. In the hour of vision, there is nothing that can be called gratitude, nor properly joy. The soul raised over passion beholds identity and eternal causation, perceives the self-existence of Truth and Right, and calms itself with knowing that all things go well. Vast spaces of nature, the Atlantic Ocean, the South Sea,— long intervals of time, years, centuries,—are of no account. This which I think and feel underlay every former state of life and circumstances, as it does underlie my present, and what is called life, and what is called death.

[26] Life only avails, not the having lived. Power ceases in the instant of repose; it resides in the moment of transition from a past to a new state, in the shooting of the gulf, in the darting to an aim. This one fact the world hates, that the soul *becomes;* for that forever degrades the past, turns all riches to poverty, all reputation to a shame, confounds the saint with the rogue, shoves Jesus and Judas equally aside. Why, then, do we prate of self-reliance? Inasmuch as the soul is present, there will be power not

confident but agent. To talk of reliance is a poor external way of
speaking. Speak rather of that which relies, because it works and is.
Who has more obedience than I masters me, though he should
not raise his finger. Round him I must revolve by the gravitation
of spirits. We fancy it rhetoric, when we speak of eminent virtue.
We do not yet see that virtue is Height, and that a man or a
company of men, plastic and permeable to principles, by the law
of nature must overpower and ride all cities, nations, kings, rich
men, poets, who are not.

[27] This is the ultimate fact which we so quickly reach on this,
as on every topic, the resolution of all into the ever-blessed ONE.
Self-existence is the attribute of the Supreme Cause, and it constitutes the measure of good by the degree in which it enters into
all lower forms. All things real are so by so much virtue as they
contain. Commerce, husbandry, hunting, whaling, war, eloquence,
personal weight, are somewhat, and engage my respect as examples of its presence and impure action. I see the same law
working in nature for conservation and growth. Power is in nature
the essential measure of right. Nature suffers nothing to remain in
her kingdoms which cannot help itself. The genesis and matura-
tion of a planet, its poise and orbit, the bended tree recovering
itself from the strong wind, the vital resources of every animal and
vegetable, are demonstrations of the self-sufficing, and, therefore,
self-relying soul.

[28] Thus all concentrates; let us not rove; let us sit at home
with the cause. Let us stun and astonish the intruding rabble of
men and books and institutions, by a simple declaration of the
divine fact. Bid the invaders take the shoes from off their feet,
for God is here within. Let our simplicity judge them, and our
docility to our own law demonstrate the poverty of nature and
fortune beside our native riches.

[29] But now we are a mob. Man does not stand in awe of man,
nor is his genius admonished to stay at home, to put itself in
communication with the internal ocean, but it goes abroad to beg
a cup of water of the urns of other men. We must go alone. I like
the silent church before the service begins, better than any preaching. How far off, how cool, how chaste the persons look, begirt
each one with a precinct or sanctuary! So let us always sit. Why

should we assume the faults of our friend, or wife, or father, or child, because they sit around our hearth, or are said to have the same blood? All men have my blood, and I have all men's. Not for that will I adopt their petulance or folly, even to the extent of being ashamed of it. But the isolation must not be mechanical, but spiritual, that is, must be elevation. At times the whole world seems to be in conspiracy to importune you with emphatic trifles. Friend, client, child, sickness, fear, want, charity, all knock at once at thy closet door, and say, "Come out unto us." But keep thy state; come not into their confusion. The power men possess to annoy me, I give them by a weak curiosity. No man can come near me but through my act. "What we love that we have, but by desire we bereave ourselves of the love."

[30] If we cannot at once rise to the sanctities of obedience and faith, let us at least resist our temptations; let us enter into the state of war, and wake Thor and Woden, courage and constancy, in our Saxon breasts. This is to be done in our smooth times by speaking the truth. Check this lying hospitality and lying affection. Live no longer to the expectation of these deceived and deceiving people with whom we converse. Say to them, "O father, O mother, O wife, O brother, O friend, I have lived with you after appearances hitherto. Henceforward I am the truth's. Be it known unto you that henceforward I obey no law less than the eternal law. I will have no covenants but proximities. I shall endeavor to nourish my parents, to support my family, to be the chaste husband of one wife,—but these relations I must fill after a new and unprecedented way. I appeal from your customs. I must be myself. I cannot break myself any longer for you, or you. If you can love me for what I am, we shall be the happier. If you cannot, I will still seek to deserve that you should. I will not hide my tastes or aversions. I will so trust that what is deep is holy, that I will do strongly before the sun and moon whatever inly rejoices me, and the heart appoints. If you are noble, I will love you; if you are not, I will not hurt you and myself by hypocritical attentions. If you are true, but not in the same truth with me, cleave to your companions; I will seek my own. I do this not selfishly, but humbly and truly. It is alike your interest, and mine, and all men's, however long we have dwelt in lies, to live in truth. Does this sound harsh

to-day? You will soon love what is dictated by your nature as well as mine, and, if we follow the truth, it will bring us out safe at last." But so you may give these friends pain. Yes, but I cannot sell my liberty and my power, to save their sensibility. Besides, all persons have their moments of reason, when they look out into the region of absolute truth; then will they justify me, and do the same thing.

[31] The populace think that your rejection of popular standards is a rejection of all standard, and mere antinomianism; and the bold sensualist will use the name of philosophy to gild his crimes. But the law of consciousness abides. There are two confessionals, in one or the other of which we must be shriven. You may fulfil your round of duties by clearing yourself in the *direct,* or in the *reflex* way. Consider whether you have satisfied your relations to father, mother, cousin, neighbor, town, cat, and dog; whether any of these can upbraid you. But I may also neglect this reflex standard, and absolve me to myself. I have my own stern claims and perfect circle. It denies the name of duty to many offices that are called duties. But if I can discharge its debts, it enables me to dispense with the popular code. If any one imagines that this law is lax, let him keep its commandment one day.

[32] And truly it demands something godlike in him who has cast off the common motives of humanity, and has ventured to trust himself for a taskmaster. High be his heart, faithful his will, clear his sight, that he may in good earnest be doctrine, society, law, to himself, that a simple purpose may be to him as strong as iron necessity is to others!

[33] If any man consider the present aspects of what is called by distinction *society,* he will see the need of these ethics. The sinew and heart of man seem to be drawn out, and we are become timorous, desponding whimperers. We are afraid of truth, afraid of fortune, afraid of death, and afraid of each other. Our age yields no great and perfect persons. We want men and women who shall renovate life and our social state, but we see that most natures are insolvent, cannot satisfy their own wants, have an ambition out of all proportion to their practical force, and do lean and beg day and night continually. Our housekeeping is mendicant, our arts, our occupations, our marriages, our religion, we have not chosen,

but society has chosen for us. We are parlor soldiers. We shun the rugged battle of fate, where strength is born.

[34] If our young men miscarry in their first enterprises, they lose all heart. If the young merchant fails, men say he is *ruined*. If the finest genius studies at one of our colleges, and is not installed in an office within one year afterwards in the cities or suburbs of Boston or New York, it seems to his friends and to himself that he is right in being disheartened, and in complaining the rest of his life. A sturdy lad from New Hampshire or Vermont, who in turn tries all the professions, who *teams it, farms it, peddles,* keeps a school, preaches, edits a newspaper, goes to Congress, buys a township, and so forth, in successive years, and always, like a cat, falls on his feet, is worth a hundred of these city dolls. He walks abreast with his days, and feels no shame in not 'studying a profession,' for he does not postpone his life, but lives already. He has not one chance, but a hundred chances. Let a Stoic open the resources of man, and tell men they are not leaning willows, but can and must detach themselves; that with the exercise of self-trust, new powers shall appear; that a man is the word made flesh, born to shed healing to the nations, that he should be ashamed of our compassion, and that the moment he acts from himself, tossing the laws, the books, idolatries, and customs out of the window, we pity him no more, but thank and revere him,— and that teacher shall restore the life of man to splendor, and make his name dear to all history.

[35] It is easy to see that a greater self-reliance must work a revolution in all the offices and relations of men; in their religion; in their education; in their pursuits; their modes of living; their association; in their property; in their speculative views.

[36] (1.) In what prayers do men allow themselves! That which they call a holy office is not so much as brave and manly. Prayer looks abroad and asks for some foreign addition to come through some foreign virtue, and loses itself in endless mazes of natural and supernatural, and mediatorial and miraculous. Prayer that craves a particular commodity,—anything less than all good,— is vicious. Prayer is the contemplation of the facts of life from the highest point of view. It is the soliloquy of a beholding and jubilant soul. It is the spirit of God pronouncing his works good.

But prayer as a means to effect a private end is meanness and theft. It supposes dualism and not unity in nature and consciousness. As soon as the man is at one with God, he will not beg. He will then see prayer in all action. The prayer of the farmer kneeling in his field to weed it, the prayer of the rower kneeling with the stroke of his oar, are true prayers heard throughout nature, though for cheap ends. Caratach, in Fletcher's *Bonduca,* when admonished to inquire the mind of the god Audate, replies,—

> "His hidden meaning lies in our endeavors;
> Our valors are our best gods."

[37] Another sort of false prayers are our regrets. Discontent is the want of self-reliance: it is infirmity of will. Regret calamities, if you can thereby help the sufferer: if not, attend your own work, and already the evil begins to be repaired. Our sympathy is just as base. We come to them who weep foolishly, and sit down and cry for company, instead of imparting to them truth and health in rough electric shocks, putting them once more in communication with their own reason. The secret of fortune is joy in our hands. Welcome evermore to gods and men is the self-helping man. For him all doors are flung wide: him all tongues greet, all honors crown, all eyes follow with desire. Our love goes out to him and embraces him, because he did not need it. We solicitously and apologetically caress and celebrate him, because he held on his way and scorned our disapprobation. The gods love him because men hated him. "To the persevering mortal," said Zoroaster, "the blessed Immortals are swift."

[38] As men's prayers are a disease of the will, so are their creeds a disease of the intellect. They say with those foolish Israelites, "Let not God speak to us lest we die. Speak thou, speak any man with us, and we will obey." Everywhere I am hindered of meeting God in my brother, because he has shut his own temple doors, and recites fables merely of his brother's or his brother's brother's God. Every new mind is a new classification. If it proves a mind of uncommon activity and power, a Locke, a Lavoisier, a Hutton, a Bentham, a Fourier, it imposes its classification on other men, and lo! a new system. In proportion to the depth of the thought, and so to the number of the objects it touches and

brings within reach of the pupil, is his complacency. But chiefly is this apparent in creeds and churches, which are also classifications of some powerful mind acting on the elemental thought of duty, and man's relations to the Highest. Such is Calvinism, Quakerism, Swedenborgism. The pupil takes the same delight in subordinating everything to the new terminology, as a girl who has just learned botany in seeing a new earth and new seasons thereby. It will happen for a time, that the pupil will find his intellectual power has grown by the study of his master's mind. But in all unbalanced minds, the classification is idolized, passes for the end, and not for a speedily exhaustible means, so that the walls of the system blend to their eye in the remote horizon with the walls of the universe; the luminaries of heaven seem to them hung on the arch their master built. They cannot imagine how you aliens have any right to see,—how you can see; "it must be somehow that you stole the light from us." They do not yet perceive, that light, unsystematic, indomitable, will break into any cabin, even into theirs. Let them chirp awhile and call it their own. If they are honest and do well, presently their neat new pinfold will be too strait and low, will crack, will lean, will rot and vanish, and the immortal light, all young and joyful, million-orbed, million-colored, will beam over the universe as on the first morning.

[39] (2.) It is for want of self-reliance that the superstition of Travelling, whose idols are Italy, England, Egypt, retains its fascination for all educated Americans. They who made England, Italy, or Greece venerable in the imagination did so by sticking fast where they were, like an axis of the earth. In manly hours, we feel that duty is our place. The soul is no traveller; the wise man stays at home, and when his necessities, his duties, on any occasion, call him from his house, or into foreign lands, he is at home still, and shall make men sensible, by the expression of his countenance, that he goes the missionary of wisdom and virtue, and visits cities and men like a sovereign, and not like an interloper or a valet.

[40] I have no churlish objection to the circumnavigation of the globe, for the purposes of art, of study, and benevolence, so that the man is first domesticated, or does not go abroad with the

hope of finding somewhat greater than he knows. He who travels to be amused, or to get somewhat which he does not carry, travels away from himself, and grows old even in youth among old things. In Thebes, in Palmyra, his will and mind have become old and dilapidated as they. He carries ruins to ruins.

[41] Travelling is a fool's paradise. Our first journeys discover to us the indifference of places. At home I dream that at Naples, at Rome, I can be intoxicated with beauty, and lose my sadness. I pack my trunk, embrace my friends, embark on the sea, and at last wake up in Naples, and there beside me is the stern fact, the sad self, unrelenting, identical, that I fled from. I seek the Vatican, and the palaces. I affect to be intoxicated with sights and suggestions, but I am not intoxicated. My giant goes with me wherever I go.

[42] (3.) But the rage of travelling is a symptom of a deeper unsoundness affecting the whole intellectual action. The intellect is vagabond, and our system of education fosters restlessness. Our minds travel when our bodies are forced to stay at home. We imitate; and what is imitation but the travelling of the mind? Our houses are built with foreign taste; our shelves are garnished with foreign ornaments; our opinions, our tastes, our faculties, lean, and follow the Past and the Distant. The soul created the arts wherever they have flourished. It was in his own mind that the artist sought his model. It was an application of his own thought to the thing to be done and the conditions to be observed. And why need we copy the Doric or the Gothic model? Beauty, convenience, grandeur of thought, and quaint expression are as near to us as to any, and if the American artist will study with hope and love the precise thing to be done by him, considering the climate, the soil, the length of the day, the wants of the people, the habit and form of the government, he will create a house in which all these will find themselves fitted, and taste and sentiment will be satisfied also.

[43] Insist on yourself; never imitate. Your own gift you can present every moment with the cumulative force of a whole life's cultivation; but of the adopted talent of another, you have only an extemporaneous, half possession. That which each can do best, none but his Maker can teach him. No man yet knows what it is,

nor can, till that person has exhibited it. Where is the master who could have taught Shakspeare? Where is the master who could have instructed Franklin, or Washington, or Bacon, or Newton? Every great man is a unique. The Scipionism of Scipio is precisely that part he could not borrow. Shakspeare will never be made by the study of Shakspeare. Do that which is assigned you, and you cannot hope too much or dare too much. There is at this moment for you an utterance brave and grand as that of the colossal chisel of Phidias, or trowel of the Egyptians, or the pen of Moses, or Dante, but different from all these. Not possibly will the soul all rich, all eloquent, with thousand-cloven tongue, deign to repeat itself; but if you can hear what these patriarchs say, surely you can reply to them in the same pitch of voice; for the ear and the tongue are two organs of one nature. Abide in the simple and noble regions of thy life, obey thy heart, and thou shall reproduce the Foreworld again.

[44] (4.) As our Religion, our Education, our Art look abroad, so does our spirit of society. All men plume themselves on the improvement of society, and no man improves.

[45] Society never advances. It recedes as fast on one side as it gains on the other. It undergoes continual changes; it is barbarous, it is civilized, it is Christianized, it is rich, it is scientific; but this change is not amelioration. For everything that is given, something is taken. Society acquires new arts, and loses old instincts. What a contrast between the well-clad, reading, writing, thinking American, with a watch, a pencil, and a bill of exchange in his pocket, and the naked New-Zealander, whose property is a club, a spear, a mat, and an undivided twentieth of a shed to sleep under! But compare the health of the two men, and you shall see that the white man has lost his aboriginal strength. If the traveller tell us truly, strike the savage with a broad axe, and in a day or two the flesh shall unite and heal as if you struck the blow into soft pitch, and the same blow shall send the white to his grave.

[46] The civilized man has built a coach, but has lost the use of his feet. He is supported on crutches, but lacks so much support of muscle. He has a fine Geneva watch, but he fails of the skill to tell the hour by the sun. A Greenwich nautical almanac he has, and so being sure of the information when he wants it, the man

in the street does not know a star in the sky. The solstice he does not observe, the equinox he knows as little; and the whole bright calendar of the year is without a dial in his mind. His note-books impair his memory; his libraries overload his wit; the insurance office increases the number of accidents; and it may be a question whether machinery does not encumber; whether we have not lost by refinement some energy, by a Christianity intrenched in establishments and forms, some vigor of wild virtue. For every Stoic was a Stoic; but in Christendom where is the Christian?

[47] There is no more deviation in the moral standard than in the standard of height or bulk. No greater men are now than ever were. A singular equality may be observed between the great men of the first and of the last ages; nor can all the science, art, religion, and philosophy of the nineteenth century avail to educate greater men that Plutarch's heroes, three or four and twenty centuries ago. Not in time is the race progressive. Phocion, Socrates, Anaxagoras, Diogenes, are great men, but they leave no class. He who is really of their class will not be called by their name, but will be his own man, and, in his turn, the founder of a sect. The arts and inventions of each period are only its costume, and do not invigorate men. The harm of the improved machinery may compensate its good. Hudson and Behring accomplished so much in their fishing-boats, as to astonish Parry and Franklin, whose equipment exhausted the resources of science and art. Galileo, with an opera-glass, discovered a more splendid series of celestial phenomena than any one since. Columbus found the New World in an undecked boat. It is curious to see the periodical disuse and perishing of means and machinery, which were introduced with loud laudation a few years or centuries before. The great genius returns to essential man. We reckoned the improvements of the art of war among the triumphs of science, and yet Napoleon conquered Europe by the bivouac, which consisted of falling back on naked valor, and disencumbering it of all aids. The Emperor held it impossible to make a perfect army, says Las Cases, "without abolishing our arms, magazines, commissaries, and carriages, until, in imitation of the Roman custom, the soldier should receive his supply of corn, grind it in his hand-mill, and bake his bread himself."

[48] Society is a wave. The wave moves onward, but the water of which it is composed does not. The same particle does not rise from the valley to the ridge. Its unity is only phenomenal. The persons who make up a nation to-day, next year die, and their experience with them.

[49] And so the reliance on Property, including the reliance on governments which protect it, is the want of self-reliance. Men have looked away from themselves and at things so long, that they have come to esteem the religious, learned, and civil institutions as guards of property, and they deprecate assaults on these, because they feel them to be assaults on property. They measure their esteem of each other by what each has, and not by what each is. But a cultivated man becomes ashamed of his property, out of new respect for his nature. Especially he hates what he has, if he see that it is accidental,—came to him by inheritance, or gift, or crime; then he feels that it is not having; it does not belong to him, has no root in him, and merely lies there, because no revolution or no robber takes it away. But that which a man is, does always by necessity acquire, and what the man acquires is living property, which does not wait the beck of rulers, or mobs, or revolutions, or fire, or storm, or bankruptcies, but perpetually renews itself wherever the man breathes. "Thy lot or portion of life," said the Caliph Ali, "is seeking after thee; therefore be at rest from seeking after it." Our dependence on these foreign goods leads us to our slavish respect for numbers. The political parties meet in numerous conventions; the greater the concourse, and with each new uproar of announcement,—The delegation from Essex! The Democrats from New Hampshire! The Whigs of Maine!—the young patriot feels himself stronger than before by a new thousand of eyes and arms. In like manner the reformers summon conventions, and vote and resolve in multitude. Not so, O friends, will the God deign to enter and inhabit you, but by a method precisely the reverse. It is only as a man puts off all foreign support, and stands alone, that I see him to be strong and to prevail. He is weaker by every recruit to his banner. Is not a man better than a town? Ask nothing of men, and in the endless mutation, thou only firm column must presently appear the upholder of all that surrounds thee. He who knows that power is inborn, that he is weak because he has looked

for good out of him and elsewhere, and so perceiving, throws himself unhesitatingly on his thought, instantly rights himself, stands in the erect position, commands his limbs, works miracles; just as a man who stands on his feet is stronger than a man who stands on his head.

[50] So use all that is called Fortune. Most men gamble with her, and gain all, and lose all, as her wheel rolls. But do thou leave as unlawful these winnings, and deal with Cause and Effect, the chancellors of God. In the Will work and acquire, and thou hast chained the wheel of Chance, and shalt sit hereafter out of fear from her rotations. A political victory, a rise of rents, the recovery of your sick, or the return of your absent friend, or some other favorable event, raises your spirits, and you think good days are preparing for you. Do not believe it. Nothing can bring you peace but yourself. Nothing can bring you peace but the triumph of principles.

EXERCISES

Emerson is often misunderstood, and the fault is partly his and partly his readers'. His diction is more general than it needs to be, and his specific illustrations are less specific than they might be. To quote his very quotable dicta out of context is disastrous, for they usually need paragraphs of elaboration and modification. His chief method of development is reiteration, and of that technique he is perhaps the world's master.

The present essay may be studied as consisting of two main parts, one on theory and one on practice.

1. What are the two main deterrents to self-reliance?
2. For what reason does Emerson believe that we can allow our thoughts and actions to be directed by our inner impulses, knowing that the results will be good?
3. When he says, in paragraph 7, "No law can be sacred to me but that of my own nature," is he justifying complete disregard of morality?
4. Would Emerson approve of the "individualist" who as a matter of principle drives the wrong way down a one-way street?
5. Would he recommend automatic non-conformity and inconsistency in all matters?

6. Was Emerson against Abolition?
7. Was he against all charity?
8. Two popular misquotations from Emerson's "Self-Reliance" are "Consistency is the hobgoblin of little minds," and "To be misunderstood is to be great." What is wrong with each?
9. Why is the sentence (in paragraph 23) beginning "These roses under my window . . ." a good summary of all that Emerson says in the first 23 paragraphs?
10. Summarize Emerson's suggestions for individual self-reliance.
11. Summarize his applications of the principle of self-reliance to social institutions.
12. Show how Emerson's discussion of consistency illustrates Huxley's "Words and Behaviour."
13. Show how Emerson's style is related to his subject matter.
14. Either in class discussion or in individual essays explain how faith in the trustworthiness of the individual insight, as Emerson explains it, is related to our American system of government. Reference to Aldous Huxley's "The Idea of Political Equality" and to Beard's "Essentials of the American System" may be useful.

Where I Lived, and What I Lived For

HENRY DAVID THOREAU

[1] At a certain season of our life we are accustomed to consider every spot as the possible site of a house. I have thus surveyed the country on every side within a dozen miles of where I live. In imagination I have bought all the farms in succession, for all were to be bought, and I knew their price. I walked over each farmer's premises, tasted his wild apples, discoursed on husbandry with him, took his farm at his price, at any price, mortgaging it to him in my mind; even put a higher price on it,—took every thing but a deed of it,—took his word for his deed, for I dearly love to talk,—cultivated it, and him too to some extent, I trust, and with-

From *Walden,* 1854.

drew when I had enjoyed it long enough, leaving him to carry
it on. This experience entitled me to be regarded as a sort of real-
estate broker by my friends. Wherever I sat, there I might live, and
the landscape radiated from me accordingly. What is a house
but a *sedes,* a seat?—better if a country seat. I discovered many
a site for a house not likely to be soon improved, which some
might have thought too far from the village, but to my eyes the
village was too far from it. Well, there I might live, I said; and
there I did live, for an hour, a summer and a winter life; saw how
I could let the years run off, buffet the winter through, and see the
spring come in. The future inhabitants of this region, wherever
they may place their houses, may be sure that they have been
anticipated. An afternoon sufficed to lay out the land into orchard,
woodlot, and pasture, and to decide what fine oaks or pines should
be left to stand before the door, and whence each blasted tree could
be seen to the best advantage; and then I let it lie, fallow perchance,
for a man is rich in proportion to the number of things which he
can afford to let alone.

[2] My imagination carried me so far that I even had the refusal
of several farms,—the refusal was all I wanted,—but I never got
my fingers burned by actual possession. The nearest that I came
to actual possession was when I bought the Hollowell place, and
had begun to sort my seeds, and collected materials with which
to make a wheeelbarrow to carry it on or off with; but before the
owner gave me a deed of it, his wife—every man has such a wife
—changed her mind and wished to keep it, and he offered me ten
dollars to release him. Now, to speak the truth, I had but ten cents
in the world, and it surpassed my arithmetic to tell, if I was that
man who had ten cents, or who had a farm, or ten dollars, or all
together. However, I let him keep the ten dollars and the farm
too, for I had carried it far enough; or rather, to be generous, I
sold him the farm for just what I gave for it, and, as he was not
a rich man, made him a present of ten dollars, and still had my
ten cents, and seeds, and materials for a wheelbarrow left. I
found thus that I had been a rich man without any damage to my
poverty. But I retained the landscape, and I have since annually
carried off what it yielded without a wheelbarrow. With respect
to landscapes,—

'I am monarch of all I *survey,*
My right there is none to dispute.'

[3] I have frequently seen a poet withdraw, having enjoyed the most valuable part of a farm, while the crusty farmer supposed that he had got a few wild apples only. Why, the owner does not know it for many years when a poet has put his farm in rhyme, the most admirable kind of invisible fence, has fairly impounded it, milked it, skimmed it, and got all the cream, and left the farmer only the skimmed milk.

[4] The real attractions of the Hollowell farm, to me, were: its complete retirement, being about two miles from the village, half a mile from the nearest neighbor, and separated from the highway by a broad field; its bounding on the river, which the owner said protected it by its fogs from frosts in the spring, though that was nothing to me; the gray color and ruinous state of the house and barn, and the dilapidated fences, which put such an interval between me and the last occupant; the hollow and lichen-covered apple trees, gnawed by rabbits, showing what kind of neighbors I should have; but above all, the recollection I had of it from my earliest voyages up the river, when the house was concealed behind a dense grove of red maples, through which I heard the house-dog bark. I was in haste to buy it, before the proprietor finished getting out some rocks, cutting down the hollow apple trees, and grubbing up some young birches which had sprung up in the pasture, or, in short, had made any more of his improvements. To enjoy these advantages I was ready to carry it on; like Atlas, to take the world on my shoulders,—I never heard what compensation he received for that,—and do all those things which had no other motive or excuse but that I might pay for it and be unmolested in my possession of it; for I knew all the while that it would yield the most abundant crop of the kind I wanted if I could only afford to let it alone. But it turned out as I have said.

[5] All that I could say, then, with respect to farming on a large scale (I have always cultivated a garden) was, that I had had my seeds ready. Many think that seeds improve with age. I have no doubt that time discriminates between the good and the bad; and when at last I shall plant, I shall be less likely to be disappointed.

But I would say to my fellows, once for all, As long as possible live free and uncommitted. It makes but little difference whether you are committed to a farm or the county jail.

[6] Old Cato, whose 'De Re Rusticâ' is my 'Cultivator,' says, and the only translation I have seen makes sheer nonsense of the passage, 'When you think of getting a farm, turn it thus in your mind, not to buy greedily; nor spare your pains to look at it, and do not think it enough to go round it once. The oftener you go there the more it will please you, if it is good.' I think I shall not buy greedily, but go round and round it as long as I live, and be buried in it first, that it may please me the more at last.

[7] The present was my next experiment of this kind, which I propose to describe more at length, for convenience, putting the experience of two years into one. As I have said, I do not propose to write an ode to dejection, but to brag as lustily as chanticleer in the morning, standing on his roost, if only to wake my neighbors up.

[8] When first I took up my abode in the woods, that is, began to spend my nights as well as days there, which, by accident, was on Independence day, or the fourth of July, 1845, my house was not finished for winter, but was merely a defence against the rain, without plastering or chimney, the walls being of rough weather-stained boards, with wide chinks, which made it cool at night. The upright white hewn studs and freshly planed door and window casings gave it a clean and airy look, especially in the morning, when its timbers were saturated with dew, so that I fancied that by noon some sweet gum would exude from them. To my imagination it retained throughout the day more or less of this auroral character, reminding me of a certain house on a mountain which I had visited the year before. This was an airy and unplastered cabin, fit to entertain a travelling god, and where a goddess might trail her garments. The winds which passed over my dwelling were such as sweep over the ridges of mountains, bearing the broken strains, or celestial parts only, of terrestrial music. The morning wind forever blows, the poem of creation is uninterrupted; but few are the ears that hear it. Olympus is but the outside of the earth every where.

[9] The only house I had been the owner of before, if I except a boat, was the tent, which I used occasionally when making excursions in the summer, and this is still rolled up in my garret; but the boat, after passing from hand to hand, has gone down the stream of time. With this more substantial shelter about me, I had made some progress toward settling in the world. This frame, so slightly clad, was a sort of crystallization around me, and reacted on the builder. It was suggestive somewhat as a picture in outlines. I did not need to go out doors to take the air, for the atmosphere within had lost none of its freshness. It was not so much within doors as behind a door where I sat, even in the rainiest weather. The Harivansa says, 'An abode without birds is like a meat without seasoning.' Such was not my abode, for I found myself suddenly neighbor to the birds; not by having imprisoned one, but having caged myself near them. I was not only nearer to some of those which commonly frequent the garden and the orchard, but to those wilder and more thrilling songsters of the forest which never, or rarely, serenade a villager,—the woodthrush, the veery, the scarlet tanager, the field-sparrow, the whippoorwill, and many others.

[10] I was seated by the shore of a small pond, about a mile and a half south of the village of Concord and somewhat higher than it, in the midst of an extensive wood between that town and Lincoln, and about two miles south of that our only field known to fame, Concord Battle Ground; but I was so low in the woods that the opposite shore, half a mile off, like the rest, covered with wood, was my most distant horizon. For the first week, whenever I looked out on the pond it impressed me like a tarn high up on the side of a mountain, its bottom far above the surface of other lakes, and, as the sun arose, I saw it throwing off its nightly clothing of mist, and here and there, by degrees, its soft ripples or its smooth reflecting surface was revealed, while the mists, like ghosts, were stealthily withdrawing in every direction into the woods, as at the breaking up of some nocturnal conventicle. The very dew seemed to hang upon the trees later into the day than usual, as on the sides of mountains.

[11] This small lake was of most value as a neighbor in the intervals of a gentle rain storm in August, when, both air and water

being perfectly still, but the sky overcast, mid-afternoon had all the serenity of evening, and the wood-thrush sang around, and was heard from shore to shore. A lake like this is never smoother than at such a time; and the clear portion of the air above it being shallow and darkened by clouds, the water, full of light and reflections, becomes a lower heaven itself so much the more important. From a hill top near by, where the wood had been recently cut off, there was a pleasing vista southward across the pond, through a wide indentation in the hills which form the shore there, where their opposite sides sloping toward each other suggested a stream flowing out in that direction through a wooded valley, but stream there was none. That way I looked between and over the near green hills to some distant and higher ones in the horizon, tinged with blue. Indeed, by standing on tiptoe I could catch a glimpse of some of the peaks of the still bluer and more distant mountain ranges in the north-west, those true-blue coins from heaven's own mint, and also of some portion of the village. But in other directions, even from this point, I could not see over or beyond the woods which surrounded me. It is well to have some water in your neighborhood, to give buoyancy to and float the earth. One value even of the smallest well is, that when you look into it you see that earth is not continent but insular. This is as important as that it keeps butter cool. When I looked across the pond from this peak toward the Sudbury meadows, which in time of flood I distinguished elevated perhaps by a mirage in their seething valley, like a coin in a basin, all the earth beyond the pond appeared like a thin crust insulated and floated even by this small sheet of intervening water, and I was reminded that this on which I dwelt was but *dry land*.

[12] Though the view from my door was still more contracted, I did not feel crowded or confined in the least. There was pasture enough for my imagination. The low shrub-oak plateau to which the opposite shore arose, stretched away toward the prairies of the West and the steppes of Tartary, affording ample room for all the roving families of men. 'There are none happy in the world but beings who enjoy freely a vast horizon,'—said Damodara, when his herds required new and larger pastures.

[13] Both place and time were changed, and I dwelt nearer to

those parts of the universe and to those eras in history which had most attracted me. Where I lived was as far off as many a region viewed nightly by astronomers. We are wont to imagine rare and delectable places in some remote and more celestial corner of the system, behind the constellation of Cassiopeia's Chair, far from noise and disturbance. I discovered that my house actually had its site in such a withdrawn, but forever new and unprofaned, part of the universe. If it were worth the while to settle in those parts near to the Pleiades or the Hyades, to Aldebaran or Altair, then I was really there, or at an equal remoteness from the life which I had left behind, dwindled and twinkling with as fine a ray to my nearest neighbor, and to be seen only in moonless nights by him. Such was that part of creation where I had squatted;—

> 'There was a shepherd that did live,
>   And held his thoughts as high
> As were the mounts whereon his flocks
>   Did hourly feed him by.'

What should we think of the shepherd's life if his flocks always wandered to higher pastures than his thoughts?

[14] Every morning was a cheerful invitation to make my life of equal simplicity, and I may say innocence, with Nature herself. I had been as sincere a worshipper of Aurora as the Greeks. I got up early and bathed in the pond; that was a religious exercise, and one of the best things which I did. They say that characters were engraven on the bathing tub of king Tchingthang to this effect: 'Renew thyself completely each day; do it again, and again, and forever again.' I can understand that. Morning brings back the heroic ages. I was as much affected by the faint hum of a mosquito making its invisible and unimaginable tour through my apartment at earliest dawn, when I was sitting with door and windows open, as I could be by any trumpet that ever sang of fame. It was Homer's requiem; itself an Iliad and Odyssey in the air, singing its own wrath and wanderings. There was something cosmical about it; a standing advertisement, till forbidden, of the everlasting vigor and fertility of the world. The morning, which is the most memorable season of the day, is the awakening hour. Then

there is least somnolence in us; and for an hour, at least, some part of us awakes which slumbers all the rest of the day and night. Little is to be expected of that day, if it can be called a day, to which we are not awakened by our Genius, but by the mechanical nudgings of some servitor, are not awakened by our own newly-acquired force and aspirations from within, accompanied by the undulations of celestial music, instead of factory bells, and a fragrance filling the air—to a higher life than we fell asleep from; and thus the darkness bear its fruit, and prove itself to be good, no less than the light. That man who does not believe that each day contains an earlier, more sacred, and auroral hour than he has yet profaned, has despaired of life, and is pursuing a descending and darkening way. After a partial cessation of his sensuous life, the soul of man, or its organs rather, are reinvigorated each day, and his Genius tries again what noble life it can make. All memorable events, I should say, transpire in morning time and in a morning atmosphere. The Vedas say, 'All intelligences awake with the morning.' Poetry and art, and the fairest and most memorable of the actions of men, date from such an hour. All poets and heroes, like Memnon, are the children of Aurora, and emit their music at sunrise. To him whose elastic and vigorous thought keeps pace with the sun, the day is a perpetual morning. It matters not what the clocks say or the attitudes and labors of men. Morning is when I am awake and there is a dawn in me. Moral reform is the effort to throw off sleep. Why is it that men give so poor an account of their day if they have not been slumbering? They are not such poor calculators. If they had not been overcome with drowsiness they would have performed something. The millions are awake enough for physical labor; but only one in a million is awake enough for effective intellectual exertion, only one in a hundred millions to a poetic or divine life. To be awake is to be alive. I have never yet met a man who was quite awake. How could I have looked him in the face? [15] We must learn to reawaken and keep ourselves awake, not by mechanical aids, but by an infinite expectation of the dawn, which does not forsake us in our soundest sleep. I know of no more encouraging fact than the unquestionable ability of man to elevate his life by a conscious endeavor. It is something to be able

to paint a particular picture, or to carve a statue, and so to make
a few objects beautiful; but it is far more glorious to carve and
paint the very atmosphere and medium through which we look,
which morally we can do. To affect the quality of the day, that is
the highest of arts. Every man is tasked to make his life, even in
its details, worthy of the contemplation of his most elevated and
critical hour. If we refused, or rather used up, such paltry information as we get, the oracles would distinctly inform us how this might
be done.

[16] I went to the woods because I wished to live deliberately, to
front only the essential facts of life, and see if I could not learn
what it had to teach, and not, when I came to die, discover that
I had not lived. I did not wish to live what was not life, living is so
dear; nor did I wish to practise resignation, unless it was quite
necessary. I wanted to live deep and suck out all the marrow of
life, to live so sturdily and Spartan-like as to put to rout all that
was not life, to cut a broad swath and shave close, to drive life into
a corner, and reduce it to its lowest terms, and, if it proved to be
mean, why then to get the whole and genuine meanness of it, and
publish its meanness to the world; or if it were sublime, to know it
by experience, and be able to give a true account of it in my next
excursion. For most men, it appears to me, are in a strange uncertainty about it, whether it is of the devil or of God, and have
somewhat hastily concluded that it is the chief end of man here to
'glorify God and enjoy him forever.'

[17] Still we live meanly, like ants; though the fable tells us that
we were long ago changed into men; like pygmies we fight with
cranes; it is error upon error, and clout upon clout, and our best
virtue has for its occasion a superfluous and evitable wretchedness.
Our life is frittered away by detail. An honest man has hardly need
to count more than his ten fingers, or in extreme cases he may add
his ten toes, and lump the rest. Simplicity, simplicity, simplicity!
I say, let your affairs be as two or three, and not a hundred or
a thousand; instead of a million count half a dozen, and keep your
accounts on your thumb nail. In the midst of this chopping sea
of civilized life, such are the clouds and storms and quicksands
and thousand-and-one items to be allowed for, that a man has to
live, if he would not founder and go to the bottom and not make

his port at all, by dead reckoning, and he must be a great cal-
culator indeed who succeeds. Simplify, simplify. Instead of three
meals a day, if it be necessary eat but one; instead of a hundred
dishes, five; and reduce other things in proportion. Our life is like
a German Confederacy, made up of petty states, with its boundary
forever fluctuating, so that even a German cannot tell you how it
is bounded at any moment. The nation itself, with all its so-called
internal improvements, which, by the way, are all external and
superficial, is just such an unwieldy and overgrown establishment,
cluttered with furniture and tripped up by its own traps, ruined
by luxury and heedless expense, by want of calculation and a
worthy aim, as the million households in the land; and the only
cure for it as for them is in a rigid economy, a stern and more
than Spartan simplicity of life and elevation of purpose. It lives
too fast. Men think that it is essential that the *Nation* have commerce, and export ice, and talk through a telegraph, and ride
thirty miles an hour, without a doubt, whether *they* do or not;
but whether we should live like baboons or like men, is a little
uncertain. If we do not get out sleepers, and forge rails, and devote days and nights to the work, but go to tinkering upon our
lives to improve *them,* who will build railroads? And if railroads
are not built, how shall we get to heaven in season? But if we
stay at home and mind our business, who will want railroads?
We do not ride on the railroad; it rides upon us. Did you ever
think what those sleepers are that underlie the railroad? Each
one is a man, an Irishman, or a Yankee man. The rails are laid
on them, and they are covered with sand, and the cars run
smoothly over them. They are sound sleepers, I assure you. And
every few years a new lot is laid down and run over; so that, if
some have the pleasure of riding on a rail, others have the misfortune to be ridden upon. And when they run over a man that
is walking in his sleep, a supernumerary sleeper in the wrong
position, and wake him up, they suddenly stop the cars, and make
a hue and cry about it, as if this were an exception. I am glad to
know that it takes a gang of men for every five miles to keep the
sleepers down and level in their beds as it is, for this is a sign that
they may sometime get up again.

[18] Why should we live with such hurry and waste of life? We

are determined to be starved before we are hungry. Men say that a stitch in time saves nine, and so they take a thousand stitches to-day to save nine to-morrow. As for *work,* we haven't any of any consequence. We have the Saint Vitus' dance, and cannot possibly keep our heads still. If I should only give a few pulls at the parish bell-rope, as for a fire, that is, without setting the bell, there is hardly a man on his farm in the outskirts of Concord, notwithstanding that press of engagements which was his excuse so many times this morning, nor a boy, nor a woman, I might almost say, but would forsake all and follow that sound, not mainly to save property from the flames, but, if we will confess the truth, much more to see it burn, since burn it must, and we, be it known, did not set it on fire,—or to see it put out, and have a hand in it, if that is done as handsomely; yes, even if it were the parish church itself. Hardly a man takes a half hour's nap after dinner, but when he wakes he holds up his head and asks, 'What's the news?' as if the rest of mankind had stood his sentinels. Some give directions to be waked every half hour, doubtless for no other purpose; and then, to pay for it, they tell what they have dreamed. After a night's sleep the news is as indispensable as the breakfast. 'Pray tell me any thing new that has happened to a man any where on this globe,'—and he reads it over his coffee and rolls, that a man has had his eyes gouged out this morning on the Wachito River; never dreaming the while that he lives in the dark unfathomed mammoth cave of this world, and has but the rudiment of an eye himself.

[19] For my part, I could easily do without the post-office. I think that there are very few important communications made through it. To speak critically, I never received more than one or two letters in my life—I wrote this some years ago—that were worth the postage. The penny-post is, commonly, an institution through which you seriously offer a man that penny for his thoughts which is so often safely offered in jest. And I am sure that I never read any memorable news in a newspaper. If we read of one man robbed, or murdered, or killed by accident, or one house burned, or one vessel wrecked, or one steamboat blown up, or one cow run over on the Western Railroad, or one mad dog killed, or one lot of grasshoppers in the winter,—we never need

read of another. One is enough. If you are acquainted with the
principle, what do you care for a myriad instances and applications? To a philosopher all *news,* as it is called, is gossip, and they
who edit and read it are old women over their tea. Yet not a few
are greedy after this gossip. There was such a rush, as I hear, the
other day at one of the offices to learn the foreign news by the
last arrival, that several large squares of plate glass belonging
to the establishment were broken by the pressure,—news which
I seriously think a ready wit might write a twelve-month or twelve
years beforehand with sufficient accuracy. As for Spain, for instance, if you know how to throw in Don Carlos and the Infanta,
and Don Pedro and Seville and Granada, from time to time in the
right proportions,—they may have changed the names a little
since I saw the papers,—and serve up a bull-fight when other
entertainers fail, it will be true to the letter, and give us as good
an idea of the exact state or ruin of things in Spain as the most
succinct and lucid reports under this head in the newspapers:
and as for England, almost the last significant scrap of news from
that quarter was the revolution of 1649; and if you have learned
the history of her crops for an average year, you never need attend to that thing again, unless your speculations are of a merely
pecuniary character. If one may judge who rarely looks into the
newspapers, nothing new does ever happen in foreign parts, a
French revolution not excepted.

[20] What news! how much more important to know what that
is which was never old! 'Kieou-he-yu (great dignitary of the state
of Wei) sent a man to Khoung-tseu to know his news. Khoung-
tseu caused the messenger to be seated near him, and questioned
him in these terms: What is your master doing? The messenger
answered with respect: My master desires to diminish the number
of his faults, but he cannot come to the end of them. The messenger being gone, the philosopher remarked: What a worthy messenger! What a worthy messenger!' The preacher, instead of vex-
ing the ears of drowsy farmers on their day of rest at the end of
the week,—for Sunday is the fit conclusion of an ill-spent week,
and not the fresh and brave beginning of a new one,—with this
one other draggletail of a sermon, should shout with thundering
voice,—'Pause! Avast! Why so seeming fast, but deadly slow?'

[21] Shams and delusions are esteemed for soundest truths, while reality is fabulous. If men would steadily observe realities only, and not allow themselves to be deluded, life, to compare it with such things as we know, would be like a fairy tale and the Arabian Nights' Entertainments. If we respected only what is inevitable and has a right to be, music and poetry would resound along the streets. When we are unhurried and wise, we perceive that only great and worthy things have any permanent and absolute existence,—that petty fears and petty pleasures are but the shadow of the reality. This is always exhilarating and sublime. By closing the eyes and slumbering, and consenting to be deceived by shows, men establish and confirm their daily life of routine and habit every where, which still is built on purely illusory foundations. Children, who play life, discern its true law and relations more clearly than men, who fail to live it worthily, but who think that they are wiser by experience, that is, by failure. I have read in a Hindoo book, that 'there was a king's son, who, being expelled in infancy from his native city, was brought up by a forester, and, growing up to maturity in that state, imagined himself to belong to the barbarous race with which he lived. One of his father's ministers having discovered him, revealed to him what he was, and the misconception of his character was removed, and he knew himself to be a prince. So soul,' continues the Hindoo philosopher, 'from the circumstances in which it is placed, mistakes its own character, until the truth is revealed to it by some holy teacher, and then it knows itself to be *Brahme*.' I perceive that we inhabitants of New England live this mean life that we do because our vision does not penetrate the surface of things. We think that that *is* which *appears* to be. If a man should walk through this town and see only the reality, where, think you, would the 'Mill-dam' go to? If he should give us an account of the realities he beheld there, we should not recognize the place in his description. Look at a meeting-house, or a court-house, or a jail, or a shop, or a dwelling-house, and say what that thing really is before a true gaze, and they would all go to pieces in your account of them. Men esteem truth remote, in the outskirts of the system, behind the farthest star, before Adam and after the last man. In eternity there is indeed something true and sublime. But all

these times and places and occasions are now and here. God himself culminates in the present moment, and will never be more divine in the lapse of all the ages. And we are enabled to apprehend at all what is sublime and noble only by the perpetual instilling and drenching of the reality that surrounds us. The universe constantly and obediently answers to our conceptions; whether we travel fast or slow, the track is laid for us. Let us spend our lives in conceiving then. The poet or the artist never yet had so fair and noble a design but some of his posterity at least could accomplish it.

[22] Let us spend one day as deliberately as Nature, and not be thrown off the track by every nutshell and mosquito's wing that falls on the rails. Let us rise early and fast, or break fast, gently and without perturbation; let company come and let company go, let the bells ring and the children cry,—determined to make a day of it. Why should we knock under and go with the stream? Let us not be upset and overwhelmed in that terrible rapid and whirlpool called a dinner, situated in the meridian shallows. Weather this danger and you are safe, for the rest of the way is down hill. With unrelaxed nerves, with morning vigor, sail by it, looking another way, tied to the mast like Ulysses. If the engine whistles, let it whistle till it is hoarse for its pains. If the bell rings, why should we run? We will consider what kind of music they are like. Let us settle ourselves, and work and wedge our feet downward through the mud and slush of opinion, and prejudice, and tradition, and delusion, and appearance, that alluvion which covers the globe, through Paris and London, through New York and Boston and Concord, through church and state, through poetry and philosophy and religion, till we come to a hard bottom and rocks in place, which we can call *reality,* and say, This is, and no mistake; and then begin, having a *point d'appui,* below freshet and frost and fire, a place where you might found a wall or a state, or set a lamp-post safely, or perhaps a gauge, not a Nilometer, but a Realometer, that future ages might know how deep a freshet of shams and appearances had gathered from time to time. If you stand right fronting and face to face to a fact, you will see the sun glimmer on both its surfaces, as if it were a cimeter, and feel its sweet edge dividing you through

the heart and marrow, and so you will happily conclude your mortal career. Be it life or death, we crave only reality. If we are really dying, let us hear the rattle in our throats and feel cold in the extremities; if we are alive, let us go about our business.

[23] Time is but the stream I go a-fishing in. I drink at it; but while I drink I see the sandy bottom and detect how shallow it is. Its thin current slides away, but eternity remains. I would drink deeper; fish in the sky, whose bottom is pebbly with stars. I cannot count one. I know not the first letter of the alphabet. I have always been regretting that I was not as wise as the day I was born. The intellect is a cleaver; it discerns and rifts its way into the secret of things. I do not wish to be any more busy with my hands than is necessary. My head is hands and feet. I feel all my best faculties concentrated in it. My instinct tells me that my head is an organ for burrowing, as some creatures use their snout and fore-paws, and with it I would mine and burrow my way through these hills. I think that the richest vein is somewhere hereabouts; so by the divining rod and thin rising vapors I judge; and here I will begin to mine.

EXERCISES

Probably most Americans are familiar with the first chapter of Thoreau's *Walden,* in which he tells why he went to live by Walden Pond, and how he built his house, and of his first experiences there. Under the heading of "Economy" he lists in minute detail his few and small expenses—for building materials (about $28), for food such as Indian meal, molasses, potatoes, etc. (about $8 for the first eight months). Such details have helped to make *Walden* popular, as E. B. White points out in the next selection. The nature of Thoreau's philosophy, which also continues to appeal to some Thoreau in all of us, is perhaps best summarized in "Where I Lived, and What I Lived For."

1. Does Thoreau seem to have believed in and practised what his neighbor Emerson had called self-reliance? Illustrate.
2. Does he seem to share Emerson's beliefs about the nature of man and the reliability of intuition?
3. What are Thoreau's main kinds of pleasures?
4. What was his purpose in living at Walden?

5. Would the kind of life he recommends be, in principle at least, available to most of us?
6. What does he consider the chief deterrents to the life he recommends?
7. If such a life were pursued, in ideal, by everyone, what would happen to civic problems?
8. Does Thoreau recommend that everyone live in the woods?
9. Point out the main difference or differences between Thoreau's style and Emerson's.

Walden

E. B. WHITE

[1] Miss Nims, take a letter to Henry David Thoreau.

Dear Henry: I thought of you the other afternoon as I was approaching Concord doing fifty on Route 62. That is a high speed at which to hold a philosopher in one's mind, but in this century we are a nimble bunch.

[2] On one of the lawns in the outskirts of the village a woman was cutting the grass with a motorized lawn mower. What made me think of you was that the machine had rather got away from her, although she was game enough, and in the brief glimpse I had of the scene it appeared to me that the lawn was mowing the lady. She kept a tight grip on the handles, which throbbed violently with every explosion of the one-cylinder motor, and as she sheered around bushes and lurched along at a reluctant trot behind her impetuous servant, she looked like a puppy who had grabbed something that was too much for him. Concord hasn't changed much, Henry; the farm implements and the animals still have the upper hand.

[3] I may as well admit that I was journeying to Concord with the deliberate intention of visiting your woods; for although I

have never knelt at the grave of a philosopher nor placed wreaths on moldy poets, and have often gone a mile out of my way to avoid some place of historical interest, I have always wanted to see Walden Pond. The account which you left of your sojourn there is, you will be amused to learn, a document of increasing pertinence; each year it seems to gain a little headway, as the world loses ground. We may all be transcendental yet, whether we like it or not. As our common complexities increase, any tale of individual simplicity (and yours is the best written and the cockiest) acquires a new fascination; as our goods accumulate, but not our well-being, your report of an existence without material adornment takes on a certain awkward credibility.

[4] My purpose in going to Walden Pond, like yours, was not to live cheaply or to live dearly there, but to transact some private business with the fewest obstacles. Approaching Concord, doing forty, forty-five, doing fifty, the steering wheel held snug in my palms, the highway held grimly in my vision, the crown of the road now serving me (on the righthand curves), now defeating me (on the lefthand curves), I began to rouse myself from the stupefaction which a day's motor journey induces. It was a delicious evening, Henry, when the whole body is one sense, and imbibes delight through every pore, if I may coin a phrase. Fields were richly brown where the harrow, drawn by the stripped Ford, had lately sunk its teeth; pastures were green; and overhead the sky had that same everlasting great look which you will find on Page 144 of the Oxford pocket edition. I could feel the road entering me, through tire, wheel, spring, and cushion; shall I not have intelligence with earth too? Am I not partly leaves and vegetable mold myself?—a man of infinite horsepower, yet partly leaves.

[5] Stay with me on 62 and it will take you into Concord. As I say, it is a delicious evening. The snake had come forth to die a bloody S on the highway, the wheel upon its head, its bowels flat now and exposed. The turtle had come up too to cross the road and die in the attempt, its hard shell smashed under the rubber blow, its intestinal yearning (for the other side of the road) forever squashed. There was a sign by the wayside which announced that the road had a "cotton surface." You wouldn't know what

that is, but neither, for that matter, did I. There is a cryptic ingredient in many of our modern improvements—we are awed and pleased without knowing quite what we are enjoying. It is something to be traveling on a road with a cotton surface.

[6] The civilization round Concord to-day is an odd distillation of city, village, farm, and manor. The houses, yards, fields look not quite suburban, not quite rural. Under the bronze beech and the blue spruce of the departed baron grazes the milch goat of the heirs. Under the porte-cochère stands the reconditioned station wagon; under the grape arbor sit the puppies for sale. (But why do men degenerate ever? What makes families run out?)

[7] It was June and everywhere June was publishing her immemorial stanza; in the lilacs, in the syringa, in the freshly edged paths and the sweetness of moist beloved gardens, and the little wire wickets that preserve the tulips' front. Farmers were already moving the fruits of their toil into their yards, arranging the rhubarb, the asparagus, the strictly fresh eggs on the painted stands under the little shed roofs with the patent shingles. And though it was almost a hundred years since you had taken your ax and started cutting out your home on Walden Pond, I was interested to observe that the philosophical spirit was still alive in Massachusetts; in the center of a vacant lot some boys were assembling the framework of a rude shelter, their whole mind and skill concentrated in the rather inauspicious helter-skeleton of studs and rafters. They too were escaping from town, to live naturally, in a rich blend of savagery and philosophy.

[8] That evening, after supper at the inn, I strolled out into the twilight to dream my shapeless transcendental dreams and see that the car was locked up for the night (first open the right front door, then reach over, straining, and pull up the handles of the left rear and the left front till you hear the click, then the handle of the right rear, then shut the right front but open it again, remembering that the key is still in the ignition switch, remove the key, shut the right front again with a bang, push the tiny keyhole cover to one side, insert key, turn, and withdraw). It is what we all do, Henry. It is called locking the car. It is said to confuse thieves and keep them from making off with the laprobe. Four doors to lock behind one robe. The driver himself

never uses a laprobe, the free movement of his legs being vital
to the operation of the vehicle; so that when he locks the car it
is a pure and unselfish act. I have in my life gained very little
essential heat from laprobes, yet I have ever been at pains to
lock them up.

[9] The evening was full of sounds, some of which would have
stirred your memory. The robins still love the elms of New England villages at sundown. There is enough of the thrush in them
to make song inevitable at the end of day, and enough of the
tramp to make them hang round the dwellings of men. A robin,
like many another American, dearly loves a white house with green
blinds. Concord is still full of them.

[10] Your fellow-townsmen were stirring abroad—not many
afoot, most of them in their cars; and the sound which they made
in Concord at evening was a rustling and a whispering. The
sound lacks steadfastness and is wholly unlike that of a train. A
train, as you know who lived so near the Fitchburg line, whistles
once or twice sadly and is gone, trailing a memory in smoke, soothing to ear and mind. Automobiles, skirting a village green, are like
flies that have gained the inner ear—they buzz, cease, pause, start,
shift, stop, halt, brake, and the whole effect is a nervous polytone
curiously disturbing.

[11] As I wandered along, the toc toc of ping pong balls drifted
from an attic window. In front of the Reuben Brown house a
Buick was drawn up. At the wheel, motionless, his hat upon his
head, a man sat, listening to Amos and Andy on the radio (it
is a drama of many scenes and without an end). The deep voice
of Andrew Brown, emerging from the car, although it originated
more than two hundred miles away, was unstrained by distance.
When you used to sit on the shore of your pond on Sunday morning, listening to the church bells of Acton and Concord, you were
aware of the excellent filter of the intervening atmosphere. Science
has attended to that, and sound now maintains its intensity without regard for distance. Properly sponsored, it goes on forever.

[12] A fire engine, out for a trial spin, roared past Emerson's
house, hot with readiness for public duty. Over the barn roofs the
martins dipped and chittered. A swarthy daughter of an asparagus
grower, in culottes, shirt, and bandanna, pedalled past on her bi-

cycle. It was indeed a delicious evening, and I returned to the inn (I believe it was your house once) to rock with the old ladies on the concrete veranda.

[13] Next morning early I started afoot for Walden, out Main Street and down Thoreau, past the depot and the Minuteman Chevrolet Company. The morning was fresh, and in a bean field along the way I flushed an agriculturist, quietly studying his beans. Thoreau Street soon joined Number 126, an artery of the State. We number our highways nowadays, our speed being so great we can remember little of their quality or character and are lucky to remember their number. (Men have an indistinct notion that if they keep up this activity long enough all will at length ride somewhere, in next to no time.) Your pond is on 126.

[14] I knew I must be nearing your woodland retreat when the Golden Pheasant lunchroom came into view—Sealtest ice cream, toasted sandwiches, hot frankfurters, waffles, tonics, and lunches. Were I the proprietor, I should add rice, Indian meal, and molasses—just for old time's sake. The Pheasant, incidentally, is for sale: a chance for some nature lover who wishes to set himself up beside a pond in the Concord atmosphere and live deliberately, fronting only the essential facts of life on Number 126. Beyond the Pheasant was a place called Walden Breezes, an oasis whose porch pillars were made of old green shutters sawed into lengths. On the porch was a distorting mirror, to give the traveler a comical image of himself, who had miraculously learned to gaze in an ordinary glass without smiling. Behind the Breezes, in a sunparched clearing, dwelt your philosophical descendants in their trailers, each trailer the size of your hut, but all grouped together for the sake of congeniality. Trailer people leave the city, as you did, to discover solitude and in any weather, at any hour of the day or night, to improve the nick of time; but they soon collect in villages and get bogged deeper in the mud than ever. The camp behind Walden Breezes was just rousing itself to the morning. The ground was packed hard under the heel, and the sun came through the clearing to bake the soil and enlarge the wry smell of cramped housekeeping. Cushman's bakery truck had stopped to deliver an early basket of rolls. A camp dog, seeing me in the road, barked petulantly. A man emerged from one of the trailers

and set forth with a bucket to draw water from some forest tap.
[15] Leaving the highway I turned off into the woods toward
the pond, which was apparent through the foliage. The floor of
the forest was strewn with dried old oak leaves and *Transcripts*.
From beneath the flattened popcorn wrapper (*granum explosum*)
peeped the frail violet. I followed a footpath and descended to
the water's edge. The pond lay clear and blue in the morning
light, as you have seen it so many times. In the shallows a man's
waterlogged shirt undulated gently. A few flies came out to greet
me and convoy me to your cove, past the No Bathing signs on
which the fellows and the girls had scrawled their names. I felt
strangely excited suddenly to be snooping around your premises,
tiptoeing along watchfully, as though not to tread by mistake
upon the intervening century. Before I got to the cove I heard
something which seemed to me quite wonderful: I heard your frog,
a full clear *troonk,* guiding me, still hoarse and solemn, bridging
the years as the robins had bridged them in the sweetness of the
village evening. But he soon quit, and I came on a couple of
young boys throwing stones at him.
[16] Your front yard is marked by a bronze tablet set in a stone.
Four small granite posts, a few feet away, show where the house
was. On top of the tablet was a pair of faded blue bathing trunks
with a white stripe. Back of it is a pile of stones, a sort of cairn,
left by your visitors as a tribute I suppose. It is a rather ugly
little heap of stones, Henry. In fact the hillside itself seems
faded, browbeaten; a few tall skinny pines, bare of lower limbs,
a smattering of young maples in suitable green, some birches and
oaks, and a number of trees felled by the last big wind. It was
from the bole of one of these fallen pines, torn up by the roots,
that I extracted the stone which I added to the cairn—a sentimental act in which I was interrupted by a small terrier from a
nearby picnic group, who confronted me and wanted to know
about the stone.
[17] I sat down for a while on one of the posts of your house
to listen to the bluebottles and the dragonflies. The invaded glade
sprawled shabby and mean at my feet, but the flies were tuned
to the old vibration. There were the remains of a fire in your
ruins, but I doubt that it was yours; also two beer bottles trodden
into the soil and become part of earth. A young oak had taken

root in your house, and two or three ferns, unrolling like the
ticklers at a banquet. The only other furnishings were a DuBarry
pattern sheet, a page torn from a picture magazine, and some
crusts in wax paper.

[18] Before I quit I walked clear round the pond and found the
place where you used to sit on the northeast side to get the sun
in the fall, and the beach where you got sand for scrubbing your
floor. On the eastern side of the pond, where the highway borders
it, the State has built dressing rooms for swimmers, a float with
diving towers, drinking fountains of porcelain, and rowboats for
hire. The pond is in fact a State Preserve, and carries a twenty-
dollar fine for picking wild flowers, a decree signed in all solemnity
by your fellow-citizens Walter C. Wardwell, Erson B. Barlow,
and Nathaniel I. Bowditch. There was a smell of creosote where
they had been building a wide wooden stairway to the road and
the parking area. Swimmers and boaters were arriving; bodies
plunged vigorously into the water and emerged wet and beautiful
in the bright air. As I left, a boatload of town boys were splashing
about in mid-pond, kidding and fooling, the young fellows singing
at the tops of their lungs in a wild chorus:

> Amer-ica, Amer-i-ca, God shed his grace on thee,
> And crown thy good with brotherhood
> From sea to shi-ning sea!

[19] I walked back to town along the railroad, following your
custom. The rails were expanding noisily in the hot sun, and on
the slope of the roadbed the wild grape and the blackberry sent
up their creepers to the track.

[20] The expense of my brief sojourn in Concord was:

Canvas shoes	$1.95	
Baseball bat	.25	} gifts to take back to a boy
Left-handed fielder's glove .	1.25	
Hotel and meals	4.25	
In all	$7.70	

As you see, this amount was almost what you spent for food for
eight months. I cannot defend the shoes or the expenditure for
shelter and food: they reveal a meanness and grossness in my
nature which you would find contemptible. The baseball equip-

ment, however, is the kind of impediment with which you were never on even terms. You must remember that the house where you practiced the sort of economy which I respect was haunted only by mice and squirrels. You never had to cope with a short-stop.

EXERCISES

E. B. White enjoys great popularity as a contemporary essayist. He persistently criticizes certain aspects of our culture, in an irrefutable but entertaining way. This account of his pilgrimage to Walden illustrates not only his amusingly disturbing style, which rewards careful study, but also his outlook on life, which comes in most appropriately here.

1. State White's attitude toward Thoreau as exactly and as fully as possible.
2. What general aspects of modern civilization is he criticizing?
3. What is the irony of the fire engine roaring past Emerson's house "hot with readiness for public duty"?
4. List several conscious allusions or parallels to Thoreau and explain the use which is made of each.
5. List some aspects of modern civilization which White considers regrettable and corrigible, some which he considers somewhat regrettable but inevitable, and some which he apparently considers natural and good expressions of human nature.
6. What aspects of Thoreau's advice about living would White respect?
7. Exactly what is the function of the shortstop in White's whole statement on Thoreau's philosophy?

The Iron String

HOWARD MUMFORD JONES

[1] I have lately been reading a Harvard author who is just now out of favor here. He has been unpopular before. He once made

An address given at the Leverett House Junior-Senior Dinner, 1950. Reprinted by permission from the *Harvard Alumni Bulletin*.

a speech at this college, a speech so disliked that he was *persona non grata* in Cambridge for thirty years. However, the alumni and the Faculty finally decided he was a solid citizen—this was after the Civil War—and so they made him an Overseer, they gave him an honorary degree, and they asked him to deliver a course of lectures. In view of this history I take some pleasure in remembering that the title of these lectures was: "The Natural History of the Intellect." Another thirty years or so drifted by, and they erected a building in his honor. On any class day in winter you can enter it and see Frank Duveneck's statue of him buried under the coats and hats. Somehow, this symbolizes what has happened to Emerson.

[2] The reasons for Emerson's current lack of favor are understandable. He was a transcendentalist, and any beginner in philosophy can tell you what is wrong with transcendentalism. As a philosophy it is inconsistent, illogical, and indefensible. Its epistemology is contrary to fact, its ethical system is unscientific, its language is confused, and its frame of reference is romantic America. It is not, as we owlishly say, for our time. All it has is imagination and insight.

[3] Another reason for Emerson's unpopularity is that he did not have a vision of evil. To count in criticism nowadays you must have a vision of evil. It seems that Herman Melville had a vision of evil in *Moby Dick,* that Nathaniel Hawthorne had a vision of evil in *The Scarlet Letter,* and that Henry James had a vision of evil in *The Turn of the Screw*. Precisely what the evil was in each case is in dispute, but it is there. Emerson had no vision of evil. His life was threatened by tuberculosis, he abandoned his pulpit, his first wife died young, his brothers were sick men, and his son perished—

> That hyacinthine boy, for whom
> Morn well might break and April bloom

he was ostracized by the conservative, he took the unpopular side in politics, he was accused of advocating atheism, he was said to be a radical, but he had no vision of evil. All he had was a vision of good. Good, he said, is something so tough, resilient, and timeless, it is indestructible. Our culture is supposed to have this vision of good as its ideal, yet Emerson is unpopular. I am not a philosopher, but merely a literary historian, and I do not pretend to explain the contradiction.

[4] A third reason for Emerson's unpopularity is that he was a liberal. A liberal, says the Oxford Dictionary, is favorable to changes and reforms tending in the direction of democracy. Emerson favored these changes. However, liberalism is dead. It is not merely dead, it was mistaken. Mr. Wallace's failure to create a liberal party in this country is proof. The latest British election, which again buried the liberal party, is proof. The liberal point of view in economics is wrong. The liberal point of view in history, or rather the point of view of liberal historians, is wrong. These historians denounced Talleyrand, but Talleyrand was a force for stability. They attacked Metternich, but Metternich was a force for order. I am afraid Emerson was a liberal; that is, he assumed that man might amount to something by and by if he would but consult his better self, and that men, taken individually, might improve themselves, so to speak, into a democratic state. This is the American dream which, through the Voice of America, we are broadcasting round the world, particularly into darkest Russia. I am not a politician, merely a literary man, and I cannot explain this contradiction.

[5] That somewhat frightened conservative, Matthew Arnold, came here in the eighties to lecture us about culture. He began the habit of depreciating Emerson. His lecture brings me to the fourth reason for Emerson's unpopularity. Arnold hinted that Emerson did not quite understand human weakness. Ours is the aspirin age, and we understand human weakness. Mr. T. S. Eliot has told us a number of times that man is full of sin. Mr. Reinhold Niebuhr has told us that man is full of sin. Monsignor Sheen has told us that man is full of sin. The bright faith in man characteristic of the eighteenth century, the bright trust in spiritual development characteristic of much of the nineteenth century, were fallacies.

[6] Arnold allowed Emerson a single virtue. Emerson, he said, is the friend and aider of those who would live in the spirit. But we are informed that our profoundest failure, individual and political, is a failure of the spirit. For example, we are not truly suc-

cessful in democratizing Germany because there is lacking a spiritual content to our democracy. Through the Marshall Plan and through military aid to Western Europe, there must glow, we are told, a radiancy of the spirit, or Communism will rush in. I do not understand how, if all men are weak, if all men are sinful, we can hope to maintain, much less improve, democratic society, I do not see how universal wickedness can be restrained except by an authoritarian church and state, I do not see how free men can be held together by mere unanimity of evil hearts. Nothing, of course, is more flattering than to think of one's self as a great sinner, irreparably lost. Byron is a case in point. A new Byronism now appears in poetry and theology, but I still suggest that some tincture of virtue is necessary for citizens of a republic. However, I am not a theologian.

[7] By now you have rightly inferred that I find something important in Emerson. I am speaking of Emerson *à propos* of our time in order to revalidate an old Harvard custom—the custom of dissent. The protection of dissent is old at Harvard. Emerson's Divinity School Address *was* delivered, whatever happened afterwards—an early example. President Lowell's refusal to discharge Münsterberg and Harold Laski, when mob feeling demanded it, is a second example. The refusal of the President and Fellows to silence Harlow Shapley at the demand of an influential alumnus is a third. If Oxford's proudest products are its rebels, the proudest tradition of Harvard is the protection of dissent. Long may it be so. I sometimes think dissent may have no other place to go if the drives for conformity continue. For a slow, irresistible drive against dissent does go forward. That is why Emerson is important. Let me briefly discuss four examples of the drive for conformity —two from politics, two from education.

[8] The British election shows what a genuine two-party system is—a system in which there is a fundamental philosophic issue. In Great Britain that issue lies between the Socialist state and the Tory state. No such issue divides the Republican state from the Democratic state. There is with us a set of persons called Democrats, some of them in office, and another set of persons calling themselves Republicans, not so many of whom are in office, but neither you nor I nor more competent observers can define the

philosophic difference between these sets of persons in terms that will really make sense. Almost nothing could be more comic, if it were not so tragic, than to watch the Republicans hunting for somebody who will tell them what to do—a party in search of a platform. The only thing just as comic and just as tragic is the Democrats hunting for somebody who will tell them what they have done—a platform in search of a party. We are afraid of political dissent. We are so afraid of it that we use every means we can to prevent the creation or continuation of a dissenting party, Communist, Progressive, or what have you. I wonder what Emerson would say to this spectacle—he who interested himself in man rather than in mass.

[9] This example of our distrust of dissent is from the national scene. My next example is from the international scene. There is a country called Russia. There is something called the cold war. There is something called the atom bomb, and there may be something called the hydrogen bomb. Now I do not care whether you think Mr. Wallace is politically naive or whether you think Mr. Wallace is an instrument of Satan, but I find nothing more characteristic of the pressure of conformity upon opinion than to compare what happened to Mr. Wallace and what happened to Senator McMahon. A few years ago Mr. Wallace was roundly smeared for urging that on the whole it would be more sensible patiently to continue to seek some accommodation with the Kremlin than to continue to slide down the terrifying spiral along which we are descending. Now that the situation has worsened, Senator McMahon—I mean no disrespect when I say he is safely ensconced in office—was a few weeks ago roundly applauded for saying very much the same thing. Mr. Wallace is on the political left and must therefore be intrinsically wrong; Senator McMahon is an administration Democrat, and must therefore be intrinsically right. We applaud the Christian sentiment of the one and denounce the identical Christian sentiment of the other. It is now, of course, clear that sensible persons were right in saying that no important military weapon and no important scientific discovery can be long kept secret, but as our emotions of conformity are always predictable when this question comes up, the Russians must be very pleased. It makes me think of what General Lee said when he

learned that General McClellan had been called back to command the Army of the Potomac. "I am very happy that General Mc-Clellan is again opposed to me," he remarked, "because I always know what he is going to do." I wonder what Emerson would tell us here about a foolish consistency, that hobgoblin of little minds.

[10] I take my third example from the world of learning. I received a week or two ago an airmail letter asking me to protest against the action of twelve regents of the University of California who, in the teeth of faculty opinion, of administrative opinion, of gubernatorial opinion, of the opinion of six members of the board, and of the opinion of many outside the university, are determined to require a new oath from a faculty which has already taken an oath, and which has declined to take the new oath by a vote of 900 to 0.[1] It is apparently supposed not only that some member of the faculty may be a Communist, but that members of the faculty may, or might, or could, or would belong to mysterious organizations not named, mysteriously threatening the peace and dignity of California. The exact language of the proposed oath is: "That I am not a member of the Communist party, or under any oath, or a party to any agreement, or under any commitment that is in conflict with my obligation under this oath." No one knows what this language means except that it is insulting. It is not proved that any member of the California faculty has perjured himself or committed treason or acted as a spy. It is provable that the faculty of no university served the country more patriotically during the war. Now a majority of the regents has discovered that this same faculty are potential liars. They infer that the faculty might take oaths only to violate the oaths they take. They therefore set up this second oath, although if the oath-taker is not bound by oath number one, he is not going to be any more bound by oath number two. The effect is simply to penalize dissent. On the other hand, a friend of Emerson's preached active disloyalty to this government, an aunt of Emerson's helped that friend to violate the laws, and when this friend eulo-

[1] Subsequent votes on related issues should not be confused with this one as reported in the newspapers. At the time of going to press, the author's summary of the situation was believed to be reasonably correct.

gized a rebel named John Brown, Emerson applauded him. Now, as we quaintly say, we "teach" Thoreau's *Essay on Civil Disobedience,* even in California. I cite these familiar facts only that you measure from what Massachusetts permitted in 1850 what California demands in 1950.

[11] Let me turn to my last example. Passing over such obvious dangers to higher education as the military control of research, the extraordinary oath proposed to be attached to the National Science Foundation, the stool-pigeon clause demanded by the Navy Department of officers in training and happily modified because of student dissent, let me briefly contrast two patterns of collegiate training.

[12] I suppose the greatest president Harvard had in the nineteenth century was Charles W. Eliot. Like Emerson he is now undervalued. He believed in the individual. His great work was to break up the cake of custom which then bound this college. He argued that if a man was old enough to go to college, he was old enough to know what he was going to college for. Mr. Eliot therefore instituted the elective system. He restored dignity both to learning and to the scholar. He knew very well that many men would not profit under his system, and that many men would abuse his system, but he also knew very well that for men worth educating, this was education worthy of men. He had got tired of educating boys. He guessed that the social gains would outweigh the social losses, and the brilliant roll call of distinguished Harvard men graduating in Mr. Eliot's time proves that he was right.

[13] I suppose the greatest president of the University of Chicago in the twentieth century is Mr. Hutchins. I honor Mr. Hutchins. He speaks his mind. He is a remarkable individual. But I am always puzzled to know why Mr. Hutchins, who speaks his mind, infers that single-mindedness is therefore the principal virtue in liberal education. Mr. Hutchins has abandoned the pattern of Mr. Eliot and gone back to the pattern of Aquinas. I do not fully understand the Chicago system, but the part I do understand is the dogma that a selected list of great books is sufficient for, or synonymous with, a liberal education. These the teacher is to

expound. The student is there to be taught. He may argue, he may debate, but he is there to master this library.

[14] But why a library? The people who wrote these books had no such library, for the most part. As Emerson said, librarians are not wiser than other men. Why is bookishness a virtue? What is a great book? Who determines when it is great enough to get in, or, what is more important, small enough to be left out? Some books in some moments for some people have great beauty, and some books for some people at some moments have great wisdom, but I submit that one gains as much pleasure and wisdom and instruction from little books as one does from big ones. Are there great books, indeed? May not one truly say there are only great readers of books, and that the great reader seldom confines himself to any restricted list? Yet it is seriously maintained at Chicago that only by bookish authority can democracy be maintained and culture be enriched.

[15] It is regrettable that Abraham Lincoln's library was meager. He never read Aquinas. He merely wrote the Gettysburg Address, which is shorter than Pericles' and just as good. Meek young men, said Emerson, grow up in libraries believing it their duty to accept the views which Cicero, which Locke, which Bacon have given, forgetful that Cicero, Locke, and Bacon were only young men in libraries when they wrote these books. It is true that Mr. Eliot put together the Harvard classics, but he did not do it to end a library; he merely thought it might be an economical way to begin one.

[16] I do not remember who first made popular the phrase: "failure of nerve." But in these several instances of a drive to conformity, I detect a failure of nerve, a failure of belief in the individual.

[17] In each case, of course, there is something to be said for conformity. There is always something to be said for conformity. I think, for example, something is to be said for the theory that whether the party in power is Democratic or Republican, we have in fact a coalition government; but a coalition government so insecure that it treats dissent as unpatriotic is not a government which Emerson, at any rate, could approve. The doctrine that "Papa knows best" troubles the presidency and the office of

secretary of state, but it is not the doctrine of Emerson. The demand for patriotic oaths contrasts with the sentiment of a president in Emerson's time who once said of a rival that he would gladly hold General McClellan's stirrup, if by so doing he could get the country through its danger.

[18] Honor is not manufactured by printed forms to be taken before a notary public; it is a function of manly self-respect—and it is a mark of the time that I feel almost apologetic for using so old-fashioned a phrase. The notion of standardized wisdom—so many parts of Plato, so many parts of Newton, so many parts of Milton; do not shake before taking—is a product of this same loss of nerve. It reveals hurry and distrust—hurry, because, when you have invented the formula, you can push the product through to its shaping, faster; distrust, because when you substitute uniformity of pattern for equality of individuals, you transfer your belief from the individuals to the pattern. A belated Emersonian, I am still, in things of the spirit, for the individual. Robert Frost reminds us that a one-man revolution is the only revolution that is coming.

[19] By this circuitous route I come back to Emerson and education. We have found out in two wars that if all we want to do is to train the young, we can do it cleverly. If all you want to do is to train the young, establish your pattern—Great Books, General Education, call it what you will—and the training may be admirable. But it will be only training. We set up these teaching patterns and then look around for somebody to make them operate instead of assuring ourselves that we first have men to teach.

[20] Like everybody else I have tinkered with the curriculum, but beyond rudimentary common sense and the baser parts of diplomacy, it does not matter what the pattern is, provided you have good scholars and students who really want to learn. The pattern seems wonderful only for a time. Ask any Harvard graduate ten years out what the catalogue outlined as proper education when he was a junior, and you will probably draw a blank; ask him who taught him, and he will instantly recur in memory to this or that powerful personality.

[21] Education is a private affair. It is as private as falling in love. There is no such thing as general education, there are only

specific individual educations. How often in the biographies of Harvard men do you find the phrase: "He studied with Agassiz, or Kittredge, or Royce, or Shaler!" How seldom does the curriculum appear except in a negative and crippling connotation!

[22] Education, I repeat, *is* a private affair. It is essentially a lonely business, which neither deans nor advisers nor proctors nor tutors nor professors can substitute for. Like religion and marriage, it is personal, the result of the impact of character upon character. My objection to some things we are trying to do here is that we have strayed away from the spirit of Emerson.

[23] When Emerson uttered his famous phrase: "Trust thyself— every heart vibrates to that iron string," he makes, if I may say so, the whole iron curtain vibrate. He did not speak to the sentimental, the lazy, the superficial men, the men who are content to get by with the aid of a tutor and skilful appeals to the dean's office. What he had in mind is the stark truth that we brought nothing into this world and it is certain we can carry nothing out, and that therefore between these poles of time lies our only opportunity to develop character. And when he said that books are for the scholar's idle time, he did not mean that nobody should enter the Lamont Library.

[24] In a democracy we count by ones and not by masses, though there are those who would define democracy by another pattern— the hatred of those who count by masses. Hate, however, is neither salvation nor statesmanship. The great contribution of Emerson is not only that he agreed to count by ones, but he also believed that one—anyone—had infinity behind him. I cannot defend this belief logically, though it looks suspiciously like Christianity, and is no more absurd than existentialism. But in education, as in the national life, how are we to fortify the individual unless we rally infinity behind him? This will, I know, be incomprehensible to many and impractical to some, and I can only point to the historic truth that this doctrine, incomprehensible and impractical, is the child of Harvard—of the great, traditional Harvard, the Harvard that I, who am merely Harvard by adoption, think we must not lose. When Lowell recited his ode for the Harvard dead in 1865, he did not celebrate the curriculum:

> Those love her best who to themselves are true,
> And what they dare to dream of, dare to do;

> They followed her and found her
> Where all may hope to find,
> Not in the ashes of the burnt-out mind,
> But beautiful with danger's sweetness round her.

[25] Perhaps if we looked more often, both faculty and students, upon the face of the statue in Emerson Hall, we might detect a smiling irony about its lips. Perhaps, if we looked at it oftener, a noble doubt, as Emerson would say, might suggest itself about our faith in advice, in pattern, in crutches, in conformity.

[26] Emerson's faith was not in machinery but in man thinking, whereas we today are proud of machines that think, and suspicious of any man who tries to. I see no reason for being as apologetic as we are about the protest of protestantism and the dissidence of dissent in a college which was founded by dissenters; and difficult though it is to make my point, I for one dissent from current notions in college and country that democracy will survive only after you have imposed a pattern and made as many persons as possible conform to it.

[27] The educational problem is not conformity to any pattern, however lofty in intent; it is how to remove obstacles from the lonely path by which education sometimes results in man thinking. As for public life, I quote Mrs. Roosevelt: "Have we really reached the point where we must fear to join any group because at some time or other a person of Communist leanings, or supposed Communist leanings, might also join it? That is a terrible thing and we should be ashamed of it." I, too, am ashamed of this pressure of conformity. I do not think it is too late in the history of the republic, whether in education or in politics, to believe that Emerson is still the most excellent spiritual catalyst we have in a democracy. It is in that spirit I have tried to speak.

EXERCISES

Howard Mumford Jones is one of the most prominent literary scholars in modern America. His choice of Emerson as the subject for the present address, delivered at the junior-senior dinner in Leverett House (Harvard), demonstrates the essential toughness of Emerson's central ideas. The address is appropriate to this position in Section E because it suggests a return to non-material values in what is thought of as a materialistic age.

1. Why is paragraph 1 a good introduction?
2. Why, probably, does Professor Jones refute the arguments against Emerson before presenting the case for him?
3. How does he refute the objections to Emerson?
4. What part does irony play in the refutation?
5. Does Professor Jones object to the restraint of specific movements or ideas as such, or to the principle mainly?
6. What positive suggestions does he make?
7. Show how the two main points of the address are related to Emerson's "Self-Reliance."
8. Analyze Professor Jones's style, explaining especially the sentence qualities which result in such great force.

The Renewal of Life

LEWIS MUMFORD

[1] One phase of civilization does not replace another as a unit, in the way that a guard assigned to sentry duty takes over its post. For a while they mingle confusedly, until a moment comes when one realizes that the entire scene has changed and all the actors are different. So with the internal change that will produce the new person. After a transition period a critical point will come when it will be plain that the new personality has at last matured and that those who wear a different mask look oddly antiquated and are "out of the picture." Though the object of this change is to make possible a new drama of culture, no one who understands the social process would pretend to write the lines or to describe, in any detail, the action and plot; for it is part of the very nature of the living drama that these things must be left to the actors. If here and there, I have ventured to anticipate the

From *The Conduct of Life,* Copyright, 1951, by Lewis Mumford. Reprinted by permission of Harcourt, Brace and Company, Inc.

next moves, it is only because the first steps have already been taken.

[2] How shall one describe the balanced man and woman, considered as an ideal type? Let me begin with a negative description. He no longer belongs exclusively to a single culture, identifies himself with a single area of the earth, or conceives himself as in possession, through his religion or his science, of an exclusive key to truth; nor does he pride himself on his race or his nationality, as if the accidents of birth were in some way specially laudable: that democratic parody of ancient feudal pride. His roots in his region, his family, his neighborhood will be deep, and that depth itself will be a tie with other men: but one part of his nature stays constantly in touch with the larger world through both his religion and his politics, and remains open to its influences and its demands.

[3] The balanced man has the mobility of the migratory worker of the nineteenth century without his rootlessness: he has the friendliness toward people of other cultures that we see most admirably in the native Hawaiian; and with the habits so engendered goes a lessening of his conceit over what is exclusively indigenous. With respect to his own region, he observes two rules: first he cultivates every part of it to its utmost, not merely because it is near and dear, but because it can thus contribute its specialties and individualities to other places and peoples; and second, when he finds his own region deficient in what is essential for full human growth, he reaches out, to the ends of the earth if need be, to bring into it what is missing—seeking the best and making it his own, as Emerson and Thoreau, in little Concord, reached out for the Hindu and Persian classics.

[4] Into the balance of the new man, accordingly, will go elements that are not native to his race, his culture, his region, even if the place he identifies himself with be as large and multifarious as Europe. The savor of his own idiosyncrasy and individuality will be brought out, rather than lessened, by this inclusiveness. So in him the old divisions between townsman and countryman, between Greek and barbarian, between Christian and pagan, between native and outlander, between Western civilization and Eastern civilization, will be softened and in time effaced. Instead

of the harsh and coarse contrasts of the past, there will be rich fusions and blendings, with the strength and individuality that good hybrids so often show: this one-world intermixture will but carry further a process visible in the rise of most earlier civilizations.

[5] The change that will produce the balanced man will perhaps occur first in the minds of the older generation: but it is the young who will have the audacity and courage to carry it through. In any event, the new person is, to begin with, one who has honestly confronted his own life, has digested its failures and been re-activated by his awareness of his sins, and has re-oriented his purposes. If need be, he has made public acknowledgment of such errors as involved any considerable part of his community. What has gone wrong outside himself he accepts as part and parcel of what has gone wrong within himself: but similarly, where in his own life he has had a fresh vision of the good or has given form to truth or beauty, he is eager to share it with his fellows.

[6] The capital act of the new man is an assumption of responsibility: he does not transfer the blame for his personal misfortunes to his parents, his elders, his associates, his circumstances: he refuses to make his own burden lighter by treating himself as a victim of processes over which he could have no control, even when he has innocently suffered: for he knows that in the moral life future intentions are more significant than past causes. On the map that science and objective investigation supply him, he superimposes his own plan of life. So the balanced person treats his own situation, however formidable or threatening, as the raw material he must master and mold. But his humility, born of self-awareness, has another side to it: confidence in his own powers of creation.

[7] *Confidence in creation:* a sense of the rich potentialities of life and of endless alternatives, beyond those that the immediate moment or the immediate culture offers. Confidence in creation, as opposed to the fixations, the rigidities, the narrow alternatives of the existing economic systems and cultural schemes: yes, here precisely is the deepest difference between the new person and the old, who gave to external conditions and external stimuli the initiative that living organisms and above all living persons must keep for themselves. Those who have this confidence are not

afraid to break with the existing patterns, however compulsive and authoritative they may seem; and they are not afraid to make departures on radically different lines, merely because they may meet with rebuff or failure. Such confidence once existed in a high degree among the great industrialists who girdled the planet with railroad lines, steamships, ocean cables, and factories; and those whose task it is to build a new world on the ruins of our disintegrating civilization must have that faith in even fuller measure. The new person, because he has not feared to transform himself, is capable of facing the world in a similar mood of adventurous amelioration.

[8] Only those who have confronted the present crisis in all its dimensions will have the strength to repent of their own sins and those of their community, to confront and overcome the evils that threaten us, and to re-affirm the goods of the past that will serve as foundation for the goods of the future that we have still to create. For those who have undergone these changes, life is good and the expansion and intensification of life is good. To live actively through every organ and still remain whole: to identify oneself loyally with the community and yet to emerge from it, with free choices and new goals: to live fully in the moment and to possess in that moment all that eternity might bring: to re-create in one's consciousness the whole in which man lives and moves and has his being—these are essential parts of the new affirmation of life. The rest lies with God.

[9] Without fullness of experience, length of days is nothing. When fullness of life has been achieved, shortness of days is nothing. That is perhaps why the young, before they have been frustrated and lamed, have usually so little fear of death: they live by intensities that the elderly have forgotten.

[10] This experience of fulfillment through wholeness is the true answer to the brevity of man's days. The awakened person seeks to live so that any day might be good enough to be his last. By the actuarial tables he knows, perhaps, that his expectation of life at birth is almost three score and ten; but he knows something more precious than this: that there are moments of such poignant intensity and fullness, moments when every part of the personality is mobilized into a single act or a single intuition, that they out-

weigh the contents of a whole tame lifetime. Those moments embrace eternity; and if they are fleeting, it is because men remain finite creatures whose days are measured.

[11] When these awakened personalities begin to multiply, the load of anxiety that hangs over the men of our present-day culture will perhaps begin to lift. Instead of gnawing dread, there will be a healthy sense of expectancy, of hope without self-deception, based upon the ability to formulate new plans and purposes: purposes which, because they grow out of a personal reorientation and renewal, will in time lead to the general replenishment of life. Such goals will not lose value through the changes that time and chance and the wills of other men will work on them, in the course of their realization; nor will the prospect of many delays and disappointments keep those who are awakened from putting them into action at the earliest opportunity. Nothing is unthinkable, nothing impossible to the balanced person, provided it arises out of the needs of life and is dedicated to life's further development.

[12] Even in his most rational procedures, the balanced person allows a place for the irrational and the unpredictable: he knows that catastrophe and miracle are both possible. Instead of feeling frustrated by these uncontrollable elements, he counts upon them to quicken the adventure of life by their very unforeseeableness: they are but part of the cosmic weather whose daily challenge enlivens every activity.

[13] Life is itself forever precarious and unstable, and in no manner does it promise a tame idyll or a static utopia: the new person, no less than the old, will know bafflement, tragedy, sacrifice, and defeat, as well as fulfillment—but even in desperate situations he will be saved from despair by sharing Walt Whitman's consciousness that battles may be lost in the same spirit that they are won, and that a courageous effort consecrates an unhappy end. While the conditions he confronts are formidable, the initiative nevertheless remains with man, once he accepts his own responsibility as a guardian of life. With the knowledge man now possesses, he may control the knowledge that threatens to choke him: with the power he now commands he may control the power that would wipe him out: with the values he has created, he may

replace a routine of life based upon a denial of values. Only treason to his own sense of the divine can rob the new person of his creativity.

[14] Harsh days and bitter nights may still lie ahead for each of us in his own person, and for mankind as a whole, before we overcome the present forces of disintegration. But throughout the world, there is a faint glow of color on the topmost twigs, the glow of the swelling buds that announce, despite the frosts and storms to come, the approach of spring: signs of life, signs of integration, signs of a deeper faith for living and of an approaching general renewal of humanity. The day and the hour are at hand when our individual purposes and ideals, reenforced by our neighbors', will unite in a new drama of life that will serve other men as it serves ourselves.

[15] The way we must follow is untried and heavy with difficulty; it will test to the utmost our faith and our powers. But it is the way toward life, and those who follow it will prevail.

EXERCISES

Lewis Mumford has spent most of his life studying Western civilization and since 1930 has worked on a series of four volumes evaluating man's technological and ideological achievements. The final volume, *The Conduct of Life* (1951), is the culmination of his life's work. Since Mr. Mumford is a highly respected scholar, philosopher, and writer, the book is one of the most outstanding interpretations of life at the mid-century. The passage you have just read is the final section of *The Conduct of Life* and may not inappropriately serve as the culmination of this book of readings.

1. List the traits which Mumford expects the new man to have.
2. What does Mumford expect will happen to the old ideal of almost unbridled individualism—as noted, for instance, by Webb?
3. Does Mumford expect a worship of the state to replace the old worship of the individual?
4. What part is individuality to play in the new person?
5. How is universalism, or awareness of all mankind, to enrich the new personality?
6. Is the new personality to be new in innately, biologically controlled traits or in habitual outlook on life?

7. What part would learning—from teachers, books, and personal observation—play in the creation and perpetuation of such a new personality?

8. How are Mumford's ideas related to those of Emerson, Thoreau, White, and Jones?

9. Write an essay in which you set forth your own conception of the ideal person and the way in which he may live most satisfactorily to himself, most efficiently in relation to his country and its resources, and most agreeably to his fellow men. The essay ought to take into account all the facts and ideas which you have encountered in Part II of this book plus your own reflections upon them. The intelligence with which you select and organize these materials and the skill with which you present your opinions and reveal your attitudes may well be taken as the best writing of which you are capable at this time.

A Glossary of Rhetorical Terms

ABSTRACT. Words which denote non-material qualities, such as *liberty,* and *truth,* or words so general as to represent only concepts deriving from material things, such as *wealth* (for *land, silver, horses,* etc.). The opposite of CONCRETE.

ADDRESS. A rather serious composition delivered orally or prepared as if it were to be delivered orally. Most important addresses are published after delivery; in published form they constitute a considerable proportion of our non-fiction reading. See page 121.

ALLEGORY. A metaphor extended into a narrative in which the obvious plot or action conveys a parallel meaning, often of a metaphysical nature.

ALLUSION AND REFERENCE. Reference is the direct mention of a subject, such as a person, place, or event; Hamlet is referred to in the sentence "I do not like Hamlet's character." Allusion is the indirect mention of a subject, or any similar way of calling attention to a subject without actually naming it; Hamlet is alluded to in the sentence "I do not like Shakespeare's gloomy Dane." Allusion and reference are useful as ornaments to style.

ANALOGY. Analogy is an extended comparison often used in explanation and argument. See page 63.

ANALYSIS. Analysis is the taking apart of a subject or the explanation of a subject by giving the details which constitute it. See page 3.

ARGUMENT. A discourse which presents evidence in proof of an assertion, against expected resistance to the assertion.

ARTICLE. A composition in which the main interest is the subject matter. See page 121.

ASSERTION. A clear, explicit, and positive statement, conveying the author's sureness of its truth. "I do not understand what has happened" would hardly be called an assertion. "It is clear that the silver has been stolen" is an assertion.

ASSONANCE. The recurrence of similar vowel sounds. Assonance may simply give unity of sound; when so used it is a means to euphony. The *i's* and *e's* are simply euphonious in the following: "Not that I can think well of every light separation . . ." (*Milton.*) When assonance is used to call special attention to important words it is a device of emphasis by repetition. The *ee* sound is so used in the phrase "meek and peaceful child." (*Milton.*)

BALANCE. A sentence structure in which two main parts, usually parallel, are equal in length. Often used with antithesis. See page 65.

BODY. The main portion of a discourse, between the introduction and conclusion.

CACOPHONY. Harsh, unpleasant sound; to be avoided except occasionally to give appropriate expression to an unpleasant idea.

CADENCE. A falling sentence rhythm in which the intervals between stressed syllables usually decrease near the end of the sentence. See page 163.

CLASSIFICATION. The analysis of a subject by groups of related details. See page 4.

CLAUSE. A group of words containing a verb form and its subject, and its object if necessary, used as part of a sentence.

CLIMATE OF OPINION. See INTELLECTUAL CLIMATE.

COHERENCE. The arrangement and connection of words and sentences in such a way that the succession of ideas is as clear as possible. It is achieved mainly by organization and the use of verbal links. See pages 17 and 34.

COMPARISON. One of the main methods of development, which operates by comparing two things for the purpose of pointing out similarities (simple comparison) or differences (contrast). See page 62.

COMPOSITION. Something put together, from various parts, into a whole; or the process of forming such a whole. In college English composition courses, *composition* means the process of assembling facts and ideas into whole, written themes having unity, full development, good organization, and appropriate emphasis, and written in a clear and effective style; *composition* is also used to designate the theme itself.

CONCISENESS. The expression of an idea in as few words as possible. See page 29, also DEADWOOD.

CONCLUSION. The conclusion is that part of a composition which follows the full development of the subject—not simply the last period. Two useful kinds of conclusion are the summary of main points and the amplification of some important theme, often by anecdote or prediction. But whatever it does, it must do well; for the conclusion holds the most emphatic position in the discourse, the end. One authority on rhetoric says that at one time the peroration (conclusion of an argument) was forbidden in the courts of ancient Athens because under its influence jurors were likely to disregard the actual facts of a case. Cicero is said to have won many pleas on the strength of his peroration. The wise writer does not waste this important position.

CONCRETE. Words which denote material things, such as *house, pumpkin,* and *cup.* Concrete words may be specific (*cow*) or general (*cattle*), but are not so general as to be abstract (*assets*). As a rule, concrete words are more vivid than abstract words.

CONNOTATION. The associated meanings or usage levels of a word, as distinguished from its denotation. *Home* means essentially the same as *domicile* but is richer in emotional associations. *Maybe* means the same as *perhaps* but has a distinctly colloquial flavor.

CONSONANCE. The recurrence of similar consonant sounds, either for euphony or for emphasis. See EUPHONY and EMPHASIS. For euphony (consonance of *l's*): "The book itse*l*f wi*l*l te*l*l us more at *l*arge." (*Milton.*) For emphasis (consonance of *s's* and *b's*): "When a city *sh*all *b*e a*s* it were *b*esieged and *b*locked a*b*out. . . ." (*Milton.*)

CORRECTNESS. Adherence to accepted standards of diction and grammar. Correctness is essential, but not all correct language is effective.

DEADWOOD. Words which could be removed without damage to meaning. "She is majoring in *the area of* sociology."

DEFINITION. That method of development which operates by placing the subject within a class and then differentiating it from other members of its class. See pages 97–99.

DENOTATION. The literal and bare meaning of a word, as listed in a dictionary. See CONNOTATION.

DESCRIPTION. The representation in words of a place, person, or thing. See Irving's description of Katrina's home.

DETAIL. A part of a whole. Development by giving details is perhaps the most frequent method of development. See ANALYSIS; see also page xi.

DEVELOPMENT. Literally, an unfolding. In composition, one of the ways in which an idea is presented. See page xi and DETAIL, EXAMPLE, COMPARISON, DEFINITION, and REITERATION.

DICTION. Word choice. See ABSTRACT, CONCRETE, GENERAL and SPECIFIC, CORRECTNESS, EXACTNESS, DENOTATION, CONNOTATION, EUPHONY, and PROPRIETY.

ECONOMY. In sentence construction, the use of as few words as will adequately convey full meaning.

In development of ideas either in the paragraph or in the whole composition, the use of only as many details or examples as are necessary to full clarity.

ELABORATION. Another term for development, ordinarily by details.

EMPHASIS. Emphasis can be given to important ideas by the attention-getting qualities which are inherent in certain positions, in repetition, in vividness, in proportion, and in contrast or singularity.

Position. Beginning and end are the most emphatic positions, in the whole composition, in the paragraph, and in the sentence. (See INTRODUCTION and CONCLUSION.) The PERIODIC SENTENCE and the CADENCE give special force to the emphatic end position in the sentence.

Repetition. In the whole composition, important ideas may be emphasized by restatement at various points.

In the sentence, repetition usually occurs in a series of *parallel elements which reiterate an idea.* (Notice that this does not include all parallelism.) A good example is Lincoln's "We cannot dedicate, we cannot consecrate, we cannot hallow this ground." *Repetition of sounds* may call attention to the words in which the repeated sounds occur; see ALLITERATION, ASSONANCE, and CONSONANCE.

In the paragraph, *parallel sentences* may, by repetition of a pattern, attract attention to the statements made in the sentences. A *recurring phrase* which appears twice or more in a paragraph also has emphatic effect.

Proportion. Emphasis by proportion is most important as it applies to the whole composition. In "Katrina's Home," for instance, Irving shows by the proportion of details concerning food that Ichabod's interests are mainly gastronomical. Little is said about whether the Van Tassel farm was money-producing, easy to manage, or lonely.

Vividness. In the whole composition, vividness results mainly from striking examples or anecdotes and from the total effect of style.

In the sentence vividness results mainly from concrete diction and from ornament. (See CONCRETE and ORNAMENT.)

Singularity, or *Contrast.* Any departure from the usual, either in form or in content, is striking. In the whole composition, a single sentence set off as a paragraph is certain to be emphatic. In the paragraph, a noticeably short sentence, an inversion, or a question, attracts special attention. In content, any idea or feeling may be given emphasis by the presence of its opposite. A gloomy day ceases to be gloomy when we have become accustomed to it. But if the sun comes out for five minutes, the gloom is even gloomier afterward. Likewise, we may remember that five minutes of sunshine on a gloomy day but forget whole days which were uniformly lovely.

ESSAY. A composition in which the main value lies in the author's interpretation of some specific aspect of a subject. See page 121.

ETYMOLOGY. The study of the origins and the original meanings of words; often helps a writer distinguish between nearly synonymous words and choose the most exact word for his purpose.

EUPHONY. Pleasantness of sound. Euphony derives from the various elements of sound, but especially RHYTHM, ASSONANCE, and CONSONANCE. Few rules can be given for achieving euphony; when language pleases the ear, it is euphonious—that is perhaps all we can know. Ordinarily it is enough to avoid harshness, except when it is appropriate to the sense. Striking and appropriate euphony can be used for important passages. See page 212.

EXACTNESS. The use of words and sentences which most accurately express the meaning intended by the author.

EXAMPLE. A method of development which operates by citing or elaborating specific instances of the idea being presented. See page 47.

EXPLICIT MEANING. Meaning which is directly expressed. See page 211.

EXPOSITION. An explanation of an idea, structure, or action. Most of the selections in this book are expository.

FIGURES OF SPEECH. Figurative language is any language which departs from normal sentence order or from straightforward statement. Figures of speech were once called *tropes,* from the Greek word meaning *a turning*—a turning from literal meaning or usual order. As time goes on, writers and critics alike seem to know less and less about figures of speech and to think that only the metaphor and other images count. Actually, more than a hundred figures can be distinguished, and they are all useful. For a beginning we shall do with those listed here.

The use of figurative language follows five principles: (1) *Usefulness*. If it is not needed to gain emphasis or to make an idea clear, figurative language is mere gingerbread, mere gymnastics before a mirror. (2) *Clarity*. The reader must be able to see the intended meaning, or the first aim of writing, communication, is thwarted. (3) *Freshness*. Trite figures—"brave as a lion," "bolt from the blue," etc.—bore the reader. (4) *Consistency*. All parts of a figure must be based on a single comparison; "The ship of state is floundering blindly in a wilderness" is not. (5) *Appropriateness*. As Aristotle observed, a figure may either exalt or degrade the subject, and the author must control this alteration. Appropriateness depends more upon connotation than upon denotation, or exactness of literal meaning. It might be quite accurate to say of a golden blonde, "Her hair is the yellow of a summer squash"; but the connotation is of course all wrong.

All figures of speech give vividness and emphasis to style. But they vary somewhat in nature and usefulness, and they may be grouped accordingly.

I. *Those figures based on imagery*. These are good for lending concreteness and familiarity to the abstract and unfamiliar. They appeal to the imagination and often to the emotions.

Antonomasia. Using the name of a prominent individual to designate another individual of the same type. A traitor may be called a Quisling. Milton was once called "our little English David" for defending the Commonwealth against criticism from the continent.

Apostrophe. An address to a person, thing, or personification, as in "O Prince of Peace," or "O Death, where is thy sting?"

Metaphor. An implied comparison, like "She's the rose of No-Man's-Land," meaning the Red Cross Nurse.

Metonymy. Naming an individual or class by something associated with it, as in "The Pentagon discloses new plans for guided missiles," meaning that Army officials disclose the plans. See *Synecdoche*.

Personification. Investing abstractions or inanimate things with human qualities; usually indicated by capitalizing the common noun, as in "Last Sunday afternoon Death rode the highways."

Simile. A stated comparison, such as "My love is like a red, red rose."

Synecdoche. The use of the part for the whole, the individual for the class, or the reverse of these. Mary Jane says "Here comes the

Army" but means "Here comes Private Joe Smith." A news report reads "General Ridgeway swept into new territory today," meaning that the General and several thousand troops and assorted weapons accomplished the feat. See *Metonymy*.

II. *Those figures based on arrangement*. These show relationship between two or more items, except inversion, which appeals only by contrast to normal order. Regression and anticlimax are often witty or humorous.

Anticlimax. The arrangement of a series of items so that the trivial follows the important or dignified. The effect is usually ludicrous, as in Byron's

"They wept for those who perished in the cutter,
And also for the biscuits and the butter."

(This figure is most properly called *bathos,* but usage seems to have appropriated that word to mean unsuccessful pathos and to have replaced it by the word *anticlimax*.)

Climax. The arrangement of a series of items in an order of ascending rank, size, importance, or other quality.

"In the new church work Anne found diversion, companionship, and peace of mind."

When items are of equal value, the arrangement may proceed from the shortest to the longest in number of words.

Gradation. A series of clauses or phrases, each building upon or stating a consequence of the preceding one. See page 266.

Inversion. A sentence which follows an inverted rather than a normal word order.

"That I cannot believe."
"A diamond she wants!"

Regression. A figure in which two words in the first part of a sentence or pair of sentences, usually balanced, are reversed in position in the second clause or sentence, with a corresponding alteration in meaning. Very useful for emphasis of close relationship between two items.

"You can take a boy out of the country, but you can't take the country out of a boy."

III. *Those figures based on contrast*. Sometimes the contrast is between the literal and the intended meaning, sometimes between two stated ideas. These figures have good possibilities for wit and intellectual appeal.

Antithesis. Antithesis consists of two contrasting elements. The placement of antithetical words in prominent positions, especially in corresponding parts of a balanced sentence, is a figure with good emphatic value.

"A woman needs loving most when she deserves it least."

See also page 65.

Hyperbole. Exaggeration for emphasis.

"She wept bucketsful of tears about it."

She probably wept a teaspoonful.

Innuendo. An indirect remark which hints at something derogatory, often something generally known, as

"The Senator's devotion to books is well known."

If the Senator's devotion is to sexy novels, the remark is an innuendo.

Irony. A statement which means the opposite of what it says, as one might say, when rain would spoil everything,

"Rain is all we need."

See also page 50.

Litotes. The expression of an idea by negation of its contrary.

"We may not unprofitably study rhetoric."

"My allowance arrived not a bit too soon."

Oxymoron. A phrase involving apparent contradiction.

"Parting is such sweet sorrow."

"There are too many well-trained fools in the country today."

Paradox. A statement which seems self-contradictory or contradictory to common sense.

"A man can't really understand success until he is thoroughly familiar with failure."

"No one is so well off as the poor."

Paranomasia, or *pun.* A play upon two words identical or very similar in sound but different in meaning, or upon the different meanings of one word. Often thought of as a low form of humor, but capable of good stylistic emphasis. See Thoreau's use, page 415.

Sarcasm. A cutting remark, as a woman's asking her angry husband,

"What are you going to do now, hit me?"

Understatement. A statement of a great deal less than the literal truth.

"The thermometer stood at thirty below. Chilly, I call it."

FORMS OF DISCOURSE. The four traditional methods of presenting the facts and interpretations of reality. See DESCRIPTION, NARRATION, EXPOSITION, and ARGUMENT.

FUNCTIONAL ORDER. A method of arranging details which follows a necessary order of occurrence. See page 34.

GENERAL AND SPECIFIC. General words denote classes or kinds of things, and specific words denote individuals or small units. *Cattle* is general and *cow* is specific. But the terms are relative. *Cow* is specific in relation to *cattle,* but it is general in relation to *Bossie* or *Elsie.* As a rule, specific words are more vivid than general words.

GRAMMAR. The system of a language, involving both the forms of words and the ways in which they are used.

IMPLICIT MEANING. Meaning which is suggested by a writer, or which clearly follows from his explicit statements. See page 211.

IMPOSED ORDER. See ORGANIZATION.

INFERENTIAL MEANING. Meaning of which the writer may be unaware, but which the reader feels justified in reading into a composition. See page 211.

INHERENT ORDER. See ORGANIZATION.

INTELLECTUAL CLIMATE, or CLIMATE OF OPINION. The body of basic assumptions and central interests of an age or group. For example, the medieval period has been called "the age of faith," the eighteenth century "the age of reason," and the twentieth century "the age of history and science." Such sweeping generalizations oversimplify each age, but they do state important characteristics too. Within one period differences exist also; there are groups interested mainly in prestige and social whirl, other groups interested mainly in cultivation of the intellect, and so on.

Intellectual climate is an important element in the background of all serious reading and writing. See page 211.

INTEREST. Interest is inherent in an especially attractive style, in originality of interpretation, in novelty of subject matter, or in immediacy of subject matter; subject matter may be said to have immediacy when it bears directly upon one of our main concerns in life—love, security, money-making, enjoyment, etc. See page 18.

INTERRUPTION. An element which temporarily interrupts the main part of a sentence or a clause. "When we reached Elyria, where we left the train to take a bus to Oberlin, we said good-bye to the Chicago students."

INTRODUCTION. That part of a discourse which precedes the actual development of the subject. It may begin directly with a statement of the subject or the issues to be treated, or it may be humorous or startling. In any case, it should attract favorable attention.

INVERSION. Putting the parts of a sentence out of their normal order. (See NORMAL ORDER.) "At such conduct as Sarah's we drew the line."

LOGIC. The study of systematic and correct reasoning.

LOOSE SENTENCE. A sentence in which the meaning is expressed progressively. (For the opposite construction see PERIODIC SENTENCE.) "The problem of financing the new park facilities kept the City Council in session for several hours yesterday."

MAIN DIVISIONS. The divisions in the body of a discourse devoted to the discussion of the main points.

NARRATION. The account of an action, detail by detail. See Ernie Pyle's "Break-Through."

NORMAL ORDER. The normal order for the main parts of an English sentence are Subject-Verb, or Subject-Verb-Object. "Lucy ran." "Joe struck the ball."

ONOMATOPOEIA. The resemblance of the sound of a word to the sound (or occasionally in modern usage to an action or idea) which the word designates. "We heard the *hum* and *whirr* of many electric motors."

ORDERS OF ARRANGEMENT. See ORGANIZATION.

ORGANIC. A structure in which each part is essential to the whole and performs a distinct function in the whole. Or, the relationship of a part to the whole in such a structure.

ORGANIZATION. Ways of arranging the content of a discourse. The main kinds are *inherent orders* (time, space function) and *imposed* or *rational orders* (climax, specific to general, concrete to abstract, cause to effect). See pages xi and xii.

ORIGINALITY. The fresh interpretation of familiar facts.

OUTLINE. A skeletal structure showing the organization of material for any discourse. See pages 21–23.

OVERSTATEMENT. Plain Exaggeration. Or, a whole composition which makes too strong an assertion about the subject. Many magazine articles on new medicines, new gadgets, and new crises are overstated.

PARAGRAPH. A division of a written discourse marked externally by indention of the first line and usually by an unfinished last line, and characterized internally by unity of subject and purpose and coherence of arrangement. Most of the exercises at the beginning of PART I of this book contain instruction in paragraphing.

PARALLELISM. Two or more parts of one sentence, or two or more sentences, similar in grammatical construction. See page 30.

PARTICULAR. The same as *detail,* but perhaps more appropriate than *detail* for abstract matters. Sometimes used, also, to mean specific examples.

PARTITION. The analysis of a subject by separate details. See CLASSIFICATION.

PERIODIC SENTENCE. A sentence in which the meaning is suspended, or not fully revealed, until the very end of the sentence. "The only protection mankind can have against the horrors of international war and the threat of total destruction is peace."

PERSUASION. Another term for argument, as one of the forms of discourse.

PHRASE. A group of words not having all the characteristics of a clause or a sentence.

PRECISION. Another term for exactness.

PROPRIETY. Language or figures appropriate to the subject and purpose of a composition.

PUNCTUATION. The separation of sentences and parts of sentences by commonly recognized marks according to rather well-defined principles. Rhetorically significant as a means of regulating sentence movement.

PURPOSE. The full meaning intended by the writer plus the intended effect on the reader.

QUOTATION. The borrowing of passages from literary compositions of any kind, either for illustration or for ornament, and indicated by quotation marks. See page 118.

REITERATION. The restatement of an idea in different ways. Once much used as a method of development; see for instance Emerson's "Self-Reliance."

RHETORIC. The systematic study and practice of effective composition, usually in written prose; distinguished from merely correct expression.

RHYTHM. Much like rhythm in verse, rhythm in prose is a more or less regular pattern of accents formed by the natural alternation of stressed and unstressed syllables. Prose rhythm should simply satisfy the ear, and no hard and fast rules can be laid down for helping it to that end. We can only say that (1) prose rhythm should not be so regular as to suggest poetic rhythm or to be monotonous, and (2) it can often be made appropriate to the meaning or feeling of a passage.

A. *Normal rhythms.* Much English prose falls naturally into iambic feet:

"Will someone please inform us why we came."

This is perfect iambic and would soon grow montonous. But rhythms like the following are also perfectly natural:

"I am quite aware they do not state their case precisely in this way." (Lincoln.)

Here the proportion of accented and unaccented syllables is about the same, but no unbroken pattern occurs.

B. *Light rhythms.* When the number of unaccented syllables is markedly greater than the number of accented syllables, the resulting rhythm is usually light and quick, as in

"O young Lochinvar has come out of the west." (Scott.)

or

"Swiftly gallop over the western plateau."

C. *Heavy rhythms.* When the number of accented syllables is markedly greater than the number of unaccented syllables, the resulting rhythm is heavy, deliberate, and often dignified, as in

"the slow moving reformation which we labor under." (Milton.)

or

"We hold these truths to be self-evident." (The Declaration of Independence.)

D. *Cadences.* A cadence is a sentence rhythm which gives a sense of falling or finality to the last two or three accent units of a sentence. Meaning undoubtedly contributes to this effect, but rhythm is a strong factor. The sentence may end in one stressed and one unstressed syllable, but a stressed syllable or even two stressed syllables is a more typical and effective pattern. Ideally the number of unstressed syllables between the stressed syllables decreases in the last two or three units or "feet" of the sentence.

Not a cadence: "The door was shut in their faces." (Churchill.)

Cadence: ". . . we arise again and take our stand for freedom as in the olden time." (Churchill.)

Since the cadence is very emphatic (see page 163), classical writers often used it just before pauses, for concluding sentences, and for especially important statements.

SATIRE. Any composition which ridicules a subject.

SELECTION. (1) The process of choosing details or examples for the development of an idea. (2) A term applied to pieces included in a book of readings.

SPACE ORDER. The arrangement of details according to their natural position in space. See page xii.

SPECIFIC. See GENERAL and SPECIFIC.

STRENGTH. Strength in sentences derives mainly from the proportion of verbs to other words and from the kinds of verbs. Linking verbs have little power. Passive voice has less power than active voice, ordinarily. Most powerful of all are the kinetic verbs, which denote overt physical action or motion.

> Weak: "The game was in the stadium."
> Weak: "The plays could not be seen well from our position."
> Better: "Joe waited for the pitcher to throw."
> Strong: "Joe slammed the ball deep into left field."

STYLE. Style is not an element in itself but the effect of a combination of different elements. It is the aspect of writing which varies most from one writer to another. The outline given here is adapted from *The Odyssey Handbook and Guide to Writing*. The relation of style to other aspects of composition is shown in the end-paper chart at the front of this reader.

A. *Grammar and punctuation.* (See in this Glossary.)

B. *Sentence qualities.*

    1. Weight. (See CONCISENESS.)

    2. Movement. Variety desirable. See NORMAL ORDER, INVERSION, INTERRUPTION, LOOSE SENTENCE, PERIODIC SENTENCE, PARALLELISM, BALANCE, and Class I of FIGURES OF SPEECH.

    3. Coherence. See COHERENCE in the Glossary and in any English handbook.

    4. Emphasis. See in this Glossary.

    5. Sound. See EUPHONY, ASSONANCE, CACOPHONY, CONSONANCE, ONOMATOPOEIA, and RHYTHM.

        These various elements of sound may be used to produce an infinite variety of effects. The sound may be pleasant, as in Shakespeare's "When to the sessions of sweet silent thought. . . ." It may be unpleasant and angry, as in Milton's sonnet "Avenge, O Lord, thy slaughtered saints, whose

bones. . . ." It may be simply vigorous, as in this quotation
from Milton's *Areopagitica:* "When God shakes a kingdom
with strong and healthful commotions to a general reforming. . . ." Ordinarily the sound of a sentence should be
pleasant unless the meaning requires some other kind of
sound; in any case it should be appropriate to the meaning.

   6. Strength. See in this Glossary.
C. *Diction*. See in this Glossary.
D. *Ornament*. See FIGURES OF SPEECH, QUOTATION, and ALLU-
   SION and REFERENCE.
E. *Tone*. See in this Glossary.

SUBORDINATION. Placing an idea in a grammatical construction not
complete and independent in itself. Ordinarily we think of subordination as the relegation of an idea to a subordinate, or dependent,
clause; but an idea may sometimes be reduced to a phrase or even
to a single word.

SYMBOL. An object or an action which represents an abstraction. Professor Jones says (page 429) that the swamping of Emerson's statue
under hats and coats symbolizes what has happened to Emerson's
ideas.

TERM. Either a single word or a phrase which designates some single
concept. The word *term* is more general than either *word* or *phrase*
and so may designate either.

THEME. Originally the subject, or one of the subjects, of any discourse.
In college composition courses *theme* usually means an assigned
prose composition.

THESIS. An assertion on a given subject, usually interpretative in nature
and requiring proof or explanation. In written compositions there
may be a main thesis and one or more subsidiary theses. The thesis
is most prominent in argument.

TIME ORDER. The arrangement of details according to their occurrence, or position, in time. See page 34.

TONE. That quality of style which reflects an author's attitude towards
his subject; it corresponds to tone of voice in speaking. The chief
components of tone are probably explicit statement and the connotative value of words and figures. Theoretically two kinds of tone
are distinguishable, objective and subjective. But most writing is
subjective in some degree. The varieties of subjective tone are infinite. See page 42.

TOPIC SENTENCE. The sentence which states the general idea of a paragraph.

UNDERSTATEMENT. A statement which asserts less than the whole truth, as when one who is completely exhausted says "I'm a bit done in." Sometimes used of whole compositions which do not explicitly assert the full significance of the subject.

UNITY. Oneness of subject and main purpose; applicable to the sentence, the paragraph, and the whole composition.

USAGE. Common practice in speaking and writing words, idioms, and grammatical constructions. Usage, mainly, regulates the status of a word or construction as to its formality or informality, correctness or incorrectness, etc.

VARIETY. Variety adds interest to style. Chiefly desirable is variety in sentence length and rhythm; but variety in diction (*e.g.,* formal relieved by touches of informal) is also good.

VERBAL LINKS. Words and phrases which connect other elements and show relationships between them. The main groups of connectives, or verbal links, are conjunctions and conjunctive adverbs. See page 17.

VOCABULARY. The entire stock of words used by an author, or the entire stock of words common to a given subject.

The Elements of Rhetoric

(All items are explained in the Glossary.)

PURPOSE: A. SUBJECT B. ASSERTION C. INTENDED EFFECT	MEANING: A. EXPLICIT B. IMPLICIT C. INFERENTIAL			
		Form of discourse	**Basic forms**	**Applied or practical forms**
			Description Narration Exposition Argument	Articles Reports Essays Addresses, etc.

		Substance	Methods of development
			    Details
			    Examples
			    Comparison
			    Definition	

		Organization	Inherent orders
			    Time
			    Space
			    Function
			
			Imposed orders
			    General to specific
			    Familiar to unfamiliar
			    Cause to effect
			    Climax
			    Special orders for
			        fixed forms and
			        occasional pieces	

		Style	Grammar and punctuation Sentence qualities Diction Ornament Tone	